D0999979

A. LINCOLN, ESQUIRE

A. Lincoln, Esquire

A Shrewd, Sophisticated Lawyer in His Time

Allen D. Spiegel

Mercer
University
Press
2002

ISBN 0-86554-739-4
MUP/H555

© 2002 Mercer University Press
6316 Peake Road
Macon, Georgia 31210-3960
All rights reserved

First Edition.

∞The paper used in this publication meets the minimum
requirements of American National Standard for
Information Sciences—Permanence of Paper for Printed
Library Materials, ANSI Z39.48-1992.

Library of Congress Cataloging-in-Publication Data
Library of Congress
Cataloging in Publication Division
101 Independence Ave., S.E.
Washington, D.C. 20540-4320

Spiegel, Allen D.
A. Lincoln, Esquire : shrewd, sophisticated litigator / by Allen D.
Spiegel.— 1st ed.
p. cm.
Includes bibliographical references and index.
ISBN 0-86554-739-4 (alk. paper)
1. Lincoln, Abraham, 1809-1865—Career in law. 2. Lawyers—Illinois—
Biography. 3. Practice of law—Illinois—History.
I. Title.

KF368.L52 S68 2001
340'.092—dc21

2001005114

CONTENTS

PREFACE

Upon retrospection, serendipity played a central role in the less traveled road being taken. In the sixth grade, I entered an essay contest and wrote about the Lincoln penny. Despite my best efforts, I came in second. Throughout school, I continually learned more about Abraham Lincoln. Much later, I investigated the first use of the paroxysmal [temporary] insanity plea in a murder trial in a US courtroom. That murder occurred on January 30, 1865 in the US Treasury building in Washington, DC. At the time, Abraham and Mary Todd Lincoln occupied the White House. In March of that year Mrs. Lincoln sent a beautiful bouquet of flowers to the imprisoned murderess. Continuing my research, I discovered that Lincoln prosecuted a man accused of murder during his law career. In his defense, his attorney's plea alleged that the murderer was insane due to an overdose of chloroform during surgery. A jury acquitted him but sent him to the lunatic asylum. As my Lincoln information accumulated, my curiosity piqued in direct proportion to the bulk of amassed papers. Eventually, I found myself in Springfield, Illinois perusing copious legal documents newly discovered by the Lincoln Legal Papers research project. These investigators scoured dark and dingy courthouse basements to unearth a multitude of previously unknown documents about Lincoln's law career. With the staff's generous assistance, I collected data about more than sixty of Lincoln's law cases. Ergo, this book evolved.

If pressed, I could answer the opening question as did one of Lincoln's defense witnesses. When cross-examined as to why he wrote a sensational book detailing how to beget male babies, this physician responded: "[I wrote and published this book to] call the attention of readers to the subject so that by putting my knowledge into practice I might benefit others and make money myself...most books are got up with the same object, viz; for the purpose of making money."

Consequently, inspirational muses arrived through all of the above mentioned—serendipity, altruism and economic considerations. Regardless of my motivation, I do hope that many, many readers will enjoy learning about Lincoln and aspects of his unique and interesting legal career.

As a lawyer, Abraham Lincoln unremittingly and simultaneously engaged in legal actions, political intrigues, and societal activities. He did not steadfastly adhere to simply handling legal matters each and every day. He did not smoothly cope with and conclude one legal case at a time. Lincoln's law work fit into his other roles in a haphazard fashion similar to his real life situations. Without hesitation, he fluidly switched from law to politics to society. Lincoln's sometimes disjointed integration of law, politics, and society is exactly what this volume portrays and I hope readers experience as much pleasure as I did in coming to know Lincoln as a litigator, as a politician, and as a citizen.

Abraham Lincoln was voted the number one president by a group of American history scholars. According to legal scholars, he could just as easily have been one of the foremost lawyers in the nation had he not become president.

Lincoln practiced law for about twenty-five years, mainly in the circuit courts of Illinois. However, he was hardly a hick country lawyer. In contrast, Lincoln was an incisive, determined and assertive litigator with a overwhelming caseload. He sought out new business for his law firm and cared about earning a comfortable living.

A ten-year research project, the Lincoln Legal Papers, discovered thousands of yellowed legal documents in musty and dusty courtroom basements. Those handwritten legal papers related to more than 5,000 cases that Lincoln handled, more than 400 before the supreme court of Illinois. In addition, Lincoln appeared before justices of the peace, circuit court judges, and even the Supreme Court of the United States.

For the first time, this book uses the newly discovered legal documents to tell the story of more than sixty of Lincoln's cases. Many of these cases have never been written about previously. This volume describes how Lincoln the lawyer handled a staggering variety of cases involving arbitration, assault and battery, bad debt, bankruptcy, bastardy, bestiality, breach of marriage, divorce, impeachment of an Illinois justice, insanity, land titles, libel, medical malpractice, murder, partnership dissolution, patent infringement, personal injuries, property damages, rape, railroad bonds, sexual slander, slave ownership, and wrongful dismissal.

There is no doubt that Lincoln was a prolific rainmaker who brought clients and fees into his firm. As a lawyer, he seldom turned away any type of client. He represented individuals and corporations, plaintiffs and defendants, prosecuted murderers and defended them, and argued for slave owners while he disagreed with the Supreme Court's Dred Scott decision that supported slave owners. In one series of trials involving the same individuals, Lincoln alternated arguing either for the defendant or the plaintiff in different trials at different levels of the court. When the Eighth Judicial Circuit judge was absent, Judge Abraham Lincoln sat in and presided in court.

This book explores Lincoln's symbiotic interdependent relation between law, politics, and society. His political and legal careers were almost interchangeable. Lincoln's activities as a lawyer, as a politician, and as a member of society blended into a unifying theme of his life and are related in narrative form in this book.

By the time Lincoln suspended his legal practice in the summer of 1860 to concentrate on the presidential election, he was one of the most eminent lawyers in Illinois and the Midwest.

It is my hope that this book will appeal to a variety of audiences. Historians can discover new information about Lincoln's legal career not published previously. This fills a gap that was overshadowed by the concentration on his years in the presidency. Obviously, lawyers will find Lincoln's cases of interest as he tells how to select a jury, how to focus on the critical aspects of cases, how to use humor in the court, how to cross-examine witnesses, how to select expert witnesses and how to appeal to jurors. Those in the medical field can read about Lincoln handling the insanity plea, about choosing expert medical witnesses, about determining usual and customary fees for medical care, about medical imposters and the wrongful dismissal of a physician administrator. Individuals and groups that focus on various aspects of Lincoln's life can find enlightening data on his legal career that covered many more years than his presidency. Educational institutions and libraries can add to their collections so students can enjoy learning about the legal career of our greatest president. This topic is seldom mentioned during the educational process. Lastly, the general public can read about Lincoln's law career and how he fit law, politics and society into his everyday life. This book presents *a slice of life*, a picture of a working mid-western lawyer in the 1800s.

Readers will note from the references and the bibliography that the research on this book was intensive. It would take forever to acknowledge all the people that aided me during the writing of this book. Suffice to say that this book benefited from their contributions that enhanced the stories. I render a heartfelt thanks collectively to many, many people and organizations.

Allen D. Spiegel

FOREWORD

Thomas R. Turner

There can be no doubt that Dr. Allen D. Spiegel's enlightening new book is at the cutting edge of the one area of Abraham Lincoln's legal and political career which can be studied utilizing formerly unavailable primary sources. During the nineteenth century, law and politics were intimately intertwined. In fact, it has become apparent that the old notion that Lincoln temporarily retired from politics after his one term in the US Congress in the 1840s is not correct. Simply because a career politician, such as Lincoln, did not hold elective office did not mean that he did not continue to be politically active. As Lincoln assiduously practiced law, he simultaneously engaged in a variety of political actions. Allen D. Spiegel's unique book provides a meaningful glimpse into the multifaceted diversity of Lincoln's twenty-four years practicing law.

I first became acquainted with Allen D. Spiegel several years ago when he submitted an article about one of Abraham Lincoln's law cases to the *Lincoln Herald*. That article was published in the summer of 1995. Since that time, Dr. Spiegel's research led him to investigate a number of cases during Lincoln's career as a lawyer that dealt with aspects of medicine. Lincoln's legal work included a sundry assortment of medically related activities. When a fellow lawyer was assaulted after he questioned whether his attending physician graduated from a regular medical school, Lincoln handled the lawsuit for damages. Called in as a consultant, Lincoln advised a fired medical superintendent of a lunatic asylum to sue to retain his job and handled the appeal to the supreme court of Illinois. He prepared material for a special legislative charter for a homeopathic medical school and politically lobbied to secure approval from the legislators. Improperly healed bone fractures engendered many medical malpractice cases during Lincoln's time as a practicing lawyer. He defended two physicians who cared for a man with two broken thigh bones and another doctor who treated a woman's broken wrist. Both patients sued the attending physicians. In an unusual twist, Lincoln assisted the state prosecutor in trying a murderer where the defense was insanity induced by an overdose of chloroform applied before surgery as an anesthetic. Lincoln even handled mundane cases such as one in which his client refused to pay the doctor's bill for medical care rendered to his nieces. Fascinatingly, the subject matter of Lincoln's legal cases remains a matter of societal concern currently: bad debts; civil versus military trials; customary medical billing; expert medical witnesses; insanity pleas; jury decisions; malpractice; politics and law; public reactions to decisions; slander; temporary insanity; and wrongful dismissal.

During a presidential review of a military commission's verdict in 1863, Lincoln had to select a medical expert to determine whether or not a convicted murderer was sane or insane. Dr. Spiegel's accounting of this particular situation revealed that Lincoln was a lot sterner man than his stereotypical image of pardoning every sleeping sentry. Evidence indicated that Lincoln deftly used his skill as a lawyer and a politician to select a medical expert who would find the convicted murderer sane and legitimate his approval of the execution. A network of political events combined to bolster the conclusion that Lincoln had to send the message, by hanging the murderer, that murdering a white officer of colored troops would not be tolerated. Coincidentally, the medical expert that Lincoln chose was a major witness at the 1882 trial of Charles J. Guiteau for the assassination of President James Garfield. Predictably, this medical expert testified that the assassin showed no signs of insanity despite abundant evidence that Guiteau was clinically insane.

In addition to the actual legal cases where Lincoln was involved, Dr. Spiegel cited the legal expertise of two of Lincoln's most influential cabinet members. In memorable and well-documented trials, Secretary of State William H. Seward defended two murderers in 1846. In both cases, Seward pleaded that severe beatings in jail caused both defendants to become insane. In 1859, Secretary of War Edwin M. Stanton played a critical role on the legal defense team for a murderer where the defense was intense emotional distress produced a temporary insanity. Obviously, lawyers do not easily forget their extraordinary cases and both Seward and Stanton likely influenced Lincoln's choices when he had to make presidential decisions regarding insanity.

To allow readers to understand the complex interactions of culture and society during Lincoln's law career, Dr. Spiegel incorporated informational chapters on America's first medical malpractice crisis from 1835 to 1865 and on insanity in the 1800s. This insanity section discusses Lincoln's "melancholy" and his "depression," Mary Todd Lincoln's confinement for insanity, and the insanity of John Wilkes Booth, although recent scholarship has tended to stress that Booth was a Southern patriot and not a madman. Furthermore, Dr. Spiegel added a chapter where the murder took place while Lincoln was still president in January 1865 but where the trial occurred after his assassination. If Lincoln had lived there is no doubt that he would have followed the trial since the verbatim transcripts were published in the daily newspapers and might have been brought to his attention by his secretaries.

It has become increasingly apparent, as Dr. Spiegel's book demonstrates, that Abraham Lincoln's law practice was a lot more sophisticated and disparate than previously thought. Like any frontier lawyer, Lincoln did take cases where he earned only a few dollars or received payment in livestock. Nevertheless, at the height of his legal career, he was one of the most widely known, busiest, and successful lawyers in the state of Illinois. He was a "star performer" on the Eighth Judicial Circuit and crowds flocked to the courthouse to watch him. When Lincoln tried medical cases, he applied a fair amount of skill, relied on expert medical testimony, and displayed some knowledge of complicated legal precedent. However, Dr. Spiegel does point out possibly helpful legal aspects that Lincoln, as well as other lawyers, overlooked during the hastily convened circuit court trials.

A major informational source for Dr. Spiegel's book has been the original documents collected by the staff of the Lincoln Legal Papers. Sponsored by the Illinois Historic Preservation Agency, the Abraham Lincoln Association, and the Center for Legal Studies, University of Illinois at Springfield, the Lincoln Legals scoured court houses and other repositories in Illinois and surrounding states where Lincoln practiced law. From his vantage point as a Lincoln Legal Papers staff member, John A. Lupton contributes an article on Lincoln as a lawyer. He comments on Lincoln's lawyerly attributes, his peers, his partnerships, his fees, his life on the circuit court, his trial preparation, and his success in his chosen profession. In preparing this article on Lincoln as a lawyer, Lupton was able to access the most complete amassed documentary record about Lincoln's legal career. These materials, generally untranscribed handwritten documents, are available in a DVD-ROM and future hard copy edition that will enable scholars to more fully examine Lincoln's legal practice. Material continuing to be collected by the Lincoln Legal Papers reinforces the patterns of Lincoln's law practice that Dr. Spiegel's book thoroughly illuminates.

Dr. Thomas R. Turner is the long time editor-in-chief of the *Lincoln Herald*, one of the two major American journals dealing with the life and career of Abraham Lincoln. In addition, Dr. Turner is a professor of history at Bridgewater State College, Bridgewater, Massachusetts. He is the author of *Beware the People Weeping: Public Opinion and the Assassination of Abraham Lincoln* [1991], *Many Faces of Lincoln: Selected Articles from the Lincoln Herald* [with C. Hubbard and S. Rogstad, 1997], and the *Assassination of Lincoln* [1999].

Earliest known image of Abraham Lincoln, circa 1846.

Lawyer Lincoln in the 1850s.

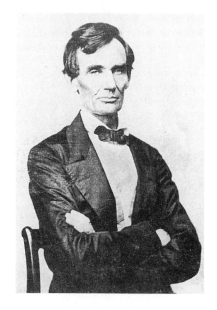

Lincoln introduces law clerk, Gibson W. Harris, to gentlemen in a courtroom.

Lincoln and law clerk, Gibson W. Harris, discuss a legal brief.

John Todd Stuart took Lincoln in as a junior partner in his law firm in 1837. This was Lincoln's first legal partnership.

Stephen T. Logan invited Lincoln to join his firm as a junior partner in 1841 after the dissolution of Stuart & Lincoln.

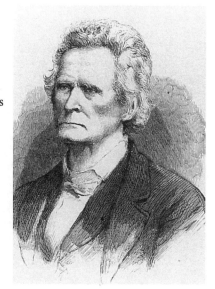

William H. Herndon, the junior partner in the law firm of Lincoln & Herndon, researched and wrote a biography of Lincoln.

Judge David Davis presided over the Eighth Judicial Circuit during Lincoln's practice. Later, President Lincoln appointed him to the Supreme Court of the United States.

Judge John D. Caton served on the Supreme Court of Illinois and heard the Higgins case.

Judge Lyman Trmbull served on the supreme court of Illinois and defeated Lincoln in his bid for the U. S. Senate seat from Illinois in 1855.

Norman B. Judd confronted Lincoln in court as both a lawyer for plaintiffs and for defendants. He worked tirelessly to secure Lincoln's nomination for president in 1860.

Admiralty lawyer Timothy D. Lincoln, no relation, opposed Abraham Lincoln in the Rock Island Bridge trial.

Dr. Frank H. Hamilton, an expert medical witness, testified about healed bone fractures.

John J. Elwell, a lawyer and a physician, wrote the first medical jurisprudence book that cited relevant malpractice cases

Clara Barton, founder of the American Red Cross, engaged in an adulterous affair with Colonel John J. Elwell during the Civil War.

Lawyer Leonard Swett traveled the circuit with Lincoln joining with him or opposing him in court. Swett worked hard to secure the presidential nomination for Lincoln in 1860.

William [Duff] Armstrong
was charged with murder and
Lincoln secured an acquittal.

Edwin M. Stanton first
encountered Lincoln when
they were co-counsel on the
patent infringement suit
filed by Cyrus McCormick
in 1855. Later, President
Lincoln selected Stanton to
be his Secretary of War.

Judge Samuel H. Treat presided in the Eighth Judicial Circuit and pioneered railroad developments.

Ward Hill Lamon, a legal associate of Lincoln on the circuit, advertised their partnership. Later, President Lincoln appointed him U.S. Marshall for the District of Columbia.

Dr. Christopher Goodbrake, Lincoln's expert medical witness, testified in his prosecution of Isaac Wyant for murder.

Dr. David Minton Wright killed a Union officer and President Lincoln reviewed the death sentence and agreed with the court. Dr. Wright was hanged on a scaffold in a public square in Norfolk, Virginia.

William H. Seward defended two murderers and entered insanity pleas alleging that brutal prison beatings caused their insanity. Later. President Lincoln selected him to be his Secretary of State.

Dr. John P. Gray was the expert medical witness selected by Lincoln to review the insanity of Dr. Wright, the convicted murderer.

Lincoln swapping and enjoying droll stories with
fellow lawyers on the circuit.

A typical office arrangement of the Lincoln & Herndon
law firm.

A sketch of Mary Harris shooting and killing Adoniram J. Burroughs in the U. S. Treasury building on January 30, 1865 appeared on the front page of a popular newspaper while Lincoln was still the president.

A sketch of Mary Harris along with a sympathetic story appeared in Harper's Magazine in March 1865.

1

REVERENCE FOR THE LAWS:

A POLITICAL RELIGION

Is there a unifying theme to Abraham Lincoln's activities as a lawyer and as a politician? "For Lincoln, they [law and politics] were complementary, interdependent, and virtually inseparable... There is no doubt that Lincoln used his political and legal careers almost interchangeably...political connections nourished his law practice and his legal work nourished his political ambitions." William H. Herndon, Lincoln's third and last law partner, similarly observed: "Mr. Lincoln was an extremely ambitious man and that ambition found its gratification only in the political field. Politics were his life and newspapers his food, merely using the law as a stepping stone to a political life and it was in this field that he seemed to be happy." Gibson W. Harris, a law student in the Lincoln & Herndon office, reinforced that viewpoint: "He took up the law as a means of livelihood, but his heart was in politics... He delighted, he reveled in it, as a fish does in water, as a bird disports itself in the sustaining air." This inextricable merging of law and politics was not unusual for lawyers in Illinois. From 1830 to 1860, forty of the forty-one practicing attorneys in Sangamon County, the Springfield area, held political office.

With a differing interpretation, a Springfield neighbor of Lincoln labeled him "the craftiest and most dishonest politician that ever disgraced an office in America." Wendell Phillips, a Bostonian, a Harvard University-educated lawyer, a renowned orator, an ardent social reformer and a fervent abolitionist sneered at Lincoln's contrivances: "A huckster in politics, a first-rate second-rate man." Lincoln himself deprecated politicians in a speech about the state bank while serving in the 1837 Illinois state legislature: "Mr. Chairman, this movement is exclusively the work of politicians, a set of men who have interests aside from the interests of the people, and who, to say the most of them, are, taken as a mass, at least one long step removed from honest men. I say this with the greater freedom because being a politician myself, none can regard it as personal."

Lincoln was a party man who adhered to his political affiliation. In his era, the moral basis of Lincoln's politics was a familiar theme. "He was an upwardly mobile striver in times bursting with economic energy and a gloomily, introspective philosopher in a culture fragrant with romantic literature. Lincoln was both a wily political operator and a stern moralizer." His political style followed "the slow, cautious building of a consensus, never going far out front" advocating a position for all to follow. Lincoln wrote about his political leadership style in an April 4, 1864 letter to Albert G. Hodges, a Kentucky newspaper editor: "I claim not to have controlled events, but confess plainly that events have controlled me." To his contemporaries, Lincoln "was a mere politician with no settled convictions. He swayed from moment to moment; he was weak; he had a deplorable tendency to wait on public opinion…[yet] his concern for the Union dominated every moral and constitutional issue." Nevertheless, Lincoln steadfastly opposed compromise to save the Union believing that the principles of democracy and freedom would be imperiled. Not surprisingly, Lincoln's philosophy emerged over the years in his speeches and writings.

Lincoln's early published speeches revealed his enduring convictions about the symbiotic interrelation between law, politics and society. This relationship existed despite the fact that society exhibited ambivalence in acclaiming honor to either profession by placing them at the top of the hierarchal societal ranking. Today, lawyers and politicians are not the most prestigious individuals in society. A 1998 poll almost duplicated results taken about twenty years earlier. Fifty-eight percent of the people polled held

A. LINCOLN, ESQUIRE

unfavorable impressions of politicians. Sixty-five percent thought people engaged in politics for personal gain and looked out for their own interests. Venturing a guess, people polled estimated that about 50 percent of the politicians were corrupt. Forty-seven percent felt that politicians didn't know what they were doing. Despite these disastrous cynical opinions, 51 percent of those polled indicated they were more likely to vote for a candidate with political experience.

In Lincoln's first political announcement on March 9, 1832 in New Salem, he ran for a seat in the Illinois General Assembly at the age of twenty-three. He told the people of Sangamon County that he supported the benefits of good roads and internal waterway improvements to make streams navigable. In addition, Lincoln advocated educational programs and urged the passage of a law regarding usury. Although Lincoln received a heavy majority in his own precinct, he lost the election running eighth in a field of thirteen.

By the time Lincoln delivered his next major speech, dramatic changes in the United States were well underway. Progress was flourishing with a significant number of invigorating happenings in water and rail transportation, in mechanical inventions, in communications, in the organization of workers, in the temperance movement, in campaigns for women's rights and in literature.

By 1825, New York's Erie Canal linked Albany to Buffalo. In the mid-west, the 308-mile-long Ohio Canal joined the Ohio River with Lake Erie to connect with New York's canal. By 1840, 3,326 miles of canals existed but few were built afterward. Robert Fulton's steamship, *Clermont*, sailed up New York's Hudson River in 1807. By 1838, steamships sailed across the Atlantic ocean.

On July 4, 1828, the Baltimore & Ohio emerged as the first important railroad line. Two years later, Peter Cooper built the first efficient American steam locomotive for the B&O and named it *Tom Thumb*. Railroads gained national prominence in transporting commerce and people. Between 1835 and 1840, the miles of railroad track available doubled to more than 2,800 miles.

Anthracite coal fueled the trains in the mid-1830s. By 1850, trains traveled regularly from Maine to North Carolina, from the Atlantic seaboard to Buffalo, and from the western end of Lake Erie to Chicago or Cincinnati.

Communication took a giant step forward when Samuel F. B. Morse invented the electric telegraph in 1835 and Richard Howe devised the rotary printing press in 1847. Mechanical labor- saving inventions applied to farming and industry multiplied the yields and provided an abundance of food and goods. Eli Whitney's cotton gin, the threshing machine, and Cyrus Hall McCormick's reaper revolutionized farming. Northern states became the centers of commerce, finance, and manufacturing involving textiles, lumber, clothing, machinery, leather and woolen goods. Southern states remained agricultural with the major products being cotton, tobacco, rice, and sugar cane. In the Midwest, wheat and meat were the staples. As technology changed the face of industry, a Workingmen's Party originated in Philadelphia in 1828 and campaigned to reduce the "sunup-to-sundown" work day to a moderate ten-hour work day.

In 1826, Boston ministers established the Society for the Promotion of Temperance to encourage a moderate or temperate use of alcoholic beverages. Temperance advocates held public meetings featuring a reformed alcoholic telling his sad tale of woe, frequently in the form of a theatrical melodrama. When that emphasis failed, the movement shifted to prohibition to curtail the sale and use of alcohol. Lincoln commented on the prohibition of liquor when he was a member of the Illinois General Assembly on December 18, 1840: "Prohibition will work great injury to the cause of temperance. It is a species of intemperance within itself, for it goes beyond the bounds of reason in that it attempts to control a man's appetite by legislation and makes a crime out of things that are not crimes. A Prohibition law strikes a blow at the very principles upon which our government was founded." Many women, denied the basic rights Lincoln mentioned, became actively involved in the temperance and abolition movements. Their participation in these and other social reform crusades

A. LINCOLN, ESQUIRE

spawned a breeding ground for the future leadership of the women's rights movement.

Elizabeth Cady Stanton and Lucretia Mott stirred up, forged, and organized campaigns to achieve basic rights for women. By July 1848, more than 200 women and 100 men attended the Seneca Falls Convention in New York. This meeting resulted in the passage of the *Declaration of Sentiments* outlining the rights that women sought with regard to voting, property, divorce, use of tax dollars, and rights of married women. However, only sixty-eight women and thirty-two men signed the document. Education for women was elevated in 1833 as Ohio's Oberlin College became the first to admit women. Two years later the college admitted blacks.

There was a great outpouring of literature articulating the spirit of national pride and societal self-confidence. Alexis de Tocqueville, the French political writer, visited the United States and published *Democracy in America in 1835*. His book received cordial praise in Europe garnering favorable attention to the United States. He commented that "one flourishing town after another...had risen from the wilderness to find...everywhere the most unequivocal proofs of prosperity and rapid progress in agriculture, commerce, and great public works." From 1829 to 1878, William Cullen Bryant combined writing poetry with being the editor of the *New York Evening Post*. Poets Henry Wadsworth Longfellow, John Greenleaf Whittier, Oliver Wendell Holmes, and James Russell Lowell created poetry with imagery portraying the glory in American history and culture that every citizen remembered. George Bancroft's first volume of the *History of the United States from the Discovery of the Continent* appeared in 1834 and became a standard text of ten volumes by 1874. Because of Bancroft's unrestrained praise for his country, critics declared that his book was like the history of the "Kingdom of God" as exemplified in the United States. Fiction writers Nathaniel Hawthorne and Edgar Allan Poe demonstrated American ingenuity as they delved into the solemnity and mysticism in the human experience. On occasion, Lincoln read items by humorist Artemus Ward [Charles Farrar Browne] to his cabinet members. John Hay's diary recorded one instance: "[Lincoln] read several chapters of the experiences of the saint & martyr Petroleum V. [Nasby] They were immensely amusing... President who read on con amore until 9 o'clock." Ralph Waldo Emerson preached individuality and the nobility of man in vigorous verse and essays. Emerson's optimistic philosophy of Transcendentalism taught that everybody had a divine spark enabling each individual to work toward perfection. Henry David Thoreau joined Emerson in warning Americans that they were too materialistic and placed too much emphasis on machines and technological values. William Lloyd Garrison began publishing the *Liberator* in 1831 as the organ of the militant abolitionist movement. After *Uncle Tom's Cabin* was serialized in the *National Era*, Harriet Beecher Stowe published the book in 1852. About 3,000 copies were sold the first day and 300,000 the first year.

As a result of these practical and cultural advancements, day-by-day living for Americans improved visibly adding to the public's enjoyment and inherent satisfaction. However, an economic panic occurred in 1837 emanating from reckless land speculation, the restriction of paper bank notes, and the granting of credit to purchase public lands. Land sales skyrocketed from $2.6 million in 1832 to $24.9 million in 1836. Average bank notes issued went from $4.5 million in 1823 to $19 million by 1831. In July 1836, President Andrew Jackson issued a specie circular stating that only gold, silver, or Virginia land scrip would be accepted by the government in payment for public lands. Jackson desired to sell up to 320 acres of public lands to each actual settler or bona fide state resident. He sought to repress "alleged frauds" from the "monopoly of the public lands in the hands of speculators and capitalists" and the "ruinous expansion" of bank notes and credit.

There were serious consequences from the Panic of 1837. New York's unemployed demonstrated against high rents and inflated food and fuel prices. One mob broke into food warehouses and sacked their supplies. Some banks suspended specie payments. Cotton prices fell by 50 percent in New Orleans. Public land sales dropped to 3.5 million acres in 1838; down from 20 million acres in 1836. This economic downturn caused some depression in the poorer industrial North while the wealthier agricultural South continued to prosper.

Population in the US increased from about 12 million in 1830 to 17 million in 1840 to 24 million in 1850; doubling in twenty years. During the 1840s there were 1,713,251 immigrants and during the 1850s an additional 2,598,214 newcomers. Large numbers of Europeans emigrated to the United States from Ireland following the potato famine and from Germany as a result of political troubles. This immigrant population combined with a massive migration of Americans on the move into the new states and territories. Hostilities toward the new immigrants increased in direct proportion to the competition for jobs and opportunities. Resultant cultural, ethnic, and economic differences stimulated adversarial regional nationalism among the inhabitants leading to a disorderly society. Zealously, Lincoln reacted to the divisive signs of distress in American society as well as to the impressive technological advancements.

Lincoln was aware of what was happening in America because he read a large number of newspapers and kept up-to-date. Gibson W. Harris, a law student at Lincoln & Herndon, considered newspapers "the most influential and potent influence that ever came into Lincoln's life in Illinois...[Lincoln] came up to the editorial office often and was a voracious reader of the [*Illinois State*] *Journal's* exchanges." His last law partner, William H. Herndon wrote about their source of information: "Lincoln and I took from 1853 to 1861 such papers as the *Chicago Tribune, New York Tribune, Charleston Mercury, Richmond Enquirer, Emancipator, Anit- Slavery Standard,* and *National Era.*" There is no reason to doubt that Lincoln & Herndon subscribed to a variety of newspapers during their years together.

Several mortifying events occurred shortly before Lincoln delivered a speech in 1838: vigilante mobs hanged gamblers in Mississippi; a barbarous rabble burned a mulatto man named McIntosh to death in St. Louis; and during November 1837 a horde of Southern sympathizers in Alton murdered Elijah P. Lovejoy, a minister who came from Maine and was the editor of the *Observer*, an Illinois anti-slavery newspaper. With these serious violations of law as a backdrop, twenty-eight-year-old Lincoln addressed the Young Men's Lyceum of Springfield, Illinois, on the *Perpetuation of Our Political Institutions* on January 27, 1838. Active in the Lyceum, Herndon extolled the civilization of the local population: "We had a society in Springfield which contained and commanded all the culture and talent of the place." Relevant to Lincoln's address, Aristotle taught his students at the original Lyceum in Athens, Greece. Specific to Lincoln's theme that evening, Aristotle's discourse *Politics* declared that "Law is a form of order, and good law must necessarily mean good order." Early in his talk, Lincoln remarked that due to good order Americans enjoyed "civil and religious liberty...a political edifice of liberty and equal rights...fundamental blessings...a legacy bequeathed us" by American revolutionary leaders. Before discussing the particular events that troubled him, Lincoln expressed his trepidation over the destruction of the rule of law as a means of sustaining social demeanor:

> I hope I am over wary; but if I am not, there is, even now, something of ill-omen amongst us. I mean the growing disregard for law which pervades the country; the growing disposition to substitute the wild and furious passions, in lieu of the sober judgment of Courts; and the worse than savage mobs, for the executive ministers of justice. This disposition is awfully fearful in any community; and that it now exists in ours, though grating to our feelings to admit, it would be a violation of truth and an insult to our intelligence, to deny.

In regard to the growing influence, and supposed superiority, of sectionalism, Lincoln pointed out the universality of the outrages against the law: they pervaded the community from New England to Louisiana without geographic restrictions; they were not the creatures of the climate; they were not confined to slave-holding or nonslave-holding states; they occurred among the order-loving citizens with steady habits; and they happened among the pleasure hunting masters of Southern slaves. "Whatever, then, their cause may be, it is common to the whole country." Continuing, Lincoln asked a rhetorical question: "What has this to do with the perpetuation of our political institutions?" His rapid and simple response: "it has much to do with it." Castigating the "mobocratic spirit," Lincoln recited a litany of actual recent vicious mob actions: They "burn churches, ravage and rob provision stores, throw printing presses into rivers, shoot editors, and hang and burn obnoxious persons at pleasure, and with impunity." Lincoln forecast that the people become tired, disgusted and alienated from a government that can not provide for the defense of their persons and property. In the end, the government will lose their strongest bulwark, the "*attachment* of the People." Logically, Lincoln delivered a simple answer to the question about fortifying the population against this disaster:

Let every American, every lover of liberty, every well wisher to his posterity, swear by the blood of the Revolution, never to violate in the least particular, the laws of the country; and never to tolerate their violation by others...Let every man remember that to violate the law, is to trample on the blood of his father... Let reverence for the laws, be breathed by every American mother...let it be taught in schools, in seminaries, and in colleges; let it be written in Primers, spelling books and in Almanacs; let it be preached from the pulpit, proclaimed in legislative halls, and enforced in courts of justice. And, in short, let it become the *political religion* of the nation.

Speaking about bad laws, Lincoln urged that they be religiously observed while in force. "There is no grievance that is a fit object of redress by mob law." Lincoln closed with a stirring appeal to the audience: "Reason, cold, calculating, unimpassioned reason, must furnish all the materials for our future support and defence— Let those materials be molded into *general intelligence, sound morality*, and in particular, a *reverence for the constitution and laws*... Upon these let the proud fabric of freedom rest, as the rock of basis." This Lyceum speech was published in the *Sangamon Journal* and provided the springboard to establish Lincoln's reputation beyond his own locality. His philosophical sentiments about law and social order were reiterated in many of his later discourses.

In preparing his notes for a law case on June 15, 1858, Lincoln recorded a pertinent point about law and order: "Legislation and adjudication must follow and conform to the progress of society." On the very next day, June 16, 1858, Lincoln addressed the Illinois state Republican convention convened in the capitol building in Springfield. Regarding the varying heated opinions on slavery, he said that "a house divided against itself cannot stand." Again, Lincoln echoed the law and social order theme. He spoke about slavery becoming "alike lawful...the almost complete legal combination-piece machinery...sacred right of self-government...people perfectly free to form and regulate their domestic institutions...except in cases where the power is restrained by the Constitution of the United States, the law of the State is supreme over the subject of slavery within its jurisdiction."

With the war clouds threatening, on December 22, 1859 Lincoln wrote to John J. Crittenden, the US senator from Kentucky, and reaffirmed his faith in the need for the people to respect and obey the law: "No law is stronger than is the public sentiment where it is to be enforced."

During Lincoln's inaugural journey to Washington, he stopped in Philadelphia at the site of the signing of the Declaration of Independence. In an impromptu speech, he emphatically stated: "I have never had a feeling politically that did not spring from the sentiments embodied in the Declaration of Independence." He particularly praised the sentiments that gave Americans and the world liberty and guaranteed Americans a promise for the future.

Lincoln delivered speeches to the New Jersey Senate and General Assembly on February 21, 1861. Pointedly, he remarked: "I am exceedingly anxious that this Union, the Constitution, and the liberties of the people shall be perpetuated in accordance with the original idea" of the American revolution. About two months later

A. LINCOLN, ESQUIRE

as he issued a proclamation calling up militia, Lincoln referred to the Southern irreverence for the national law: "Laws of the United States...now are opposed and the execution thereof obstructed...[action must be taken] to cause the laws to be duly executed."

On March 4, 1861, Lincoln delivered his first inaugural address in Washington. Significantly, Lincoln "swore in his presidential oath to take care that the laws be faithfully executed...[Lincoln] staunchly defended law, liberty and the constitution." This speech is replete with numerous mentions of the Constitution, lawful rights, abiding by the law, and appeals to reasoned decision-making and patience. "I have no purpose, directly or indirectly, to interfere with the institution of slavery where it exists. I believe I have no lawful right to do so, and I have no inclination to do so...Why should there not be a patient confidence in the ultimate justice of the people? ...that truth and that justice will surely prevail...there still is no single good reason for precipitate action." However, after the South attacked Fort Sumter in April 1861, Lincoln summarily suspended the writ of habeas corpus [you have the body] which allowed people who were arrested to challenge an illegal detention. Commenting on his restriction of civil liberties and his presidential oath to faithfully execute the laws, Lincoln said: "Are all the laws, but one to go unexecuted, and the government itself go to pieces, lest that one be violated?" As conditions changed, Lincoln's position softened. On April 2, 1864, Lincoln responded to a request from the Maryland district attorney about a Federal treason case. In 1861, Josiah Grindall, a thirty-six-year-old Baltimore resident, took part in a mob that blocked Massachusetts troops heading for Washington. Since the *writ of habeas corpus* was suspended, Grindall was arrested and held. His trial was coming up in 1864 and Lincoln sent a carefully worded reply: "In this case, not as a precedent for any other case, the District Attorney will be justified by me, if in his discretion, he will enter a *Nolle Prossequi*. A. Lincoln." *Nolle Prossequi*, sometimes spelled *Prosequi*, means no further prosecution and effectively dismisses charges in a criminal case.

Anticipating actual sensational events affecting President William J. Clinton at the end of 1998, a mock trial impeaching President Lincoln occurred on January 29, 1998 at the University of Arizona's law school in Tucson. All four articles of impeachment related to Lincoln's suspension of the *writ of habeas corpus* and demonstrated his violation of the First Amendment of the Constitution and his exceeding the emergency powers of the president:

Article One: On May 10, 1861, the President suspended the writ of habeas corpus, which led to the May 25 arrest of John Merryman, a citizen said to be drilling Marylanders in a scheme to take them south and join the Confederate army.

Article Two: In the summer of 1861, the President caused the arrest of sixteen members of the Maryland legislature, fearing they would pass an ordinance to secede from the Union.

Article Three: On August 8, 1862, the President issued an order to suspend the writ of habeas corpus in respect to all persons arrested and detained for violating the draft...arrested for disloyal practices... A further order permitted the arrest and imprisonment of anyone engaged in discouraging volunteer enlistment... Between August 8 and September 8, at least 354 civilians in the North became prisoners as a result of such orders including Charles Anderson and Samuel Strantzenheiner for giving a cheer and a hurrah for Jefferson Davis; Lewis Bobson for saying that Lincoln was a damn fool and the South's cause was just; and Dr. Israel Blanchard for attending a meeting of the Knights of the Golden Circle and making disloyal remarks.

Article Four: On May 5, 1863, the President had Representative Clement L. Vallandigham arrested, tried, and sentenced to close confinement in a United States fortress for publicly expressing disloyalties toward the U.S. government, for expressing sympathies for those in arms against the U.S. government, and for aiding and abetting the insurgents who gave aid and comfort to rebels against the authority of the U.S. government.

Mark E. Neely, professor of history and American studies at St. Louis University, Missouri, was the expert witness for the prosecution. Neely noted that Lincoln was told by his own assistant attorney general, Titian Coffey, that he did not have the power to suspend the *writ of habeas corpus*. Additionally, Chief Justice Roger B. Taney of the Supreme Court held that the president had no power to suspend the writ and an arrest was unconstitutional. In summary at the end of his cross-examination, Neely evaluated Lincoln: "I think history will record him as a very successful Commander-in-Chief and as a failed steward of the Constitution." Eric Foner, professor of history at Columbia University in New York, was the expert witness in Lincoln's defense. Foner eventually concluded that the impeachment was all about politics. On cross-examination, the questions and responses illuminated Foner's reasoning:

> Q: Professor Foner, is it fair for us to conclude, based upon your last remark, that you see this as a political prosecution?
> A: Yes, I do.
> Q: You do not accept, I take it, then, the proposition that there may be merit to the claims that the President engaged in the commission of high crimes and misdemeanors?
> A: That is right.
> Q: You find no substance in the accusations that his conduct was in direct violation of the Constitution?
> A: That is right. I think some of his subordinates were overzealous at times, but it is hard to believe that the President, while conducting the war, had an obligation to oversee every single action of every colonel and major in the Union Army. And, as we heard, in some cases when they went beyond the bounds of what was necessary, he reversed those orders.

In closing, the prosecution stressed that Lincoln denied the most basic rights to US citizens and ignored legal opinions stating that the president did not have the power to suspend the *writ of habeas corpus*. In defense, Lincoln's lawyer argued that the impeachment was about law, politics, and history. Commenting on the motives of the elected representatives, Lincoln's lawyer declared that "they want to tear the President down. Why? Not because of the law. Because of politics." After the members of the Senate voted, the judge spoke: "It is obvious from the polling of the Senate that the conviction is not confirmed and that a judgment of not guilty should be entered in the trial of the impeachment of President Abraham Lincoln." To set the record straight, Neely indicated in a footnote his personal view that Lincoln should not be impeached.

It appears that Lincoln's exigencies of war justified the public attitude that *inter arma silent leges* [in time of war the laws are silent]. Paradoxically, Lincoln acted with a disregard for personal liberty, but still had an overriding love for majority rule. Lincoln did not suspend the congressional elections in 1862 and 1864 nor the presidential election in 1864. Expressed in his own words, Lincoln said: "If there is anything which it is the duty of the whole people to never entrust to any hands but their own, that thing is the preservation and perpetuity, of their own liberties, and institutions."

At the end of 1862, Lincoln's concluding remarks to Congress in his annual message discussed his plan for voluntary colonization of slaves and compensated emancipation. He asked a rhetorical question: "Is it doubted that it would restore the national authority and national prosperity, and perpetuate both indefinitely?"

About one year later, Lincoln issued a thanksgiving proclamation, written by Secretary of State William H. Seward. That proclamation noted that despite the severity and magnitude of the Civil War "peace has been preserved with all nations, order has been maintained, the laws have been respected and obeyed, and harmony has prevailed everywhere except in the theatre of military conflict."

On August 18, 1864, Lincoln spoke to the 164th Ohio Regiment and admitted that "there may be some irregularities in the practical application of our system." Specifically, Lincoln spoke about citizens paying a fair share of taxes and about mistakes made by government officials. Nevertheless, he urged his audience to perpetuate the great, free government of the United States.

Shortly after Lincoln's reelection to a second term, the College of New Jersey [later Princeton University] conferred the honorary degree of Doctor of Laws on him. On December 27, 1864, Lincoln wrote to the college president, Dr. John Maclean, and reaffirmed his concern for good government. He acknowledged receiving the honor from "a body of gentlemen of such character and intelligence...I am most thankful if my labors have seemed to conduce to the preservation of those institutions under which alone we can expect good government." Lincoln received two other honorary Doctor of Laws degrees. One from Knox College (Galesburg, Illinois) on July 4, 1860 and another presented by Dr. Francis Lieber, president of Columbia College (NY) on June 26, 1861.

In Lincoln's second inaugural address on March 4, 1865, he was concise and biblical. "Both parties deprecated war; but one of them would *make* war rather than let the nation survive; and the other would *accept* war rather than let it perish... With malice toward none; with charity for all; with firmness in the right, as God gives us to see the right, let us strive on to finish the work we are in; to bind up the nation's wounds...to do all which may achieve and cherish a just and lasting peace, among ourselves, and with all nations." In his last public address on April 11, 1865, Lincoln mentioned the "re-inauguration of the national authority" and he revealed his thoughts on reconstruction.

These philosophical themes about obeying the law and applying reason continuously recurred throughout Lincoln's career as a lawyer and as a politician. Judge Sidney Breese addressed these themes based on his frequent experiences presiding when Lincoln appeared in various courts. "I have, for a quarter of a century, regarded Mr. Lincoln as the fairest lawyer I ever knew…a professional bearing so high-toned and honorable…He was besides, an honest lawyer, practicing none of the chicanery of the profession…presented to the profession as a model well worthy of the closest imitation." Notwithstanding, Lincoln's ideas and behavior were not unique. David Barnes, a law student at the University of North Carolina in 1840, compiled a notebook with a lofty philosophical entry about the law:

> The true spirit of the law is all equity, and justice. In a government based on true principles, the law is the sole sovereign of the nation… None are high enough to offend it with impunity, none so low that it scorns to protect them… The light of the law illumines the palace and the hovel…The power of the law crushes the power of men… It is the bulwark of piety—the upholder of morality—the guardian of the right—the distributor of justice. Its power is irresistible—its dominion indisputable. *It is above us, and around us, and within us we cannot fly from its protection.*

A frequently engraved phrase on public courthouses first appeared in John Locke's *Second Treatise of Government* in 1690: "Wherever Law ends, Tyranny begins." Captain Oliver Wendell Holmes, Jr., the future Supreme Court justice, who ordered Lincoln to get down from an exposed dangerous site at Fort Stevens during the Civil War, commented in an 1881 lecture: "The law embodies the story of a nation's development through many centuries." In 1893, Woodrow Wilson made a similar point during a lecture at Princeton University: "Law is the crystallization of the habit and thought of society."

Lincoln's law practice reflected the culture and society of his times just as the practice of law today mirrors the current status of civilization. Ambivalence existed at the time, and still does today, about using the justice system to resolve disagreements. Americans recognize the law as a necessary part of the fabric of our culture.

Yet, the formal imposition of legal action is ofttimes construed as a contentious act that is contrary to acceptable standards of gentility. Throughout time, people always sought justice to recover debts, to stop people from spreading base rumors about them, to settle matrimonial disputes, to register legal real estate deals, and a host of daily business and personal interactions between individuals. Even the Codex Hammurabi, carved in stone circa 1700 BCE, dealt with the minutiae of dispensing justice on all ordinary matters in a civilized society. Throughout his life, Lincoln maintained an utmost faith in "the sober judgment of Courts" and the ability of the people to arrive at reasoned decisions that sustained the social order. For Lincoln, there was a dynamic and symbiotic relation between his thoroughly compatible legal and political activities.

2

A. LINCOLN, ESQUIRE:

THE EVOLUTION OF A LAWYER

by John A. Lupton

He was not a folksy, down-home kind of guy. Instead he was a shrewd, sophisticated, tough and aggressive litigator with a staggering caseload who cared about making money and signed his legal papers as...*A. Lincoln.*

During the approximately twenty-five years that Abraham Lincoln practiced law, a rapid transformation of the legal system occurred in Illinois and throughout the nation. Meaningful aspects of the legal system began during the antebellum period: "the rise of a truly independent judiciary; the advent of state court reports, periodicals and legal treatises; major case law changes in tort, contracts, property and corporations; a strenuous effort toward codification; a flood of new state constitutions; and the emergence of a national pantheon of legal superstars which included John Marshall, James Kent, Lemuel Shaw, Daniel Webster and others."

Courtroom trials, along with politics, provided prime entertainment for the community. Isaac N. Arnold, a legal contemporary of Lincoln, commented that courtrooms were always crowded because the drama, tragedy, and comedy of real life occurred there. With judges and lawyers as the star actors, the courtroom substituted for the theater, the concert halls, and the opera. Spectators in the courtroom expected a good show from the lawyers, the judges, the witnesses and the other participants. Living up to his reputation, Lincoln seldom disappointed the crowd.

Lincoln practiced law mostly in the courts in central Illinois. In contrast to the myth that he was just a country lawyer who defended the underprivileged and downtrodden, Lincoln's legal reputation carried his practice far beyond the boundaries of Illinois. Furthermore, Lincoln used the vocation of law as a stepping stone to achieve his political aspirations. Like other attorneys such as Henry Clay, Andrew Jackson, and Daniel Webster, Lincoln "juggled law and politics so effectively that they nourished and reinforced each other." As he practiced law, Lincoln cemented legal and political connections in Illinois and throughout the nation. Lincoln evolved from an insecure self-taught lawyer in the 1830s to a confident and respected attorney. By 1860, his law practice provided a generous income, professional identity, and community stature.

In his courtroom appearances, Lincoln used logic, oratory, and his native intelligence to become a leading attorney in Illinois despite less than one year of formal education. William H. Herndon, Lincoln's third and last law partner, meticulously described how Lincoln acted before a jury:

> When he rose to speak to the jury...he stood inclined forward, was awkward, angular, ungainly, odd and, being a very sensitive man, I think that it added to his awkwardness.... Sometimes his hands, for a short while, would hang by his side...he used his head a great deal in speaking, throwing or jerking or moving it now here and now there, now in this position and now in that, in order to be more emphatic, to drive the idea home. Mr. Lincoln never beat the air, never sawed space with his hands, never acted for stage effect; was cool, careful, earnest, sincere, truthful, fair, self-processed, not insulting, not dictatorial; was pleasing, good-natured; had great strong naturalness of look, pose, and act.

As Mr. Lincoln proceeded further along with his oration, if time, place, subject, and occasion admitted of it, he gently and gradually warmed up; his shrill, squeaking, piping voice became harmonious, melodious, musical, if you please, with face somewhat aglow; his form dilated, swelled out, and *he rose up a splendid form.* erect, straight, and dignified....

Arnold, a prominent attorney himself, discussed Lincoln's ability as a litigator:

Lincoln was, upon the whole, the strongest jury lawyer in the state. He had the ability to perceive with almost intuitive quickness the decisive point in the case. In the examination and cross-examination of a witness he had no equal. He could compel a witness to tell the truth when he meant to lie, and if a witness lied he rarely escaped exposure under Lincoln's cross-examination....His legal arguments...were always clear, vigorous, and logical, seeking to convince rather by the application of principle than by the citation of cases....He seemed to magnetize everyone. He was so straight-forward, so direct, so candid, that every spectator was impressed with the idea that he was seeking only truth and justice. He excelled in the statement of his case. However complicated, he would disentangle it, and present the real issue in so simple and clear a way that all could understand.... His illustrations were often quaint and homely, but always apt and clear, and often decisive. He always met his opponent's case fairly and squarely, and never intentionally misstated law or evidence.

A summary of Lincoln's forensic and rhetorical style succinctly characterized the elements of his legal approach: "simplicity and economy of language, empathy, illustrative anecdotes or analogies, calculated dramatic outbursts, a taste for verbal antitheses, and a talent for riveting audience attention on fundamental issues of logic or equity." When he became president, Lincoln continued to apply these lawyerly characteristics to national matters of state.

Similar to today, the legal system in the antebellum period in the United States reflected life in general. An anecdote by Herndon illustrated Lincoln's thoughts about the law mirroring society. A newly elected justice of the peace in Sangamon County asked Lincoln for advice on forming his own judgments when acting as a justice. In response, Lincoln said: "There is no mystery in this matter...listen well to all the evidence, stripping yourself of all prejudice...and throwing away all technical law knowledge, hear the lawyers make their arguments...ask yourself: What is justice in this case?... Law is nothing else but the best reason of wise men applied for ages to the transactions and business of mankind." Lincoln's legal career was firmly imbedded within the larger social and legal framework of the antebellum era in Illinois and in the United States.

Antebellum Illinois was a litigious society. Cases in the courts throughout central Illinois depicted problems that local residents deemed aggravating enough to hire a lawyer and to bring into the legal system for dispute resolution. Legal issues included assault and battery, bankruptcy, contract disputes, debt, divorce, medical malpractice, mortgage foreclosure, personal injury, slander, and trespass. Courts did not exclude paupers, children, or women, although a married woman could not sue without her husband's consent under the law of coverture. During coverture, a married woman was civilly merged with her husband and could make no contracts without his consent.

As a consummate general practice attorney, Lincoln handled a broad spectrum of litigation from collecting a debt for a three-dollar hog before a justice of the peace to arguing state constitutional questions before the supreme court of Illinois to pleading bankruptcy cases before the federal courts. One of Lincoln's state constitutional issues involved the impeachment of a supreme court of Illinois justice in 1843. Thomas C. Browne, a Whig, was a supreme court justice since October 9, 1818. After twenty-five years on the bench, a politically motivated Democratic-majority legislature charged that he was "incompetent...ill-trained in the law" and voted to impeach him. Impeachment was the political means to the end of forcing out an unpopular Whig judge to replace him with a Democrat. Legislators even tried to redistrict the circuit courts to force Browne to hear cases four hundred miles away from his home. Browne hired Lincoln, a prominent Whig politician, to defend him. At one point in the 1843 case, Lincoln spoke with impassioned eloquence before the legislators about Browne's constitutional rights. Lincoln was so convincing that unfriendly legislators quickly passed a resolution forbidding further speeches at the hearings except by members of the House and by Browne. In the end, Lincoln successfully blocked the impeachment attempt. Browne continued to serve on the supreme court until January 11, 1847.

During Lincoln's time, lawyers knew enough about various types of legal actions to competently argue their cases. Throughout his long legal career, Lincoln was involved in at least 5,000 cases. However, Lincoln did not specialize in any one area of the law. More than half of Lincoln's cases [55 percent] involved debt collection at all levels of court: justice of the peace, county, circuit, appellate, and federal. His remaining caseload included, among others, inheritance-related matters (15 percent), mortgage foreclosure (7 percent), divorce (3 percent), slander (2 percent), and medicine (less than 1 percent). Only 4 percent, about 160 of his cases, involved railroads. Although minor in number, Lincoln's railroad litigation resulted in major consequences in the formative age of railroads and railroad law.

While Lincoln did develop a large practice, he was not immediately successful in his chosen career. Initially, the Sangamon County Circuit Court issued Lincoln a certificate of good moral character, and the supreme court of Illinois examined him. On September 9, 1836, Lincoln received his license to practice law in the courts of Illinois. John Todd Stuart, a cousin of Lincoln's future wife, Mary Todd, and a prominent citizen and politician in Springfield, asked Lincoln to join him in the practice of law as a junior partner. Stuart was a college graduate who commenced practice in Springfield in 1828 and became a successful lawyer. During the Black Hawk War in 1832, Stuart was a major in Lincoln's battalion. When Stuart and Lincoln both represented Sangamon County in the Illinois General Assembly from 1834 to 1836, Stuart lent law books to Lincoln and influenced him toward the study of law. In the spring of 1837, the two began their legal partnership and regularly published advertisements in the *Sangamo Journal* such as the front page professional card that appeared on April 15, 1837:

J. T. STUART AND A. LINCOLN, ATTORNEYS AND COUNSELLORS AT LAW, WILL PRACTICE CONJOINTLY IN THE COURTS OF THIS JUDI-CIAL CIRCUIT. OFFICE NO. 4, HOFFMAN ROW, UPSTAIRS.

Stuart & Lincoln handled at least seven hundred cases in the four years that they practiced together. Of those cases, nearly 67 percent concerned debt collection. *Herndon v. Smith* was a typical debt case. Thomas Smith gave John Herndon a promissory note for $100 for a debt. In turn, John Herndon owed money to William Herndon, an uncle of Lincoln's future law partner, and assigned the promissory note to him. Smith paid $29.75, but failed to pay the balance. William Herndon heard that Smith planned to leave Illinois without paying his debts. He hired Stuart & Lincoln to sue Smith. In July 1837, William Herndon sued Smith to attach his real and personal property. This legal maneuver gave Herndon a lien on Smith's property if he left the state. Smith could not take his possessions with him because the sheriff seized them. After Smith defaulted, the court ruled for Herndon and awarded him $73.75. Other people also sued Smith because he owed them debts. To settle the litigation, the court sold the seized property and the proceeds were prorated among Smith's creditors. Herndon received $9 from the sale of the land and $26.78 from the sale of the personal property. Many creditors in antebellum Illinois, such as Herndon, did not receive full pecuniary satisfaction from their victory in the courtroom. Typically, Stuart & Lincoln received five dollars for their legal services.

In 1838, Stuart continued to concentrate on politics and was elected as a Whig to the Twenty-sixth Congress. After Stuart left for Washington in November 1839, Lincoln wrote in their partnership fee book: "Commencement of Lincoln's administration 1839 Nov 2." With only eighteen months experience at the bar, Stuart's departure left the novice Lincoln running a leading legal firm in Springfield. Somewhat overwhelmed in his new capacity, Lincoln handled the business as best he could. However, he sorely missed the opportunity to learn from the empirical legal experience of Stuart's twelve years of practicing law. Although managing the partnership by himself was initially burdensome, Lincoln probably relied on his instincts and power of persuasive speech to win cases rather than his legal acumen.

After Stuart's reelection to Congress in 1840 and two years of practicing law by himself, Lincoln began to question his abilities and vacillated about his decision to become a lawyer. In a letter to Stuart, Lincoln replied to a suggestion: "the matter you speak of on my account, you may attend to as you say, unless you shall hear of my condition forbidding it. I say this, because I fear I shall be unable to attend to any business here, and a change of scene might help me. If I could be myself, I would rather remain at home with Judge Logan." This letter was written three weeks after the "fatal first" of January 1841, at which time Lincoln broke his engagement to Mary Todd. Although much of Lincoln's letter to Stuart is of a personal nature, parts of it may relate to his legal career. No doubt, Stuart recognized that their long-distance partnership was not working out for Lincoln. He possibly suggested that Lincoln pursue a legal partnership with Stephen T. Logan.

On April 14, 1841, Stuart and Lincoln formally dissolved their partnership. Stuart remained in the US Congress until March 3, 1843. After the breakup of the Whig Party in 1854, Stuart became a Democrat and opposed Lincoln on many policies. During Lincoln's presidency, Stuart served in the US House of Representatives as a Democrat from March 4, 1863 to March 3, 1865.

A. LINCOLN, ESQUIRE

Early in 1841, new professional prospects rejuvenated Lincoln's slow-moving career. Logan saw an opportunity to become a leading bankruptcy attorney in Illinois and solicited Lincoln's help. Congress passed *An Act to Establish a Uniform System of Bankruptcy Throughout the United States* on February 1, 1842. In the thirteen months that the bankruptcy law was in operation, Logan & Lincoln handled at least seventy bankruptcies for people from nearly thirty counties in Illinois. Only three other lawyers or law partnerships handled more bankruptcies than Logan & Lincoln. Bankrupts came from all over Illinois. Logan & Lincoln handled twelve bankruptcies from Sangamon County, Lincoln's home county, and ten from Boone County, on the Wisconsin border. In handling these cases all over Illinois, Lincoln began to make political alliances.

Logan served a crucial mentoring role for the unpolished Lincoln as he showed him how to pay attention to the methodical details of a case. In the eyes of his colleagues Logan was "one of the ablest and most successful lawyers of the state, and at that time universally recognized as the head of the bar at the capital." Logan was Scotch, dour, and not loveable. Herndon described Logan:

> a little shriveled-up man, a thoroughly read man in all the departments of the law, quick as lightning and as technical as technicality itself; he was the best circuit court *nisi prius* lawyer on the circuit; he could gain a case where no other man could, unaccommodating in his practice, cold, ungenerous, snappy, irritable, fighting like a game fowl every point of his case and, when whipped at this point, he would grumblingly fall back on his next point.... Logan fought a five-cent case just as energetically and as well as he fought one for ten thousand dollars, rather better because such a big pile of money broke him down through fear of losing the case.

Herndon observed that Logan was an orderly and technical lawyer and Logan's example "had a good effect on Lincoln." Later,

Herndon concluded that Lincoln's loose habits of practicing law eventually overcame Logan's influence.

Despite Logan's unruly hair and disheveled clothing, he had an orderly mind crammed with legal lore. Logan saw potential in the unseasoned Lincoln, and their partnership propelled Lincoln into new areas of law. At this time in his life and in his career Lincoln needed guidance and Logan's influence was one of the main reasons that Lincoln became a successful attorney. As the senior partner, Logan described how Lincoln worked and learned the law:

> He would get a case and try to know all there was connected with it...he got to be quite a formidable lawyer... So far as his reading knowledge of law went he had a quite unusual grasp of the principles involved. When he was with me, I have seen him get a case and seem to be bewildered at first, but he would go at it and after a while he would master it. He was very tenacious in his grasp of a thing that he once got hold of.

Herndon, then studying law in the Logan & Lincoln office, agreed Lincoln "was in every respect a case lawyer." Lincoln "never studied law books unless a case was on hand for consideration." He did not concern himself with a legal question until he had a case involving that question. In addition to bankruptcy, Logan & Lincoln handled numerous cases in the federal district court in Springfield. Their law partnership became one of the more sought-after firms to handle appeals before the supreme court of Illinois.

Logan & Lincoln handled approximately 850 cases in the four years that they practiced together. In the 1830s, Logan was a circuit-riding lawyer. After entering into partnership with Lincoln, Logan remained in Springfield, while Lincoln expanded his circuit travels. Geographically, Lincoln ventured beyond the boundaries of the Eighth Judicial Circuit and handled cases in Clark County, on the Indiana border, and in Madison County, on the Missouri border. Frequently, Lincoln traveled to Coles County, which was not on his circuit, because his father, stepmother, and family lived there. About 70 percent of the litigation of the Logan & Lincoln firm was debt collection. This increase in business from the Stuart & Lincoln partnership probably can be attributed to the bankruptcy act.

Lincoln began his supreme court of Illinois practice during his partnership with Stuart, but had few cases of any importance. Stuart & Lincoln only handled ten cases in the supreme court of Illinois during their partnership. Lincoln's appellate practice blossomed during his partnership with Logan. In part, this increase occurred when the supreme court of Illinois moved to the new state capital at Springfield in 1839 from its former site at Vandalia. Logan was well known for his ability to argue a case in the supreme court and he set an outstanding legal example for Lincoln to imitate. In each term of the supreme court, the firm of Logan & Lincoln averaged twenty-five cases. Attorneys from all parts of Illinois asked Logan & Lincoln to handle their appeals before the supreme court. In terms of practical economics, Logan introduced Lincoln to a more prestigious supreme court of Illinois and federal practice.

Logan and Lincoln did not divide fees equally. Lincoln probably got a one-third share. In comparison with the Stuart & Lincoln partnership, the average number of cases per year nearly doubled in the Logan & Lincoln partnership. This increased workload began to provide Lincoln with a lucrative income. During his Logan & Lincoln partnership, Lincoln married Mary Todd and rented a second-floor room in Springfield in a combination hotel and stagecoach office. Lincoln wrote to his friend Joshua F. Speed: "We are not keeping house, but boarding at the Globe Tavern, which is well kept now by a widow of the name of [Sarah] Beck. Our room (the same Dr. [William S.] Wallace occupied there) and boarding only costs us four dollars a week." They ate their meals in the common dining room of the boardinghouse. On August 1, 1843, their son Robert was born at the Globe Tavern. Shortly thereafter, the Lincolns rented a small three-room frame cottage on South Fourth Street in Springfield for $100 per year. Less than a year later, Lincoln bought his only house at Eighth and Jackson Streets.

In contrast to the, at times, careless approach that Stuart & Lincoln assumed in collecting fees, Logan took the matter of fees seriously and diligently pursued delinquent clients. In one case, Justin H. Butterfield, the United States attorney for the district of Illinois, sued Perah Farnsworth to recover a penalty on a bond. John Atchison, one of the defendants in the case, signed the bond as a surety for Farnsworth and retained Logan & Lincoln. In its verdict, the court ruled for Farnsworth and his sureties. Logan & Lincoln charged Atchison $100 for their legal services. However, Atchison failed to pay them and Logan & Lincoln immediately sued Atchison to recover the $100 debt. Atchison defaulted, and the court ruled for Logan & Lincoln and awarded them $100. Lincoln learned his lessons and continued to pursue clients that did not pay his fees throughout his legal career.

After almost four years of practicing law together, Logan & Lincoln dissolved their partnership amicably in the fall of 1844. Logan wanted to begin a partnership with his son David. Fortunately, this coincided with Lincoln's desire to form his own law firm after seven years of serving as a junior partner. In 1844, Lincoln asked Herndon, then twenty-six years old, to be his junior partner. In 1841, Lincoln encouraged Herndon to read law at the Logan & Lincoln office. Herndon read law for three years, received a certificate of good moral character on November 27, 1844, and was admitted to the bar on December 9, 1844.

During the time that Lincoln and Herndon practiced together, the state of Illinois underwent dynamic and historic changes. Railroads went from being a curiosity to a popular and common mode of transportation. People migrated into Illinois and the population increased dramatically. Economically, the state gradually changed from a subsistence economy to a market economy. A new state constitution was adopted and the law changed in concordance. As a citizen and as a lawyer, Lincoln experienced these changes within the state. Along the way, Lincoln evolved into one of the best attorneys in Illinois. Lincoln's peers considered him a "lawyer's lawyer" and enlisted his aid in litigation involving everything from homicides to railroads. Using the pseudonym Cog, a reporter for the Danville *Illinois Citizen*, complimented lawyer Lincoln's abilities:

> In his examination of witnesses, he displays a masterly ingenuity and a legal tact that baffles concealment and defies defeat…. And in addressing a jury, there is no false glitter, no sickly sentimentalism to be discovered…[s]eizing upon the minutest points, he weaves them into his argument with an ingenuity really astonishing…. Bold, forcible and energetic, he forces conviction upon the mind, and by his clearness and conciseness, stamps it there not to be erased…. Though he may have his equal, it would be no easy task to find his superior.

Lincoln & Herndon set up office in the Tinsley building, a handsome Greek Revival structure at Sixth and Adams Streets in Springfield. Seth M. Tinsley owned the building and operated a mercantile business on the first floor. He leased space for a federal post office on the ground floor and a federal courtroom on the second floor along with offices for the court clerks and chambers for the judges. Lincoln retained the third floor office from his partnership with Logan. Lincoln & Herndon's office fronted the state capitol across the square, a prime location. Their law office was directly above the US Circuit and District courtroom and had a trap door in the floor, which Lincoln or Herndon could open and listen in on the proceedings. Directly across the square, the supreme court of Illinois met in the state capitol and the court had the most comprehensive law library in the state. Lincoln and Herndon frequently borrowed books or conducted research at this library. A block north on Sixth Street, the Sangamon County Circuit Court conducted their business. Across Sixth Street, Springfield's finest hotel, the American House, provided lodging for lawyers, legislators, and lobbyists. "Mr. Lincoln usually called his partner Billy and Mr. Herndon always addressed his partner as Mr. Lincoln." "Not even Judge David Davis or any of his other intimates felt sufficiently free and easy to call him *Abe* or slap him on the shoulder."

After Lincoln was elected to the US Congress and moved to Washington in 1847, Herndon rented a smaller office on the opposite end of the third floor in the same building. When Lincoln returned in March 1849, he resumed his law practice in the smaller office. Disappointed at their meager library, Herndon purchased $168.65 worth of books and charged half of the cost to Lincoln. By late 1852, Lincoln & Herndon moved from the Tinsley building and advertised their firm in an office on the west side of the public square. During their partnership, Lincoln & Herndon occupied at least three law offices on the state capitol square in Springfield.

Gibson Harris, a law student and clerk at Lincoln & Herndon in 1845, described the Tinsley building office:

> The furniture, somewhat dilapidated, consisted of one small desk and a table, a sofa or lounge with a raised head at one end, and a half-dozen plain wooden chairs. The floor was never scrubbed...Over the desk a few shelves had been enclosed; this was the office bookcase holding a set of Blackstone, Kent's Commentaries, Chitty's Pleadings, and a few other books. A fine law library was in the Capitol building across the street to which the attorneys of the place had access.

John Littlefield, a law student and clerk in the same law office, cleaned up the premises one day and found that seeds sprouted in the dirt on the floor. Generally, all the offices were poorly maintained. Four large unscrubbed windows barely illuminated the dark and dingy office. Two worktables, one long and one short, formed a T and were covered with baize, a felt-like wool, to make it easier to write with the quill pens. Often, Lincoln sat at the end of the table reading aloud. After reading material about a case, Lincoln would put down the papers and declare: "Do you know what this case makes me think of?" He would then tell a humorous story.

A systematic lack of an office management system was obvious. Disorder was apparent in the scattered papers, bulging desk drawers and the overflowing pigeonholes atop the desk.

Lincoln had poor organizational skills and left papers all over the office. He haphazardly stuck important notes and documents into his elongated black stovepipe hat converting it into a makeshift filing cabinet. Both partners had difficulty finding documents and even had to admit that papers were lost or destroyed or could not be found. When a client complained that Lincoln did not answer his letter, Lincoln apologized. His explanation averred that he put the letter "in my old hat and buying a new one the next day the old one was set aside, and so the letter was lost sight of for a time." One bundle of papers on his desk had a notation written by Lincoln: "When you can't find it anywhere else, look in this."

Lincoln was a hard-working attorney who was self-reliant and rarely consulted other lawyers for advice. After the dissolution of their partnership, Lincoln did maintain a close legal relationship with Logan, who was one of the few lawyers that Lincoln consulted. Herndon said that often Lincoln worked from seven or eight in the morning until midnight. Albert T. Bledsoe, a lawyer who practiced in Springfield in the 1840s and later became an ardent Southern nationalist, claimed that Lincoln "did his reading...by *proxy*, by his Good-Man Friday, William H. Herndon, who, with creditable zeal and industry, would collect all sorts of cases and authorities for him. From these he would make his selections and prepare his arguments...." Using the firm's commonplace book, similar to a composition book, Herndon maintained a listing of various legal topics classified by subject, with supporting case citations and legal treatises. However, Herndon was not simply Lincoln's law clerk; he maintained a thriving practice himself, consistently traveled to neighboring counties for legal work, and argued many important cases before the supreme court of Illinois. Lincoln did not solely rely on Herndon and performed much of his own research if working on a particular legal subject.

In seventeen years of practicing law, Lincoln & Herndon handled nearly 3,400 cases. Seventeen hundred (50 percent) of these cases concerned the collection of debts. Although this is still an extraordinary number, it is considerably less than the percentage during Lincoln's partnerships with Stuart and with

Logan. As he practiced, Lincoln continually expanded the breadth of his legal knowledge. Herndon noticed a change in Lincoln's habits after Lincoln returned from his term in the US Congress in 1849. On the surface, Lincoln devoted more time to law and less time to politics. Courts became more serious and learned as judges and lawyers acquired and applied their various expertise. Lincoln excelled at new areas of law. Railroad companies sought out Lincoln & Herndon to handle their cases. Land titles were critical to people, and Lincoln was successful at proving ownership of land. However, Lincoln continued to handle simple debt cases for nominal fees throughout his legal career. Despite their success, Herndon expressed doubts about Lincoln as a lawyer: "Yet Mr. Lincoln in a certain sense was a great lawyer, and in another sense an exceedingly little one."

Lincoln continued and refined his appellate practice. In the course of their seventeen-year partnership, Lincoln & Herndon averaged fifteen cases per year on appeal to the supreme court of Illinois. Lincoln handled a number of notable cases before the supreme court of Illinois. In *Barret v. Alton and Sangamon Railroad*, Lincoln argued that stock subscribers to a railroad company must pay their obligations despite the fact that the railroad altered the course of the road. Significantly, this case "emphasized the necessary subordination of individual shareholder interest to those of railroad management in making corporate decisions." In part, Lincoln's success at the supreme court was attributed to his slow thinking. Herndon said that Lincoln "thought slowly and acted slowly; he must have his time to think, analyze the facts, and then wind them into a whole story." In Herndon's opinion, Lincoln was at his best in the supreme court:

> But it was in the Supreme Court of the State of Illinois that he [Lincoln] was truly a great lawyer, and nowhere else. The Supreme Court has its rules and gives time, ample time, to read the record and gather up the facts of the case, the issues and the law arising thereon, abstracts of the case and the lawyers' briefs, stating the facts in a condensed form and the issues made

thereby. No man can be caught by surprise here and thrown out of court. In this court there is, except on special occasions, no oral evidence admitted. The written record as made up alone goes to the court. The lawyers see each other's briefs, arguments, and the quoted law; they have ample time to hunt up the law and to argue the case, and in this court alone Lincoln was great truly and indeed.

In federal court, Lincoln & Herndon's litigation consisted mainly of debt collection by out-of-state creditors who sued Illinois residents. More than half of the creditors came from major metropolitan areas such as Boston, Cincinnati, New York, Philadelphia, and St. Louis. In the 1840s, Lincoln handled several noteworthy land-title cases that went to the Supreme Court of the United States. While in Washington, DC, shortly after the end of his term in Congress, Lincoln argued for the defendant Thomas Lewis in *Lewis for use of Broadwell v. Lewis*. Lincoln claimed that the statute of limitations prevented William Lewis from suing his client. Chief Justice Roger B. Taney ruled against Thomas Lewis declaring that the statute of limitations had not expired. In the 1850s, Lincoln traveled to Chicago for sessions of the federal district court in addition to maintaining a strong presence in the Springfield federal court. Lincoln even planned to argue several more cases before the Supreme Court of the United States in 1860, but instead focused on the upcoming presidential nomination and election.

Lincoln was considerably knowledgeable about federal law. Illinois attorneys who were not familiar with federal practice wrote Lincoln asking for advice in the federal court. Lincoln made additions and corrections on the pertinent documents and filed them for other lawyers. During the late 1850s, Lincoln was among the leaders of the bar in Illinois. East Coast attorneys and potential clients sought him out requesting legal assistance. These people may have been familiar with Lincoln's politics, may have had previous legal experience with him, or may have asked someone for a referral. Whatever the reason, Lincoln was well known as an effective attorney, at least in the eastern and mid-western states. After Lincoln delivered the Cooper Union Address in New York in February 1860, Erastus Corning, the president of the New York Central Railroad, offered Lincoln a job with the railroad as general counsel at a salary of $10,000 per year. Lincoln refused the position to concentrate on his pursuit of the US presidency.

Lincoln probably gained much of his income from his federal practice. A case could not be heard in the US Circuit Court unless it involved a dispute exceeding $500. As a result, Lincoln could charge more. He received $350 for a fee in the sand bar case, *Johnston v. Jones & Marsh*, in 1860. This case included detailed maps and consumed five federal trials and two US Supreme Court appeals to determine title to valuable accreted land at the mouth of the Chicago River. Allegedly, Lincoln accepted $600 for his fee in the McCormick reaper case. Cyrus McCormick, the inventor of the reaper, claimed that Manny and Company infringed on his patent. These two examples illustrate the higher end of Lincoln's legal fee scale. Average fees in federal court were generally larger than the standard $10 to $20 fee that Lincoln charged while riding the circuit.

Arnold, a fellow lawyer, estimated Lincoln's annual income at $2,000 to $3,000 per year. However, this figure is misleading because Arnold extrapolated Lincoln's activity at a particular time to the whole of his career. Based on the number of cases in each of Lincoln's partnerships, he probably earned around $750 to $1,000 per year with Stuart and $1,000 to $1,500 per year with Logan. Over the course of the seventeen-year partnership with Herndon, Lincoln's income gradually rose. By the late 1850s, Lincoln most likely earned around $4,000 to $5,000 per year. Lincoln's total property was valued between $10,000 and $20,000. Comparative annual salaries in 1849 had Illinois Supreme Court justices earning $1,200, circuit judges earning $1,000, and the governor earning $1,500.

Unlike many of his fellow attorneys, Lincoln did not engage in land speculation. As a result, many of his associates such as Judge Davis and Clifton H. Moore became wealthy from their land transactions. However, Lincoln was content to earn his living from the law. Occasionally, he earned large fees for cases. However, as one of the hardest-working lawyers, Lincoln earned his living from the sheer quantity of his cases. Lincoln & Herndon had one of the largest practices in the Sangamon County Circuit Court. At times, they handled more than a third of the cases in a given court term. While on the circuit, Lincoln worked hard as well, and earned from $150 to $325 in a given term.

Circuit traveling was a vital aspect of Lincoln's legal career. Lawyers, judges, and clerks traveled from county seat to county seat holding court for a week or so in each location. Courts met every day except Sunday. Courthouses were frame or brick structures usually topped by a cupola and surrounded by verandas with huge columns. Inside, the courtroom walls were painted a hard white with unpainted wood trim. Stark wooden benches and a platform for the judge sat atop the pine floors. Huge Franklin stoves heated the courtroom as yards of stovepipe traveled along the walls and ceilings seeking an exit.

When the circuit-riding lawyers entered the town square, local people in need of legal representation and local lawyers needing help sought them out. Lincoln "occupied very much the position of an English Barrister, being called on by other lawyers to try cases for them." During his partnership with Stuart, Lincoln began to ride the circuit and he expanded his territorial range during his partnership with Logan. However, it was during his partnership with Herndon that Lincoln's circuit riding covered the most terrain.

During the last seventeen years that Lincoln practiced law the Eighth Judicial Circuit expanded and contracted. When the Illinois General Assembly created the eighth circuit in 1839, it contained nine counties. In 1845, the circuit contained fifteen counties. During the period 1849 to 1853, Lincoln traveled to fourteen counties on the circuit—a 500-mile trip. After a few years of this extensive traveling, Lincoln concluded that the circuit was too large. Travel was still cumbersome since railroads had not yet connected county seats. Although he was not a member of the

Illinois General Assembly, Lincoln wrote the bill to reduce the eighth circuit and removed many of the counties that traditionally were Democratic strongholds. From 1853 to 1857, only eight counties comprised the eighth circuit. In 1857, Lincoln's home county of Sangamon moved into the newly created Eighteenth Judicial Circuit, but Lincoln continued to travel to the five remaining counties on the eighth circuit.

Generally, the circuit judge, the state's attorney, and Lincoln were the only people to travel the entire circuit. Most lawyers practiced in their own county and a few neighboring counties. They traveled with the group to the next county but returned home afterwards. However, Lincoln kept moving to the next county and was on the road for a total of four to five months per year. In 1850, Lincoln was on the circuit 175 days and in 1852 for 155 days.

Circuit riders traversed the area on horseback with an extra shirt or two in their saddlebags along with two or three law books. Later, the circuit riders used a horse and buggy. They endured the hard fare at miserable country taverns, slept on the floor or shared a room and often a bed with other lawyers. Horrible travel conditions included muddy or dusty roads, swollen streams that had to be forded, and fallen trees to bypass. Despite the hardships, Lincoln enjoyed the circuit life. To occupy their time while staying in neighborhood taverns or farmhouses, the men told stories, read books, and discussed politics. Judge Davis, who presided on the Eighth Judicial Circuit from 1849 to 1862, often held an informal orgmathorial, a made-up word, court to try circuit travelers for a breach of decorum. In one session, Davis found Lincoln guilty of "impoverishing this bar by your picayune charges of fees. You are now almost as poor as Lazarus, and if you don't make people pay you more for your services, you will die as poor as Job's turkey."

Upon arriving in a county seat, circuit-riding lawyers set up ambulatory law offices on the sunny side of the courthouse or under a shady tree. Prospective clients approached Lincoln and asked him to write a legal document for a case. Local attorneys asked Lincoln to assist them with a case or make the arguments before a jury. Usually, Lincoln prepared for five or six cases in a three-or four-day term of court. When court adjourned, Lincoln preferred to be paid in cash by his clients. However, he accepted promissory notes and hoped to be paid at the next term of court. Lincoln then rode out of town on his horse or in his buggy and headed toward the next county seat. By the late 1850s, railroads linked most major towns and Lincoln often traveled to a county seat, returned to Springfield, and then continued to the next county seat.

Circuit riding portrays a romantic image of a cadre of legal professionals coming into town to dispense frontier justice and to argue cases on issues of right or wrong. In contrast, the common law was a strictly structured legal system. Courts followed precedent and dismissed cases for minor technicalities. In 1858, Lincoln took advantage of an inexperienced state's attorney in a murder case. James B. White held the office of state's attorney for less than a year. During a drunken brawl, an incensed John Bantzhouse, a tavern-keeper in Sangamon County, fired a shotgun through a window and hit and killed Walter Clark. Without objection from White, defense lawyer Lincoln secured a change of venue and a continuance to locate witnesses. Significantly, White unwittingly violated the statutory limit specifying that a murder suspect must be tried within two consecutive court terms. On Lincoln's motion, the court dismissed the case on this technical violation of the speedy trial rule.

On one occasion, Lincoln's hardball tactics led to a jury acquittal and an indicted murderer walked free. When Judge Edward Y. Rice excluded critical evidence, Lincoln angrily protested. He told the judge that he "had never heard of such law" and inaccurately challenged the rulings as "absurd and without precedent in the broad world." Herndon said that Lincoln spoke "fiercely and contemptuously" of the court's decision. In the face of this "withering attack," Judge Rice retracted his ruling and admitted all the substantiation. Lincoln's evidence showed that the victim threatened to beat up the defendant. His dying confession acknowledged the blame and granted forgiveness to the defendant: "Yes, I have brought it upon myself, and I forgive Quinn."

Almost all of the local attorneys on the circuit worked with Lincoln at one time or another. There is no evidence to show that Lincoln favored local lawyers affiliated with the Whig or Republican parties. He had close relations with Democratic attorneys on the circuit as well. Although Lincoln enjoyed traveling the circuit because it allowed him to make political connections throughout central Illinois, when he stepped into the courtroom, politics was irrelevant. Along the Indiana border, in Vermilion County, Ward Hill Lamon and Lincoln established an informal partnership. Lamon became a state's attorney on the eighth circuit, and they handled more than 150 cases together. When Lamon advertised their partnership in local Danville newspapers, Lincoln did not object. Yet, this partnership did not prevent Lincoln from working with other attorneys in Danville and even from opposing Lamon in a handful of cases. As president, Lincoln appointed Lamon the United States Marshal for the District of Columbia. Lincoln claimed that other lawyers had wanted to become his junior partner and "hoped to secure a law practice by hanging to [Lincoln's] coat-tail."

Content with traveling the circuit as an advocate, Lincoln did not have any aspirations to seek high-profile positions such as judge or state's attorney. At times, Judge Davis had to leave a county while circuit court was still in session. Between 1854 and 1859, Davis appointed Lincoln acting judge in his place to try cases or finish the term. Although this was not legal, it was common practice. In many of the 300 pending cases, Lincoln simply continued them to the next term. In other cases, Lincoln "decreed divorces, awarded settlements, granted foreclosures, allowed motions, accepted dismissals, approved reports, acknowledged proof and in general performed all of the duties of a judge." Lincoln assisted and wrote documents for David Campbell, the state's attorney, and his successor Lamon. In the Logan County Circuit Court, Lincoln drafted an indictment for Lamon. Shortly thereafter, Lamon wrote to Lincoln, who was in Chicago for another case, that the defense attorney filed a motion to quash the indictment on a technicality. Lincoln responded: "If, after all, the

A. LINCOLN, ESQUIRE

indictment shall be quashed, it will only prove that my forte is as a Statesman, rather than as a Prossecutor [sic]."

During his circuit travels and while working at home in Springfield, Lincoln became exposed to many different types of litigation. Some counties, such as Shelby, had an extraordinary number of slander cases. Counties that contained railroads had a large number of railroad lawsuits. Lincoln was in favor of the building of railroads ever since he served in the Illinois General Assembly in the 1830s. Although it took nearly fifteen years before railroads in Illinois became feasible, Lincoln continued to support them. He even bought stock subscriptions to a railroad scheduled to run from Springfield to Alton, Illinois. Despite his personal interest in railroads, however, Lincoln opposed railroads in the courtroom as often as he represented them.

Lincoln's railroad practice was particularly notable. One of the biggest constitutional issues to come before the Illinois court system concerned the question of whether a county was able to tax the land on which the Illinois Central Railroad ran its tracks. While Lincoln had no preference for either the county or the railroad, he wanted to be involved in the case so that he would not "miss a fee altogether." Eventually, McLean County assessed its tax and threatened to sell the railroad's land to pay the taxes. Quickly, the railroad retained Lincoln and sued for an injunction to stop the sale of the railroad's real property. After losing in the lower court, Lincoln won the case on appeal before the supreme court of Illinois. Lincoln charged the railroad $5,000 for his legal services. However, the railroad refused to pay because only Eastern attorneys were paid that much. Finally, Lincoln sued the railroad for his fee and won the case with the testimony of other attorneys. This was Lincoln's largest known legal fee for one case.

Most of the railroad cases in which Lincoln was involved concerned more mundane matters than vital constitutional questions. Wilson Allen, a DeWitt County farmer, owned land along the Illinois Central Railroad and brought several damage suits against the railroad. While building the railroad, workers destroyed his land, despoiled his crops, and left stagnant pools of water near his house. Lincoln represented the Illinois Central in five cases in which Allen requested a total of $9,300 in damages. Juries found for Allen in three cases and awarded him a total of $1,063 in damages. One case was dismissed by the court. In the final case, the jury found for Allen and awarded him $25. Lincoln appealed that case to the supreme court of Illinois because Allen had already received an award from the court in an earlier case. In agreement, the supreme court reversed the decision. Even though Lincoln lost three of the five cases, he mitigated the damages for the railroad. In this example, Lincoln was a successful railroad attorney despite his won-loss record.

Another legal area in which Lincoln excelled was land titles. Land was a valuable commodity in antebellum Illinois and inhabitants wanted a clear title to their property. Lincoln had more than 130 ejectment cases that determined who possessed proper title to a tract of land. Because of his reputation, litigants sought Lincoln to handle their title disputes, particularly in the federal courts. Four of Lincoln's five cases that reached the Supreme Court of the United States dealt with land disputes. J. H. Cheney, a client of Lincoln's from Bloomington, claimed that Lincoln could untangle "knotty land cases," particularly title work. In 1856, another client, Herring Chrisman, asked Lincoln for his opinion on some land claims in Illinois. Chrisman reported that Lincoln gave him an honest answer and charged a low fee for his services.

Most of Lincoln's criminal cases concerned economic interests of local citizens such as larceny or moral problems such as liquor violations. Criminal law comprised only about 5 percent of Lincoln's total caseload. Nevertheless, murder trials attracted widespread attention from local citizens, who probably knew either the victim or the defendant. Although murder trials were a small percentage of Lincoln's criminal caseload, several of his most famous litigations were criminal murder cases. In *People v. Armstrong*, Lincoln used a farmer's almanac to discredit the prosecution's star witness and secured an acquittal in a murder charge. In *People v. Goings*, Lincoln defended seventy-year-old Melissa Goings on a charge that she murdered her husband, seventy-seven-year-old Roswell Goings. During a drunken argument, Roswell began choking Melissa and she defended herself by hitting him with a piece of stove wood on the side of his head. He died four days later from the injury. Allegedly, Bob Cassell, the court bailiff, accused Lincoln of telling his client to leave the state to avoid prosecution. Lincoln responded, "Oh no, Bob, I didn't run her off. She wanted to know where she could get a good drink of water, and I told her there was mighty good water in Tennessee." Melissa was not pursued. After a meeting with the state's attorney, Lincoln arranged to have the murder stricken from the docket on May 24, 1859. Four years later, Lincoln's assistant secretary, John Hay, made a relevant diary entry about a variation of this case: "He [Lincoln] told one devilish story about U. F. Linder's getting a fellow off who had stolen a hog by advising him to go & get a drink & suggesting that the water was better in Tennessee &c. &c."

Moral and economic issues blended in criminal litigation involving bastardy. Lincoln had eight bastardy cases. Bastardy laws punished the guilty father by making him pay for the education and welfare of the illegitimate child. Thus, the local community was not liable for the child. Louvinia Neighbor, an unmarried woman, became pregnant. She claimed that George Hall was the father of the child and informed the state's attorney. A grand jury indicted Hall for bastardy. At the same time, Neighbor initiated a civil lawsuit against Hall. She declared that Hall promised to marry her but then reneged on his promise. Neighbor retained Lincoln & Herndon and sued Hall in an action of *assumpsit* for breaching the marriage contract. Seeking to prevent the sordid details from being presented in open court, Hall and Neighbor reached an agreement in both cases. Neighbor dismissed the *assumpsit* case against Hall, and Hall pleaded guilty in the bastardy case. In response to the guilty plea, the court ordered Hall to pay Neighbor $50 per year for seven years for the education and support of the child.

Lincoln preferred to settle a case rather than go to trial. Judge Davis stated that Lincoln hated long trials and was fond of settlements. When Littlefield was a student reading law at Lincoln & Herndon, he made a similar observation: "I have heard him tell would-be clients again and again—You have no case; better settle." In fact, about 33 percent of Lincoln's cases were dismissed and many of those can be attributed to settlements.

Slavery-related legal cases plagued the American courts and were difficult to settle. Lincoln did not necessarily seek slavery cases, but there were few slavery cases in Illinois. John Bunn, a friend and client of Lincoln's, claimed that Lincoln appeared in few suits because of his unwillingness to be a party to the violation of the Fugitive Slave Law. This law required slaves to be returned to their owners. Being politically sensitive, Lincoln possibly avoided the issue. On the other hand, Herndon did handle several fugitive slave cases without success and apparently without Lincoln's assistance.

In one of Lincoln's better-known cases, he defended Robert Matson, a slave owner. In 1847, Matson transported five of his slaves, Bryant and her four children, from Kentucky into Illinois to work on his farm in Coles County. After living in Illinois for two years, the slaves sought refuge with Gideon M. Ashmore and Dr. Hiram Rutherford. Matson declared them runaways and the sheriff imprisoned the slaves until the court was ready to sell them to the highest bidder. On behalf of the slaves, Ashmore sued for their freedom. Representing Matson, Lincoln and Usher F. Linder resisted the application for freedom and argued that a slave owner could take his property all over the country. In disagreement, the court ruled that the slaves were free. Matson was billed for $111.05 by the sheriff for "Keaping and Dieting five negrows [sic] forty Eight [sic] Days at thirty-seven cents each per day." Rebuffed, Matson allegedly returned to Kentucky and failed to pay Lincoln his legal fee. Ironically, Lincoln's argument in the Matson case predated by nine years one of the Supreme Court of the United States' rationales in ruling that Dred Scott remained a slave in Missouri. Lincoln protested against the Supreme Court's decision in *Dred Scott v. Sandford* arguing that there was a conspiracy to nationalize slavery.

As an attorney who took cases as they came along, Lincoln represented opposing viewpoints on the same question. He argued against the freedom of five slaves in Illinois in the Matson case despite his personal dislike for the institution of slavery. Taking the opposite side, Lincoln criticized the *Dred Scott* decision that agreed with his earlier Matson argument. In another pair of cases, Lincoln argued on behalf of the water transportation interests one time and the railroad transportation interests the other time. In 1853, Lincoln represented the water transportation businesses in a situation that occurred on the Illinois River. A steamship pulling cargo boats passed under the bridge spanning the river at Peoria. One of the cargo boats hit a pier and sank into the river. Boat owners filed a claim with their insurance company and received compensation for the loss. In turn, the insurance company retained Lincoln and sued the bridge company to recover damages for the lost boat and cargo. In arguing one of the larger issues in *Columbus Insurance Company v. Peoria Bridge Company*, Lincoln "challenged the power of the state to authorize a total obstruction of a navigable stream running within its territorial limits." This jury failed to agree on a verdict and the court dismissed the case.

In *Hurd v. The Rock Island Bridge Company*, a steamship on the Mississippi River hit a bridge, caught fire instantly, and sank into the river. Hurd sued to recover damages charging that the railroad bridge was an obstruction to river navigation. The bridge company, supported by railroad companies, hired Lincoln to argue its case. This time Lincoln took exactly the opposite position as in the Peoria case. Now, Lincoln argued in favor of unfettered water crossings for railroads. In 1857, the jury was unable to agree on a verdict, and the court dismissed the case. Although Lincoln did not win either of the commercial transportation cases, he effectively argued opposing viewpoints about a bridge being an obstruction to river navigation. Personally, Lincoln favored railroads, internal improvements, and the advancement of their transportation interests.

In a bizarre example of Lincoln's representing both sides of an argument, he appeared for both the plaintiff and the defendant in a series of cases. Elisha Perkins sold Samuel Hall several acres of land in Tazewell County for $1,150. Hall gave Perkins $650 in cash and promissory notes for $200 and for $300. Perkins did not give Hall a deed to the land. Consequently, Hall refused to pay him the remaining $500. In 1841, Perkins retained Lincoln and sued Hall in an action of *assumpsit*, breach of contract, to recover the $500. Initially, the circuit court ruled for Perkins, but Hall appealed the case to the supreme court of Illinois. Lincoln continued to represent Perkins at the appellate level. In 1844, Lincoln lost the case when the supreme court of Illinois reversed the circuit court decision because Perkins did not give Hall a deed to the land. This ruling prohibited Perkins from suing Hall in an *assumpsit* action. Taking another tack, Perkins again sued Hall to recover the $500 in 1850 in an action of debt. In a reversal of clients, Hall retained Lincoln to defend him. This time, the jury found for Perkins and awarded him $544 in damages. Lincoln won the *assumpsit* case for Perkins at the circuit level, lost the supreme court appeal for Perkins, then lost the debt case for Hall at the circuit level. Appearing for both sides of the same issue, Lincoln lost both cases.

Lincoln was not a perfect attorney. He made frequent mistakes early in his career but learned from his errors as time passed. Contrary to the folklore about Lincoln, not everyone recommended him as a lawyer. Allen B. Clough, a physician from Champaign County, Illinois, observed Lincoln in the courtroom although they were only involved in three cases together. Nevertheless, Clough declared that he has "seen and heard *Old Abe* at the legal bar...and I never saw him do a good thing yet in his profession, and I have seen him whipped several times by young lawyers of no great pretensions and [Lincoln] is certainly not considered a third rate lawyer...."

Although he was born four years after Lincoln's death, Edgar Lee Masters, the composer of the *Spoon River Anthology*, denigrated Lincoln's lawyering abilities. Masters was a partner of the famous defense attorney, Clarence Darrow and the son of Hardin W. Masters, a legal contemporary of Lincoln's. In belittling Lincoln, Masters said that while other lawyers might read law books, Lincoln would not because he was too busy telling stories and talking politics with local farmers and townspeople. Lincoln "did not prepare his cases [and] would go into court and lose a case that anyone should have won." However, Masters accurately recognized that Lincoln did not simply take cases that were just and morally correct, and that a "lawyer who would take no bad case is pure unctuous twaddle."

Many of Lincoln's contemporaries agreed that he was a very good lawyer. Leonard Swett stated that Lincoln "was as hard to beat in a closely contested case as any lawyer I have ever met." His fellow circuit-riding colleague believed that Lincoln used his down-to-earth qualities to win juries over. Swett rode the Eighth Judicial Circuit with Lincoln for many years and became nationally celebrated as a criminal lawyer. Based on his experience with Lincoln in his courtroom, Judge Davis was unstinting in praise: "In all of the elements that constitute the great lawyer, he had few equals." Lincoln avoided superfluous arguments and advised fellow lawyer Usher F. Linder that "it is good policy to never plead what you need not, lest you oblige yourself to prove what you cannot."

Speed, Lincoln's steadfast friend, commented on Lincoln's legal philosophy: "One would think, to hear him present his case in the court, he was giving his case away. He would concede point after point to his adversary." Swett also commented about Lincoln's tactic of conceding points. Whitney, a fellow circuit-riding lawyer, explained their relationship: "[Swett] was not a profound lawyer, but he was a most adroit, ingenious and brilliant advocate; and I personally knew, that in a jury case, Lincoln preferred association with him to any other lawyer in the State." Swett elaborated on Speed's observation about Lincoln's giving the case away:

> As he entered the trial, where most lawyers would object he would say he "reckoned" it would be fair to let this in, or that; and sometimes, when his adversary could not quite prove what Lincoln knew to be the truth, he "reckoned" it would be fair to admit the truth to be so-and-so. When he did object to the Court, and when he heard his objections answered, he would often say, "Well, I reckon I must be wrong." Now, about the

time he had practiced this three-fourths through the case, if his adversary didn't understand him, he would wake up…too late and find himself beaten. He was wise as a serpent in the trial of a cause, but I have had too many scars from his blows to certify that he was harmless as a dove. When the whole thing was unraveled, the adversary would begin to see that what he was so blandly giving away was simply what he couldn't get and keep. By giving away six points and carrying the seventh, he traded away everything which would give him the least aid in carrying that. Any man who took Lincoln for a simple-minded man would very soon wake up with his back in a ditch.

Frequently, Lincoln & Herndon received letters from aspiring lawyers who wanted to read law in their office. Lincoln generally referred those matters to Herndon but occasionally offered advice. Several weeks before Lincoln won the election for the presidency in 1860, he received a letter from William Gilbert, a New York attorney, who wanted to move to Illinois. Gilbert heard that Lincoln "had a large practice in your profession" and wondered if anyone was going to take over his practice. "If not, I would like to know whether I could make arrangements with you." There is no evidence that Lincoln responded.

Lincoln had a reputation as an honest man. However, Lincoln's personality should not be generalized to his legal career. Lincoln represented his clients without regard to the justness of their claim. Had Lincoln only taken cases with which he was in moral agreement, he never would have appeared for Matson, the slave owner, or parlayed technicalities in the Bantzhouse murder case. There are examples of Lincoln's not taking cases because he believed in particular issues as well as examples of Lincoln's not charging his clients a fee. However, these examples are few and cannot be generalized to the whole of Lincoln's legal career. In all probability, he would have been an unsuccessful practitioner if he only accepted specific types of clients.

One aspect of Lincoln's personality that remained with him in the courtroom and in the White House was his sense of humor.

Judge Davis found that an "unfailing vein of humor never deserted him" in the courtroom. While traveling the Eighth Judicial Circuit in McLean County, Illinois, Lincoln opposed John Scott, a young lawyer who did not like to be beaten. Lincoln and Scott made their respective arguments before the jury. Early the next morning, Lincoln met Scott at the courthouse and asked him what had happened in the case. Scott replied, "It's gone to h-- l." Lincoln responded, "O well, then you'll see it again."

Often, Lincoln used humor in and around the courtroom to emphasize a point of law or simply to be funny. Judge Davis observed that he "never failed to produce joy and hilarity" on the circuit. People keenly awaited his arrival on the circuit. From a political viewpoint, there was some question as to whether Lincoln's "unusual sense of humor and fondness at times for off-color jokes might derail him" while heading upward politically.

On a hot, humid day in court, Lincoln opposed Logan, his former partner. As the arguments heated up, both lawyers removed their coats and vests to become comfortable. At that time, shirts with buttons in back were unusual. Lincoln immediately saw an opening to deflate Logan's advantageous grasp of the law. Aware of the prejudices of the jurors toward any social pretension or affectation, Lincoln arose and addressed the jury: "Gentlemen, you must be careful and not permit yourselves to be overcome by the eloquence of counsel for the defense. Judge Logan, I know, is an effective lawyer. I have met him too often to doubt that; but shrewd and careful though he be, still he is sometimes wrong. Since this trial has begun I have discovered that with all his caution and fastidiousness, he hasn't knowledge enough to put his shirt on right." Everyone then noticed that Logan had his shirt on backwards, laughter flowed, and Lincoln won the case.

Lincoln explained self-defense to a jury by telling the story of a man who killed a vicious dog with a pitchfork:

Lincoln: That reminds me of a conversation between the man who was attacked by a farmer's dog, which he killed with a pitchfork.

Farmer: What made you kill my dog?

Man: What made him try to bite me?

Farmer: But why didn't you go at him with the other end of the pitchfork?

Man: Well, why didn't he come at me with his other end?

Using humor, Lincoln could discredit an opposition witness. An opposing counsel asked his witness, a surveyor, questions about a plat map. Without objecting, Lincoln blurted out: "It looks very much like it represents a fancy bed quilt." On the surface, this remark seems harmlessly humorous. However, by criticizing the surveyor's expertise before the jury, Lincoln purposefully discredited an opposing witness. Apparently, the opposing attorney did not take notice of Lincoln's jibe by raising an objection. Unaware of the damage Lincoln may have inflicted on the witness and the case, he continued as if Lincoln had said nothing.

In 1859, Lincoln represented the defendant in the US Circuit Court in a suit involving a bond, *Farni v. Tesson.* Charles M. Chase, editor of the *DeKalb County Sentinel* in northern Illinois, served on the jury and observed Lincoln in the Chicago courtroom. Chase reported on the case in a June 25, 1859 letter in the *Sentinel:* "Lincoln tries a suit well. By his genial spirit he keeps the Court, the jury and the opposite counsel in good humor, and sometimes by a comical remark, or a clever joke, upsets the dignity of the court." Abram Bergen, who observed Lincoln at work in the courtroom, asserted that Lincoln was skilled at "acting" in court to produce a desired effect, especially laughter.

In his monograph on Lincoln the lawyer, John Frank evaluated Lincoln as a lawyer. He concluded that Lincoln was an "outstandingly able and successful lawyer for his own time and place." Lincoln possessed five characteristics that contributed to his success and reputation: a personality that attracted clients and the confidence of juries, the ability to go quickly and briefly to the heart of a matter, restrained but effective verbal expression, a highly retentive mind, and a willingness to work very hard.

How did humor, skill before the jury, and Lincoln's legal characteristics translate into effectiveness as a lawyer? Lincoln's success rate is difficult to establish. His won-lost and dismissed percentages representing the plaintiff or the defendant can be examined in a simple chart.

	Won	Lost	Dismissed
For Plaintiff	60%	8%	32%
For Defendant	15%	53%	32%

A number of Lincoln's victories as a plaintiff's attorney were due to a default by the defendant. A number of his losses as a defendant's attorney were in debt-related cases in a legal system that favored creditors over debtors and were probably impossible to win. These percentages only partially answer the question of how effective Lincoln was as an attorney. There is no doubt that Lincoln had the respect of his fellow attorneys. Prospective clients from Illinois and beyond approached Lincoln for his assistance. Judges and lawyers referred various issues to Lincoln for a legal opinion. On the circuit, local attorneys evoked a preference for a partnership with Lincoln. In the more significant and constitutional cases, Lincoln was largely successful. These factors, more important than simple numbers, indicate that Lincoln was a successful attorney in antebellum Illinois.

In the course of twenty-five years of legal practice, Lincoln matured as an attorney. He began his legal career as an unpolished and insecure novice lawyer and evolved into a confident and flourishing attorney. His peers respected his hard work and knowledge and sought his advice on a variety of legal matters. Lincoln's legal career was one of the fundamental building blocks that made him one of the most effective presidents in United States history. By the time Lincoln suspended his legal practice in the summer of 1860 to concentrate on the presidential election, he was one of the most eminent lawyers in Illinois and the Midwest.

John A. Lupton is assistant director and an assistant editor with the Lincoln Legal Papers. He has degrees in history from Southern Illinois University at Carbondale [BA] and from the University of Illinois at Springfield [MA]. A frequently requested speaker, he discusses Lincoln's legal career and antebellum legal history. Lupton directed the research at Washington's Library of Congress and the National Archives to discover records relating to Lincoln's legal career. His publications include his thesis on Lincoln's law practice in Carlinville, Macoupin County; "Abraham Lincoln: Pension Attorney" in the *Lincoln Newsletter* [Winter 1996]; "In View of the Uncertainty of Life: A Coles County Lynching" in the *Illinois Historical Journal* [Autumn 1996]; an article on document collection in *Documentary Editing* [June 1996]; and "Basement Barrister: Abraham Lincoln's Practice Before the US Supreme Court" in the *Lincoln Herald* [Summer 1999].

3

LINCOLN'S CLIENT ASSAULTED:

HE QUESTIONED HIS PHYSICIAN'S MEDICAL SCHOOL GRADUATION

In 1851, Abraham Lincoln represented Edward Jones in his *Trespass Vi Et Armis* suit against Dr. Joseph S. Maus for $5,000 in damages. Essentially, Jones alleged that Maus assaulted him with force of arms. A heated imbroglio ensued between the two over Maus's claim that he graduated from the Jefferson Medical College in Philadelphia. Jones persisted in questioning whether Maus really graduated from that medical school. In turn, an enraged Maus ferociously assaulted Jones. In his defense, Maus said that he was not guilty, contended that Jones was the aggressor, and he merely defended himself.

William B. Parker, co-counsel with Lincoln, filed Jones's affidavit with the Tazewell County Circuit Court on July 24, 1851. On the same day, a money bond assured that Joseph S. Maus would appear at the trial in Pekin on September 10, 1851: "We Joseph S. Maus and William S. Maus of the County of Tazewell and State of Illinois are holden and firmly bound unto William Gaither, Sheriff of said County of Tazewell in the final sum of four thousand dollars good and lawful money of the United States."

At one point during their conversation immediately preceding the assault, Maus told Jones that his Jefferson Medical College diploma was at his house. In his declaration, Jones swore that this statement by Maus was "infamously false, the said Maus at said time being neither a graduate of said Jefferson Medical College nor of any other chartered medical school." According to Jones, the assault by Maus developed "without any natural provocation whatever." Jones swore that Maus "made an assault upon affiant [Jones] and struck him either with his fist or some felonious weapon on or over the left eye and has discharged the sight thereof...affiant [Jones] believes that he can prove from the character of the injury sustained that it is not probable that it was done with the fist." While Jones did not see any weapon used by Maus, he said that a few days later Maus was boasting and exhibited an instrument "used by none other than felonious and cowardly highway men, murderers and house-breakers" such as a colt gun. Furthermore, Jones contended that he was informed and believed that "such an instrument may be used in a manner so as not to be perceived." Jones declared that "by profession affiant [he] is an attorney and counselor-at-law in good practice and was so at the time of the commission of said assault. That his family and himself depend upon the income derived from the practice and that the loss of the sight of said eye injured by said Maus affects materially the ability of the affiant [Jones] to perform his professional duties." He sued for $5,000.00 in damages.

On September 1, 1851, Parker filed Jones's terse one page complaint against Maus:

> Edward Jones, Plaintiff, by Parker his attorney, complains of Joseph B. Maus, defendant in custody, of an action of trespass vi et armis. That said defendant here-to-fore to wit on the first day of December in the year of our Lord of eighteen hundred and fifty at the county and circuit aforesaid made an assault upon said plaintiff and beat and wounded him...against the peace and laws of the State of Illinois.

While Parker filed the complaint, the firm of Lincoln & Herndon was busy in Sangamon County Circuit Court. Five of their cases were called on Tuesday, September 8, 1851. One case was dismissed by agreement, one case was dismissed by Lincoln & Herndon, another case was dismissed by their opponents, and the remaining two cases were continued. Immediately thereafter,

Tazewell County Circuit Court convened in Pekin on September 9 and Lincoln and Parker filed a motion in the *Jones v. Maus* case. They moved that the damages demanded in the declaration be made to conform to the writ.

On September 23, 1851, two of Lincoln's cases were called in Pekin and both were continued. In the debt case of *Perkins v. Hall*, Lincoln wrote an affidavit for Samuel Hall and had it sworn by the defendant. On the same day in the same court, Horace P. Johnson, Benjamin S. Prettyman, and James Haines, Maus's lawyers, filed a response to Jones's complaint. Almost exactly one year earlier, Haines was co-counsel with Lincoln in the defense of George W. Hawley, who was indicted for the obstruction of a public road in Tazewell County. Although Haines was just beginning his legal career, Lincoln proposed that he deliver the opening speech. Sensing his reluctance, Lincoln put his hand on Haines's shoulder and gave him some practical legal advice: "I want you to open the case, and when you are doing it, talk to the jury as though your client's fate depends on every word you utter. Forget that you have any one to fall back upon, and you will do justice to yourself and your client."

In the reply to Jones's complaint, Maus said that "at said time of the beating, wounding and other misfortune" Jones attacked him with a "large cane...wherefore he the said defendant did then and there defend himself against the said plaintiff, as he lawfully might for the cause aforesaid." In defending himself, Maus stated that he "did necessarily and unavoidably strike with his hand the said plaintiff and slightly wounded him doing no further unnecessary damage to said plaintiff on the occasion aforesaid...which is the same supposed mishap in said declaration mentioned and whereof the said plaintiff hath above complained against him." Maus said he was ready to verify the facts and his lawyers "prayed for judgment" in his favor.

Six days later, Lincoln appeared in Bloomington at the opening of the McLean County Circuit Court. Lincoln, William H. Holmes, and John M. Scott represented David C. Thompson in a suit against George W. Henline for slander. Henline's defense was that the statement was factual. In truth, Thompson "did have sexual intercourse or carnal knowledge with a cow." Asahel Gridley and John T. Stuart, Lincoln's former partner, defended Henline. On this day, Judge Davis granted a continuance. On October 2, Lincoln moved to amend his client's declaration, but the motion was denied. On the following day, a trial was held and the jury could not agree on a verdict. Judge Davis continued the case.

Although the law firm of Lincoln & Herndon existed since December 1844, Lincoln frequently accepted cases with other lawyers as co-counsel as he went from courthouse to courthouse on the Eighth Judicial Circuit. At least seventy-five other lawyers were associated with Lincoln on the circuit. By this time, Lincoln had practiced law in three firms: Stuart & Lincoln, Logan & Lincoln, and Lincoln & Herndon. Within a seven-year period, Lincoln was the junior partner to Stuart and to Logan. When he changed law firms, there was a bit of confusion. Lincoln succinctly noted one change: "Judge Logan & myself are doing bussiness [sic] together now."

In an April 18, 1842 letter to George W. Hawley of Dixon, Lincoln wrote about the bankruptcy suit that Logan & Lincoln was handling for Dixon in the US District Court in Springfield. Logan & Lincoln had cash accounts of $10.00 each at the state bank and the Shawneetown Bank. Lincoln reported on the expenditures: "Of this we have expended of State Bank $6.00 leaving on hand $4.00. Of the Shawnee, we have expended for these papers $3.00, for postage on your letter 37 1/2 cents; for 70 day publication $4.00. In all $7.37 1/2 leaving on hand $2.62 1/2."

Furthermore, some cases dragged on for a number of years. In 1850, Lincoln explained three separate bills totaling $40.00 that he submitted to David M. Irwin, a Springfield merchant, that he represented from 1844 to 1850:

1844 to Logan & Lincoln
ejectment suit against Hall Sangamon Circuit Court $20.00

1845-6 to A. Lincoln
attending same suit Supreme Court $10.00

1846-7-8-9 & 50 to Lincoln & Herndon
attending to Chancery in Sangamon Circuit Court $10.00

Lincoln's third and last law partner, William H. Herndon, presented a sharp physical and mental contrast with the senior partner. In appearance, Herndon was about seven inches shorter than Lincoln with jet-black hair and a dark-skinned complexion. Bony and lean, Herndon always stood upright. His face was dominated by piercing black eyes glaring out from cup-like rings. Nervous energy bristled throughout his body as he moved and walked quickly. He was quick- tempered, rash, and unpredictable. A rapid thinker, writer, and speaker, Herndon reached conclusions swiftly. Yet, as he compiled pertinent legal information and prepared legal documents, Herndon's literary style was verbose and pompous. In his dress, Herndon affected a special finery. At times, he wore shiny black patent leather shoes, gloves of smooth kid leather, and a tall black stovepipe silk hat. Having a pronounced and well-cultivated fondness for liquor, Herndon frequently indulged in drinking sprees and sometimes ended up drunk. Although Herndon "was an excellent student and became an able attorney, he seems never to have liked the law."

Mary Todd Lincoln hated Billy Herndon with an enmity that was formidable. On the rare occasion when she visited the Lincoln & Herndon office, Mrs. Lincoln "pointedly drew her voluminous skirts aside that they might not touch him. They never exchanged a greeting." In a March 4, 1867 letter to Judge David Davis, then administrator of Lincoln's estate, she reacted to a November 16, 1866 evening lecture by Herndon. He spoke to a meager audience at the Springfield courthouse on *Abraham Lincoln, Miss Ann Rutledge, New Salem, Pioneering and the Poem [Immortality].*

Without prudence, Herndon said that his investigation proved that Lincoln loved Ann Rutledge. Mrs. Lincoln brandished a robust vocabulary in her response: "This is the return for all my husband's kindness to this miserable man! Out of pity he took him into his office when he was almost a hopeless inebriate and although he was only a drudge in the place—he is very forgetful of his position and assumes a confidential capacity towards Mr. Lincoln."

Herndon dabbled in politics and on April 4, 1854 a heavy majority of the voters, including Lincoln, elected him the mayor of Springfield, then a city of 6,218 inhabitants. He was a reform-minded mayor who initiated efforts to attain a public school system and uncharacteristically, and totally unexpectedly, imposed a citywide prohibition on liquor. That measure aroused intense emotional reactions from the residents. Herndon served his one year-term and was not suggested for reelection.

In court, Herndon battled for every point and was considered an effective lawyer. Lincoln was the primary litigator and Herndon did the "drudge" work, handled the office, supervised the law students, and attended cases in Springfield and the immediate surrounding areas. Charles S. Zane, a law student at Lincoln & Herndon, commented on their individual legal style:

> I also heard them examine witnesses and argue questions of law and fact in court.... Mr. Lincoln, as a reasoner, was careful as to his premises and drew his inferences cautiously and with great clearness.... [He] considered them [questions] more in the concrete. [Lincoln] had great capacity for analysis and generalization. He was adept in drawing reasonable inferences. As a rule they both did not engage in the trial of the same case.... Mr. Lincoln was more methodical and systematic.

Lincoln developed a reputation as a "rainmaker" as he eagerly sought, and found, new business for his law firm. Consequently, Lincoln was almost entirely a litigation man with negligible office practice. His pleas were thoroughly adequate and briefs followed that simply and concisely concentrated on the simplification of the case to one or two points. Given the time constraints on the circuit, Lincoln consistently demonstrated his precise skill in interviewing to collect data and his extremely effective direct and cross-examination of witnesses. He had a major talent in speaking to the jury and putting the entire case into focus in an appealing manner. A colleague recalled Lincoln's individuality: "Mr. Lincoln was the plainest man I ever heard. He was not a speaker, but a talker. He talks to jurors and to political gatherings plain, sensible, candid talk, almost as in conversation, no effort whatever in oratory. But his talking had wonderful effect. Honesty, candor, fairness, everything that was convincing, was in his manner and expressions."

As the junior partner, Herndon repeatedly said that Lincoln did not confide in him. He found Lincoln to be the "most reticent & mostly secretive man that ever existed." However, the partners adhered strictly to a sharing of their fees equally regardless of who appeared in court. *Jones v. Maus* was just such a situation.

Despite Lincoln's reputation and ability as a lawyer, his political opponents printed a dubious broadside depicting his business card. Obviously, the Democrats ridiculed Lincoln's common man characteristics implying his unfitness to be president. Supposedly, this business card regularly appeared in the pages of local newspapers ro inform the citizens when the services of an affable lawyer would be available in their community:

A. LINCOLN ATTORNEY AND COUNSELOR AT LAW
SPRINGFIELD,—ILLINOIS
TO WHOM IT MAY CONCERN. My old customers, and
others, are no doubt aware of the terrible time I have had in
crossing the stream, and will be glad to know that I will be
back, on the same side from which I started, on or before the
FOURTH OF MARCH NEXT, when I will be ready to SWAP
HORSES, DISPENSE LAW, MAKE JOKES, SPLIT RAILS

A major legal issue for Lincoln in *Jones v. Maus* concerned medical education and practice. Considering the status of medical education and practice at the time, it is quite possible that Maus did not earn a diploma from a chartered medical school. He may have appeared medically incompetent to Jones. Even in the mid-1850s, physicians often made diagnoses without taking the patient's pulse, without the benefit of a clinical thermometer or without using a stethoscope. A fading treatment mode used by physicians educated at orthodox medical schools involved reducing the "convulsive action" via blistering, blood-letting and/or the use of calomel for purging."

In 1848, Lincoln was an elected Congressman from Illinois who was extremely active in the House of Representatives in the capitol. He took a strong position against President James K. Polk's waging the Mexican War. This position was much to the discomfort of many of Lincoln's Illinois associates, including Herndon. Early in the year, on January 3, Herndon notified Lincoln that he deposited $500 in his bank account as his share of the fee from Siter Price & Co. At the end of the year, on December 25, Lincoln replied to Speed's letter about an uncollected judgement against Judge Thomas C. Browne. Speed felt that Logan & Lincoln were to blame. Lincoln denied that they were at fault, but told Speed he'd rather lose a fee than create hard feelings.

Several rationales possibly explained Maus's alleged lack of a Jefferson Medical College diploma: he attended some lectures but not all; he left before he met the school's graduation requirements; he didn't serve his apprenticeship with a practitioner; or he purchased the admission tickets to the medical lectures and attended none. In an illuminating history of the medical profession published in 1901, the author claimed that nine out of ten practitioners never graduated from any institution. Often, admission tickets to the lectures served as the only proof of the medical student's attendance and met the requirements for graduation.

By 1899, there were 156 schools of healing with 24,119 students in the United States. Despite the misgivings about medical education, only three states (Alabama, North Carolina, Virginia) required more than a diploma for evidence of competency to obtain a license to practice. State license requirements for physicians started to collapse in the 1830s. As late as 1876, Dr. Austin Flint observed that there are "no legal restrictions for practicing without a diploma or license."

Lincoln was well aware of the contemporary condition of the art and science of medicine. During his years in New Salem, Illinois, he was an active participant in a discussion group convened by his good friend, Dr. John Allen. He was well acquainted with Drs. Charles Chandler and Francis Regnier. Two of Lincoln's brothers-in-law were physicians, Drs. George Todd and William Wallace. A number of Lincoln's political associates were active physicians such as Drs. Anson Henry, William Jayne, John Logan, Charles Ray, and J. A. Vincent. He had more than a fleeting knowledge of the public's attitudes toward physicians that ranged from hostile to skeptical to ungrateful to dubious to appreciative to forever grateful.

Lincoln probably realized the futility of arguments at a trial in this assault case. Most likely, he urged both Jones and Maus to settle the problem out of court. In his notes for a law lecture, Lincoln described the role of the lawyer as an honest peacemaker:

> Discourage litigation. Persuade your neighbors to compromise whenever you can. Point out to them how the nominal winner is often a real loser—in fees, expenses, and waste of time. As a peacemaker the lawyer has a superior opportunity of being a good man. There will still be business enough.
>
> Never stir up litigation. A worse man can scarcely be found than one who does this. Who can be more nearly a fiend than he who habitually overhauls the Register of deeds, in search of defects in titles, whereupon to stir up strife, and put money in his pocket? A moral tone ought to be infused into the profession, which should drive such men out of it.
>
> There is a vague popular belief that lawyers are necessarily dishonest. I say vague, because when we consider to what

extent confidence, and honors are reposed in, and conferred upon lawyers by the people, it appears improbable that the impression of dishonesty is very distinct and vivid. Yet the impression is common—almost universal. Let no young man, choosing the law for a calling, for a moment yield to this popular belief. Resolve to be honest at all events; and if, in your own judgement, you cannot be an honest lawyer, resolve to be honest without being a lawyer. Choose some other occupation, rather than one in the choosing of which you do, in advance, consent to be a knave.

Peacemaking was not unusual among principled honest lawyers in the nineteenth century. In referring to lawyers who swindled their clients, Lincoln was adamant: "I never want the reputation enjoyed by those shining lights of the profession *Catch'em & Cheat'em.*" In 1845, the *New York Legal Observer* declared that "the respectable attorney...is almost always a peacemaker and a settler of disputes, without litigation, where it is practicable." Despite these lofty legal tenets urging compromise, trials during Lincoln's years as a practicing attorney clearly demonstrated a litigious disposition in the community. That ready disposition to sue continues to the present day.

During the September 1851 term of the Tazewell County Circuit Court, Judge Davis presided when *Jones v. Maus* was scheduled to be heard. Davis's most prominent feature was his girth. He was short, portly to an extreme, and weighed more than three hundred pounds. However, he was a perfectionist who was impeccable in his choice of clothing and in his attention to cleanliness. Davis presented a perfectly groomed and appropriate judicial picture. In contrast, in his early years at the bar, Lincoln was nondescript and dressed carelessly. His "attire and physical habits were on a plane with those of an ordinary farmer. His hat was innocent of a nap. His boots had no acquaintance with blacking. His clothes had not been introduced to the whiskbroom."

After graduating Kenyon College (OH), Davis attended the New Haven Law School (later Yale) for one year. In 1836, Davis moved to Bloomington (IL) and two years later he married the daughter of a judge. In 1848, Davis was elected the judge of the Eighth Judicial District. He and Lincoln had a most cordial relationship and at times Lincoln substituted for the judge when Davis was unexpectedly called away.

When the *Jones v. Maus* case was called, Lincoln informed the judge that both parties reached an agreement and the court dismissed the case. There is no record of exactly how Jones and Maus came to an agreement. However, Lincoln encountered Jones as an adversary almost immediately during the same September 1851 term of the Tazewell County Circuit Court. Jones represented the plaintiff in *Jacobus v. Kitchell et ux.* while Lincoln argued for the defendants. Allegedly, Milden Kitchell and his wife Elizabeth slandered Mary Ann Jacobus. They called her a whore who got her fine clothes by whoring.

As to Maus's being a physician, the 1850 federal census of Tazewell County does list two physicians named Maus in the city of Pekin. Both were born in Pennsylvania with Joseph being forty years old and William S. being forty-three. However, census information is provided by the individual and is not checked for accuracy. Lincoln was probably correct to believe his client's statement that Maus was not a physician who graduated from Jefferson Medical College. A perusal of the list of 4,018 graduates of the Jefferson Medical College beginning with the first graduating class in 1826 and going to 1858 did not reveal a single person with the surname of Maus and no one named Joseph S. Maus.

This bombastic problem of medical education, medical practices, and the animosity between regular and irregular physicians arose a number of times during Lincoln's law practice. Four years after *Jones v. Maus*, Lincoln helped prepare a special legislative charter for a proposed homeopathic medical college to be located in Chicago. Six years later in a medical malpractice case, he cross-examined a parade of physicians of all persuasions who were willing to castigate the therapeutic regimens of their regularly trained colleagues. In an 1857 murder trial, Lincoln cross-examined the defense's expert medical witnesses who testified that an overdose of chloroform caused insanity. Two years later, in 1859, Lincoln presented legal citations to support his contention that a single expert medical witness is not sufficient to establish what is usual and customary payment for medical services rendered. Even during his presidency, Lincoln considered a pardon for a convicted murderer and selected a medical expert to determine the condemned man's sanity or insanity. In all of these examples, Lincoln was keenly aware of the differences in medical education, the biases in everyday medical practice and in the contradictory testimony engendered by the animosity between orthodox and irregular doctors.

4

FIRED FOR INCOMPETENCY:

ASYLUM'S MEDICAL SUPERINTENDENT SUES

David A. Smith and Murray McConnell, attorneys for Dr. James M. Higgins, consulted Logan & Lincoln about an appeal to the supreme court of Illinois. Higgins was removed as medical superintendent by the trustees of the Illinois State Hospital for the Insane. When Higgins sued, a circuit court jury found that Higgins's removal as medical superintendent by the trustees was illegal. In disagreement, the trustees appealed the lower court's decision to the supreme court of Illinois. Higgins's lawyers sent him to confer with Logan & Lincoln. Afterward, Lincoln sent Higgins back to his lawyers with a letter stating that they thought Higgins's removal was invalid:

> We have had Dr. Higgins' case under consideration; and, inasmuch as, by the law "he shall be subject to removal only for infidelity to the trust reposed in him, or incompetency in the discharge thereof"—we think the resolution of removal, not placing the removal on either of these grounds, is, on it's [sic] face void; and we further think, that any removal, without giving the Dr. a chance to be heard in his defence, on the questions, of infidelity and incompetency, one or both, will be void. Quo warranto, we think, is the way; and we think it some better that he should hold on, and leave his adversaries to proceed; but if his holding on would embarrass the institution,

he might, without much disadvantage, leave, and commence the proceedings himself. Yours &c.

Quo warranto is a legal proceeding to remove a person from public office and to prevent that person from exercising unlawful authority. Trustees of the asylum claimed to be in possession of the superintendent's office by state law. Sticking to the precise language of the law, Lincoln opted to compel the trustees to demonstrate how they applied *Quo warranto*. Since Lincoln was deeply immersed in politics in Illinois, he realized that political considerations were frequently the clandestine motivation for *Quo warranto* lawsuits. Later events proved that politics definitely precipitated the action to fire Higgins. As medical superintendent, Higgins controlled a sizeable business enterprise and monetary flow: he hired and fired a number of employees; selected firms when he purchased asylum furnishings and supplies; sold surplus food and livestock from the asylum farms to commercial establishments; and managed construction and rehabilitation monies. If so inclined, those sweeping uncontested administrative powers offered ample opportunity for Higgins to participate in the political spoils system through patronage.

Disguised in *Quo warranto* legal terminology, this type of political action against asylum superintendents was not uncommon. Asylum superintendents, through their professional organization, the Association of Medical Superintendents of American Institutions for the Insane (AMSAII), characterized public complainants as "evil-minded or misguided persons," "impractical idealists," and "lawyers on the make" who were possessed of a "questionable mental integrity" and inspired by "gross misrepresentation and ignorance." Relevantly, Higgins, who was a member of the AMSAII, looked to the association for assistance. However, the AMSAII was reluctant to support fellow superintendents entwined in politically motivated actions. An overwhelming majority of asylum superintendents enjoyed good relations with their own governing boards and thought that their formal protest could jeopardize their own positions. Since the beleaguered Higgins was not a long-standing or prominent member of the organization, the AMSAII had little to gain and much to lose by supporting him with a formal protest.

Illustrative of *Quo warranto*-type lawsuits, Dr. Charles H. Nichols, endured numerous politically motivated sieges. He was superintendent of the Government Hospital for the Insane in Washington, DC, since its conception in 1852. In contrast to Higgins, Nichols was a prominent long-standing AMSAII member and the association membership thought that criticizing politicians for political interference did not carry any personal threat for them. Formally and forcefully, the AMSAII supported Nichols on a number of occasions. They did so even in one incident in 1861 when President Lincoln considered the allegations against Nichols. AMSAII members felt free to do this because they were coming into conflict with an *advisory* board of visitors rather than a *governing* board. Nichols was directly accountable to the US secretary of the interior, rather than to his advisory board.

In 1858, Nichols was labeled a "rank abolitionist" when Democrats from Southern and border states sought his removal. By 1861, he somehow turned completely around into a "secessionist" as a former patient appealed to President Lincoln to remove Nichols. In 1868, Nichols was labeled a "copperhead" (Southern sympathizer) by the wife of a former employee dismissed by Nichols. She alleged that he detained people in the asylum whose political views differed from his own.

Claiming that Nichols was incompetent, in 1869, a group of citizens including such prominent physicians as Nathan S. Davis, J. Marion Sims and Joseph Toner, urged the secretary of the interior to remove Nichols. Their action cloaked an ulterior motive. They had a candidate ready to replace Nichols, a Dr. Christopher Cox, a Baltimore gynecologist and professor of medical jurisprudence. All the charges were given orally to the secretary of the interior, likely motivated by the medical politicians. In this case, the AMSAII confronted physicians limited in experience with mental illness, but testing the political waters. An outrageous litany of charges confronted Nichols and included anything his political opponents could conjure up: thirteen instances of fraud; three instances of individual fraud; misappropriation of funds; twice preparing false annual reports; four counts of extravagance; two examples of injustice and tyranny; seven examples of poor patient care; no accounting; and having rebel proclivities. At the hearings, the specifics of the charges were detailed and minuscule.

Despite making no headway, Nichols' political foes did not despair and tried again in 1876, even as Nichols was elected president of the AMSAII. He hired Daniel W. Voorhees, a respected attorney and a representative from Indiana in the US Congress, to defend him. Lincoln and Voorhees were well acquainted. Just after Voorhees graduated from college, during the October 1851 term of the Vermilion County Circuit Court, Judge David Davis entered an order: "On motion of A. Lincoln it is ordered that Daniel W. Voorhees, an Attorney of Indiana, be admitted to practice as such in this Court."

Lincoln and Voorhees opposed each other in court. In *Martin v. Underwood*, Lincoln, Oliver L. Davis, and Oscar F. Harmon represented the plaintiff, Nancy M. Martin, while Voorhees and five other lawyers were the attorneys for Achilles M. Underwood. Martin accused Underwood of slander and the trial took place in Danville during the April 1858 term of the Vermilion County Circuit Court. At the end of the plaintiff's sensational slander complaint, Lincoln's signature is first followed by Davis and Harmon's. Although the section was stricken from the record, the content summed up the accusations: Underwood boasted about having sex with Martin and "used, uttered, spoke and published...false, scandalous, malicious and defamatory words [about Martin]...`By God, Nance *has* been *fucked* more times than I've got fingers and toes for dammed if it ain't so big I can almost poke my fist in'...meaning that the said plaintiff had been guilty of fornication...said plaintiff is otherwise much injured and damnified...the damage of the said plaintiff of five thousand dollars and therefore she brings her suit." Signed by E. S. Terry, John C. Moses, G. W. Lawrence and D. W. Voorhees, Underwood's lawyers entered ten pleas in answer to Martin's declaration. More than ten individuals were named who had sexual intercourse with Martin. In closing, the tenth plea commented that "the said plaintiff was of general bad character for chastity among the citizens...was generally suspected and believed to be guilty of fornication, and this the said defendant is ready to verify." Responding to Underwood's answer to the complaint, on October 30, 1857, Lincoln wrote a demurrer challenging his allegations. On November 2, 1857, Voorhees and Lincoln argued the demurrer. After the argument, Voorhees withdrew five pleas and filed a not guilty plea. As they began trial proceedings, Voorhees filed an affidavit asking for a continuance and the court granted the request. Four months later, the trial took place and the verdict was tersely delivered by the jury foreman, Jacob N. Ashwood: "We the jury find for the Plaintiff two hundred and thirty-seven dollars damage." Lincoln won for his client. He described her in the declaration as a "good, true, honest, just and faithful citizen...esteemed and accepted...a person of good name, fame and credit...said plaintiff hath not been guilty of fornication."

Again, nothing came from these hearings and Nichols remained on the job. In 1877, he resigned as superintendent. Surprisingly, while Nichols condemned appointing asylum superintendents on political grounds, he felt that many were appointed "because they were political supporters of the appointing party had made excellent superintendents... For this reason I have no objections to urge against these appointments...in most cases they appear to be remarkably good ones."

As superintendent of the Illinois State Hospital for the Insane, Higgins had the potential to be a valuable political ally. Through patronage, there could be rewards for the party faithful looking for a job, seeking a business connection or promoting any profitable scheme. Substantial sums were paid out by the institution for furniture, shrubs, and supplies. In 1851/1852 the total was $61,852.16 and in 1853/1854 the expenditures totaled $100,533.29. These purchases took place when a government employed male clerk was delighted to earn $1,200 a year and a female clerk $700. With the economical overtones clearly evident, Lincoln realized the probable divisive political nature of the governing board's lawsuit. Taking a strictly technical approach, Lincoln concentrated on the explicit language in the legislative act in his appeal to the supreme court of Illinois.

Trustees Fleming Stevenson, William Brown, William Butler, Richard Henry, Charles H. Lanphier, and Benjamin Pyatt, Jr., were named in the lawsuit initiated against Higgins when he refused to vacate his office as medical superintendent. Trustees Simeon Francis, William L. Craven, Pleasant L. Ward, and Darius Dexter were not included in the suit by name. Significantly, the omission of Craven and Dexter takes on importance in view of their later protest against "irregular meetings of the trustees" and what they labeled as the "unlawful" action of the trustees.

Created as a government institution, the legislature passed *An Act to Establish the Illinois State Hospital for the Insane* to accommodate 250 patients. This Act was signed by Governor Augustus C. French on March 1, 1847 and supported with state funds. In the Act, it states that the trustees

> shall have charge of the general interests of the institution; they shall appoint the superintendent, assistant physician and steward, and shall fix the amount of their salaries. The superintendent shall be a skillful physician, and shall be appointed for a term of ten years, during which time his salary shall not be reduced; he shall be subject to removal only for infidelity to the trust reposed in him or incompetency to the discharge thereof; he shall be a married man and with his family reside in the institution.

In their first biennial report, the trustees reported: "On the twelfth August, 1848, Doct. James H. Higgins of Griggsville, was appointed medical superintendent, and by a resolution of the board he is not to enter upon the duties of his office before the first of March, nor until the board shall thereafter direct." Since the asylum was first being built, the time delay was necessary. Higgins was chosen "after many contentious ballotings, in which a bare majority was secured over several rival candidates." There is no indication that Higgins had any training or experience in the care and treatment of the insane when he was named superintendent of the hospital at the age of forty-one. Higgins was appointed "with a salary of $800.00 per annum, and the privilege of employing a mechanical assistant to the amount of $400.00 more; thus making the whole expense of supervising the work, $1,200.00 per annum." With prognostication, the trustees described the preexisting turmoil that eventually led to Higgins downfall: "The successful candidate inherited, as a matter of course, a plentiful legacy of ill will from his rivals and their friends, which attended him during all of his incumbency of office, giving rise to a permanent division of the trustees, and a scene of bitter discord, in which the best interests of the institution were sacrificed to the passions of the contending parties."

John Henry was appointed steward of the asylum in 1851 and revealed details about the controversy in his memoirs. He related that "long before the building [of the asylum] there were two opposing parties in Jacksonville that could not agree. They were so hostile to each other that neither side could please the other." Henry said that Higgins let their battles enter into the affairs of the institution and he "took strong grounds in favor of one of the parties which was the means of his removal as Medical Superintendent... The position he took in the affair was unfortunate for the institution as well as for himself as he was a man of excellent qualities and kind to all in the institution."

Higgins was born in Montgomery County, Maryland on July 30, 1808. He attended the Rockville Academy and graduated in medicine from Columbia College (Washington, DC) on March 11, 1829. Based upon his site of medical training, Higgins remained an honorary member of the Medical Society of the District of Columbia. He relocated in Jacksonville, Illinois, and on January 25, 1831. Practicing in Jacksonville, Higgins was said to be the first physician in Illinois to successfully tie the common carotid artery. In 1834, Higgins settled in Griggsville with his family. Entering politics, Higgins was elected to represent Pike County in the Illinois legislature from 1846 to 1847. In the issue of the *Sangamo Journal* that listed the members of the Illinois legislature, there was also a legal advertisement published by Lincoln & Herndon. In the column directly under the listing of Higgins' name, Lincoln & Herndon represented the complainant in the divorce case of *Robert O. Paranteau v. Ann C. Paranteau* and served notice, dated August 10, 1846, upon the defendant to appear in Logan County Circuit Court.

On August 29, 1848, Higgins accepted the appointment as medical superintendent of the Illinois State Hospital for the Insane. He indicated that he would spend the fall and winter visiting asylums in other states to acquaint himself with the treatment of patients as well as the plans and arrangements of buildings. More than seven months later, on April 16, 1849, Higgins and his family took up residence at the asylum in Jacksonville in Morgan County. Higgins bolstered his professional stature by attending and reading a paper at the fifth annual meeting of the AMSAII on June 18, 1850. Significantly, AMSAII President Dr. William M. Awl from the Ohio Lunatic Asylum requested that Higgins read his paper *On the Necessity of a Resident Medical Superintendent in an Institution for the Insane.* His paper was "called up for consideration and the whole subject was fully discussed" at the meeting. In view of the trustees's actions to remove Higgins about three years later, it is pertinent to note the six points his paper discussed: the role of the superintendent as the *paterfamilias* of a vast household; the superintendent's ability to treat patients; securing the confidence of the patients; methods to control maniacs; the control of restraints by attendants; and the vital character of the attendants.

On March 1, 1851 the newly appointed trustees met at Higgins' office and an imbroglio developed over the naming of a specific trustee. There was an appointment for James Morton that should have been for Joseph Morton. That dispute about the number of trustees required by law expanded into acrimonious discussions about a number of subjects that lasted through June 1851. Angry words peppered the drawn out discussions between the politically appointed old and new trustees: "intrigue or fraud...doubts and fears...possession of books and papers...render accounts...acted in good faith...errors and utter inconsistencies... solemn protest...legal order." About ten weeks later Higgins continued his professional education.

There is no doubt that political events led to Higgins's problems with the trustees. Although both Illinois Governors were Democrats, it is significant that Higgins was appointed under the administration of Governor Augustus C. French and terminated during the subsequent administration of Governor Joel A. Matteson. Members of the board of trustees of the asylum were totally different under each governor and the composition of the Illinois legislature also changed during this time period. There were ensuing legislative actions to amend the law and reduce the number of trustees of the asylum. In their third biennial report for 1851-1852, the trustees took the legislature to task using blunt language:

> Did the authors and concoctors of that inimitable bill really think it important...or had they certain sinister ends to accomplish?... If the plain object was not revolution without legislative scrutiny, it would trouble a sensible man to divine what it could be. Why all this bungling confusion of objects and ends? Was it ignorance or awkwardness? Or what is more probable, an attempt to be cunning, in which, it must be confessed, they were temporarily successful.

In an open letter to the newspapers in 1852, trustees J. T. Holmes, Joseph Morton, Aquilla Becraft and J. B. Turner responded to the following six specific legislative criticisms of the asylum:

1. Extravagant and useless appropriation of rooms to officers and attendants to the "serious detriment of the unfortunate Insane."
2. The "quartering of large families on the Institution."

3. "Extravagant expenditures in furniture and other conveniences for the officers and their families."
4. "Supporting families and persons, who cannot, or do not contribute in the way of labor or otherwise, anything to the benefit of the Institution or its inmates."
5. "Employing an unnecessary number of persons in and about the Institution."
6. Insinuation as regards the incompetency of the officers and board, as well as their predecessors in office.

While the trustees lambasted the legislature, they complimented Higgins for his work as medical superintendent: "gratifying results presented in the superintendent's report will compare favorably with even the oldest and most thoroughly equipped and experienced institutions in the land…thirty percent of all received into the institution have experienced its most beneficent results, at a cost highly creditable to the superintendent under the circumstances."

Mentioning a series of attacks on the asylum trustees and officers, the third biennial report noted that "The superintendent has been represented as totally unfit for his duties." That charge against Higgins was likely related to two catastrophic incidents at the asylum: the death of a patient in July 1852 that resulted from her clothing catching fire and another incident in which a patient inadvertently burned down the barn. Admitting the complexity of their duties and enumerating a litany of innuendos and derogatory rumors, the trustees sarcastically concluded that "no one ought to expect that the ship could be sailed successfully by such a crazy crew for a single week, even if successfully launched…. The various officers of such an institution, like the generals of the army, must be judged not by any pre-conceived notions of etiquette, or fitness, or propriety, but by their actual practical success."

Higgins received a request on January 20, 1853 from a state senator asking for the names of patients and the counties from which they came. Nine days later, Higgins sent an up-to-date list of the names of 148 patients admitted. His report to the state Senate listed four various circumstances for the "apparent inequality… from the various counties."

Adding to the turmoil, the legislature installed their own selections as trustees. On February 11, 1853, the legislature appointed nine trustees for the Illinois State Hospital for the Insane: David Brainard of Cook County; William Butler of Sangamon County; William Craven of Morgan County; Darius Dexter of Pope County; Richard Henry of Morgan County; James Mahon of Wabash County; Fleming Stevenson of Morgan County; Timothy R. Young of Clark County; and Pleasant L. Ward of Gallatin County.

On April 14, 1853, the board of trustees of the Illinois State Hospital for the Insane met pursuant to adjournment in the room over Mr. F. Stevenson's store in Jacksonville. Alexander McDonald presented his bond and was approved as secretary of the board, replacing Higgins. Mr. Butler offered a preamble and resolution that recited the existence of sundry complaints involving Higgins and the institution and the need for a new superintendent:

> [W]hereas, this board, after mature reflection, and acting without regard to men, but solely with a view to the good of the institution, are fully convinced that the said medical superintendent [Dr. James M. Higgins] does not possess the kind of qualifications, which are necessary to the discharge of the duties of said office; and that the harmony, good, management, usefulness and prosperity of the institution, demand a change in said office of medical superintendent….

Trustees Stevenson and Butler were appointed as a committee "to report to a subsequent meeting of the board, the name or names of a suitable person or persons to fill said office, as medical superintendent…committee is instructed to report the name of no person as a candidate for such office, whose associations heretofore have involved him in the slightest degree, in any of the difficulties or divisions connected with the institution; and that they report the name of some individual whose high character for integrity, capacity, medical reputation and experience, cannot admit of a question..." After adopting Butler's resolution and setting the next meeting for the first Tuesday in May in Jacksonville, the board of trustees adjourned.

At the board meeting on May 3, 1853 in the back room of Stevenson's store, trustees Craven and Dexter, opposed the resolution offered by Butler regarding Higgins. Significantly, their protest was tabled until the next meeting. Actions taken at the April 14, 1853 meeting were reiterated and the vote recorded. Only Craven voted against the following resolutions:

> 2d.   *Resolved,* That James M. Higgins, medical superintendent of the Illinois State Hospital for the Insane, be, and hereby is, removed from said office; and the said office of medical superintendent for the Illinois State Hospital for the Insane is declared vacant.
>
> 4th.   *Resolved,* That Dr. H[enry] K. Jones, assistant physician of the institution, be authorized and required to perform the duties of superintendent...until a superintendent shall be appointed and enter upon the performance of his duties...he shall receive the same salary as was received by the late superintendent.

At the conclusion of the May 3, 1853 meeting, the board's secretary was ordered to furnish copies of the appropriate resolutions to the individuals concerned and did so immediately.

A week later, on May 10, 1853, Lincoln was the prosecutor in *People v. Thomas Delny* in Tazewell County Circuit Court in Pekin. Delny was accused of raping a seven-year-old girl who lived with her widowed mother in Wesley. Lincoln wrote the indictment: "That Thomas Delny, a male person above the age of fourteen years...on the seventh day of May in the year of our Lord one thousand eight hundred and fifty-three, with force of arms...in and upon Jane Ann Rupert, a female child under the age of ten years, to wit of the age of seven years...violently and feloniously did make an assault, and her, the said Jane Ann Rupert, then and there violently, and against her will, feloniously did ravish and carnally know; contrary to the form of the statute in such case made and provided, and against the Peace and dignity of the said people of the State of Illinois." Witnesses included Jane Ann Rupert, the little girl who was raped, and Paul N. And Catherine Rupert. Coincidently, Joseph S. Maus testified in this case. Lincoln sued Maus in 1851 representing Edward Jones. Nevertheless, two years later Maus most likely testified as a physician for prosecutor Lincoln.

With no doubt in their minds, the jurors speedily brought in a verdict of guilty. After the conviction, the judge sentenced Delny to eighteen years in the state penitentiary at Alton. An article in the Springfield *Daily Register* reported that a horde of vengeful citizens, inflamed by the hideous crime, sought swift justice at a convenient tree. "A mob came very near getting possession of the base wretch and hanging him." Subsequently, Delny was "hired out" by the prison to work at a local factory run by S. Wise. Later, Delny was scheduled to be transferred to a new prison at Joliet. On February 11, 1859, Wise petitioned Governor William H. Bissell to grant a pardon. "Will your Excellency, then, extend to Delny the clemency, of which I think him well worthy and deserving." On the next day, February 12, 1859, Governor Bissell wrote to his secretary of state, Ozias M. Hatch: "Please let this man be pardoned as within requested by the 22 or 23 inst." Delny was released at the end of February 1859 after serving five years and nine months, less than one-third of his eighteen year sentence for his "awful crime."

At the next monthly meeting, on Saturday, June 4, 1853, the board of trustees of the Illinois State Hospital for the Insane convened for a regular meeting. Higgins was requested to report on the "amount of indebtedness of this institution; the amount of expenditures likely to accrue the present year; and also an estimate of monies to be received from the State." This meeting was adjourned until seven o'clock next Monday morning.

On June 6, 1853, the governing board reconvened their regular meeting. "Dr. Higgins asked the privilege of making a statement to the board, which was accorded to him. Dr. Higgins then made a statement and presented a report containing charges against the Steward of the Institution; which was ordered to be filed, and copies of same be furnished Dr. Higgins and Mr. Henry—the subject to be acted upon at the next meeting of the Board." In closing, Higgins made a conciliatory statement to the board. Recounting the events at the April 14, 1853 meeting, the board reiterated and approved the resolutions removing Higgins from his position as superintendent. It was ordered "That Dr. James M. Higgins be allowed the sum of two hundred dollars for the deduction made by a former Board in his salary of one thousand dollars, which deduction took place since the opening of the Institution."

On July 19, 1853, the trustees met at the hospital and Mr. Francis made several corrections in the minutes of the last meeting. It was added that "J. M. Higgins, late superintendent, was present at the former meeting of the board, held on the 6 of June, 1853, when the following resolutions were introduced and acted upon, to wit:" Resolution number one was unchanged. However, resolution number two added significant legal language having a direct impact upon the subsequent lawsuits. After "declared vacant," the resolution continued:

> and whereas, while the said resolutions were pending, the said James M. Higgins was present and discussed the matters embraced in the same, making an argument against the passage thereof; and whereas, after said argument, said resolutions were passed, said Higgins asking no postponement of action upon the same; therefore, it is ordered, that the records of the last meeting, be, and are hereby amended, so as to show the foregoing facts,—which corrections of the journal of the last meeting of the board were unanimously adopted.

Clearly, if the board's minutes are believed, Higgins did have the opportunity to defend himself against the charges before the resolutions ordering his removal were considered. Furthermore, there is no indication that Higgins expressed any desire to postpone the vote of the trustees on his removal. Therefore, the trustees contended that Higgins unlawfully usurped and intruded into the duties of the medical superintendent by remaining on the premises after the board removed him.

In the October 1853 term of the Morgan County Circuit Court, Cyrus Eppler, the state's attorney, and William Brown, Benjamin S. Edwards and Richard Yates, attorneys for the trustees, sued and charged that Higgins was not qualified for the position of medical superintendent of the hospital for the insane and was legally removed by the trustees. Higgins was accused of defiance of the authority of the trustees, unlawfully residing in the hospital with his family, unlawfully intruding into the management of the affairs of the hospital and acting "contrary to the legislative act against the peace and dignity of the people of the State of Illinois." Eppler addressed Judge David M. Woodson, the presiding magistrate: "State's attorney prayeth the consideration of the court...that due process of law may be awarded against the said James M. Higgins to make him answer to the said people of the State of Illinois and shew by what authority he claims to have use and enjoy the office aforesaid." In contrast, Higgins's lawyer argued for a strict interpretation of the exact language of the legislative act. A convinced jury ruled in favor of Higgins that the board could not remove him for the reasons stated. Edwards and Yates, attorneys for the trustees, disagreed with the verdict and the court gave the approval to appeal to the supreme court of Illinois.

During the December 1853 term of the supreme court of Illinois, Judge John D. Caton presided over the appeal. Caton considered Lincoln "equally potent before the jury as with the court." Smith and McConnell were joined by Lincoln to represent Higgins. John T. Stuart & Benjamin Edwards and William Brown represented the trustees of the hospital. Lincoln argued for a strict adherence to the language of the legislative act appointing the medical superintendent. In doing so, Lincoln legally demonstrated that he "could split hairs as well as split rails." From a legal standpoint, Lincoln contended that the legislative act did not specifically say who had the right to remove the superintendent. He argued that the superintendent's removal can only be exercised by the legislature, the governor, the members of the legislature and by the members of the supreme court of Illinois, as visitors of the institution. This referred to the last section of the act which declared: "the governor, the judges of the supreme court and members of the legislature shall be, *ex officio*, visitors of the institution." In addition, Lincoln contended that the trustees could not remove Higgins for any reason except breach of trust or incompetency. In their removal resolution, the trustees stated that Higgins was "not qualified for the position." Lincoln declared that precise reason was not in the act and the trustees failed to meet the two conditions specified in the act. His argument contended that an asylum superintendent was considered a person in a high and responsible position. Continuing, Lincoln noted that the legislature, in their wisdom, placed the superintendent beyond the whims of the hanging by political parties or other inferior considerations by conclusively delineating the only two causes for removal.

Judge Caton ruled that the legislature bestowed on the trustees all the powers necessary for managing the hospital. Those powers included the authority to remove the superintendent for breach of trust or incompetency. In disagreeing with Lincoln, Judge Caton stated that "the substance is the same, though, perhaps, expressed in more delicate or less offensive terms."

Referring to the legislative act and the power of the trustees, governor, legislature, and supreme court of Illinois judges, the court found that the legislature has the power of amotion, with or without the law, to remove the superintendent for any reason. Therefore, the court found that the removal power with the specified limitations must refer to some other authority created by the Act. "We have no doubt it was the clear intention of the legislature that they [trustees] should have the power of removing the superintendent as well as appointing him, and otherwise properly managing the institution." When either of the two specific causes existed, the trustees are the appropriate body to make that removal. It would not be compatible with the "highest interests of the institution" to delay action until the legislature could assemble or the governor or supreme court of Illinois judges could act. Judge Caton commented: "I do not believe that the legislature intended to organize such a tribunal by the seventeenth section; but that we need not decide."

In continuing, the court proceeded on the fact that the trustees did have the power of removal. Two questions remained: Was a legal manner followed in the removal? Was the removal made for a legal cause? Lincoln made four arguments relative to due process of the proceedings: Higgins was not served with specific and formal charges; he did not receive a formal notice of the time and place of those charges; he should have had a regular trial based upon the testimony of witnesses; and he was entitled to a trial by jury. In responding, Judge Caton found that the statute made none of those formalities necessary and the common law did not interpose or attach them to the statute. "In cases of this sort, where the law is silent as to the mode of preceding...they are not bound down by any legal rule of evidence...they may determine that question [of qualifications] upon their own observation, and exercising their own best judgment." To emphasize that point, the judge presented the examples of immediate action required by the trustees in outrageous and abusive discipline and treatment of patients or aggravated cases of misconduct by superintendents. Inaction or formal proceedings would merely allow the same abuses to continue. "Such a proceeding, instead of promoting the ends of justice and the objects of the law, would be but a mockery of the one and an abuse of the other."

By the Act, the trustees were authorized to evaluate the qualifications of the medical superintendent prior to their appointment. If so, the trustees must also be competent to do likewise as to the removal of the superintendent. Judge Caton juxtaposing the specific language of the statute on "removal only for infidelity to the trust reposed in him or incompetency" against the reason of the trustees that Higgins "does not possess the kind of qualifications" to discharge his duties. "Unless the board were bound to adopt the precise language of the statute, it can not well be denied that the cause assigned for the removal was sufficient." Simply put, if Higgins did not possess the qualifications to discharge the duties of the office, he was incompetent. In expanding that view, the court detailed the superintendent's activities and concluding "Competency includes every necessary qualification."

In conclusion, Judge Caton found that it was not necessary for the trustees to use the precise language of the statute. "If it substantially embraced it, that was sufficient. Such was the case here... The judgment of the circuit court must be reversed and the cause remanded." Higgins was removed as superintendent in December 1853. On February 13, 1854, in support of Higgins, trustees Craven and Dexter submitted a nine-page special minority report of the trustees of the Illinois State Hospital for the Insane to the Illinois General Assembly. They cited a number of pressing reasons for "the immediate attention and interference of your Honorable Body in your legislative and visitorial capacity." Their report called attention to: irregular illegal meetings of the trustees; "grave and serious charges of incapacity and delinquency against the Steward"; violations by law and by contract; "precipitate, unlawful, unjust and unwise actions disastrous to the institution;" "alarming detriment" to the institution; and the "incorporation of evils" preventing the institution from achieving "its rue [common] weal and destiny." Apparently. politics prevailed and there was no further action by the General Assembly.

Trustees of the Illinois Hospital for the Insane recorded their selection of a new superintendent in their Fourth Biennial Report : "Dr. Andrew McFarland, late Superintendent of the New Hampshire Asylum for the Insane; and on the 16 of June of the present year [1854], he arrived at the institution, and assumed its superintendence."

McFarland was born in Concord, New Hampshire in 1817, graduated from Dartmouth College and received his medical degree from Jefferson Medical College (Philadelphia). He was asylum superintendent in New Hampshire from 1845 to 1852 and then spent some time in Europe studying methods of treating mental diseases. A little less than three years after he was appointed superintendent of the Illinois asylum, McFarland was cross-examined by Lincoln during a murder trial. In 1857, McFarland was the chief medical expert testifying that an overdose of chloroform caused the insanity of Isaac Wyatt, an accused murderer whom Lincoln was prosecuting in cooperation with the state's attorney. In 1875, McFarland was employed by Lincoln's only surviving eldest son, Robert T. Lincoln, to evaluate the mental status of his mother, Mary Todd Lincoln.

Lincoln continued to be a political advisor to Richard Yates, one of the lawyers opposing him in the *People ex rel. Stevenson v. Higgins* case. Toward the end of 1854, Lincoln wrote to Yates about an upcoming election:

> I would like, by your leave, to get an additional paragraph into the *Journal,* about as follows:
> "Today we place the name of Hon. Richard Yates at the head of our columns for re-election as the Whig candidate for this congressional district. We do this without consultation with him and subject to the decision of a Whig convention, should the holding of one be deemed necessary; hoping however, there may be unanimous acquiescence without a convention."
> May I do this? Answer by return mail.

Four days later, the following item appeared in the *Illinois State Journal:* "Hon. Richard Yates has yielded to the solicitations of his friends and consented to be a candidate for re-election to Congress." While in Congress, Yates forcefully spoke against the extension of slavery into the Kansas and Nebraska territories. His fellow legislators considered him odd because he favored women's suffrage. In an autobiography that Lincoln prepared, he wrote that "In the autumn of that year [1854], he took the stump with no broader practical aim than to secure, if possible, the reelection of Hon. Richard Yates to Congress." As a politician, Yates was charismatic, genial, handsome, an eloquent orator, and more emotional than intellectual. On the negative side, he was "convivial," a euphemism for a heavy drinker or an alcoholic. During the nineteenth century, people in public life in America consumed an "incredible quantity of hard liquor. Drunkenness in Congress was so common that leaders found it hard to keep intoxicated members off the floor." During the campaign for election to Congress, Yates professed temperance but there were rumors that he was a drinking man. Lincoln replied to the allegation in a letter to Richard J. Oglesby, a fellow lawyer from Decatur who was later elected Illinois governor three times (1865-1869, 1873, 1885-1889) and also served in the US Senate. In that confidential September 8, 1854 letter, Lincoln directly answered the rumor about Yates' temperance:

In view of later events, Lincoln hedged his bet by stating that his vote did not depend on whether or not a candidate drank liquor. Yates lost the congressional election to Thomas L. Harris, a Democratic lieutenant of Stephen A. Douglas. In a November 12, 1854 post-election letter to Orville H. Browning, Lincoln blamed a portion of Yates's defeat on the legal battle over the firing of Higgins: "Yates is beaten 100 to 150. The whole thing was done in Morgan & Scott counties...The quarrel over the Insane Asylum...did the work for him."

After leaving Congress, Yates became president of the Tonica and Petersburg Railroad. Aiming for higher office, Yates refused to run for Congress again. In 1855, he promised Lincoln that he would run for senator only "in the event you do not succeed." At the first Republican convention, Yates made a "stirring speech" and was an official. In 1860, Yates ran against Norman B, Judd of Chicago and Leonard Swett of Bloomington for the Republican nomination for Illinois governor. Lincoln had close ties to Yates, Judd and Swett and justifiably remained neutral in the politicking. He expressed his dilemma to Lyman Trumbull, a lawyer who won election to the US Senate over Lincoln in an 1855 appointment by the Illinois legislature. Trumbull served on the supreme court of Illinois from 1849 to 1854, converted from an anti-Nebraska Democrat into a Radical Republican, served three terms as a Senator (1855-1872), helped to draft the Thirteenth Amendment, and was one of seven Republicans who voted to acquit President

Andrew Johnson of impeachment charges. In an April 7, 1860 letter to Trumbull, Lincoln wrote that "I am trying to keep out of the contest among our friends for the Gubernatorial nomination; but from what I hear, the result is in considerable doubt." On the fourth ballot, Swett threw his support to Yates, who became the compromise candidate of the party. Francis A. Hoffman of DuPage County, who was declared ineligible to be William H. Bissell's lieutenant governor in 1856, got the nomination to run with Yates. In the November election, Yates won by 12,943 votes over circuit court Judge James C. Allen to became the thirteenth governor and continued the Republican dominance of the state. As Lincoln and other dignitaries waited at his inauguration, Yates was too drunk to deliver his address. He staggered down the aisle one-half hour late, collapsed in a chair and the clerk read his long speech. Despite Lincoln's considerable assistance to his political career, Yates preferred Edward Bates of Missouri over Lincoln for the Republican presidential nomination in 1860. Yates was the Civil War governor who was instrumental in sending 197,360 men into the Union armies. Governor Yates did not hesitate to voice his disapproval of Lincoln's administration. In 1862, he told a Brooklyn audience that "Old Abe was too slow for me…I was for the [emancipation] proclamation, for confiscation, for the arrest of rebels and traitors, and for every measure be which we could put down the rebellion." Yates's term as governor expired on January 15, 1865 and he was succeeded by Richard J. Oglesby. Prior to the end of his term, Yates was elected to the US Senate and joined the Radical Republicans. Senator Yates convinced Mrs. Mary T. Lincoln that President Lincoln should be buried in Springfield, Illinois. In line with the Radical Republicans, Senator Yates voted to impeach President Andrew Johnson. Today, a life-size statue of Yates stands on the lawn of the Illinois State Capitol. When that statute was dedicated, Yates's son, also named Richard Yates, had already served as the twenty-fourth governor of Illinois from 1901-1905.

LINCOLN SECURES A CHARTER FOR A HOMEOPATHIC MEDICAL COLLEGE AND REPRESENTS RAILROADS

In 1854, the law firm of Lincoln & Herndon prepared a proposed special legislative charter to establish a homeopathic medical college in Chicago. Coincidentally, after the legislature approved the charter on February 14, 1855, the May 1855 meeting of the House of Delegates of the American Medical Association (AMA) passed a resolution concerning teaching in medical schools and denigrated homeopathy. A particularly obnoxious resolution was placed in the section on cults and healing:

> *Resolved,* That any such unnatural union such as the mingling of an exclusive system, such as homeopathy, with scientific medicine in a school, setting aside all questions of its untruthfulness, cannot fail, by the destruction of union and confidence, and the production of confusion and disorder, unsettling and distracting the mind of the learners, to so far impair the usefulness of teaching as to render every school, adopting such a policy, unworthy of the support of the profession.

While Abraham Lincoln drafted the charter, his complex legal task was exacerbated by the deep-seated animosity and vigilant opposition of organized orthodox medicine to the "cult" of homeopathy. A comment at the AMA meeting revealed the practical side of the protracted and caustic quarrel: "We never fought the homeopath on matters of principle; we fought him because he came into the community and got the business." Organized medicine furthered their own ends by establishing a code of ethics that allowed for the expulsion of member physicians who consulted with, or even associated with, non-regular practitioners. On April 14, 1865, US Surgeon General Joseph K. Barnes was denounced by the AMA for treating Secretary of State William H. Seward after he was severely wounded during Lincoln's assassination conspiracy plot. This attack occurred simply because Seward's personal physician was a homeopath.

A number of Chicago's most influential citizens and politicians participated in the creation and furtherance of the proposed Hahnemann Medical College including William H. Brown, Joseph B. Doggett, John H. Dunham, George A. Gibbs, Thomas Hoyne, Norman B, Judd, Orrington Lunt, George E. Shipman, M.D., David S. Smith, M.D., and John M. Wilson. These ten men were named as trustees in the act to incorporate the Hahnemann Medical College. In addition, Van H. Higgins, Edson Keith, Benjamin Lombard, Jonathan Young Scammon, E. H. Sheldon, and Henry M. Smith collaborated and served on the college's board of trustees a bit later. Because of the powerful individuals supporting the establishment of the homeopathic medical college, Lincoln realized that an opportunity existed for attracting more business to his law firm. In fact, that did happen.

Homeopathy originated in Europe in the early 1800s and became spectacularly popular in the United States. Women, in particular, sought care from homeopaths and became lay and professional practitioners. In 1848, the first women's medical college in the world, the homeopathic Boston Female Medical College, was founded. Advocates included some of the most respected members of American society: novelist Louisa May Alcott; poet and journalist William Cullen Bryant; newspaper editor Horace Greeley; novelists Nathaniel Hawthorne and William James; poet Henry Wadsworth Longfellow; politicians William H. Seward and Daniel Webster; and abolitionist Harriet Beecher Stowe. Some of the popularity evolved from the public's distaste for the harsh orthodox therapeutic regimens of bleeding, blistering, and purgatives. Dr. Benjamin Rush, the father of American medicine, taught medical students that bloodletting was useful in all general and chronic disease. In 1856, two American firms imported 800,000 leeches for medical bloodletting. In addition, orthodox physicians used medicines compounded from arsenic, lead, mercury and strong herbs to purge the body of disease-causing matter. Individuals who became ill frequently avoided orthodox physicians because the offered treatment was ineffective and possibly more dangerous than the illness itself.

Dr. Samuel Hahnemann's homeopathic therapeutic regimen built upon the "law of *similia*" expressed in the Latin dictum *similia similibus curantur* stressing that "like cures its like, and not that which is contrary." Therapy applying Hahnemann's principle of the "law of infinitesimals" involved the patient taking minuscule watered-down medication doses that produced the same signs and symptoms in healthy people as those present in people ill with a specific disease. For the sum of $5.00, people purchased their own domestic homeopathy kit consisting of numbered vials of infinitesimals along with a therapeutic guidebook. Hoyne and Scammon "were among the earliest of the homeopathic laymen." Hoyne's wife, Leonora, was the daughter of a prominent homeopath, Dr. John T. Temple.

Illinois emerged as a major center of homeopathy. Between 1857 and 1859, 40 percent of all the homeopaths in the world were said to be located in the Cook County area, which included Chicago. By 1905, Chicago educated more homeopathic physicians than any other American city.

America's first national medical society, the American Institute of Homeopathy, was founded on April 10, 1844. Two years later, in opposition and in contrast, the American Medical Association evolved, focused on the orthodox or regular approach to medical care and vowing to put a halt to the growth of homeopathy. Organizationally, a rancorous conflict developed between the homeopaths and the allopaths. Overt animosities between the differing practicing physicians appeared in concrete form in an exchange of open letters in the October 1850 issue of the *Northwestern Journal of Homeopathy*:

Dr. N. S. Davis — *Sir*: I am a homeopathist from a conviction of the truth of the principles and the efficacy of the practice of homeopathia. With these views, will you graduate me if I comply with the ordinary requisitions of the faculty?
Yours, etc.,
M. DANIEL COE

Mr. DANIEL COE--*Dear Sir*: I am directed to inform you that the faculty of Rush Medical College will not recommend you to the trustees for a degree so long as they have any reason to suppose that you entertain the doctrines, and intend to trifle with human life on the principles you avow in your letter. To do otherwise would involve both parties in the grossest inconsistency.
Very respectfully yours,
N.S. DAVIS,
Secretary of the Faculty of Rush Medical College

While the homeopaths rationally realized the need for a medical college of their own, the members of the local Homeopathic Society advised caution: "Your committee thinks that the time is not yet ripe for the establishment of a Homeopathic College in Chicago." When necessary, people had multiple choices of medical healers. Ill patients could select from a variety of curative therapies: botanics and herbs, eclectic remedies, hydrotherapy, mesmerism, phrenology, spiritualism, steam vapors, or vegetarianism. All of the healing sects furiously battled to overturn the preeminence of the orthodox and/or regular physicians. Intense competition among the medical healers made it difficult for practitioners to earn a living. For a large part of the nineteenth century, medical practice in the US was a hodgepodge of regular medicine, unorthodox theories, irregular healers, and dubious remedies.

This deleterious situation worsened due to the deplorable state of medical education in the 1800s. Medical students tended "to rush into practice with the least expenditure of money, time, brains and knowledge."

In view of the dominance of the proprietary auspices of medical education in the 1850s, Lincoln prepared a document requesting that the state legislature grant a charter to a private corporation as a stock company. Section 6 of the act did so: "Fifty thousand dollars shall constitute the capital stock of said institution, to be hereafter increased to one hundred thousand dollars, if deemed necessary by the trustees...whenever one thousand dollars of the capital stock shall have been paid in; and the said trustees shall have all necessary power to convert and use said money for the benefit of the institution." Although the proposed medical school was a private corporation, no dividends were ever paid out. All the profits were reinvested into improvements to the college. Lincoln did the legal work on behalf of Dr. Davis S. Smith, Thomas Hoyne, and Norman B. Judd. Smith was a pioneer homeopathic physician in Chicago; Judd was his patient and a distinguished Chicago lawyer; while Hoyne was an active and influential politician in Illinois. Hoyne was the primary actor in bringing Lincoln and the others together in this legal undertaking related to a business venture. Smith met Hoyne in Springfield, explained the predicament, and "Hoyne took the Doctor to the law office of Abraham Lincoln" where the new charter for the Hahnemann Medical College was drafted.

Thomas Hoyne was born in New York City on February 11, 1817 and came to Chicago about September 1, 1837. In 1853, President Franklin Pierce appointed him the US attorney for the Northern District of Illinois. When the US circuit and district courts convened in Springfield with Justices John McLean and Thomas Drummond on the bench, Lincoln met Hoyne in his official capacity. As noted in the July 5, 1853 issue of the *Illinois Register*: "Mr. Hoyne, the district-attorney, arrived in town.... But few of the lawyers had arrived last evening." Lincoln & Herndon had a thriving practice in the federal courts in Springfield.

A Democrat, Hoyne supported Stephen A. Douglas rather than Lincoln in their political contests. For more than forty years, Hoyne was an influential political force, a mover and shaker, in Illinois politics and particularly in Chicago. He helped to establish the Chicago Public Library, the Chicago Astronomical Society and arranged for the purchase of the Clarke telescope for the observatory of the University of Chicago. Hoyne was a founder of the Hahnemann Medical College and Hospital and remained an "active and efficient member of the Board of Trustees" for twenty-eight years. Much of the success and growth of the medical school and hospital resulted from Thomas Hoyne's labors and influence. He exhibited "constant fidelity to one of the oldest charitable and educational institutions in Chicago." His son, Temple S. Hoyne, attended the college, became a prominent homeopathic physician, a faculty member as professor of materia medica and therapeutics, and the registrar at the Hahnemann Medical College. Dr. Hoyne delivered the valedictory address to the medical school's graduating class in 1873.

In 1876, Hoyne was elected mayor of Chicago as an independent under "singular" circumstances. Chicago was reorganized in April 1875 and the election for mayor was switched from November 1875 to April 1876. A series of administrative omissions and commissions resulted in inadvertently bypassing mayoralty election requirements. Nevertheless, a popular vote ensued and Hoyne was overwhelmingly elected mayor of Chicago on April 18, 1876. A month later, Hoyne delivered his inaugural address. However, the prior mayor, Harvey D. Colvin, legally contested the election and refused to yield possession of the office. Hoyne served as mayor for about four months until the court declared his election null and void. Therefore, Hoyne is usually not counted among the ranks of Chicago's legal mayors. A special election was held on July 12, 1876 to select a Chicago mayor and Hoyne was not elected. Seven years later, Hoyne died in a train collision on the Rome, Watertown, and Ogdensburg railroad near Carlton Station in New York on July 27, 1883. He was sixty-six years of age.

Judd first encountered Lincoln during a July 1-3, 1847 River and Harbor Convention in Chicago to protest President James Polk's veto of an appropriation for development. Lincoln's address to the meeting impressed Judd. From that point, Lincoln and Judd got to know each other quite well from their mutual political and legal activities. When president, Lincoln told his Secretary of War, Simon Cameron, that "he was more indebted to Judd than any other one man for his nomination [in 1860]." Judd was born in Rome, New York, and arrived in Chicago in 1836 to form the law firm of (John D.) Caton & Judd. Later, Caton served as a supreme court of Illinois justice from 1842 to 1864. When that partnership dissolved, Judd joined with Jonathan Young Scammon. Active in politics, Judd was a former Independent Democrat who switched parties and became a political stalwart in Republican circles in Illinois. Judd served several terms in the state legislature. In their respective unsuccessful campaigns in 1859, both he and Leonard Swett lost their bids for the Republican nomination for Illinois governor to Richard Yates.

Judd was heavily involved in Lincoln's campaign for the Republican nomination for president. At this time, Lincoln was annoyed by his law partner's political meddling. William H. Herndon upset Lincoln's need to maintain his equal friendship with Judd, Swett, and Yates. Herndon said that Judd, as Republican state committee chairman, used party funds to promote his own political prospects. Immediately, Judd complained bitterly to Lincoln on July 31, 1860: "I am advised that Herndon is…talking about misapplication of funds by me etc., etc….This ought not to be and is not true-cannot you set him right."

Even before Lincoln received Judd's protest, he heard the rumors. Lincoln responded to Judd: "…I mentioned it to him; he rather denied the charge, and I did not press him about the past, but got his solemn pledge to say nothing of the sort in the future…. I impressed upon him as well as I could, first, that such was untrue and unjust to you; and, second, that I would be held responsible for what he said.

During Judd's gubernatorial campaign, he was accused of being unfair and unfaithful to Lincoln during the canvass for the US Senate in 1858. Lincoln wrote about their personal relations in a December 14, 1859 letter that spoke about his avowed friends during the political Senatorial canvass: "There is not one of them in whose honesty, honor and integrity I to-day have greater confidence than I have in those of Mr. Judd." Judd actively campaigned for Lincoln's presidency in 1860. After Lincoln won the presidential election, he wrote to Judd: "If it shall not incommode you, your company, on the whole, or any part of my journey to Washington, shall be very agreeable to me. Yours as ever A. Lincoln." An uncommoded Judd accompanied Lincoln on the railroad ride from Springfield to Washington in 1861. Shortly after his inauguration, on March 4, 1861, Lincoln appointed Judd minister to Berlin. He served there until Lincoln's death and his summary removal by President Andrew Johnson.

Judd was a prominent lawyer specializing in railroad law with high positions and at least seven railroad companies as clients: Chicago & Milwaukee Railway (Director); Chicago & Rock Island Railway (attorney and director); Michigan Southern Railway (attorney); Mississippi & Missouri Railway (attorney and director); Peoria & Bureau Valley Railway (president); Pittsburgh, Fort Wayne & Chicago Railway (attorney); and the Rock Island Railroad Bridge Company (president).

Throughout his legal career, Lincoln knew Judd both as co-counsel and as an opposing attorney. For instance, Judd represented the plaintiff in the case of *Scammon v. Cline*. On November 19, 1836 Cornelius Cline signed a promissory note: "One year after date I promise to pay D. N. Whitney or bearer fifty-two dollars with use. Value received in goods, &c."

Whitney assigned the promissory note for $52.50 over to Jonathan Young Scammon who sued to recover the debt. Scammon was appointed a reporter for the supreme court of Illinois in 1839 and held that position at the time of this suit. Justice of the Peace Alexander Heely was scheduled to hear the case in Belvedere. However, Cline managed to have the case transferred to Hiram

Waterman, another justice of the peace in the same county. No reason for the change was given. It can be assumed that Cline felt he would do better with Waterman. Cline was an early settler in the Belvedere area and was well known. Without any explanation, the court found the promissory note not valid and binding and ruled in Cline's favor on February 21, 1839. There is speculation that the justice's of peace ruling routinely supported Cline, the long time Belvedere resident over the outsider. Immediately, Judd filed an appeal to the Boone County Circuit Court on March 1, 1839 for a *de novo* trial, a new trial. Cline's lawyers argued that the Boone County Circuit Court did not legally exist when Judd filed his appeal. He should have filed with the court clerk of Jo Daviess County. In agreement, circuit court Judge Dan Stone dismissed the appeal on the technical ground that the Boone County Circuit Court was not yet in existence. In fact, Seth Whitman was appointed as court clerk before March 2, 1839, the date set by statute for the opening of the new court. Still in disagreement, Judd moved to the higher court and filed an appeal with the supreme court of Illinois. On June 10, 1840, Lincoln was hired as co-counsel by Cline's attorney, James L. Loop, to argue the case in the supreme court and opposed Judd. Lincoln concentrated on upholding the calendar technicalities of the prior decisions. He presented the same argument offered previously in the lower court: the appeal papers were filed one day too early with the court clerk in Boone County. Lincoln's technical hair-splitting argument was rejected by the supreme court of Illinois. Chief Justice William Wilson wrote the unanimous opinion of the court on February 24, 1841:

> The court is of the opinion that this case was improperly dismissed altho' the appeal bond appears to have been taken by the Clerke before the time fixed by law for holding the Court, yet the court itselfe must be considered in existence at the time, otherwise there would have been no Clerke by whom the appeal could be allowed, until the Legislature fixed the time for holding court; This authority was by a prior law vested in the

judge, and whether he exercised the authority by designating a time is immaterial.

The existence of the court and the right to take an appeal to it, must be regarded as having commenced with the appointment of a Clerke of the court by the Judge thereof.

As respects the jurisdiction of the Court (for the want of which this case was dismissed) we are also inclined to think that if the Court had had jurisdiction at the time its process was issued it ought to have entertained and tried the case. Jugt. therefore is reversed and the case remanded to the C.C. for trial.

Lincoln took no part in the retrial in Boone County Circuit Court. Despite the apparent lack of merit in Cline's claim, the jury rendered a verdict in his favor on April 27, 1841. Perhaps the Boone County jury was prejudiced against the Chicago capitalist, Scammon, and favored a fellow Booneite, Cline.

Coincidentally, when Robert T. Lincoln served his law apprenticeship. he did so in Scammon's law office. Scammon's son, Charles T. Scammon, became a partner in Robert T. Lincoln's law firm.

Judd, Lincoln, and Lincoln's senior partner, Stephen T. Logan, appeared together in the United States district court in Springfield, Illinois. They represented Chicago merchant Charles H. Chapman against a charge of perjury in obtaining his discharge under the bankruptcy act. This was the last case tried by Logan & Lincoln. However, it does not appear that Judd actually took part in the trial. A famed Chicago lawyer prosecuted the case for the government. A four-day trial ensued that was "conducted with great ability on the part of Justin Butterfield, Esq., United States Attorney, and Messrs. Logan and Lincoln on behalf of the prisoner." On December 14, 1844, the jury was "out but a few moments, when they returned into court a verdict of GUILTY against the prisoner." About one week later, Lincoln argued a motion for a new trial. Judge Nathaniel Pope denied the new trial and sentenced Chapman to five years in the federal penitentiary.

As a spin-off of Lincoln's professional and political network, Lincoln & Herndon acted as a corporate attorney representing a significant number of railroad companies in their law practice. In February 1837, the Illinois legislature passed the *Internal Improvement Act* allocating $12,000,000 for railroad improvements. Three and a half million dollars went to the Illinois Central Railroad (ICRR). Being a member of the state legislature and its committee on finance, Lincoln played an important part in the passage of this legislation. Sidney Breese, then a legislator and later a judge, was chief counsel and lobbyist for a competing investment group seeking a charter. For his effective work, Breese became known as "the Father of the Illinois Central" and his tombstone records his major achievement, "He who sleeps beneath this stone projected the Illinois Central Railroad." William Bissell, later an Illinois Governor, and Mason Brayman became the first attorneys for the ICRR. In the early 1850s, Lincoln was put on a retainer by the ICRR, one of the largest corporations in Illinois. Subsequently, Lincoln handled numerous and diverse cases in his practice of corporate law. Evidence suggests that Lincoln lobbied legislators in connection with the charter grant for the ICRR in 1851. One of Lincoln's earlier cases for the ICRR was tried in 1853 and involved taxation of railroad property by McLean County.

In August 1853, McLean County proposed to levy a tax on railroad property within their jurisdiction. Under the terms of the ICRR charter, the railroad agreed to pay a 7 percent tax on their gross earnings plus a 2 percent tax on their property. Earlier, Lincoln did some legal work for Champaign County that was of a similar county taxation nature. Keeping his professional and personal obligations in mind, Lincoln wrote to Thompson R. Webber, clerk of the Champaign County Circuit Court, on September 12, 1853. He offered his legal services for "the largest law question" in the state, if the fee was adequate: "As this will be the same question I have under consideration for you...you have first right to my services, if you choose to secure me a fee somewhat near such as I can get from the other side…therefore in justice to myself, I can not afford, if I can help it, to miss a fee altogether."

There can be no misreading the intent of Lincoln's words. A deft appraisal of Lincoln's law practice runs contrary to the mythology that he was a country lawyer: "He was an absolute hustler as a lawyer—he wanted to make money and he had a terrific work ethic…many lawyers speculated in real estate, but Lincoln didn't. He made his money from his law practice, by taking a prodigious number of nickel-and-dime cases…. He was a real lawyer's lawyer." Lincoln never heard from Champaign or McLean County and he sent a letter to the attorney for the railroad, Mason Brayman, on October 3, 1853: "I am now free to make an engagement for the Road; and if you think fit you may *count me in.*"

ICRR chief counsel James F. Joy, Brayman and Lincoln legally sought to enjoin McLean County from imposing the additional tax. McLean County was represented by Lincoln's former law partners, John T. Stuart and Stephen T. Logan. In their February 28, 1854 argument, Stuart and Logan claimed that the railroad's charter applied only to state taxes. Legally, the state constitution prohibited an ICRR exemption from county taxes. After hearing the case, the McLean County Circuit Court agreed with McLean County's position. About two years later, Lincoln successfully argued for the railroad before the supreme court of Illinois in *Illinois Central Railroad Company v. The County of McLean.* In their ruling, Chief Justice Walter B. Scates found the tax exemption "within the constitutional power of the legislature." This ruling of the supreme court of Illinois affirmed the right of the legislature to make exceptions and to mandate a variant of the levy. In an October 22, 1858 speech at Carthage, Lincoln ventured his opinion: "The decision, I thought, and still think, was worth half a million dollars to them [the ICRR]."

Despite winning the case, Lincoln had trouble collecting his $2,000 fee for representing the railroad. Railroad management complained that the amount was more than Daniel Webster would charge. Lincoln consulted with Judd and other lawyers about this unpaid fee problem. They persuaded Lincoln to increase his fee to $5,000 and to sue the company. At first, Lincoln revised his bill and forwarded the new bill along with endorsements by prominent attorneys:

Bill for Services Rendered the Illinois Central Railroad Company:

For professional services in the case of the Illinois Central Railroad Co. against the County of McLean, argued in the Supreme Court of the State of Illinois at December term 1855..............$5,000.00

We, the undersigned members of the Illinois Bar, understanding that the above entitled case was twice argued in the Supreme Court, and that judgment therein decided the question of the claim of counties and other minor municipal corporations to tax the property of said railroad company, and settled said question against said claim and in favor of said railroad company, are of opinion the sum above charged as a fee is not unreasonable.

Grant Goodrich	N. H. Purple
N. B. Judd	O. H. Browning
Archibald Williams	R. S. Blackwell
Isaac N. Arnold	S. T. Logan

Lincoln sued and on June 23, 1857, a trial took place where Lincoln read the jury depositions from leading lawyers, including Judd, about the value of his services. Impressed, the jury rendered a verdict for Lincoln for $4,800, the full amount minus Lincoln's $200 retainer. However, the ICRR still did not pay. Lincoln did not collect his fee until the railroad was served with a sheriff's execution notice and threatened with the seizure of the company's property on August 1, 1857. Incidentally, Joy was paid $10,000 per year by the ICRR as chief counsel in 1854. He resigned before the

McLean County case was resolved and nevertheless received $1,200 for his legal work on this case. For a comparison of Lincoln's largest fee, $5,000, annual earnings in 1857 listed the Illinois governor at $1,500, supreme court of Illinois justices received $1,200 and circuit court judges got $1,000.

Later, in fall of 1857, Lincoln joined the railroad company lawyers, Judd and Joseph Knox, in defending the railroad in the *Hurd v. The Rock Island Bridge Company* case. In 1855, Rock Island built the first bridge across the Mississippi River to allow railroads to transverse the water between Rock Island in Illinois and Davenport in Iowa. Captain John S. Hurd commanded the fastest and most up-to-date side-wheeler ship on the Mississippi. Inadvertently, he ran his ship, *Effie Afton*, into the drawbridge hitting one pier after the other on May 6, 1856. In the space of five minutes, his ship caught fire, flames completely demolished a span of the drawbridge which collapsed, and destroyed the vessel before it sank into the murky waters of the Mississippi. Hurd sued for $50,000 in damages. He charged that the bridge caused the accident by obstructing navigation by not having piers parallel to the river current. Three lawyers represented Hurd: Hezekiah M. Weed of Peoria, an authority in river practice, and a former circuit court judge; Corydon Beckwith of Chicago, an able attorney and later a supreme court of Illinois justice; and Timothy D. Lincoln of Cincinnati, no relation, and an admiralty practitioner.

With Judge John McLean presiding, the trial began on September 8, 1857 in the US District Court for the Northern District of Illinois. This accident and the ensuing court confrontation focused on the acrimonious battle between the competing self-interested businesses promoting railroad transport and those advocating water transport. Essentially, the litigation was a contest between commercial interests in Chicago and St. Louis to become major transportation hub cities. Newspapers in each city championed their own prejudiced regional concerns. Local newspapers in St. Louis published meeting announcements for "merchants, river-men and all others interested in the removal of the bridge at Rock Island and the obstruction formed by it to the navigation of the upper Mississippi." Allegedly, at a meeting on December 16, 1856, "half a million dollars had been subscribed under the lead of the St. Louis Chamber of Commerce by the river interests between Pittsburgh and St. Paul to prosecute this suit to the bitter end."

By this time in 1857, West Point graduate George B. McClellan was the chief engineer for the ICRR and in 1858 he was named a vice-president of the company. Lincoln continued to work on taxation problems including a lower valuation for railroad property. On November 18 and 19, 1859, McClellan accompanied Lincoln to Mt. Vernon , Illinois, to appeal to the supreme court of Illinois. Applying unbelievable legal skill, Lincoln managed to induce the court to reduce the railroad's 1857 property valuation of $19,711,559.59 to merely $4,942,000.00. At the state tax level of 67 cents per $100, the ICRR paid about 2 percent on its gross receipts. Disbelievers in the legal system pointed out the possibility of a packed supreme court of Illinois because the sitting justices had ties to railroads while considering this case: Justice Breese was a director of the Baltimore and Ohio railroad and Chief Justice John D. Caton was president of the Illinois & Mississippi Telegraph Company which he transferred to the Western Union Company in 1867. Justice Pinkney H. Walker was a Democrat appointed by Bissell, a Republican governor with a strong allegiance to the ICRR. Additionally, Lincoln was Bissell's chief advisor. However, Breese, Caton, and Walker were able, independent, uncontrolled, and judges of high reputation. There is no evidence of any disposition to favor the ICRR.

In preparing for the *Effie Afton* trial, Lincoln and the railroad's bridge engineer, Benjamin Brayton, made a personal study of the rebuilt drawbridge on September 1, 1857. On the next day, the *Rock Island Weekly Argus* commented on Lincoln's visit: "Hon. A. Lincoln.—This distinguished lawyer who is employed by the bridge company to defend that mammoth nuisance is expected in Davenport in a few days, for the purpose of examining that huge obstruction to the free navigation of the river." In addition, Lincoln researched the navigation of the river and questioned other captains about the high and low tides, tricky currents, water velocity, drifts, rocks, sand-bars, and snags. He believed that the disaster occurred due to mishandling, negligence, and incompetence by the ship operator's in moving the *Effie Afton* between the piers of the bridge. Lincoln discovered that fewer than 1 percent of the boats passing under the bridge had any problem. Relevantly, the *J. B. Carson* went through immediately before the *Effie Afton* without any difficulty. Commenting on Lincoln's activities, Judd sent him a letter enclosing a voucher for his legal services in a different case : "My Dear Mr. Lincoln: I sincerely hope you suffered no ill effects from your trip to Rock Island, and your inspection of the Mississippi river bridge last Tuesday. I also hope you were successful in securing the information of which you were in search."

In his opening, Judd clearly emphasized the importance of this trial: "Every bushel of wheat from east to west would be affected." During the trial, Lincoln's impressive arguments vividly illustrated his extensive grasp of the navigation of rivers. He used a model of the *Effie Afton* to demonstrate the accident. Lincoln claimed that "people along the river had the right to cross it in common intercourse...and it was the manifest destiny of the people to move westward and surround themselves with everything connected with modern civilization." Voluminous evidence, mainly by deposition, steadily increased each day as the trial continued. An article in the September 17, 1857 *Cincinnati Enquirer* found the trial exciting but slowly progressing. Depositions of Pittsburgh captains George Neare and David Brickell "united in saying that the Rock Island bridge was the greatest obstruction on the western waters, —worse than the rapids." Lincoln sat on a bench in the back of the court room and chipped away at a piece of wood with his knife until he rose and demanded that the defense produce the original notes to support their statistics. Starting on Tuesday afternoon September 22 and continuing through Wednesday morning, the thirteenth and fourteenth days of the trial, Lincoln delivered his meticulous, information packed summation. He began by telling the jurors that he "had no prejudice against steamboats" and would be earnest "but not ill natured." Lincoln revealed that 12,586 freight cars and

74,179 passengers passed over the bridge from September 8, 1856 to August 8, 1857. Rhetorically, Lincoln asked: "What mood were the steamboat men in when this bridge was burned?" He answered: "Why there was a shouting, a ringing of bells and whistling on all the boats as it fell. It was a jubilee, a greater celebration than follows an excited election." He technically described the position of the piers detailing the angles, as measured in degrees, to consider the nature of a "material obstruction." Referring to the role of Captain Hurd, Lincoln asked: "What is reasonable skill and care? This is a thing of which the jury are to judge." To help the jurors judge, Lincoln reviewed his investigations into the average velocity of the current and cross currents in the river. He concluded that the average speed was five and one-half miles an hour. "The next thing I will try to prove is that the plaintiff's boat had power to run six miles an hour in that current." Reading from the testimony of witnesses, Lincoln said it was undisputed that the *Effie Afton* "did not move one inch ahead while she was moving thirty-one feet sideways...only explanation is that her power was not all used—that only one wheel was working." After stopping, Lincoln told the jury: "Gentlemen, I have not exhausted my stock of information and there are more things I could suggest regarding the case, but as I have doubtless used up my time, I presume I had better close." Newspapers carried comprehensive reports on the trial. Judge McLean's charge to the jury was published in full in the *Chicago Daily Press* on September 25, 1857 and took up almost four columns in the newspaper. In the full account of the trial in the same newspaper, an obviously sectionally biased report evaluated Lincoln's litigation: "Mr. A. Lincoln in his address to the jury was very successful, so far as a clear statement and close logic was concerned." Lincoln's contentions were reported by Robert R. Hitt, the first official stenographer in Illinois, and disclosed each day in the Chicago *Daily Democratic Press.* Plaintiff's attorney Timothy D. Lincoln subjected the jury to a seven-hour summation focusing on the technical aspects of the case. After retiring and deliberating for several hours, the jury was unable to reach a verdict. A hung jury had nine jurors for the Rock Island Bridge Company and three for the water transport interests. Judge McLean dismissed the case and discharged the jury.

Hurd went no further with his case. However, the river interests continued to attack the Rock Island bridge with a suit in the US District Court for the Southern District in Iowa. James Ward, a St. Louis steamboat captain, charged that the bridge was a nuisance. This federal court ruled that the bridge was "a common and public nuisance" and ordered the Rock Island to remove that part of the bridge in Iowa. Rock Island appealed to the Supreme Court of the United States. In the 1862 December term of the court, the justices ruled that there could be no public nuisance produced by a public benefit, provided the bridge was reasonable for passage by boats. This Iowa district court order to remove a part of a railroad bridge spanning a waterway was set aside. That case ended litigation over railroad bridges spanning waterways.

There is speculation about Lincoln's fee for this case with $50 or $400 being mentioned. In either case, those fees do not appear to be appropriate. While the specifics are unknown, Lincoln may have loaned Judd $3,000 during this trial. As collateral, Lincoln took a mortgage on land Judd owned in Council Bluffs, Iowa. In reality, this mortgage may have been part of Lincoln's fee for his services in the Rock Island Bridge case. Judd may have personally reimbursed Lincoln for his legal aid.

In an intriguing aside, it was rumored that Hurd was bribed by the water transportation interests to purposely run his ship into the bridge to make a case for obstruction of navigation. This was angrily denied by the water lobbyists. However, when the *Effie Afton* burned, all the river craft gathered at the scene and blasted their ear piercing whistles repeatedly in sheer joy at the disaster. During the trial Lincoln asked and answered a pointed rhetorical question on the mood of the boatmen to influence the jury.

Returning to the homeopathic medical school charter, Lincoln learned more about his employers. Dr. Smith was born in Camden, New Jersey on April 28, 1816 and earned his medical degree from a regular medical school, Philadelphia's Jefferson Medical College, in 1836. He opened his practice in Chicago and immediately became interested in homeopathy. In 1844, Smith opened the first homeopathic pharmacy in Illinois in his office. In addition to Judd and Hoyne, Smith energetically enlisted the support of additional Chicago influentials such as John Wentworth and William B. Ogden. Smith founded and served as the first president of the Illinois Homeopathic Association. In 1851, he was a founder of the Western Institute of Homeopathy. Extremely active in the American Institute of Homeopathy, Smith was elected general secretary in 1857, chairman in 1858 and treasurer in 1865. He was thirty-nine years old when he and Lincoln cooperated to draft and secure a charter for the Chicago Hahnemann Medical College and Hospital. Obviously, Smith, Hoyne, and Judd headed a formidable combination of political influentials able to persuade and inveigle the members of the state legislature to favorably look upon their charter request.

In drafting the charter, Lincoln and Smith covered all aspects of a "body politic and corporate," a private medical school: operations, style, location, objects, general powers, trustees, terms of office, vacancies, course of studies, compensation, expelling of students, buildings, homeopathic proviso, removal of officers, quorum, and capital stock. Lincoln stated that the school is to be located in Chicago, county of Cook, state of Illinois and he delineated the purposes: "to give instruction, by lectures and otherwise, in surgery, anatomy, physiology, obstetrics, pathology, chemistry, materia medica and the theory and practice of the Homœopathic system of medicine; to which may be added dispensary and hospital departments." Continuing, Lincoln said that the medical school could "make, create and endow as many professorships as may be deemed necessary for the benefit of said institution; to appoint curators; to appoint any one or more of the medical faculty or other physicians who may be deemed competent to take charge of and superintend the hospital or dispensary departments, and to confer on such persons as may be found worthy such honorary degrees as are usually conferred by similar institutions.... No person shall be appointed...who has not graduated at some reputable medical institution and received his or their diploma as a graduate of such institution, and who is not, at the time of his or their appointment, a practicing physician of the Homœopathic school of medicine." This proviso regarding medical school appointments assured that homeopathic instruction would prevail. Trustees could "prescribe and regulate the course of studies...fix the rate of tuition...appoint instructors...fix their compensation...displace or remove them...erect necessary buildings...purchase books, chemical, philosophical and such other apparatus, instruments and implements as may be necessary...make rules for the general regulation...suspend or expel any students whose habits are idle or vicious or whose moral character is bad or who refuse to obey the rules of the institution."

As Lincoln prepared the charter document, he kept the acrimonious opposition of the orthodox or regular physicians firmly in mind. His draft of the charter proposal used precise verbiage to guarantee equity and justice for the contemplated homeopathic medical school:

all rights, privileges and powers not herein enumerated, mentioned or declared, which may have been or may at this time be conferred upon or enjoyed by any medical institution heretofore or at this time incorporated by an act of the legislature of this state, shall be taken and enjoyed by this institution, said institution to be placed upon as favorable a footing in all respects as the most favored medical institution heretofore or at this time incorporated by an act of the legislature of this state.

Lincoln, Smith, Hoyne, Judd and their influential cohorts presented, promoted and lobbied the special charter for a medical school. To nobody's great surprise, the legislature approved and granted the charter for the Hahnemann Medical College on February 14, 1855.

When Lincoln represented physicians in medical malpractice cases, his understanding of the varied approaches to regular and irregular medical treatment therapies helped him to plan his legal strategy. He realized the complex details involved in selecting a medical expert to testify on behalf of his client. In this legal encounter, unlike the *Jones v. Maus* case, Lincoln's client, Dr. Davis S. Smith, really did graduate from Jefferson Medical College.

Shortly after the Civil War began, one of Lincoln's legal adversaries in the *Effie Afton* case, Beckwith, asked a favor of the president. On May 28, 1861, Lincoln wrote to Gideon Welles, the Secretary of the Navy: "A friend of mine" from Chicago, Mr. C. Beckwith wants a lady relative, Miss Elizabeth Smith of St. Marks, Florida brought away from there. Can any vessels do so without too much trouble? "I shall be obliged." On August 7, 1861, Welles replied that the Navy was unable to remove Miss Smith.

6

VICTORIAN LAWYERS, IMPROPERLY HEALED FRACTURES, AND AMERICA'S FIRST MEDICAL MALPRACTICE CRISIS, 1835-1865

During most of Abraham Lincoln's career as a busy attorney-at-law, a medical malpractice crisis epidemic existed in the United States. On two occasions, Lincoln defended physicians when dissatisfied patients sued for medical malpractice because their broken bones did not heal properly. Both cases, *Fleming v. Rogers and Crothers* and *West v. Ritchey*, typically demonstrated the legal components of a medical malpractice case during the mid-1800s: medical literature research by lawyers; selection and use of medical experts as witnesses; courtroom techniques to motivate lay jurors toward the correct verdict; legal approaches to influence the judge's rulings; and informational procedures to secure the backing of the public.

Cultural changes and the passage of time do not appear to have substantially differentiated the first American medical malpractice crisis from those that ensued subsequently. An overwhelming majority of malpractice claims initially arose from improperly healed fractures. That continues to be a reappearing cause in a number of current lawsuits. Heated interactions, malevolent accusations, and acrimonious verbal assaults between physicians and lawyers continue unabated up to the present time. This enduring hostility results from the intrinsic differences between law and medicine: "Much of the hostility existing between the professions of law and medicine is caused by the fact that medicine is a prospective profession, whereas law is retrospective.

When a physician does anything to any patient, he is experimenting or medically speculating. But if the patient suffers adverse results and sues, then the court applies what is by definition a retrospective judgment of a particular course of treatment."

Medical malpractice in the United States was virtually unknown between 1800 and 1835. Cases that did not pertain to amputation or death were particularly infrequent and patients and/or their families seldom won in court. Within the thirty-year period from 1835 to 1865, medical malpractice lawsuits inundated the courts. Numerous editorials and comments on the subject appeared in professional medical journals. A contagion of malpractice suits emanated from western New York State, spread east throughout New England and then traveled into the upper Midwest. "A respected Buffalo [NY] surgeon and a perpetual witness," Dr. Frank H. Hamilton, estimated that nine out of every ten physicians in western New York suffered charges of malpractice by the mid-nineteenth century. In agreement, an 1853 issue of the *Western Journal of Medical and Physical Sciences* lamented that malpractice suits "occur almost every month in the year and everywhere in our country." By 1860, a book on medical jurisprudence asserted: "There can hardly be found a place in the country, where the oldest physicians in it have not, at some periods in their lives, been actually sued or annoyingly threatened."

Although America's first medical malpractice crisis evolved in the 1800s, many of the impinging variables remained constant over the years. Legal concepts of medical negligence were founded upon the British jurisprudence system which the colonists adapted. As the American law suits meandered through the US judicial system, case law created original malpractice principles Additionally, trial experiences molded the opinions and attitudes of the participants: the physicians, the judges, the attorneys, and the jury members. An onerous majority of the early malpractice law suits were related to the outcomes of orthopedic therapy for fractures and dislocations. Further complicating the malpractice crisis, conflicts arose regarding the adversarial expert medical testimony of contradictory witnesses for the defendants and the plaintiffs. Professional disagreements between lawyers and physicians spawned caustic medical opinions about malpractice suits.

American judges and lawyers, including Lincoln, were familiar with, and relied upon, the *Commentaries on the Laws of England* by William Blackstone, first published in 1767. Later editions were commonly available in the US. However, Blackstone categorized malpractice under private wrongs, not under contract or mercantile law. In his definition of *mala praxis*, Blackstone's last sentence is almost verbatim from a 1697 ruling in the Dr. Grovenvelt case:

> 4.Injuries affecting a man's health are where, by any unwholesome practices of another, a man sustains any apparent damage in his vigor or constitution…. As by…or by the neglect or unskillful management of his physician, surgeon, or apothecary. For it hath been solemnly resolved, that *mala praxis* is a great misdemeanour and offence at common law, whether it be for curiosity and experiment, or by neglect; because it breaks the trust which the party has placed in his physician and tends to the patient's destruction.

Using a common law remedy, a solicitor could file a suit for damages caused by a breach of duty, negligence, or carelessness. In the United States, lawyers filed a writ of trespass for direct injuries or a trespass on the case for indirect injuries.

In 1794, the earliest recorded US appellate court decision in a medical malpractice suit occurred in *Cross v. Guthrie*. One of Mrs. Guthrie's breasts was surgically removed by Cross, a Connecticut physician, and she died three hours later. In his malpractice suit alleging negligence in the performance of an operation, her husband sued Cross for £1,000 for "his costs and expense, and deprivation of the service and company of his wife." Plaintiff's arguments stated that the undertaking on the part of the surgeon to perform a mastectomy safely and skillfully was ignored by the physician in that his professional performance was unskillful, ignorant, and cruel, "contrary to all the well-known rules and principles of practice in such cases, and that the patient survived by but three hours, and that the defendant had wholly broken and violated his undertaking and promise to the plaintiff to perform said operation skillfully and with safety to his wife." Notwithstanding the jury's verdict favoring the surviving husband, he was only awarded £40 in damages for the loss of companionship.

Despite the surge in malpractice suits, there was a lack of systematically recorded statistical data about cases resolved in local courts without an appeal. A legal investigation found twenty-seven malpractice suits in sixteen randomly distributed states that were adjudicated in appeals to the respective state supreme courts between 1794 and 1861. Most of the states used the existing English common law as a basis for decisions or as an analogous reference. Fundamental legal principles about medical malpractice evolved in the United States as state justices rendered judicial opinions. An analysis of *stare decisis* (case law) classified twenty-one pre-Civil War appellate court decisions between 1845 and 1861 into five groupings of legal rationales for medical malpractice that Lincoln and other lawyers used in court:

1. Dealing with education and knowledge: A physician was held legally responsible for what he professed he was able to do. In 1856, the supreme court of Tennessee held that a physician "contracts with those who employ him that he has such skill, science, and information as will enable him properly and judiciously to perform the duties of his calling."

2. Opinions about the nature of the skill: Ordinary, not extraordinary, skill was all that was required by law. In 1860, the supreme court of Illinois held that "the principle is plain and of uniform application, that when a person assumes the profession of physician and surgeon, he must, in its exercise, be held to employ a reasonable amount of care and skill. For anything short of that degree of skill in his practice, the law will hold him responsible for any injury which may result from its absence. While he is not required to possess the highest order of qualification, to which some men attain, still he must possess

and exercise that degree of skill which is ordinarily possessed by members of the profession."

3. Nature of care: Physicians contract to use reasonable and ordinary care in their application of their knowledge and skill. In 1860, the supreme court of Georgia observed that "he [the physician] undertakes that he will bring to the work a fair, reasonable and competent degree of care and skill in reference to the operation to be performed." He does not undertake that he will, in all events, safely and without injury care for the patient.

4. Dealing with mistakes or errors of judgment: When reasonable grounds for diagnostic doubts and differences of opinion about treatment existed, the physician who exercised his best judgment was not responsible for errors of judgment or mistakes. However, errors of judgment were not excused when what was well known and clearly indicated was not used in treatment. An 1853 New Hampshire decision asserted that "freedom from errors of judgment is never a part of a contract with a professional man."

5. Opinions about cure: Legally, physicians were not required to guarantee or insure a cure. While the law did not prevent the writing of contracts for cure warranties, the law would not uphold compensation claims if there was no absolute cure. In addition, the law would not support a malpractice defense by a physician if an absolute cure had been promised.

Prior to 1860, none of the medical jurisprudence books commonly used as references by lawyers discussed medical malpractice, most dealt with aspects of forensic medicine. Widely circulated works on medical jurisprudence included the first text in English, Samuel Farr's *Elements of Medical Jurisprudence* (1788). In the US, the first notable work was Theodoric Romeyn Beck's *Elements of Medical Jurisprudence* (1823). Henry Coley's *A Treatise on Medical Jurisprudence Comprising the Consideration of Poisons and Asphyxia* (1832) typically dealt with metallic poisons, earths, alkalies, mineral acids, vegetable acids, vegetable poisons, aqarics, and poisonous fish. Additional popular references included Joseph Chitty's *A Practical Treatise on Medical Jurisprudence* (1834), Alfred Swaine Taylor's *Elements of Medical Jurisprudence* (1836), Isaac Ray's *A Treatise on the Medical Jurisprudence of Insanity* (1838), Amos Dean's *Principles of Medical Jurisprudence: Designed for the Professions of Law and Medicine* (1850), and lawyer Francis Wharton and physician Moreton Stillé's *A Treatise on Medical Jurisprudence* (1855). Lincoln frequently mentioned Chitty's book in his legal documents.

John J. Elwell, a lawyer and a physician, was the first expert to intensively examine the mid-nineteenth century medical malpractice crisis. Citing the surge of malpractice suits since 1845 and using excerpts from recent cases, Elwell's *A Medico-Legal Treatise on Malpractice, Medical Evidence and Insanity, Comprising the Elements of Medical Jurisprudence* (1860) aimed "to furnish the medical man that necessary information respecting his legal responsibility as a practitioner." Almost uniformly, medico-legal experts hailed Elwell's book as filling a huge void in medical and legal literature. A review of Elwell's book in the *New York Medical Press* commented that "law and medicine had evolved into mutually incompatible professions." Continuing, the *Press's* remarks reflected the abiding attitude of the medical profession toward medical malpractice: "None of the previous works on medical jurisprudence have been at all sufficiently practical.... It is necessary that [a physician] knows what he should say and do in a contingency which may happen unexpectedly, any time, especially in civil suits for malpractice...[while valuable for lawyers, Elwell's material was absolutely] paramount to our medical brethren."

Battle lines between physicians and lawyers that emerged during the nineteenth century malpractice crisis became deeply entrenched in American society as lawsuits continued to rise in absolute numbers as well as in rates. Likewise, judges were affected by the medical malpractice onslaught. Judges displayed divergent attitudes towards medicine and physicians as they and the jury pondered if the medical treatment was rendered with "due and proper care, skill, and diligence." In an extreme opinion, a judge contended that the number of unqualified practitioners would be reduced if patients were encouraged to bring malpractice accusations more frequently.

Juries did not escape the ploys of lawyers and the wrath of physicians. Lawyers for plaintiffs often exploited the anti-professional and anti-social class prejudices of the public in fervent statements to the jury. Disgraceful aspects of a jury trial occurred in malpractice trials. In the 1857 New Hampshire case of *Leighton vs. Sargent*, a sick juror was allowed to drink brandy while the verdict was being decided. Upon appeal, the defendant was acquitted "for the cause that brandy was furnished to the jury, and drank [sic] by several of them while deliberating upon the cause, after retiring to form their verdict. We think the verdict must be set aside."

Throughout history, medical and nonmedical healers treated fractures using a variety of splints and mechanical devices. Pertinently, and with relevance to Lincoln's defense arguments in *Fleming v. Rogers and Crothers*, a sixteenth-century English physician, Peter Lowe (or Love), warned against refracturing a vicious union: "Better suffer a little deformity of the part than loss of the whole body." Most eighteenth-century physicians agreed that the standard treatment for compound fractures was immediate amputation. "It was generally believed that sacrificing the limb before wound complications ensued would enhance the chance of survival." In contrast, in 1780, Scottish physician, Dr. Thomas Kirkland, exclaimed that it takes more skill to save a limb than to sever it: "A man must be very ignorant, who cannot take off a leg, an operation to be performed by any blockhead." Nevertheless, despite occasional digressions, primary amputation remained the treatment of choice for some time to come well into the nineteenth century. "Compound fractures of the limbs with attendant sepsis remained mostly unmanageable and staggering morbidity and mortality could be anticipated."

Dr. Astley Paston Cooper's 1822 book, *A Treatise on Dislocations and On Fractures of the Joints*, was the principal medical reference in the US and the United Kingdom for thirty years. In 1830, famed Philadelphia physician, Dr. Samuel D. Gross, authored a 389-page book, *The Anatomy, Physiology and Diseases of the Bones and Joints*, the first American book on orthopedics.

In 1835, Dr. Cooper discussed perfunctory amputations in cases of compound fracture: "Formerly, and with my recollection, it was thought expedient for the preservation of life by many of our best surgeons to amputate the limb in these cases, but from our experience of late years, such advice would in a great majority of instances be now deemed highly injudicious." After 1835, improperly healed fractures became the most common reason for a malpractice suit. Elwell claimed that "nine-tenths of all the cases of malpractice that come before the courts for adjudication arise either from the treatment of amputations, fractures, or dislocations." Litigation involved patient dissatisfaction with less than perfect results following dislocations and fractures: deformities such as a frozen position following a compound fracture; deformed or crooked limbs; or noticeably shorter limbs. With ease as they played to the jurors, disgruntled patients demonstrated for the court their unequivocal and measurable damage as a result of the physician's unskillful treatment. Technological advances in the treatment of fractures generated unrealistic public and professional expectations and stimulated medical malpractice suits.

With the introduction of ether in 1846 and chloroform in 1847 as anesthetics, the complications involved in setting bones and doing surgery eased somewhat. To prevent sepsis and avoid subsequent amputation, improved bandaging, splinting, and packing techniques were used. Concepts of antisepsis were not introduced until Joseph Lister's series of articles appeared in the *Lancet* in 1867. In his 1860 book on medical jurisprudence, Elwell also elucidated a change in the standard treatment of fractures by amputation: "An amputation that would have been justified by the rules of surgery and the operator protected in the court, twenty years ago or even less time than that, would now be repudiated by the best authority and the operator justly charged with malpractice."

Profound professional differences existed between regular or orthodox physicians and irregular physicians regarding the scientific treatment of compound fractures and dislocations. These conflicts surfaced in malpractice litigation as expert medical witnesses of various persuasions berated each other's therapeutic remedies.

Regular or orthodox physicians received their training at medical schools, perhaps loosely linked to a university. Supposedly a three-year program, medical schools followed varying curriculums that required a series of two separate four to five months of academic lectures including surgical demonstrations and a one-year apprenticeship in a practitioner's office. Although an outspoken critic of medical education, by 1851 Dr. Nathan S. Davis declared that regular medical school graduates were "tolerably well-versed in the ordinary details of medical and surgical practice." Yet, a regular medical education was of notoriously low quality, unevenly regulated, and disorganized enough to allow students to earn a medical degree in fewer than three years.

Irregular physicians included "[American] Indian doctors, urine doctors, root doctors, water doctors, steam doctors, and homeopaths...." John Ordronaux, a lawyer and a physician and author of a 1869 book on medical jurisprudence, declared that "the quack, the pill-vender, the life-elixir compounder, the panacea concocter...may permanently injure health, or even steal the breath from a man's nostrils without being charged with misdemeanor or felony." In discussing jury trials for medical malpractice, the *Western Medical and Surgical Journal* communicated the professional opinion "that the chances are altogether better for the acquittal of an ignorant, uneducated pretender to medical knowledge, who is really guilty, than that of an intelligent, well-educated surgeon to whom no fault can justly be charged."

In the early nineteenth century, most of the state medical licensure laws were either weak or nonexistent. Competition for patients and fees among regular physicians and between regular and irregular doctors provoked the early increase in medical malpractice litigation. To improve their own status, individual physicians willingly denigrated the therapeutic practices of their competitors. Such public criticism undoubtedly encouraged patients to file lawsuits.

Efforts to regulate the profession of medicine were initiated during the late 1840s as the newly organized American Medical Association recommended reforms in medical education. "Ignorant and impudent pretenders, under a great variety of humbugging titles, come before the public with equal rights, and a better chance for popular favour, than the regular practitioner… Hence, ignorance and charlatanism become the rule, and intelligence the error." Ironically, the most knowledgeable and technologically advanced physicians became frequent targets of medical malpractice suits involving the care of fractures. Several factors resulted in the better physicians being sued more often rather than the host of amateurs and alternative doctors.

1. *Improved techniques and more careful training produced advances in therapeutic measures.* With the adoption of professional advances, physicians opted to try to save limbs in difficult cases. About twenty years earlier, there is no doubt that the majority of patients with compound fractures endured the amputation of their affected limbs. Physicians could choose to follow safe and standard amputation procedures and avoid any danger of a malpractice suit.

2. *To avoid internal infection, the physician required sophisticated knowledge of wound dressing and bone setting.* Often, better regularly trained physicians tried to save the limb in difficult compound fracture cases, even if the result was less than perfect. In making this decision, a physician rationalized that even a slightly deformed limb was better than no limb. In contrast, amateur or inexperienced healers never pretended to possess the skill to properly dress the wound and to set the fracture.

3. *Irregular healers could not be sued for malpractice since no established procedures existed.* Regular physicians utilized educational textbooks and manuals that constituted evidence of norms or standards in court suits. On the other hand, irregular physicians could not be sued for undesirable results because no

such standards existed. Each patient came for the individualized herbal drugs, hot baths, or water therapies. A regular physician expressed his frustration: "It is better to be without a diploma; for then, besides having the sympathies of the community, the practitioner can say, 'I make no pretensions, I offer no certificate of ability, and only gave my neighbour in his sufferings such aid as I could.'"

4. *A deep pockets theory already existed.* Patients were not inclined to sue irregular doctors who had few assets. Regular practitioners were more prosperous and the award might actually be collected. Part of this attitude arose from the anti-professional and social class ethos of the period. In addition, there was "the avarice of those disposed to escape their doctor's bill, and willing to take the chance of making money out of their injuries."

To avoid this swindle, physicians found it easier to forgive the bill or settle a claim rather than legally fight the accusation and risk dire consequences. In reflecting on the frequency of medical malpractice suits in the Northern states, Dr. Hamilton claimed "that many men abandoned the practice of surgery, leaving it to those who, with less skill and experience, had less reputation and property to lose." Trepidation about a possible malpractice suit generated passionate emotional feelings among regular physicians.

While some patients continue to be regarded with suspicion as larcenous opportunists, a majority of physicians tend to blame the "ambulance chasing" lawyers for instigating the gullible, or perhaps greedy, patients to sue. Attorneys counter that people are entitled to sue if they are harmed. Battle lines between the "mutually incompatible professions" of the mid-1800s, physicians and medical malpractice lawyers, still appear to be as hostile as they were when Lincoln was practicing, during America's first medical malpractice crisis.

DEFENSE LAWYER, A. LINCOLN, USES CHICKEN BONES IN A MALPRACTICE CASE

Around midnight on October 16, 1855, a fire erupted in the livery stable behind the Morgan House in Bloomington, Illinois and rapidly engulfed the entire area. As thousands of people milled about mesmerized by the flames, firemen battled the conflagration. By four in the morning, all but two buildings in the block south of the McLean County Courthouse were burned to the ground. William Green, a wagon driver, was killed and Samuel G. Fleming, a carpenter, had both thighs broken when the Morgan House chimney fell on him. Drs. Thomas P. Rogers, Eli K. Crothers, and Jacob R. Freese first examined Fleming in Crothers's drug store. They were not optimistic about his recovery from such a serious injury. His left thigh suffered a break straight across (a square fracture) the femur while his right thigh had an oblique fracture, almost a compound fracture.

Fleming was carried to the house of his brother, John C. Fleming, where the doctors attended him. Before the splints were affixed, both thigh fractures were carefully reset. Both limbs were bandaged by first applying an unbleached muslin roller bandage beginning at the foot and extending to the uppermost portion of the thigh. Next, short splints, about eight inches long and three inches wide, were applied above and within and a long splint, known by surgeons as a Desaultes extension splint, was applied outside, around the inner and outer splints. Then, another roller bandage was applied. Both outer long splints were carefully wadded with raw cotton, and strips of old muslin to adapt them to the inner surfaces of the limbs. Crothers adjusted and dressed the right leg assisted by Rogers and Freese. At the request of the other two physicians, Freese adjusted and bandaged the left leg himself. In his deposition Freese commented on the procedures: "The dressing of both limbs was done with care and in the same manner as I have seen it done by some of the most celebrated surgeons of this Country, and in the same manner as is recommended by some of the best authors on surgery."

Fleming's sister, Cynthia Ann Fleming, first saw her brother on October 20 and remained with him as his nurse until April 15, 1856. She was instructed in how to move Fleming and told to try to keep his toes pointed inward. Doctors told her Fleming would be confined from four to six weeks. Under the doctor's direction, she gave her brother morphine to alleviate his pain. In her testimony, Fleming's sister contradicted the attending physicians' recollection of events, the treatment of his fractures and the statements of those involved. She stated that the doctors did not complain about the nursing care and Rogers said the nurses did their duty.

According to Fleming's sister, at least one of the doctors came almost every day, examined her brother and measured the length of his legs. A few days after the first dressing, Rogers and Freese carefully examined both limbs and found them all right. Fleming told the doctors that he "was getting along first rate and that were it not for his confinement he would scarcely know that his thighs were broken, so little did he suffer." He expressed himself as entirely satisfied with all aspects of the care rendered by the doctors.

Almost a month after his accident, Fleming complained considerably about a pain in his side. His sister called Dr. Edward R. Roe, whom Rogers had left in charge for a time. Roe said that the legs were all right and gave Fleming morphine. Crothers came the next morning to examine Fleming and said that the legs were all right. Regarding Fleming's pain, Crothers said that he was suffering from an attack of pleurisy that caused pain in his ribs, difficulty in breathing and a dry cough. Fleming made no particular complaints to Freese about his limbs, but did say that he thought he was getting along as well as could be expected under the circumstances.

Around mid-November, Rogers examined Fleming. Upon removing the bandages, Rogers found the left leg straight and healing well but the right one had a considerable bend at the point of the fractures. Fleming's sister recalled that Rogers said "they were crooked as a Ram's horns." Originally, the right thigh fracture was oblique with the lower sharp point of the upper portion of the thigh bone bending outward from a proper alignment of the bone. A considerable amount of bone adhesion had already taken place since October when the leg was bandaged and splinted. At this time, Fleming's right leg measured 3/4 of an inch shorter than his left leg. Rogers sent for Crothers and Freese to come and assist in resetting Fleming's right thigh fracture. After sitting by the stove talking among themselves for a while, the doctors proposed to Fleming that they break up the adhesions and reset the right leg applying strong pressure to bring back the bend significantly. Fleming agreed and his brother and sister assented.

Assisted by his medical student, Isaac M. Small, Freese administered chloroform to Fleming until he was sufficiently anesthetized for Crothers to go ahead. Crothers manipulated the right leg to break up the adhesions and to readjust the fracture. Rogers held the right foot and tugged to produce the proper amount of extension. Suddenly, Fleming began to holler very loudly and begged Crothers: "For God's sake, hold on!" "Being present and much excited," Fleming's brother and sister insisted that Crothers stop trying to break the adhesions. Crothers let go of the leg before the adhesions were broken up and told Fleming that he would not stand responsible unless the leg was broken and reset. An emotional conversation ensued between Fleming, his brother and sister, and the three doctors. Fleming's sister claimed that her brother said "he would not have it broke unless they would send to town and get a counsel of physicians and if they ordered, he would resubmit. He also said he would hold them responsible whether it was so broke or not." Fleming "swore that he would not be hurt any more and asked whether the leg would get strong enough for him to walk upon, providing it was left go as it was." In responding, all three doctors agreed that the leg would most likely be strong enough, although the leg would always be crooked. Fleming said "he would rather have a crooked limb than suffer any more pain in letting us [doctors] again try to adjust it." Freese summarized the events in his deposition:

> I then understood and from the conversation I supposed that both the plaintiff and the defendants understood that the adhesions had not been broken up at their first attempt and that another—more powerful effort would have to be made before they were broken up and that the plaintiff preferred to have a crooked limb all his life rather than subject to second attempt. I understood the defendants as ready to make a second attempt provided the plaintiff would submit to it. After it was determined not to make a second attempt at breaking up the adhesions, the dressing was again applied and we each left for our homes.

After this aborted attempt to reset Fleming's right leg, the doctors continually visited him and assured him that the fractures were healing. For a short time, the doctors used an inclined plane on the right leg. At one point, the doctors made a starch bandage to allow Fleming to walk. His sister described the bandage: "A layer of muslin dipped in starch—a layer of doubled-board and starch and then three layers of bandages dipped in starch. After this dried, he tried to walk and failed." About five months after the initial fractures, the legs healed but the right leg was misshapen, crooked and shorter just as the doctors had told Fleming.

On March 28, 1856, Fleming's lawyers filed a complaint in the McLean County Circuit Court against Rogers and Crothers in a plea of *trespass on the case,* essentially a medical malpractice claim for $10,000. Freese and Small were not included in the complaint, perhaps because they were no longer living in Illinois. Eventually, three law firms represented Fleming: Asahel Gridley & John H.

Wickizer, William H. Hanna & John M. Scott, and William Ward Orme & Leonard Swett.

Rogers and Crothers hired two law firms to defend them: David Brier & Jesse Birch and L. L. Strain & Andrew W. Rogers. In turn, these law firms retained John T. Stuart & Abraham Lincoln. Typically, Lincoln bore the main weight for the defense while Swett led the plaintiff's case.

At the time of the fire and Fleming's accident, public sentiment reflected widespread anti-professional and anti-social class biases. Jurors holding these prejudices might naturally favor Fleming. A physician commented in a professional journal that "the interests and prejudices of the whole class [lower socio-economic] are against the acts and doings of the regular [medical] practitioner." Discussing the prosecution of surgeons, the *Boston Medical and Surgical Journal* emphasized that "juries have seemed to act with a determination to cripple the profession." A juror in a 1856 malpractice trial confirmed these observations:

> A jury of laboring men...go into the jury box with feelings excited against the surgeon, because they think his business should produce no better pecuniary returns than his own; the surgeon's bill is ways deemed exorbitant by them; and he is generally looked upon as almost a swindler, and living luxuriously upon their hard earnings; therefore they are always inclined to render a verdict against your profession, and in favor of one of their own class.

As the spring term of the McLean County Circuit Court opened on April 7, 1856, the three defendant law firms responded to the complaint: "And the said defendants come and defend the wrong and injury when, where, etc, and say plaintiff action now because they are not guilty in manner and form as in the declaration alleged; and of this the defense puts forth themselves upon the county etc."

Lincoln realized that time was the best defense for the doctors because of the prevailing biased attitudes of the citizens of

Bloomington. Two days later, Lincoln & Stuart filed an affidavit requesting a continuance: "Rogers visited said plaintiff much more frequently than did said Crothers and that he, said Rogers, has the more intimate acquaintance with, and perfect knowledge of the whole case... Rogers is now so unwell as to be unable to attend at the present term of this court, and that affiants believe his personal presence at the trial is necessary to enable them to conduct the defense of the case properly."

Judge David Davis granted the request on April 10, 1856 and ordered that "this cause stand continued at the costs of said defendant. And on motion of said plaintiff by his attorney leave is granted him to amend his declaration herein filed." Fleming's complaint was amended on August 27, 1856. In a long handwritten declaration, several phrases relating to the care provided by the physicians were redundantly reiterated:

"negligent, unskillful and improper manner" [eight times]; "did not use due and proper care, skill, and diligence [seven times]; "ignorant, unskillful and negligent manner" [four times]; "intending and contriving to injure and aggrieve" [twice]; legs "so unsightly and unnatural" [twice]; legs "crooked, misshapen and useless" [once]; and "unnecessary pain and anguish" [twice].

In this declaration, Hanna & Scott, Gridley & Wickizer & others concluded that Fleming "expended a large sum of money to wit $1,000 for treatment...so prolonged and increased by means of negligent unskillful and improper conduct...to the damage of said plaintiff of...ten thousand dollars."

In preparation for an anticipated trial at the fall term of the court, Swett had the court clerk, William McCullough, prepare a notice in which the sheriff was "commanded to summon" witnesses, including expert medical witnesses for Fleming. On September 8, 1856, summons were served on Drs. Ballard, Dunn, Elder, Luce, Major, Martins, and Niccolls. In addition, Swett summoned E. V. Augustus, Miss C. A. Fleming, J. C. Fleming, J. S.

Ireland, Mott [drayman], Isaac Pilcher, and J. Ricketts. Two days after the fall term of the McLean County Circuit Court opened, on September 10, 1856, Lincoln prepared an affidavit for Crothers to sign requesting another continuance:

> The defendants can not safely go to trial at the present term, because of the absence of J. R. Freese who is a material witness for them…witness was present when plaintiff's limb was first set, and knows that it was properly set; that at the end of fourteen days witness was present, saw the limb examined, and saw that it was right then, that on or about the twenty-second day witness was again present when the displacement of the fracture was observed, and at plaintiff's request, a contemplated effort to correct it was postponed a few days to ascertain if it would improve without rebreaking…expects to prove by said witness, that the injury was an oblique fracture and only lacked the cutting of the skin of being a compound fracture…defendants can not prove the same facts so fully by any other witness…defendants first learned of his intention to remove, less than ten days elapsed before he actually left, so that they could not give notice and take his deposition in the regular way…the application is not made for delay, but that justice may be done.

Judge Davis again continued the case to the April 1857 term of the court "at the costs of said defendants." With these two continuances, defense lawyers postponed the trial for a year and Lincoln gained time to prepare for the trial.

Usually, the rapid pace of circuit court trials didn't allow enough time for the lawyers to seek out national medical experts as witnesses, to study legal and medical jurisprudence reference material or to acquire detailed medical knowledge. Lincoln's calculated and justified continuances provided extra time in this case.

Neither Lincoln or Swett mentioned, communicated or sought out as a witness a leading American authority on fractures and their treatment, Dr. Frank H. Hamilton of nearby Buffalo (NY). In the late 1840s, Hamilton was a surgeon on the faculty at the University of Buffalo medical school. He collected and analyzed statistical data on the treatment and the outcomes of almost 500 fracture and dislocation cases. Using the data, he compiled "fracture tables" noting imperfect alignments, shortened limbs, malformations, and legal aspects. His data emphasized that oblique fractures commonly heal with a deformity and a shortening of the limb; twenty-six of thirty cases resulted in union with deformity. In one study, forty of the fifty fractures (80 percent), of the lower extremities healed with deformities or shortening of the limbs. By 1853, a Hamilton publication contained data about 461 fracture cases. Hamilton's statistical data were published in pamphlets, medical journals, and books and reached a wide audience. A series of three articles in *Transactions of the American Medical Association* in 1855, 1856, and 1857 totaled almost 500 pages and included drawings and a listing of treatments. Often, expert witnesses and defense attorneys relied on Hamilton's publications or even used him as an expert witness. An 1860 review of Hamilton's investigations evoked a hope that his work would "erect something like a standard which may be generally agreed upon for the protection and satisfaction of all parties who may hereafter be involved…in the miseries of a prosecution for 'malpractice.'"

However, this wish was not achieved and uncertainty remained in approaches to treatments for fractures. Hamilton's data were not irrefutable and his selected treatments were not unanimously embraced. Despite the lack of a consensus, Hamilton's prominence led him to become president of a number of professional organizations: the New York State Medical Society (1855); New York Medico-Legal Society (1875-1876); and the New York Society of Medical Jurisprudence (1880-1884).

Relevant to this malpractice suit, Hamilton's 1855 book, *Deformities After Fractures*, explained that a "fracture of the thigh bone is always a severe accident, as the broken bones are retained in proper contact with great difficulty." He dispelled the myth that properly treated bones unite perfectly and debunked the alleged perfection of the surgeons:

> Neither in Great Britain nor in the United States, nor in any other part of the world, has the art of treating fractures attained that degree of perfection which surgeons have almost universally claimed for it.
>
> Students will continue to go out from our hospitals with a belief that perfect union of broken bones is the rule, and that exceptions imply generally unskillful management.
>
> Physicians testify that they have seen and treated ten fractures of the femur, in adult persons, and not one of them (the limbs) is in any way shortened or deformed.

Implying that surgeons may not tell the truth in the courtroom, Hamilton observed: "They may hesitate to regard the sanctity of an oath!" He attributed these medical actions to a combination of self-preservation and the silence of practitioners about the true outcomes. As a defense witness, Hamilton commiserated: "Surgeons themselves have believed, and taught, and testified that in a large majority of cases, broken limbs may be made perfect, while the fact is not so!"

Practicing lawyers, especially those who traveled on the laborious circuit court route, relied upon the few legal references they could easily carry with them. "On the circuit Lincoln cited but few authorities in the argument of a legal proposition." However, this was a generic problem for the lawyers: "It is true that Lincoln rarely took time on the circuit to systematically prepare for trial, but this was equally true of his peers." Most of Lincoln's research was conducted by proxy through his junior partner, William H. Herndon, who "toted books and hunted up authorities." Lincoln's customary legal references are reflected in his advice to aspiring attorneys to read and reread William Blackstone's *Commentaries on the Laws of England,* Joseph Chitty's *Pleadings,* Simon Greenleaf's *Evidence,* Joseph Story's *Equity* and Story's *Equity Pleadings.* For medically related cases, references included Blackstone's section in the *Commentaries,* "Of Wrongs and Their Remedies, Respecting the Rights of Persons, in Private Wrongs"; Chitty's *A Practical Treatise on Medical Jurisprudence*; Alfred Swaine Taylor's *Elements of Medical Jurisprudence*; and lawyer Francis Wharton and physician Moreton Stillé's *A Treatise on Medical Jurisprudence.*

There was an 1850 copy of Amos Dean's *Principles of Medical Jurisprudence. Designed for the Professions of Law & Medicine* in the Lincoln & Herndon law office. Lincoln may have consulted this book in his preparation for this malpractice case. However, Dean's 629-page book did not even mention medical malpractice and stayed within the scope of forensic medicine.

An 1856 *Report on Difficulties Growing Out of Alleged Malpractice in the Treatment of Fractures* by an Ohio State Medical Society committee on surgery could have helped Lincoln's case. Citing six case studies, the report dealt with oblique fractures, femur fractures, and the need for standards. In conclusion, the report praised Hamilton's fracture tables and stated: "It abundantly proves what every surgeon of experience must attest, that *imperfection* is a rule as regards these cases, to which *perfection* is a mere occasional exception."

Prior to 1860, none of the legal scholars dealt with the issue of medical malpractice in the medical jurisprudence books commonly used as references. John J. Elwell, a physician and a lawyer, was the first expert to discuss the surge of malpractice suits and to cite excerpts from case law. In 1860, he published *A Medico-Legal Treatise on Malpractice, Medical Evidence and Insanity, Comprising the Elements of Medical Jurisprudence* designed "to acquaint physicians about their legal responsibilities and to provide relevant information."

With these two continuances in Fleming's malpractice suit, Lincoln postponed the trial for a year and gained time to prepare. In the interim, Crothers coached Lincoln on the physiology and chemistry of bone growth, bone structure, and the changes in organic matter brought on by advancing age. Since Fleming was a middle-aged man, Crothers explained how bones healed in the young as compared with older people. Lincoln and Crothers devised the idea of using chicken bones to demonstrate the age concept to the jury. Bones taken from young pullets were pliant and supple, less liable to break and healed quicker when fractured. Bones from older chickens were brittle and crisp and took longer to heal because of slower bone regeneration.

Swett was not idle during the continuance. On February 20, 1857, he asked the court clerk to issue summons for witnesses. This time he listed Dr. Ballard, Dr. Dunn, Wm. Elder, Albert Luce, Dr. Major, Dr. Martin, Dr. Niccolls, Dr. George W. Stipp, Dr. Ward, and Dr. Worrell. Additional witnesses included Eli V. Augustus, Sam B. Carrollton, Miss C. A. Fleming, J. S. Ireland, Mott (drayman), Isaac Pilcher, and J. Ricketts. Swett had the court clerk issue summons for Dr. Christopher Goodbrake and Dr. Edmonson on March 6, 1857. Twelve days later, Swett summoned Drs. Harrison Noble and Sabin as witnesses for the plaintiff.

Lincoln and Swett were legal adversaries in a murder trial in the first case of the spring term of the McLean County Circuit Court. On March 30, 1857, Lincoln was appointed by the local state's attorney to assist in the prosecution of Isaac Wyant for the murder of Anson Rusk. Using an insanity defense, Swett argued that an overdose of chloroform administered to Wyant during surgery induced insanity. Six physicians and thirteen other witnesses were called by the defense. Swett consulted with Dr. Luther V. Bell, a leader in the field and superintendent of McLean Asylum (Boston, Massachusetts), secured the superintendent of the Illinois State Hospital for the Insane (Jacksonville, Illinois), Dr. Andrew McFarland, as a star witness, and read the most highly regarded book on the subject, *A Treatise on the Medical Jurisprudence of Insanity* by Dr. Isaac Ray. Lincoln rebutted with sixteen witnesses including three physicians, one of whom was the president of the Illinois State Medical Society. Jurors found Wyant not guilty by reason of insanity a little after midnight on Sunday April 5. After the verdict, Lincoln revealed that at first he thought Wyant was "possuming insanity" but later realized that he may "have been too severe and that the poor fellow may be insane after all." When president, Lincoln intervened in a review of a military commission verdict and chose a medical expert to decide whether or not the convicted murderer was sane or insane.

Immediately after concluding the *People v. Wyant,* the malpractice case of *Fleming v. Rogers & Crothers* finally came before Judge Davis, one year after the complaint was filed. With the trial beginning, on April 7, 1857, Lincoln subpoenaed ten medical experts: Drs. W. J. Ballard, Chew, Crist, Dickison, Freese, Hoover, Parke, Roe, Spencer, and Worrell. As the trial progressed, two days later, Lincoln added Drs. Fowler and J. L. Ballard to his witness list to summon. This case went to trial despite the fact that the defense lawyers were unable to locate Freese, a material eyewitness, and to take his deposition. As adversaries, Lincoln and Swett continued to argue about medical issues in the week-long malpractice trial. Swett enhanced his reputation as the leading central Illinois practitioner in medical litigation as he presented the testimony of fifteen physicians plus twenty-one other witnesses. Testimony was solicited from Fleming, his brother and sister, from Isaac Pilcher, who saw Fleming the day after he was injured, and from local townspeople who observed and/or visited Fleming. Importantly, Swett relied upon jurors knowing or being familiar with their peers and their doctors who appeared in court. Lincoln relied mainly upon the attending physicians and the expert medical testimony.

Swett's medical experts for the plaintiff were selected from physicians who were willing to denigrate the therapeutic practices of their competitors to improve their own status in the community. They were not immune to self-service as they charged Rogers and Crothers with incompetence in treatment modalities such as bandaging and splinting. Perhaps the fierce economic competition between the physicians for patients and fees fueled the eager acrimonious testimony. Additionally, the animosity between regular or orthodox physicians and irregular doctors stimulated the voluminous expert opposition testimony.

There were a large number of physicians for Lincoln and Swett to consider as expert medical witnesses. In 1857, the Bloomington *Weekly Pantagraph* featured paid advertisements, usually on the front page, from a number of physicians: Drs. Dunn and Weed practiced as homeopaths; Mrs. Hall was a hydropath; Drs. Brown and Major were eclectics; and Drs. Elder, Lemon, Martin, Reeves, Smith, Young, and Worrell appeared to be regular practitioners. Drs. Ballard, Crist, Cromwell, Dodson, Espy, Holmes, Hoover, Hubbard, Miller, Minor, Schroder and Stipp were listed in the 1855-1856 Bloomington, Illinois city directory. In addition, Drs. Chew, Crist, Dunlap, and Luce were mentioned in a bibliographic history of McLean County. These medical expert witness possibilities totaled twenty-eight medical healers. In addition to the already mentioned Drs. Hoover and Roe, Swett used Drs. Edmonson, McFarland, Parke, and Spencer in the *People v. Wyant* trial that had just concluded in the first week of April. In that same trial, Lincoln had Drs. Goodbrake and Warner as witnesses plus Dr. Lemon already cited. Rogers and Crothers testified in their own behalf as well as Freese and Small by deposition later. These possible medical witnesses brought the potential pool to about thirty-seven.

Pertinently, Dr. Silas Hubbard, who was in a practice partnership with Freese in 1857, probably knew Dr. Hamilton, the medical expert on fractures. They were both practicing in Buffalo from 1846 to 1855 when Hubbard moved to Bloomington. Of course, the question is did Hubbard mention Hamilton to Lincoln?"

During the trial, Lincoln did not remember Crothers's medical descriptions about the lime and calcium deposited in the bones of older people. Instead, in showing the flexibility of the bone of a young chicken to the jury, he used the expression: "This bone has the starch all taken out of it, as it is in childhood." When he easily snapped the bone of an older chicken, the jury quickly understood the age differential.

A dialogue during Lincoln's cross examination of Fleming may have impressed the jury and aggravated their dilemma in reaching a verdict:

Lincoln: Can you walk at all?
Fleming: Yes, but my leg is short so I have to limp.

Lincoln: Well! What I would advise *you* to do is get down on your *knees* and thank your Heavenly Father, and also these two Doctors that you have any legs to stand on at all.

Lincoln impressed upon the jury that Fleming's serious injury could just as easily have resulted in the doctors amputating one or both of the badly injured legs. If they did so, the physicians would probably not have been sued because they followed that still acceptable professional choice. However, Lincoln contended that the doctors exercised their considerable skill and opted to try to save Fleming's legs and did so. Instead of Fleming complaining, Lincoln reasoned for the jury that "the slight defect that finally resulted, through Nature's methods of aiding the work of surgeons, is nothing compared to the loss of the limb altogether."

At this time, statutory law regarding the medical profession was in its infancy despite the fact that between 1835 and 1865 the courts were inundated with medical malpractice law suits. Evidently Lincoln was unfazed by this lack of medical case law and used logical analysis and rhetorical flourishes to argue his points. However, both Lincoln and Swett could have profited from knowledge of specific case precedents.

Lincoln could have bolstered his argument by citing an 1854 Massachusetts malpractice case of a patient with compound leg fractures. In his testimony, medical expert, Dr. Abner Phelps, made exactly the same argument about the plaintiff's shorter leg: "...the skill, ingenuity and strong judgment employed...in the cure of such a limb...entitled him [the physician] to far greater and more lasting honor and reputation than he could have acquired by fifty successful amputations."

An 1854 malpractice case in New Hampshire, *Leighton v. Dr. Sargeant,* could have been used by both Lincoln and Swett. A man suffered a compound fracture-dislocation of his ankle and lower leg and the joint became frozen in an awkward position. His leg healed but he had to walk with a cane. Leighton sued the physician for malpractice. Lincoln's defense could have cited the impressive testimony of medical experts that this type of injury previously required amputation. Dr. Henry J. Bigelow, professor of surgery, Harvard Medical School (Boston), testified from his personal experience with similar cases: "After all one can do, the surgeon is glad to get off with any foot that will do to walk on." Dr. Valentine Mott (New York City). "one of the most distinguished surgeons in the world" at the time, stated "compound dislocations of the ankle-joint are very formidable accidents.... No surgeon ought to be prosecuted and fined for such a result. The patient ought to be thankful that it is so favorable, and pay his surgeon for services, as the defect can readily be remedied by a high heel, or some mechanical contrivance."

Citing the same case, Swett could have countered Lincoln's argument that Fleming should be grateful to the doctors for being able to walk at all. Despite the similar plea that eventually proved successful for Lincoln, the New Hampshire jury found the physician guilty of malpractice. Swett could inform the jury that Dr. Sargeant was found guilty in two trials: fined $1,500 and costs in the first and $525 in the second and the costs of both trials.

One Pennsylvania judge did instruct juries that the attending physician was required to use the skill necessary "to set the leg so as to make it straight and of equal length with the other." This decision against the physician was overturned by the state supreme court as it reiterated that the implied contract with the physician is to treat the case with care, diligence, and skill, not to cure.

Lincoln might have cited an 1844 case in Erie County (Pennsylvania). William Tims suffered an oblique fracture of his thigh bone in a fall off a building and was treated by Dr. James P. White. Tims's leg healed but the limb was crooked and there was a bony protuberance at the point of the injury. Tims sued the doctor for malpractice but the jury was deadlocked. In 1845, he sued again with the same result. Finally, in 1848, the jury decided the case in favor of the physician.

Closer to home, Lincoln could have cited an 1856 case in Cincinnati, Ohio, in which the plaintiff broke both bones in his lower leg. As an expert witness, Hamilton testified that in only about 50 percent of his recorded cases of this nature were the outcomes satisfactory. Jurors refused to award damages to the plaintiff and rendered a verdict for the doctor.

A farmer serving as a juror in a 1856 malpractice trial described the reaction of a working-class jury to the testimony of expert medical witnesses: "After a few questions are answered, they [jurors] sneer and laugh at you [physicians] and make up their minds long before they leave the box."

Apparently, the *Fleming v. Rogers & Crothers* jury was overwhelmed by the contradictory expert medical testimony from twenty-seven local physicians. Combining all of the existing court subpoenas for expert medical witnesses in this case Swett summoned twelve physicians. Lincoln called seven medical experts. Both Lincoln and Swett summoned five of the same physician witnesses. There is no documentation to indicate who actually testified for whom. Late in the afternoon on Friday, April 10, 1857, the jury returned a verdict which was read by the judge:

> Thereupon came a jury...[a]nd having heard the evidence produced before them and the arguments of counsel retire to consider upon their verdict and being unable to agree upon a verdict return into court and pray to be discharged. And thereupon it is ordered by the court that the jurors aforesaid be wholly discharged from rendering any verdict on the premises aforesaid. And it is further ordered that this cause stand continued to the next term of this court.

Judge Davis ordered the case to stand continued to the next term of the court, a special session called for June 1857. On Saturday morning, April 11, 1857, the Bloomington *Daily Pantagraph* reported on the trial and the jury's verdict:

THE DAILY PANTAGRAPH
Bloomington, Illinois April 11, 1857

Circuit Court. The jury in the case of Fleming v. Drs. Crothers and Rogers were—after being out 18 hours, and failing to agree on a verdict—discharged yesterday at four o'clock. Mr. Fleming, as most of our readers know, was badly injured by the falling of a wall at the time of the great fire in Bloomington, in October 1855. The alleged malpractice consisted in the mode of treatment pursued by his physicians, the defendants. As the case may be tried again, we do not deem it proper to publish the evidence or comment upon it now. The trial excited much interest, and kept the court house [sic] well filled during its continuance.

Since the newspaper did "not deem it proper " to write about the trial and most of the records perished in courthouse fires, there are only fragmentary documents about *Fleming v. Rogers & Crothers.*

Lincoln secured a continuance to the fall term of the court on June 15, 1857. Defense lawyers located Freese in New Jersey during July 1857. Freese was not practicing as a physician but was "at present engaged in editing the *Daily and Weekly State Gazette and Republican.*" On August 1, 1857, Lincoln prepared seven questions for Freese's deposition:

> 1stWhat is your name and occupation in life?
>
> 2ndDid you see the plaintiff while he was in charge of the defendants with his broken thighs? And if yes, state how often you saw him during this time? Giving the day on which you saw him during this time—giving the day on which you saw him each time beginning from the time he received the injury—What was done in the case each time you saw him, by the defendants, by yourself (if anything) and by others—the particular manner in which each limb was dressed and who did it and each part of it?
>
> 3edState the condition you found the plaintiff in each time, and the condition of the injured limbs, and the manner of the splints, bandages, extensions, etc.?
>
> 4thGive a particular account of all that was done with or about the injured limbs upon the occasion of the first

　　　　A. LINCOLN, ESQUIRE

unbandaging them and doing them up again, with all that was said by the plaintiff or to him or in his presence, by the defendants, yourself and every other person?

5thWas anything said…adhesion of the broken bones? and Who said it?

6[th]Was the adhesion broken up? and if not was any objection made to breaking it up? and if yea by whom was such objection made? State particularly what each person said about it.

7thDid you hear the plaintiff say anything about pleurisy and if yea, when was it? and what did he say about it?

Anticipating a new trial, Swett summoned his witnesses "to be holden at the Court House [sic] in Bloomington on the first Monday in the month of September next to testify and the truth to speak." He called ten physicians: Drs. Ballard, Dunn, Elder, Luce, Major, Martin, Niccolls, Parke, Spencer and Stipp. In addition, Swett summoned Eli V, Augustus, Samuel Carlton, Miss C. A. Fleming, J. C. Fleming, J. S. Ireland, Mrs. J. C. Ireland, and J. Ricketts.

Small was located in Nashville, Tennessee and on August 21, 1857, Lincoln prepared five interrogatories for him dealing with Fleming's treatment, the breaking of adhesions, and the outcomes of the treatment. Swett provided four questions for the cross examination dealing with Small's occupation and his medical therapeutic skills.

On August 24, 1857, Freese answered the questions under oath in the office of William C. Howell, a justice of the peace in Trenton, New Jersey. In his deposition, Freese corroborated the testimony given by Rogers and Crothers as to what happened and who said what. Swett's thirteen additional cross-examination interrogatories aimed to discredit Freese's reputation as an expert medical witness. Only two questions dealt with his practice and occupation. Eleven of Swett's questions dealt with Freese's authorship of a sensational popular book. With a feel for the jurors' attitudes in the Victorian culture of America at the time,

Swett's questions took direct aim at the most scandalous section of that book.

Freese began his written responses by detailing his professional education. He studied medicine with Dr. Joseph Hedges from July 1843 to August 1845. Afterward he attended one course of medical lectures in Philadelphia during the winter of 1845-1846. He became a pupil of Professor Bryan up to 1857 while attending another full course of lectures. After receiving his medical diploma, he attended medical lectures in New York City paying special attention to hospital practice After relocating westward, he attended the St. Louis medical college and reviewed his knowledge of anatomy and surgery. Freese did not enter into full office practice until he moved to Illinois in the summer of 1852. He practiced there until he moved to Cincinnati, Ohio. He practiced there until spring 1857 when he moved to this Trenton, New Jersey.

Getting to Swett's main point of contention, Freese admitted being the author of a book entitled *Freese's Combined System of Practice for Physicians in Families*. Freese's book was published in 1856 by Smith, Small & Company of Cincinnati and consisted of three parts: Part 1, The physician's handbook and family guide to health; Part 2, Special treatise: a practical treatise on the diseases peculiar to the genital organs of the male sex; and Part 3, Special treatise: a practical treatise on diseases peculiar to the genital organs of the female sex. Continuing, Freese admitted that he was the author of an article or chapter in the book "treating upon the mode and means of begetting male and female children at the pleasure of the parents." Furthermore, Freese stated that he still believed the information to be true and that his advice "was beneficial and proper."

Seeking to discredit Freese, Swett put forth questions to embarrass the physician and for his responses to influence the jurors:

> 7th Is there any means, in your opinion as a professional man, by which…a child of the male sex can be begot at the will

of the parents except by repeated efforts and taking the chances of nature?

Ans: Yes. There are means that may be properly used and with a reasonable hope of success [of begetting a child of your choice].

8th Why did you write and publish the chapter referred to?

Ans: [I wrote & published book t]o call the attention of readers to the subject so that by putting my knowledge into practice I might benefit others and make money myself.

9th Have you in the course of your practice advised persons in relation to the particular means of begetting a child of either sex? And if yea, will you state if you have no objection the means advised by you?

Ans: I have advised in such cases. The advice was always suited to each particular case.

Swett tried to get Freese to admit that he said the book was "a mere humbug" for the purpose of making money. Strenously, Freese denied that his book was a humbug although he did say that "most books are got up with the same object, viz; for the purpose of making money." Continuing to attack, Swett accused Freese of stating that his medical advice would not be "honest and fair" regarding begetting children. Emphatically, Freese denied that he swore to any such thing and blamed the confusion on "unfair questioning." In concluding this line of questioning, Swett requested a copy of the book but Freese "declined to part with it." Swett ended his interrogatories with a simple question. "What is your present occupation and how long have you been engaged in the same?" Freese answered, "Since the first of July last, I have been editing a daily and weekly newspaper."

On September 8, 1857, Judge Davis declared that the court being "fully advised on the premises doth order that this cause be continued at the costs of said defendants." Lincoln and Stuart informed the court about the need for Small's testimony and prepared an affidavit for Crothers to sign:

Eli K. Crothers cannot safely proceed to the trial because of the absence of Isaac M. Small, who is a material witness.... Small was a student of medicine and present when the limbs' adhesions were to be broken up and when determinations were made to rebreak and readjust the right broken limb. Small heard plaintiff at first consent to adjustment and later say he would rather have a crooked leg all his life rather than endure the pain of rebreaking and readjusting the limb. Defendants had forgotten that Small was present and that he now lived in Tennessee and that his testimony is vital to this case.

Justice of the Peace Egbert A. Raworth took Small's deposition on November 10, 1857 in Nashville. There were five interrogatories and Small's answers were written by Raworth. Small said that he was a cabinet maker and saw Fleming only once about three weeks after his injury while his physicians cared for him. After the doctors examined Fleming, Small said they measured his legs and found the right leg to be shorter than the other. At this time, the doctors proposed to break up the adhesions to restore the shorter leg to its former length. Next, Small said that he and Dr. Freese went to office to procure the necessary splints and chloroform preparatory to the operation. When they returned, Small acted under the directions of the doctors and administered the chloroform to Fleming. As soon as Fleming was supposed to be under the influence of the chloroform, the doctors attempted to break up the adhesions. However, the pain and strain proving too much for Fleming to bear. He screamed and told the doctors to let him alone because he had suffered enough. Small noted that Fleming's brother and sister were present and very much excited. They insisted that the doctors desist from breaking up the adhesion. While the doctors did stop, Dr. Crothers remarked at the time that he would not be responsible for the result unless the adhesion was broken. Small described what happened next:

They then commenced to drape the leg by rolling a bandage around the leg from the foot up to the thigh. They put on an extension splint on the outside of the leg, and shorter ones on the—and inside of the leg. They then commenced a roller bandage extending from the foot up to the thigh, commencing at the foot. I do not think the other leg was unbandaged by the defendants at all. This took place between the hours of 2 and 4 o'clock PM. Dr. Crothers applied the bandages and splints assisted by Drs. Rogers & Freese.... It seemed to be a unanimous opinion among the doctors present that the adhesion of bones should be broken, and they all so expressed themselves to the plaintiff.

Small declared that he did not see the limb unbandaged or what was done subsequently. As far as he could tell, the adhesions were not broken up from what he saw and heard on that occasion. He concluded by repeating that there were objections made by Fleming himself and by his brother and sister.

Swett again prepared for a re-trial after the depositions of Freese and Small were completed. On November 16, 1857, the sheriff was commanded to summons witnesses for the plaintiff. Again, Lincoln requested and was granted another continuance. After the fourth continuance, on December 20, 1857 Brier & Birch prepared an affidavit for Rogers and Crothers to sign requesting a change of venue. Grounds for the change declared:

By our petitioners Thomas P. Rogers & Eli K. Crothers, defendants in the above entitled suit do say that the above suit against them as is alleged by plaintiff's declaration for malpractice in the treatment of plaintiff's broken legs that they so informed by counsel and verify herein that they are not guilty of said malpractice; that they have a complete defence to said action of plaintiff. These defendants say that the inhabitants of this county are so prejudiced against them that they cannot expect a fair trial in this county & further that these defendants say that it is absolutely necessary to their legitimate defense in said cause to introduce the testimony of practicing physicians who are skilled in surgery and that the inhabitants of said county as these defendants believe are so prejudiced against the testimony of physicians given in such cases and account of some recent trials in said court that they do not expect due weight will be given to said testimony. These defendants believe the same indifference to the inhabitants, in respect to the testimony of physicians, exists. And further these defendants say that the prejudice, alleged above as existing, has caused to their knowledge harm to these defendants as in the last September term of this court and further that their affidavit is not made for delay but that justice may be done. These defendants respectfully ask that your Honor will award them a change of venue to some other county where the aforesaid cause against them do not exist.

On the next day, December 21, 1857, the court granted the request and ordered "the venue of this case be changed to the County of Logan," about thirty-five miles southwest of Bloomington.

Almost two and one-half years after Fleming was injured, this malpractice case came to an end after four continuances, one hung jury trial, and a change of venue. Although Lincoln did not win this medical malpractice case, he was probably grateful to secure an out of court settlement, a draw. *Fleming v Rogers and Crothers* posed a contradiction when considering evaluations of Lincoln as a lawyer. When Lincoln jumped into a case "he was not more than ordinarily successful" but "Lincoln was great [as a lawyer] when he had time to think and study." In this medical malpractice case Lincoln jumped in, had time, and secured a settlement out of court.

However, this legal settlement was quickly relegated into history during the drawn out litigation. In June 1857, Lincoln's suit for payment for legal services for the Illinois Central Railroad from 1854 to 1856 resulted in the highest fee he ever earned, $5,000, minus his $200 retainer. Three years later, in 1860, Lincoln represented another physician in a malpractice appeal before the supreme court of Illinois.

Lincoln got to know Crothers and his wife, Marie, quite well during the time they spent together. At the time of this law suit, Crothers was thirty-one years of age and was an organizer of the

Republican party in Illinois. Lincoln appointed Crothers a medical examiner for a large part of central Illinois. Practically without pay, he examined soldiers who were home on furloughs due to wounds or disease and authorized furlough extensions when medically necessary.

One of the medical experts, Dr. George Stipp, did not hesitate to write to President Lincoln about his situation during the Civil War. He was suspended from duty as a surgeon due to some incapacity. Stipp asked Lincoln to have him assigned to a specific location. Lincoln wrote to Secretary of War Edwin M. Statnton on June 24, 1863: "[Dr. Stipp] is my old personal friend." Assign him where he wants. By December 19, 1863, Lt. Col. Stipp was assigned to the Department of the Gulf.

Lincoln also continued to be in touch with Dr. Jacob R. Freese. From 1861 to 1863, Freese was an assistant captain and assistant adjunct general of volunteers. He made Lincoln aware of his desires and Lincoln sent a note to Secretary of War Edwin M. Stanton on November 11, 1863: "I personally wish Jacob R. Freese, of New Jersey to be appointed a Colonel for a colored regiment—and this regardless of whether he can tell the exact shade of Julius Caesar's hair." When that appointment failed to materialize, Lincoln made another request of the secretary of war on February 24, 1864: "I will be personally obliged if the appointment of an additional Paymaster shall be given to J.R. Freese of New Jersey."

There is no record of that appointment ever being made either. But Freese continued to push for a position. On September 19, 1864, Lincoln wrote to US Senator John C. Ten Eyck of New Jersey: "Dr. J. R. Freese, now editor of a leading Union journal in New Jersey, resided for a time in Illinois, when & where I made his acquaintance, and since when I have enjoyed much of his friendship. He is somewhat wounded with me now, that I do not recognize him as he thinks I ought. I wish to appoint him a Provost-Marshall in your State. May I have your approval?" About a week later, Lincoln followed with a letter to Provost-Marshall-General James B. Fry on the same subject: "Please let the appointment of Jacob R. Freese, as Commissioner of Board of

Enrollment for 2nd District of New Jersey, in place of Mr. Wilson resigned, be made at once. Senator Ten Eyck is agreed to it. I have his letter to that effect, though I can not at this moment lay my hands on it." Freese finally got an appointment. James Wilson resigned on September 2, 1864 and Freese was appointed the same day that the provost-marshall-general received the president's letter. Freese served on the draft board until his discharge on April 30, 1865.

8

BROKEN WRIST WITHOUT DUE CARE:

LINCOLN DEFENDS THE PHYSICIAN

Keziah West sued Dr. Powers Ritchey of Carthage for *trespass on the case* during the October term of Hancock County Circuit Court in 1855. Her complaint cited injuries resulting from Ritchey's lack of skill and negligence in the practice of his profession as a physician and surgeon. Allegedly, Ritchey treated West's fractured and dislocated wrist. He applied splints and bandages and promised to return to examine her the next day. In her testimony, West claimed Ritchey failed to reexamine her the next day and her wrist was subsequently deformed due to the doctor's improper wrapping. Ritchey's negligence resulted in a deformity and the inability to use one of her hands. During the trial, several physicians testified for West that Ritchey's medical treatment was faulty. They said that Ritchey did not extend the splints and bandages below the injured wrist and that caused West's deformity and continuing disability. Furthermore, Ritchey used splints that were allegedly not wide enough or long enough to treat the fracture. In addition, Ritchey did not observe or treat the dislocation, which was noticed by doctors and non-medical people later on. Similar to the *Fleming v. Rogers & Crothers* case, local physicians were not reluctant to castigate their brethren in the business of healing. Physicians testified against Ritchey for the same rationales they denigrated Rogers and Crothers: to gain status in the competitive market for patients and to perpetuate the animosity between the various types of orthodox/regular and irregular medical healers.

In the three to five months preceding this medical malpractice trial, Lincoln first encountered Edwin McMasters Stanton, his later secretary of war. In 1855, Lincoln and Stanton were both defense counsel in the *McCormick v. Manny et al.* patent infringement case. Cyrus Hall McCormick, inventor of the original reaper, sued John H. Manny for $400,000 in damages for manufacturing mechanical reapers that allegedly used McCormick's patented improvements to his reaper. Patent lawyer Edward N. Dickerson of New York and Reverdy Johnson, legendary trial attorney from Baltimore, represented McCormick. Manny's counsel were patent attorneys George Harding of Philadelphia and Stanton of Pittsburgh. Harding hired Washington lawyer Peter H. Watson to promote Manny's interests because of his reputation as a good legal "fixer" and influence peddler. Because the case was scheduled for the US district court in Chicago, Illinois, Watson solicited Lincoln to be the designated local lawyer. Lincoln was hired to make the closing argument on the home court and was given a retainer of $400. However, the case was unexpectedly moved to Cincinnati, Ohio, for the convenience of the presiding Supreme Court of the United States Justice, John McLean, who lived there. At that point, Lincoln began to experience difficulty securing documents from his co-counsel. In a July 23, 1855 letter to Watson, Lincoln complained about not being sent the pertinent documents and depositions. He told Watson that he secured his own copies of the complaint and answer when he was at the US court in Chicago. In preparation for the case, Lincoln did his own investigation: "During my stay in Chicago, I went out to Rockford and spent half a day, examining and studying Manny's Machine." Still experiencing difficulty getting information, Lincoln sent a sharply worded letter directly to Manny & Co.

> Since I left Chicago about the 18th of July, I have heard nothing concerning the Reaper suit. I addressed a letter to Mr. Watson, at Washington, requesting him to forward me the evidence, from time to time, as it should be taken, but I have received no answer from him.

Is it still the understanding that the case is to be heard at Cincinnati on the 20th inst.?

Please write me on the receipt of this.

On September 20, 1855, the trial began. When Lincoln arrived in Cincinnati, he stayed at the city's leading hotel, the Burnett House. When he went to confer with his legal associates, Lincoln was greeted in a boorish and discourteous manner. Stanton expressed his displeasure in his crude description of Lincoln: "A long, lank creature from Illinois, wearing a dirty linen duster for a coat, on the back of which the perspiration had splotched wide stains that resembled a map of the continent." Combining that attire with heavy boots, Lincoln appeared to be a typical western farmer. Usurping the role of chief counsel with characteristic haughtiness, Stanton asked Harding: "Why did you bring that d--n long armed Ape here? He does not know anything and can do no good…. If that giraffe appears in the case, I will throw up my brief and leave." Stanton's tactless outburst and antagonistic demands forced Lincoln to withdraw from the case. However, Lincoln remained in Cincinnati to attend the trial and saw Stanton win the case. Sitting in the courtroom, Stanton's masterful presentation, brilliant logic, and careful preparation deeply impressed Lincoln. He resolved to study the law all over again. When he arrived back in Springfield, Lincoln told his partner, William H. Herndon, that he was "roughly handled by that man Stanton." Despite the outrageous insult from Stanton, Lincoln did not carry a grudge. At the opportune time, he appointed Stanton secretary of war because he was the best man for the job and for the country.

On Monday, October 8, 1855, the Hancock County Circuit Court docket recorded that "On motion and by agreement ordered that this cause stand continued until the next term of this court." At the March 1856 term of the court, Ritchey requested security for the costs: "Now comes the defendant by his attorney and on his motion and affidavit filed ordered that the plaintiff be ruled to show cause by the meeting of the Court on Thursday morning next why she should not be required to give security for costs herein."

On Thursday, Ritchey filed his pleas and West filed her security: "Now comes the defendant by his attorney and files his pleas, one, two, three, four, five, six and seven herein—And hereinfrom the plaintiff came and filed security for costs in this cause." Next day, West responded to Ritchey's pleas with a demurrer challenging his allegations: "Now comes the plaintiff by her attorney and files her demurrer to the second, third, fourth, fifth, sixth and seventh plea of the defendant filed herein."

On the following Tuesday, the court rendered an opinion on West's demurrer: "Now come to be heard the demurrer to the second, third, fourth, fifth, sixth and seventh pleas of the defendant and the Court being fully advised on the premises doth consider the said demurrer to said pleas be sustained and that leave be given the defendant to amend his said pleas." On June 9, 1856, Ritchey's attorneys moved for a continuance, but the judge denied the request and the trial took place during the next three days.

Between June 10 and June 12, 1856, jurors heard evidence, the arguments of counsel, and instructions by the court. With the consent of the parties it was agreed that when they should decide upon a verdict they might seal the same, disperse and meet the Court tomorrow morning at half past seven o'clock.

The next morning, the jury reported to the Court that they could not agree upon a verdict. After discharging the jury, the judge continued the case until the next term of the Court.

While the *West v. Ritchey* trial was going on, Lincoln & Herndon appeared in many cases during the Summer 1856 term of the Sangamon County Circuit Court in Springfield. In *Currier v. North American Insurance Company*, they won a judgment of $1,000 plus costs. When the defendant defaulted in *Cass v. Showers*, Lincoln & Herndon secured $215.23 for their client. In *Bunn v. Bays*, the case was settled by agreement and the estate of Bannister Bays paid $100 to Lincoln's client. On the last day of the court session, Lincoln & Herndon secured a divorce degree for their client and settled an *assumpsit* suit for breach of contract for $550.45 in favor of their client.

At the next term of the Hancock County Circuit Court, on October 7, 1856, Ritchey asked for a change of venue. After the hearing on the motion, the court agreed and the case was assigned to the Adams County Circuit Court. Trail was set for Monday of the second week of the 1857 spring term. Following the granting of the change of venue, Ritchey quickly submitted a motion to the Adams County Circuit Court for a continuance, which was granted. Fee books for the Hancock County Circuit Court recorded that Ritchey paid $18.00 to the sheriff to serve subpoenas, $17.00 for witnesses Sarah E. Stewart, E. D. Rogers, T. R. Montgomery, and George W. Hall, each of whom received one dollar per day, $7.45 for court paperwork, a jury fee of $3.00 and $4.40 for the change of venue. West expended $12.50 for the court paperwork., $18.00 to serve the subpoenas, and $92.00 for witnesses James K. Moore, A. J. Griffith, Thomas McCellan, Thomas Bond, H. P. Griswold, J. J. Crawford ,and George W. Hall. These seven witnesses spent a total of ninety-two days at the October, March and June terms of the Court. Her Hancock County Circuit Court costs totaled $122.50.

At the same time that *West v. Ritchey* changed its venue from Hancock County to Adams County, Lincoln was extremely busy campaigning for Republican candidates. In the fall of 1856, Lincoln made more than fifty speeches enthusiastically supporting John C. Frémont and William L. Dayton for president and vice-president and William H. Bissell and John Wood for Illinois governor and lieutenant governor.

West v. Ritchey continued to drag on for some time through the courts. Another trial occurred during the March 1858 term of the Adams County Circuit Court with Judge Joseph Silbey presiding. On Tuesday, March 23, 1858, different jurors were empaneled to retry the case. For three days the jury heard the case. By Thursday, March 25, the trial ended with a verdict for West: "We the jury find the defendant guilty in manner and form as the said plaintiff hath thereof complained against him and assess the said plaintiff damages by reason thereof of seven hundred dollars."

Ritchey's lawyers immediately asked for a new trial and gave reasons for doing so.

A few days afterward, on March 30, 1858, Lincoln appeared in Woodford County Circuit Court in Metamora representing Samuel W. Beck, the bondsman who assured the $1,000 bail for Melissa Goings. Goings accidentally killed her abusive husband during a drunken brawl as she defended herself from his choking. Lincoln represented her and Goings disappeared during her trial. Supposedly, Goings asked Lincoln where to get a drink of water and he replied that the water in Tennessee was pretty good. She took his advice and skipped bail to leave Illinois. A *scire facias* writ requiring the bondsman to show cause why the court record should not be enforced was issued by the court. On behalf of his client, Lincoln wrote and filed a plea of confession and avoidance. On the strength of Lincoln's pleadings, the proceedings were continued. When Lincoln visited Metamora to deliver a political speech on October 4, 1858, he conferred with Henry Miller, the state's attorney. On the following day, the court ordered the case against the bondsman stricken from the docket on a motion from the prosecutor.

Judge Sibley heard Ritchey's motion for a new trial on Saturday, April 10, 1858 and rendered his opinion denying the motion for a new trial. Ritchey was ordered to pay West the sum of $700 in damages, plus her costs, and charges expended by her in execution of this suit. However, Judge Sibley did allow Ritchey to appeal to the supreme court of Illinois. As a condition of the appeal, Ritchey had to file an appeal bond with security in the sum of $1,500 within thirty days.

Abraham Lincoln, William H. Herndon, and Elliott B. Herndon, his law partner's brother, were retained by Ritchey to appeal to the supreme court of Illinois. Two years younger that his brother, Elliott was admitted to the bar in the winter of 1842-1843. He served as the attorney for Springfield, the attorney for Sangamon County and the US attorney for the Southern District of Illinois. In 1858, he was appointed governmental disbursing agent for Illinois. In sharp contrast to his brother, Elliott was active in

Democratic politics and edited the *Illinois State Democrat* newspaper from 1857 to 1860. True to his politics, he supported John C. Breckinridge for president in 1860 and participated as a Peace Democrat in anti-war activities during the Civil War. Williams, Grimshaw & Williams represented West in the supreme court of Illinois appeal during the January 1860 court term.

Lincoln & Herndon's law office on the west side of the public square faced the imposing Greek Revival state capitol building. Four formidable columns on the portico and a stately circular domed tower atop the building dominated the square. Entering the state capitol, Lincoln made a sharp left turn to enter the first floor room housing the supreme court of Illinois. There were four rows of long plain wooden benches with spindle backs providing seating for spectators. A wood and coal burning stove against the right wall heated the room. Lincoln entered past the railing, commonly called the bar, that separated the court from the spectators, to take his place in front of the judges. Both plaintiff and defendant lawyers sat together at one long table directly inside the bar. A green velvetlike cloth covered the table creating a smooth surface so the lawyers could write clearly with the quill pens. Three justices sat on a raised dias directly in front of the table for the lawyers. Legislative charters called for four justices in 1819; nine justices after 1841; and three justices after 1848. Incongruously, a floor to ceiling, three foot square painted white column obstructed the view of the lawyers as well as the chief justice, who sat in the middle of the three members of the court. (Earlier, this architectural flaw stimulated one chief justice to order the provoking column removed. However, the upper floor legislative chamber began to buckle and the column had to be returned to its offending, but necessary, supporting position.) To the left of the lawyer's table, the court clerk sat at an oversized desk and struggled to rapidly write everything down. Adjoining the courtroom, a large spacious room housed a number of clerks and the repository for the filed documents. Each hand written document and printed form was folded into a letter size and placed in small containers resembling mailboxes. When the container was full, the documents were tied into bundles and usually stored helter-skelter in the basement.

Another room on the first floor served as the library of the supreme court of Illinois. A number of tall bookcases with glass doors housed the most extensive legal library in the state. Books were expensive and a majority of lawyers did not have their own sizable library. Lawyers regularly borrowed books and did research in preparation for their cases. However, this library did not require silence and members of the bar used it as a convenient social meeting place. Attorneys swapped stories with each other and with the ever-present politicians. Playing cards were available at one table. Another table had game boards for chess or checkers. There was a black pot-bellied stove in the middle of the room. Like many others, Lincoln often stayed at the library late into the night to swap stories and to talk about law and politics.

Despite Lincoln's exhausting political campaigns as he poised himself for the impending campaign to select a Republican candidate for president, Lincoln represented Ritchey in his appeal to the supreme court of Illinois in January 1860. Lincoln believed that Ritchey's case was fatally botched in the Adams County Circuit Court and he tried to salvage the malpractice defense. In a deja vu situation, Lincoln probably relived his experiences during the *Fleming v. Rogers & Crothers* medical malpractice case of 1857. Similarly, the conflicting expert medical testimony most likely confused the jury. Similarly, Ritchey's attorneys neglected pertinent scientific evidence to rebut West's claims of malpractice. To repair the botched lower court defense, Lincoln could have cited Dr. Frank H. Hamilton's data on the outcomes of wrist fractures as evidence. In nine of the ten wrist and hand related fractures that Hamilton cited, the bones united but were imperfect. Four additional cases resulted in amputations for three patients and death for the remaining patient.

Valiantly, Lincoln tried his legal best to present a sound case in the appeal. However, Lincoln was not able to challenge the medical testimony given in the lower court because Ritchey's lawyers did not enter a bill of exceptions. At that time, lawyers themselves had to laboriously write out, in longhand, a transcript of all the relevant testimony given at the trial. However, the supreme court of Illinois would not review questions not raised in a bill of exceptions. Justice Pinckney H. Walker wrote the opinion for the court. "No question can arise on the correctness of the decisions of the court below in admitting or rejecting evidence, in this case, as no exceptions were preserved in the record: We shall therefore decline their examination." For whatever their reason, Richey's lower court lawyers did not enter a bill of exceptions to the expert medical testimony being presented for the plaintiff.

During the earlier trials, physicians testifying for the plaintiff agreed that it is customary and necessary for the surgeon to pay a second visit to check the patient's progress and to determine if additional treatment is needed. This was interpreted by the supreme court of Illinois as a professional duty of the attending physician. There was no dispute that Ritchey was asked to revisit West, that he agreed to do so, and that he never did return afterwards. This professional duty was explained in the court's opinion:

> [Omission of this duty established] a want of reasonable care and diligence, which, together with his [Ritchey] failing to comply with his agreement to return, must render him liable for all injury which has resulted from its non-observance.... Had he returned...in all probability the visit would have resulted in his detecting the true situation of the injury, and relief might have been obtained by the employment of the necessary surgical aid.

This longstanding legally established medical care principle was reiterated in the court's opinion:

> [a physician] must be held to employ a reasonable amount of care and skill. For any thing short of that degree of skill in his practice, the law will hold him responsible for any injury which may result from its absence. While he is not required to possess

the highest order of qualification...he must possess and exercise that degree of skill which is ordinarily possessed by members of the profession. And whether the injury results from a want of skill, or the want of its application, he will in either case, be equally liable.

In reviewing the testimony of the expert physicians appearing for West, the court found that they concurred that the splints and bandages were not properly applied, were too short and were not of sufficient width. Furthermore, the physicians testified that even if Ritchey had applied the splints and bandages midway between the wrist and elbow as alleged, the treatment was improper. Evidence seemed to indicate that if the splints and bandages extended below the wrist, the wrist would have been confined to its proper place. In Justice Walker's opinion for the supreme court of Illinois, the court concluded:

> [proper splinting and bandaging] would have tended, notwithstanding the fracture, to have held the broken bone more nearly to its place until a union was formed, and thus have prevented, to some extent, if not altogether, the deformity and disability to use the hand...it would seem that there must have been a great want of ordinary skill, or great negligence in the treatment of the case, in not detecting the dislocation of the wrist joint...there was a want of ordinary care, or skill, or both, manifested in the treatment of this case.

In his more than 200th appearance before the supreme court of Illinois, Lincoln filed a writ of error and attempted to secure a new trial by claiming newly discovered evidence that West's wrist was not injured when Ritchey attended her. According to the supreme court of Illinois, the new evidence would only have shown that "the wrist received no injury at the time he [Ritchey] was called for medical advice." A ruling of the supreme court of Illinois declared that "a new trial will not be granted for newly discovered evidence that is merely cumulative, and if the affidavit in support of the motion fails to state that the newly discovered evidence is true, it will be fatally defective.... It is not sufficient for the party to state that he has been informed and believes that the witness will testify to the facts, but the truth of such facts must be verified by affidavit." Evidently, Lincoln did not present any affidavits affirming the new evidence. In truth, there may not have been any substantial new evidence.

In conclusion, the supreme court of Illinois said: "Upon the whole of this record, we are unable to perceive any error for which the judgment of the court below should be reversed, wherefore the same is affirmed." A judgment order was rendered in the January 1860 term using a legal form with blank spaces to fill in the appropriate terms [in italics]:

> On this day come again the said parties, and the Court having diligently examined and inspected as well the record and proceedings aforesaid, as the matters and things therein assigned for error, and being now sufficiently advised of and concerning the premises, for that it appears to the Court now here, that neither in the record and proceedings aforesaid, nor in the rendition of the *Judgment* aforesaid, is there any thing erroneous, vicious, or defective; and that that record is no error: Therefore, it is considered by the Court that the *Judgment* aforesaid be Affirmed in all things, and stand in full force and effects notwithstanding the said matters and things therein assigned for error.
>
> And it is further considered by the Court that the said *Defendant in error* recover of and from the said *Plaintiff in error* costs by *her* in this behalf expended, and that *she* have execution therefor.

In settling her suit, West received $700 in damages, $206.30 for her costs and $77.05 for the fees she paid, for a total of $983.35.

Politically, Lincoln won election to the Illinois General Assembly as a member of the Whig party in 1834, 1836, 1838, and 1840. In 1846, Lincoln ran against Peter Cartwright, a Methodist circuit rider preacher and politician, for election to the US House of Representatives. Cartwright could not, or would not, distinguish preaching from politicking as he ministered to a far-flung constituency. By issuing a public appeal for pious schoolteachers to volunteer to educate students in common schools, Cartwright stirred up heated reactions from the populace. In response to the outcry, Cartwright wrote a letter to the editor of the *Sangamo Journal* published under the heading, "The Valley of the Mississippi, or the Moral Waste, No. 1." In his letter, Cartwright strongly took to task those who denigrated the poor heathens in this Valley. Using a pseudonym, Lincoln composed a satiric response for the *Beardstown Chronicle*. At that time, anonymous and pseudonymous letters to the editor were the norm for political disputes. However, Samuel Hill agreed to sign the letter and the editor printed a back-page notice that the communication was inserted by request and paid for by Samuel Hill. Much to Cartwright's dismay, Lincoln "dismantled his shifty political rival with ruthless wit and logic." Regarding Cartwright's educational suggestion, Lincoln was personally scathing and brutal: "But being thoroughly satisfied that it is wholly a political manoeuvre [*sic*], and being equally satisfied that the author is a most abondoned [*sic*] hypocrite...in politics, I venture to handle it without restraint... Poor ghost of ambition! He must have two sets of opinions, one for his religious, and one for his political friends; and to put them together smoothly, presents a task to which his feverish brain is incompetent." During the election, rumors circulated that Lincoln was an infidel or unbeliever. Nevertheless, Lincoln won and served one term.

At the end of August into early September of 1859, Logan & Hay, Shelby M. Cullom and Lincoln & Herndon defended Peachy Quinn Harrison against a murder charge. Harrison was the grandson of Pete Cartwright, the Methodist preacher and politician who ran against Licoln in the 1846 House race. Harrison got into a quarrel over politics with his brother-in-law, Greek Crafton, in a drugstore in Pleasant Plains, fifteen miles northwest of Springfield. Harrison used the four-inch blade of a white-handled knife and stabbed Crafton in the chest during the altercation. Crafton died of his wounds three days later. For four sweltering days, the trial was intensively contested in Sangamon County Circuit Court. Judge Edward Y. Rice, a lifelong Democrat with a probable bias against Republican Lincoln, presided. In a cross-examination of Crafton's brother, John, Lincoln tried to prove that Greek threatened to beat up Harrison, who then feared for his life. John only admitted that he said that Greek could whip him. In the courtroom, Lincoln demonstrated the fracas between Greek and Harrison for the benefit of the jurors. Lincoln knew that Reverend Cartwright went to see the dying man, held his hand, expressed regret, and was privy to a deathbed confession. Crafton told Cartwright: "Yes, I have brought it upon myself, and forgive Quinn and I want it said to all my friends that I have no enmity in my heart against any man." Rice heard and discussed the deathbed confession without the jury being present. In his ruling, Rice said that there was no proof that Harrison knew beforehand of any retaliation threats, that the confession was hearsay testimony and denied Lincoln's repeated efforts to introduce the critical evidence. Herndon, perhaps overzealously, commented on Lincoln's argument to the judge: "[speaking] fiercely, strongly, contemptuously of the decision of the Court, Lincoln in his anger and contempt, kept just inside the walls of the law, did not do anything, say anything, that would be a contempt of court; he was careful and yet the scoring that he gave the Court, through its foolish decision, was terrible, blasting, crushing, withering." After Lincoln's heated aggressive protests, Rice relented and allowed Cartwright to testify about the confession. Obviously impressed with Cartwright's revelation of the deathbed confession, the jury retired and took a little more than an hour to return with a not guilty verdict. Cartwright was Lincoln's star witness and his testimony about the confession was instrumental in securing an acquittal.

Returning to Illinois from Washington after his term as a congressman, Lincoln was again elected to the Illinois General Assembly in 1854. He declined the seat, sought the US Senate seat instead and was not successful. On May 29, 1856, Lincoln helped organize the new Republican party of Illinois. About one month later, the first national Republican convention met and Lincoln received 110 votes for the vice-presidential nomination. He did not become the candidate, but campaigned energetically for the chosen candidates although the Democrats won the presidency.

About this time, the Supreme Court of the United States issued its opinion in the case of *Dred Scott v. John F.A. Sanford*. In a decision that caused a sensation throughout the nation, the Court made two major points: [1] "Negroes, whether slave or free, that is, men of the African race, are not citizens of the United States, by the constitution" and [2] "the provision of the act of 1820, commonly called the Missouri Compromise, so far as it is understood to exclude Negro slavery from and communicate freedom and citizenship to Negroes in the northern part of the country was not and never was constitutional." In effect, the Supreme Court of the United States declared that Scott was not a citizen of Missouri and therefore could not sue for his freedom in the courts of the United States, and the suit must be dismissed for want of jurisdiction. This Supreme Court decision was mediated by the fact that the Missouri Compromise was repealed three years earlier and Dred Scott was freed shortly after the trial. On June 7, 1857, Stephen A. Douglas spoke in Springfield in support of the Court's decision. On June 26, 1857, Lincoln spoke out in a speech in Springfield against the Supreme Court of the United States' Dred Scott decision. He said that the Court must be respected and obeyed, but the decision was erroneous. By 1858, Douglas and Lincoln, in that order, were among the most conspicuous men in Illinois. Notwithstanding a profusion of politics swirling about him, Lincoln still attended to his legal business.

During May 1858, Lincoln defended William [Duff] Armstrong against a charge of murdering James P. Metzker. James H. Norris and Armstrong were charged with the atrocious crime of savagely beating and killing Metzker. On Saturday night, August 29, 1857, a bad-tempered Armstrong engaged in a raucous drunken frolic and brawl with Norris and Metzker on the outskirts of a religious camp meeting at Virgin's Grove near New Salem. Young toughs had set up makeshift bars on the rowdy fringes of the camp meeting. Armstrong, Norris and Metzker went from bar to bar and drank copiously. They quarreled and fought in the afternoon and again later at night. An indictment charged Norris and Armstrong of acting in concert. Norris hit Metzker on the back of the head "with a certain piece of wood about three feet long," possibly a cart-rung; and Armstrong "with a certain hard metallic substance called a slung-shot struck Metzker in the right eye… mortal bruises from which Metzker died." A slung-shot is a striking weapon consisting of a small mass of metal or stone fixed on a flexible handle or strap. At a speedy trial in the same October term, William Walker of Havana was assigned to represent Norris, who had a wife and four children and no money for a lawyer. With the public still caught up In the emotional heat of the killing, Norris was rapidly convicted of manslaughter and sentenced to eight years in the penitentiary. Dillworth & Campbell, Armstrong's lawyers, sought a severance, a separate trial from Norris, and a change of venue. "He [Armstrong] fears that he will not receive a fair and impartial trial in this court on account of the minds of the inhabitants of said Mason County being prejudiced against him." Both requests were granted by the judge and the case was transferred from the Havana courthouse in Mason County to the Cass County Circuit Court in Beardstown. On September 18, 1857, Lincoln wrote to Mrs. Hannah Armstrong:

> *Dear Mrs. Armstrong:* I have just heard of your deep affliction, and the arrest of your son for murder. I can hardly believe that he can be capable of the crime alleged against him. It does not seem possible. I am anxious that he should be given a fair trial at any rate; and gratitude for your long-continued kindness to me in adverse circumstances prompts me to offer my humble services gratuitously in his behalf.
>
> It will afford me an opportunity to requite, in a small degree, the favors I received at your hand, and that of your lamented husband, when your roof afforded me a grateful shelter, without money and without price.

When Lincoln first came to New Salem, Jack and Hannah Armstrong befriended him and made him part of their family. While he lived with them, Lincoln played with Duff and even rocked him to sleep. Jack Armstrong died shortly after his son was indicted for murder.

During November 1857, Lincoln sought bail for the twenty-four-year-old Armstrong. Bail was denied and Armstrong remained in jail until the trial began. On May 6, 1858, Lincoln traveled about forty-five hard miles northwest of Springfield to arrive in Beardstown. On the next day Armstrong's trial took place on the second floor in the Beardstown courthouse. Prosecutors included Hugh Fullerton, the state's attorney and J. Henry Shaw, a special prosecutor hired by Metzker's family. Lincoln was assisted by Walker, Norris's lawyer, and Caleb J. Dillworth, Armstrong's lawyer. Judge James Herriott of Pekin presided.

Armstrong was a young man and Lincoln took pains to select young men as jurors believing that they could understand youthful hot blood and be sympathetic. Lincoln succeeded and the average age of the jurors was under thirty. On picking the jurors, Lincoln avoided blue-eyed, blond haired men. He believed them to be inherently nervous and more likely to side with the prosecution in murder cases. Lincoln felt that dark-haired men with high foreheads made up their minds about the case beforehand. He did not select them unless he knew where they stood. Lincoln considered fat men the ideal jurors. They were jolly by nature and easily swayed.

Twenty-five witnesses testified. On direct examination by prosecutor Shaw, house painter Charles Allen presented the most damaging evidence giving an eye-witness account of the fight. Allen swore that he saw Armstrong strike Metzker about the right eye with a slung-shot about ten or eleven o'clock on the evening in question. Lincoln listened intently but he took no notes. Abram Bergen, a young Cass County lawyer just admitted to the bar and later a judge, was in the courtroom and described Lincoln's reaction as Allen was questioned: "[Lincoln] sat with his head thrown back, his steady gaze apparently fixed upon one spot of the blank ceiling, without the single change in the direction of his dull expressionless eyes, and without noticing anything transpiring around him and without any variation of feature, or movement of any muscle of his face." Finally, Lincoln slowly pulled his lanky body out of his chair, hooked his thumbs under his gallus straps that held up shapeless trousers, strolled up and down in front of the witness stand and began his seemingly casual cross-examination of Allen:

Q: Did you actually see the fight?
A: Yes
Q: And you stood very near to them?
A: No, it was one hundred fifty feet or more.
Q: In the open field?
A: No, in the timber.
Q: What kind of timber?
A: Beech timber.
Q: Leaves on it rather thick in August?
A: It looks like it.
Q: What time did all this take place?
A: Eleven o'clock at night.
Q: Did you have a candle there?
A: No. what would I want a candle for?
Q: How could you see from a distance of one hundred fifty feet or more, without a candle, at eleven o'clock at night?
A: The moon was shining real bright.
Q: Full moon?
A: Yes, a full moon, and as high in the heavens as the sun would be at ten o'clock in the morning.

Continuing his nonchalant cross-examination, Lincoln made Allen repeat his allegation in minute detail a dozen or more times until it was impossible for the jury to forgot the eye-witness testimony. Again and again Allen recounted what he saw by the light of the full moon. "Lincoln, with his usual care, had brought with him from Springfield the almanac then regarded as the standard in the region." During a court recess, Lincoln gave the blue covered 1857 *Ayer's American Almanack* to sheriff James A. Dick to hold until he asked for it. Now, during his cross-examination of Allen, he paused and asked the sheriff for the almanac. Slowly, Lincoln exhibited the almanac to the prosecuting lawyers and opened it to the astronomy table for the night in question. Placing the almanac before Allen, Lincoln continued his cross-examination:

> Q: Does not the almanac say that on August 29th the moon was barely past the first quarter of being full?
> A: [No audible answer from the witness]
> Q: Does not the almanac also say that the moon had disappeared by eleven o'clock?
> A: [No audible answer from the witness]
> Q: Is it not a fact that it was too dark to see anything from so far away, let alone one hundred fifty feet?
> A: [No audible answer from the witness]

During the questioning, Allen became flustered and confused. There was a tremendous sensation in the courtroom as the revelation resulted in a combination of a roar of laughter and undisguised astonishment. Lincoln had the sheriff hand the almanac to the jury for their inspection. After the verdict, several jurors said that "the almanac floored the witness."

Being thorough, Lincoln did not rely solely upon the almanac. He called witnesses to testify to Duff's good reputation. One witness testified that after the beating, the injured Metzker rode off and fell from his horse at least twice. Nelson Watkins swore that the slung-shot belonged to him and he had it in his home the night of the murder. Furthermore, Watkins said that he threw the slung-shot away. On the next day, it was found exactly where he threw it the previous night. Exhibiting some knowledge of anatomy in his questioning, Lincoln's principal medical witness, Dr. Charles

Parker answered hypothetical questions. Parker testified that falls from a horse or the blow from Norris possibly caused the fatal injury. He stated that while the blow to the forehead resulted in internal injury to the brain, Metzker's death was caused by a blow to the back of the head. Evidence showed that Norris delivered that blow and Armstrong was not acting in concert with him. Afterward, Judge Herriott said that Parker's testimony was the most persuasive on the defendant's behalf. In rebuttal, the prosecution called Dr. Benjamin F. Stephenson to respond to the reasonable doubt raised by Lincoln's medical expert witness. Apparently, Stephenson did not convince the jurors that Armstrong's blow was mortal.

On a hot, sultry day with Armstrong's mother audibly sobbing in the courtroom, Lincoln began his summation. As "he began to talk his eyes flashed and every facial movement helped express his idea and feeling. Then involuntarily vanished all though or consciousness of his uncouth appearance, or awkward manner, or even his high keyed, unpleasant voice." With compelling eloquence, Lincoln reviewed the "whole testimony and picked it all to pieces for one hour." He showed that everything did not depend upon Allen's eye-witness testimony. Dramatically, Lincoln stated that Allen never saw Armstrong strike Metzker by the light of the moon because the full moon was not in the heavens between ten and eleven in the evening. There was not enough moonlight for Allen to positively identify Armstrong. Recalling the testimony of the physician and Watkins, Lincoln declared that Metzker probably died from his spills from his horse or from Norris' blow to the back of his head. In concluding, Lincoln did something uncommon. In unabashedly sentimental language, Lincoln told the court he represented Armstrong for no fee and he explained his indebtedness. With tears coming to his eyes, Lincoln told the court that when he was a poor, friendless boy in New Salem, Jack and Hannah Armstrong took him in, fed him, clothed him, and made him part of their family. Lincoln told the jurors that Hannah even mended his trousers and buckskins. When Hannah, now a widow, asked him to help her son, Lincoln could not refuse. There was considerable sympathy in the courtroom and members of the jury were sorely affected. Lincoln's co-counsel, Walker commented on the summation: "I have never seen such mastery exhibited over the feelings and emotions of men as on that occasion."

In his instructions for the jury, Lincoln made two points to consider reasonable doubt and to shift the blame to Norris, who was already convicted and in jail:

> The Court instructs the jury that if they have any reasonable doubt as to whether Metzker came to his death by the blow on the eye, or the blow on the back of the head, they are to find the defendant *Not Guilty*, unless they further believe from the evidence, beyond all reasonable doubt, that *Armstrong and Norris acted by concert*, against Metzker, and that Norris struck the blow on the back of the head. That if they believe from the evidence that Norris killed Metzker, they are to acquit Armstrong, unless they also believe from the evidence, beyond a reasonable doubt, that Armstrong acted in concert with Norris in the killing, or purpose to kill or hurt Metzker.

As the jury filed out, Lincoln spoke to Armstrong's mother: "Aunt Hannah, your son will be free before sundown." On the first ballot, the jurors agreed with Lincoln. One hour later Armstrong was discharged as not guilty.

At some point after the trial, apocryphal questions were raised about the authenticity of the almanac Lincoln used in the trial. There were allegations that Lincoln used a dubiously dated almanac to deceive the court. Milton Logan, jury foreman, and juror John T. Brady concurred that Lincoln really used an 1857 almanac. In response to an inquiry in 1905, the US Naval Observatory reported that on August 29-30, 1857 the moon set at 7 minutes, 5 seconds after midnight, and at culmination during the preceding 24 hours, the moon "was 2 days, 9 hours and 46.1 minutes past the first quarter." Expert astronomers proved that the August 27, 1857 moon was low and setting at eleven in the evening just as Lincoln said it was. There was absolutely no reason for Lincoln to falsify the truth printed in the 1857 almanac.

Lincoln's legal reputation was enhanced by his defense in the Armstrong trial. About three months after the jury verdict, Lincoln received a request from William H. Grigsby to study law in Lincoln's office. On August 3, 1858, he responded: "If you wish to be a lawyer, attach no consequences to the *place* you are in, or the *person* you are with; but get books, sit down anywhere, and go to reading for yourself. That will make a lawyer of you quicker than any other way."

When he was president, Lincoln was again involved with the Armstrong family. Lincoln received a letter from Hannah asking him to discharge her son, who was ill in a Union army hospital. Duff was in Company C, 85th Illinois volunteers at the time. Lincoln responded: "I have just ordered the discharge of your boy William, as you say, now at Louisville, Ky."

A few weeks after Ritchey hired Lincoln to handle his appeal to the supreme court of Illinois, on June 16, 1858, Lincoln was nominated as the Republican candidate for the US Senate. His opponent was the two-term incumbent US Senator from Illinois, Stephen A. Douglas, the little giant. Both Lincoln and Douglas were politically active and first met about twenty-five years earlier in 1834. In 1854, Democratic Senator Douglas was responsible for the passage of the Kansas-Nebraska Act allowing the new states and territories to use popular sovereignty to accept or prohibit slavery.

On August 12, 1858, Lincoln returned to Beardstown to mount a platform in the park across from the courthouse to deliver a speech as the Republican candidate for the US Senate. On the following day, Senator Douglas spoke in the same location. When Lincoln and Douglas debated at Glenview, Illinois in April 1858, the nine cents admission ticket carried a colorful advertisement: "Come see Stephen 'razzle dazzle' Douglas vs 'Simple' Abe Lincoln." Earlier Lincoln and Norman B. Judd, chairman of the Republican central committee, proposed a series of joint discussions to Douglas and he accepted. Eight days after Douglas spoke in Beardstown, the Lincoln-Douglas debates began. Since both spoke previously in Chicago and Springfield, debates were scheduled in each of the seven remaining congressional districts in Illinois: Washington Square, Ottawa on August 21; Freeport on August 27; Union County Fairgrounds, Jonesboro on September 15; Coles County Fairgrounds, Charlestown on September 18; Old Main, Knox College, Galesburg on October 7; Washington Park, Quincy on October 13; and at Broadway and Market Streets in Alton on October 15.

All the debates took place outdoors in "broiling summer heat and gusty autumn chill." An agreed upon debate format called for an opening speech of one hour, replies of an hour and a half, and a rebuttal of thirty minutes. Audiences stood for a total of three hours listening to the candidates discuss the predominant divisive and abrasive issues: popular sovereignty; local self-government; obedience to the supreme court of Illinois ruling on slavery in the Dred Scott case; and the fate of the Union regarding the extension of slavery into the new territories. Crowds congregated well in advance of each debate to watch parades and listen to marching bands. People ate picnic lunches, drank to excess, got into fights with strangers, and shouted loudly. Political partisans in the audience routinely interrupted the debaters to cheer or jeer or heckle. They laughed at "Douglas' withering sarcasm and roared at Lincoln's droll stories." When the audience was not yelling and shouting, "onlookers set off cannons to punctuate each speaker's best hits." There was no moderator, the speeches were seldom eloquent, and the candidates' language tended to be bickering, cutting, nitpicking, and slashing. After the first debate, Lincoln said: "The fire flew some and I am glad to know I am still alive." In his own critical review Lincoln found arguments in Douglas's speeches as thin as a homeopathic soup "made by boiling the shadow of a pigeon that had starved to death." Newspaper reporters freely gave their evaluations: The pro-Lincoln *Chicago Tribune* admitted the "[debate} gave great satisfaction to our side." Headlines in the pro-Douglas *Chicago Times* read, "Lincoln's Heart Fails Him! Lincoln's Legs Fail Him! Lincoln's Tongue Fails Him! Lincoln's Arms Fail Him! LINCOLN FAILS ALL OVER!"

More than 78,000 people attended the seven debates. Douglas's overall campaign expenses totaled about $50,000 while Lincoln parsimoniously spent only $1,000. On election day, November 2, 1858, Lincoln received 125,430 popular votes to Douglas's 121,609. However, the Illinois state legislature, not the voters, determined which candidate became a US Senator. In the first week of January in 1859, the legislators chose Douglas over Lincoln strictly along party lines, 54 Democrats to 46 Republicans. In March 1860, the Lincoln-Douglas debates were published.

About six months after Lincoln and Ritchey lost their appeal, on May 18, 1860, Lincoln was nominated to be the Republican candidate for president of the United States. Douglas was the candidate of the Northern Democrats and John C. Breckinridge the choice of the Southern Democrats. Even as the political campaigning intensified, Lincoln still carried on as a lawyer. About a month before the election, on September 25, 1860, Lincoln took time to write a letter of advice to a young teacher aspiring to be a lawyer. John M. Brockman desired to know "the best mode of obtaining a thorough knowledge of the law" and Lincoln responded: "The mode is very simple, though laborious and tedious. It is only to get the books and read, and study them carefully. Begin with *Blackstone's Commentaries*, and after reading it carefully through, say twice, take up *Chitty's Pleadings*, *Greenleaf's Evidence*, & *Story's Equity* &c. in succession. Work, work, work, is the main thing."

In November, Lincoln was elected the first Republican president with 40 percent of the popular vote and 180 electoral votes. Coincidentally, historian Ken Burns conjectured that Lincoln could not be elected today. Many people would not find him photogenic; certainly not telegenic. "So awful ugly" was one contemporary man's description of the rough-hewn man from the backwoods of what was then the frontier. On February 11, 1861, Lincoln bid farewell to his friends and supporters in Springfield as he left by train for Washington.

After Lincoln's departure, a Lincoln & Herndon shingle continued to creak above the office entrance on the west side of the public square. A professional card continued to appear in front page advertising columns in Springfield newspapers until January 1862. At the end of January 1862, Herndon wrote to Lincoln suggesting a division of the fees collected. On February 3 Lincoln replied: "Yours of January 30th is just received. Do as you say about the money matter. As you well know, I have not time to write a letter of respectable length. God bless you, says your friend, A. Lincoln." Dutifully, on February 11, 1865, Herndon sent Lincoln a draft for $133 on the First National Bank of Springfield, one-half of the fees collected from cases where he was involved. An announcement in *Everybody's Advertiser* alerted the public to changes: "Upon the election of Mr. Lincoln the further existence of the firm of Lincoln & Herndon terminated without a formal dissolution, and it was succeeded by the firm of Herndon & Zane." Charles S. Zane was a former law student in the Lincoln & Herndon office and as early as July 1861, he and Herndon handled cases together.

After Lincoln's election, the new president had a private conversation with Herndon at their office before he left for Washington. As they spoke, Lincoln noticed the weather beaten wooden Lincoln & Herndon sign swinging on rusty hinges in the stairwell. Perhaps with prescience, he told Herndon: "Let it hang there undisturbed. Give our clients to understand that the election of a President makes no change in the firm of Lincoln and Herndon. If I live I'm coming back some time, and then we'll go right on practicing law as if nothing happened."

9

LINCOLN'S CASES OF SEX, SLANDER, AND SUNDRY SUITS

As a lawyer, Abraham Lincoln represented commercial businesses such as banks, insurance companies, mercantile firms, railroads, and manufacturers involved in patent suits. His law firm handled civil suits as well as criminal cases. Ordinarily, his cases included sex, slander, libel, and a motley variety of suits such as debts, divorce, foreclosure, fraud, property issues, personal damage suits, and wills. Lincoln's everyday cases illustrate the diversity of his law practice as well as the commonplace litigation being contested.

During his legal career Lincoln handled at least sixty-eight slander cases; thirty-four for plaintiffs and thirty-four for defendants. Libel is similar to slander except the malicious defamation is expressed in printing or writing, or by signs and pictures, tending to expose someone to public hatred, contempt, or ridicule. Antebellum lawyers worked within the following slander guidelines:

> Slander is defined as the speaking of base and defamatory words tending to prejudice another in his reputation, office, trade, business, or means of livelihood. The essential elements are a false and defamatory statement concerning another, an unprivileged communication; fault amounting at least to negligence on the part of the person making the statement; and either actionability of the statement, irrespective of harm, or the existence of special harm.

Two Bloomington physicians were involved in a slander suit. On the recommendation of his lawyer, Dr. Julius Lehman wrote to Lincoln to retain him in the case of *Lehman v. Schroeder.* Lincoln's reply was concise: "Mark me down on your side." No lawyer is listed for Schroeder.

While the specific nature of the slander in this case is not known, Lehman sued Schroeder in the McLean County Circuit Court. On Saturday, January 8, 1859, the court docket recorded the outcome:

> And now at this day come the parties, by their attorneys, and here in open court make argument the judgment be rendered herein against said defendant for the sum of five thousand dollars. And that execution be stayed herein for three months. and thereupon comes the plaintiff and here in open court remits to said defendant the sum of four thousand nine hundred and fifty dollars. It is therefore considered by the court that said plaintiff recover of said defendant the sum of fifty dollars damages and also his costs herein expended. and that he have execution therefor. And it is further ordered by the court that execution herein be stayed for three months.

This practice of the winning party remitting most of the money awarded back to the loser occurred frequently in the slander suits. Evidently, the suing parties were more concerned with winning to regain their good names rather than with receiving only a fraction of the monetary award. Lincoln used this device in quite a few of his cases to render justice.

Frequently, charges of slander involved gossip and idle talk about improper sexual activities. During the cases that combined slander and sex, Lincoln demonstrated that he was by no means a prudish lawyer. Lincoln's slander cases addressed adultery, bestiality, fornication, and prostitution. In court, witnesses recited the specific slander with relish and graphically described the detailed sexual acts using explicit sexual behavior language.

Lincoln & Herndon represented three male clients who sued for slander because they were accused of bestiality. A sow, a cow, and a female dog were the alleged recipients of sexual attention from the respective plaintiffs in these law suits.

During the June 1848 term of the Christian County Circuit Court in Taylorville, William Torrence sued Newton Galloway for *trespass on the case* for slander. On August 1, 1847, Torrence said that Galloway spoke or published "false, scandalous, malicious, and defamatory words [accusing Torrence] of an infamous crime against nature with a beast." Lincoln & Herndon represented Torrence, and Silas W. Robbins defended Galloway. Judge Samuel H. Treat presided. In preparing the plaintiff's declaration, Lincoln colorfully and explicitly quoted exactly what Galloway said in public discourse with Aaron Vandeveer and "diverse good and worthy citizens." "He [Torrence] caught my old sow and fucked her as long as he could.... He knocked up my old sow and it is now bellying down and will soon have some young *bills*... [Torrence] had been and was guilty of the infamous crime against nature with a beast." Obviously, Galloway intended a pun on Torrence's first name in talking about the impregnated sow's litter of young Bills. Lincoln wrote that the "false, scandalous, malicious and defamatory words by the said defendant... plaintiff hath been injured and so greatly injured to the damage of said plaintiff of one thousand dollars and therefore he brings this suit." Later, Torrence dismissed the case and paid the court costs. Lincoln & Herndon received $25 for their legal services.

David L. Thompson sued George W. Henline for slander in the September 1851 term of the McLean County Circuit Court in Bloomington. Thompson requested $3,000 for damages caused by the slander. Lincoln, William H. Holmes, and John M. Scott represented Thompson, while Asahel Gridley and John T. Stuart defended Henline. Judge David Davis presided. In his defense, Henline pled justification for the slander because he spoke the truth. Thompson actually "did commit the infamous crime against nature with a beast...did have sexual intercourse or carnal knowledge with a cow." This suit was tried twice and each time there was a hung jury. Both parties agreed to dismiss the case after the second trial and each party paid his own costs.

Lincoln assisted Asahel Gridley during the 1852 April term of the Woodford County Circuit Court in Metamora. Beverly Davidson sued George McGhilton for *trespass on the case* for slander that ruined his "good name, fame and credit." In public discourse with "good and worthy citizens," McGhilton "falsely and maliciously charged him [Davidson] of an infamous crime against nature with a beast, to wit a female dog bitch." McGhilton contrived and "wickedly and maliciously intended to bring Davidson into public scandal, infamy and disgrace" amongst his neighbors. In their declaration, Davidson's lawyers explicitly repeated the "false, slanderous, malicious and defamatory words [that McGhilton used] in the presence and hearing of good and worthy citizens." Reacting to the "infamous crime against nature," Davidson suffered great distress and the "good and worthy citizens" refused to have any transactions with him. On behalf of the plaintiff, Gridley and Lincoln requested subpoenas for witnesses: Benjamin Kelly, Old man Upshaw, Francis Upshaw, Thomas S. Davidson, William J. Davidson, and John Arterberry. Gridley and Lincoln described Davidson as "a good, true, honest, just and faithful citizen of the State of Illinois…known to be a person of good name, fame and credit." McGhilton defaulted and failed to present a defense. Judge Davis ruled for Davidson and ordered a writ of enquiry. Gridley and Lincoln won for their client and the jury awarded Davidson $2,000 in damages.

In the September 1851 term of the Tazewell County Circuit Court in Pekin, Lincoln & Herndon defended Milden Kitchell and his wife Elizabeth against a charge of *trespass on the case* for slandering May Ann Jacobus. Edward Jones represented Jacobus and Judge Davis presided. In her sworn affidavit, Jacobus claimed that Elizabeth "graphically, falsely and maliciously, without any cause of justification…reputed that affiant [Jacobus] was a whore, that she got her living by whoring and that she and her sisters got their bonnets and fine clothing by whoring." Damages in the sum of $4000 were requested. In entering a plea and demurrer, Lincoln repeated the slander and said that "Elizabeth is not guilty of the speaking of said words in manner and form" and the evidence "is not sufficient in law" for the plaintiff's charges. He pleaded *actio non* that the plaintiff ought not to have or maintain her aforesaid action against the defendants. In an affidavit prepared by Jones, Jacobus swore that Milden Kitchell had valuable property and "will either leave the state or place his property out of his hands " to avoid her recovering anything in her suit. She requested that the Kitchells "be compelled to give special bail." Each of the defendants posted their individual surety bonds. Jones subpoenaed twelve male witness to testify for Jacobus. In view of the overwhelming witnesses for Jacobus, Lincoln persuaded his clients to make open denials in the Tazewell County Circuit Court that "they or either of them ever made any charge against the chastity of the plaintiff…neither of them has ever had any knowledge, information, or reasonable belief, of any want of chastity on the part of the plaintiff." Both parties reached an agreement with the Kitchells agreeing not to make any allegations about Jacobus's chastity. This public affirmation of Jacobus's good reputation repaired her standing in the community and settled the case. With the consent of both parties, Davis dismissed the case and sought court costs from the plaintiff. Milden Kitchell came to the support of Jacobus. He swore that he knew Jacobus "for a considerable length of time and has not known of her having any property whatever beyond her wearing apparel…said plaintiff is wholly unable to pay the costs in this suit."

In another case, Dr. Francis Regnier disparaged Eliza Cabot's moral laxity and gossiped to townspeople that she engaged in fornication with Elijah Taylor. Cabot, a young schoolteacher originally from the New England area, brought an action of slander against Regnier. She sued for $5000 in damages in the November 1843 term of the Menard County Circuit Court. In his pretrial declaration, Regnier said that Taylor mischievously "rogued" Cabot. He was "after skin and he got it [with Cabot]… the captain has got some skin there as much as he wanted." Both Cabot and Taylor denied the allegation. Lincoln, Thomas L. Harris, and Edward D. Baker represented Cabot. Silas W. Robbins defended Regnier. Judge Samuel H. Treat presided when the case was heard by a jury in Petersburg. In a letter to Herndon, Samuel C. Parks, a lawyer from Logan County, commented on the case: "...and his [Lincoln's] denunciation of a defendant [Regnier] who had slandered a small, friendless schoolmistress, was probably as bitter a Philippic as was ever uttered." Lincoln knew Regnier from when they both lived in New Salem.

After hearing testimony from about twenty witnesses, the jury foreman rendered the verdict: "We the jurors find a verdict in favor of the plaintiff of twelve dollars and costs." Shocked by the meager award, Cabot's lawyers moved to set aside the verdict. Lincoln wrote and filed five affidavits, including his own, alleging jury misconduct. Bennett Abell's affidavit stated that "he did not believe Miss Cabot ought to recover much, if anything, off of Dr. Regnier." When Abell made that remark, he was a sitting juror in the ongoing trial of *Cabot v. Regnier*. On the basis of the affidavits, Baker moved for a new trial. That motion was granted as well as a change of venue to Morgan County Circuit Court for the new trial.

On March 14 and 15, 1844, a new trial took place in Jacksonville with Judge Samuel D. Lockwood presiding and the lawyers and the witnesses remaining the same. Lincoln wrote and filed exceptions to the defendant's deposition and a demurrer to his amended plea. On the next day, the case was tried before a jury. Maria Bennett, Cabot's landlady at her Petersburg hotel, gave damaging evidence in her March 12, 1844 deposition. Supposedly, Cabot's acts of fornication were committed at this hotel. A sampling of Bennett's questions and answers support Regnier's allegations:

> Q: Do you not think that the conduct which came under your view between Mr. Elijah B. Taylor and Miss Eliza S. Cabot was highly improvident for a virtuous female?
> A: I certainly did.

Q: Do you believe Miss E. S. Cabot to be a lady of veracity?

A: I did not.

Q: Did not her conduct appear while living with you to substantiate the charge which Francis Regnier has against her as regards Mr. E. Taylor?

A: I never approved, from the first, of her conduct with Mr. Taylor, but the latter part of the time fully convinced me of the impropriety of it, and left not a shadow of a doubt on my mind of the charge advanced against her by Francis Regnier.

Q: Did you not some time previously to her leaving your house request her to do so?

A: I did so.

Regnier's lawyers tried to enter evidence about a specific act of fornication by Cabot. On the technical grounds that the evidence contradicted Regnier's plea of general denial, Lincoln was able to exclude that particular fornication evidence. After hearing the case, this jury found for Cabot and awarded her $1,600 in damages. In seeking to void the award, Regnier alleged that the "jury separated contrary to law." His lawyers contended that John D. Bowen, one of the jurors, left the deliberations and was approached by the plaintiff's side. Lincoln responded by submitting Bowen's affidavit in which he swore that he "went out to find a place for his horse, and while going and returning and during his absence he spoke to on one." Judge Lockwood denied the motion to void the award and the judgment stood.

Unsuccessful in voiding the award, Regnier appealed to the supreme court of Illinois with a writ of error citing erroneous exclusion of certain evidence Regnier introduced concerning Eliza. Martha Cogdill testified for Regnier that she saw Taylor in Cabot's bedroom "at a late hour in the night, she sitting in the window in her night clothes, no other person being in the room." On Lincoln's technical objections, Judge Lockwood excluded Cogdill's testimony. Regnier's lawyers also cited the exclusion of evidence of Eliza's bad character.

This appeal was heard in the December 1845 term of the supreme court of Illinois. Regnier was represented by Robbins, A. K. Smede, and William Thomas. Cabot had Lincoln, Harris, and Stephen T. Logan as her lawyers. Justice Norman H. Purple wrote the opinion of the court. By this time Cabot was married to Erastus C. Torrey. Purple said that there was some conflict about how much evidence a defendant in a slander case can offer to cast guilt on the plaintiff. He said that "by the weight of authority, now to be, that where a defendant does not justify, he may mitigate damages in two ways only; first, by showing the general bad character of the plaintiff, and second, by showing any circumstances which tend to disprove malice, but do not tend to prove the truth of the charge." Neither of the two ways applied in this case and the court ruled that Regnier's evidence was properly excluded. Regnier's lawyers asked a witness about the general character of Cabot for chastity. He responded that all he knew resulted from conversations with his brother and two sisters. Purple made an emphatic legal point: "In my judgment, character is too valuable to permit it, in a court of justice to be destroyed, or even sullied by a report derived from a majority of three persons only. It is general, and not partial, reputation in the neighborhood where the party resides which, in legal contemplation, establishes character for good or evil.... No doubt can be entertained but that the court decided correctly in rejecting this evidence." In concluding, Purple was firm: "Upon the whole, the court is of the opinion that there is no error in the record, and that the judgment of the circuit court should be affirmed with costs."

Ultimately the courts found in favor of Cabot, awarding her $1,600. After reviewing the information about the *Cabot v. Regnier* case, John J. Duff, a practicing New York lawyer for more than thirty years and an author of a book on Lincoln's law career, wondered if there was a modicum of truth to Regnier's charges. He suspected that Cabot was not quite the innocent young maiden Lincoln made her out to be. Specific to this case, Duff came to an irreverent conclusion. He was sometime "struck by the shockingly irreverent thought that Lincoln would appear to have been a most dangerous adversary, even when, to put it politely, the justice of his client's cause was not readily apparent." Like any conscientious lawyer, Lincoln put forth his best effort regardless of what he thought of the client's guilt or innocence.

Lincoln & Herndon continued to legally duel with Regnier. In the May 1855 term of the Menard County Circuit Court, Regnier sued James Druet to collect a past due $300 account for his "labor, care, diligence & attendance" in rendering medical services. William H. Herndon and Thomas L. Harris appeared for Druet, while Albert I. Brooks and Augustus K. Riggin acted for Regnier. Judge David M. Woodson presided during the trial. After hearing the evidence and the lawyers, the jury delivered their verdict: "We of the jury find for the plaintiff two hundred and sixty-two dollars and sixty-two cents his damages" plus his costs. While the jurors obviously did some calculation to arrive at the odd dollar amount of damages, the jury's verdict does not explain their machinations. Herndon quickly moved to set aside the judgment. Judge Woodson granted the motion and continued the case to the next term of the court. There is no information about the final outcome of this case.

Dr. Charles Winn sued Frederick Stipp on April 19, 1841 to collect a $32.75 debt for medicine and services. Winn subpoenaed F. S. Harrison, Charles Maltby, Catherine Stipp, and David Wheeler. Stipp summoned Nancy Griffin. After hearing all the evidence, Justice of the Peace David Montgomery ruled: "it appeared there was due from the defendant to the plaintiff twenty-eight dollars. Judgment for $28.00 and cost of suit" bringing the award to $33.60. Stipp appealed to the DeWitt County Circuit Court on May 11, 1841. During the October 1841 term of the court, Winn spent $5.81 while Stipp spent $5.80 in fees including two days for his witness, James Lemon, at fifty cents per day. In the May 1842 term of the court, the fee book showed that Winn spent $12.53 for assorted court fees including one day for witness Charles Maltby at fifty cents per day. Some time after this docket entry,

Stipp dismissed his appeal. In all probability, the parties settled out of court. Lincoln wrote an account of the case, but his role in the suit is unknown and no other attorneys are noted in the documents.

Dr. Squire Powell sued Iven Worth in the court of Justice of the Peace Josiah B. Smith in November 1845 to collect an unsettled debt for $26.75. This debt was for medical services to Worth, his children and his wife. Powell made seventeen visits to Worth's home between December 18, 1843 and December 5, 1844. Usually, each of Powell's medical visits cost one dollar. If medicine was given to the patient, the cost went up twenty-five or fifty cents. On December 5, 1844, Powell charged five dollars for "delivering wife." On January 17, 1845, Powell noted that he received one dollar from Worth. In a later bill for the same services Powell listed five dollars for "delivering lady" and added $5.38 for "medicine & reducing tumor for lady" on January 27, 1845 and $10 for "sewing and dressing boy's lip" on February 24. That brought Worth's debt up to $42.13.

After a trial, the jury found for Worth: "We the jury find for the defendant—judgment four dollars 66 cents." This judgment covered Worth's court costs of $3.16 plus fifty cents per day for three witnesses. Powell retained Lincoln and appealed to the Menard County Circuit Court. Judge Samuel H. Treat presided and Thomas L. Harris represented Worth during the trial in June 1846. Lincoln's old friend from New Salem, Dr. Regnier provided the surety for Worth. After hearing from witnesses John G. Douglass, Colbey Knapp, Jacob Loutzenhiser, William Sammons, Thomas Simpson, and Jacob Wing, the court affirmed the judgment of Justice of the Peace Smith. Worth's court costs totaled seventeen dollars and fifty-three cents including fifty cents per day for four witnesses serving at the trial for seven days. Two of the witnesses received five cents per mile for their travel to the court: sixty-six miles for three dollars thirty cents. Powell's costs were $23.00.

Almon L. Robinson owed Alfred Cassell $100. In turn, Cassell transferred the $100 debt to Dr. Roland Crocker for medical services rendered. Robinson failed to pay the debt. When Robinson did not pay, Cassell became the nominal plaintiff and Crocker the true plaintiff. in a suit against Robinson before Justice of the Peace Thornton Parker in the Woodford County court in June 1843. Parker ruled for Cassell and awarded him $65. Robinson was unable to appeal in time because Parker failed to handle matters promptly. Filing a *writ of certiorari*, Robinson sought to command "said justice [Parker] to certify to the Circuit Court for Woodford County a true and perfect transcript of said judgment and all proceedings relating thereto." At first, Robinson petitioned James Robinson, no relation, probate justice of the peace for Woodford County. He explained the reasons for his not meeting the twenty-day deadline for filing an appeal and offered an appeal bond as security. After the *writ of certiorari* was quashed by the court, Robinson petitioned "the Hon. Samuel H. Treat, associate justice of the Supreme Court of the State of Illinois and Judge of the Circuit Court of Woodford County" on September 15, 1843. Robinson pled his case to Treat: "said judgment is unjust and erroneous...said services were not rendered on the request or employment of your petitioner and were not rendered for him in any manner...can show these facts on trial...[petitioner offered] good & ample security to take an appeal.... Your petitioner therefore prays that a writ of certiorari may be granted." Treat signed a notice that Robinson posted an appeal bond of $130 with the court clerk. During the April 1844 term of the Woodford County Circuit Court in Metamora, Treat heard the case. Cassell and Crocker retained Lincoln. William H. Leonard and John S. Holland represented Robinson. William Blanchard, Jared Keyes, Charles Molitor and Justice of the Peace Parker appeared as witnesses. Evidently, Robinson showed "these facts on trial" and convinced the jurors that he did not owe Cassell $100. This time the jury found for Robinson.

In the October 1851 term of the Vermilion County Circuit Court, Dr. William Fithian sued George W. Casseday for libel and asked for $25,000 in damages. Fithian and Casseday each owned a competing seminary in Danville and were bitter rivals who frequently engaged in personal quarrels. At one point, Casseday wrote a scathing article attacking Fithian. This printed article combined zealous unmistakable political overtones along with the libelous calumny, dishonor, and ignominy. A headstrong man of considerable means, Fithian was a political ally of Lincoln and frequently sought his legal counsel. Lincoln, Usher F. Linder, and Oliver L. Davis represented Fithian. Linder was a former Illinois attorney general and legislator and Davis was then a state legislator. In easily legible handwriting and colorful language, Davis prepared a fourteen-page declaration specifying that Casseday did "falsely, wickedly and maliciously compose and publish of and concerning said plaintiff, a certain false, scandalous, malicious and defamatory libel in which he said: 'Now suppose, Doctor, I was to ask you if you ever abandoned the corpse of your wife at Paris [IL] and left her to be buried at the mercy of others.'"

Casseday knew that Fithian went to Georgetown to care for his sick son. However, his son was better when Fithian arrived. Subsequently, Fithian went to Danville before returning to Paris. Fithian's accounting of the events included Casseday's vicious political attack along with his objectionable moral interpretation of what happened:

And now, fellow citizens, Whigs and Democrats, I ask you, would Fithian have laid down and slept securely if a political election had been on hand in place of a dead wife, and his presence had been wanting at Paris? I fancy I hear the answer coming up in thunder tones from every voter in the District, No Sir! He would have mounted his horse and with energy and perseverance almost superhuman he would have faced fire and tempest in order to be there.... No, Doctor, soon as the eyes of her you had sworn never to forsake were closed upon you, soon as her lips were sealed in death, ere the warm current of life had settled cold about her heart, you hastened to leave the spot where her sickness had detained you for a few unwilling days; surely Doctor you must feel the burning fires of shame pass over your countenance at the remembrance of such inhumanity.... Go and cast yourself down at her grave, water the green sod with tears of regret and penitence, then perchance Heaven may forgive you for abandoning the lifeless body of her that now lies in yonder graveyard. Fellow Citizens, Dr. Fithian should be frowned upon by every good and virtuous man and woman for thus forsaking the corpse of her whom he had sworn at the alter of Heaven to love, cherish and keep in his inner heart.

Casseday's legal team included Ward Hill Lamon, John H. Murphy, Joseph Peters, and Edward A. Hannegan. Recently from Virginia, Lamon became Lincoln's Danville law partner one year after this trial and later President Lincoln appointed him marshal of the District of Columbia. Earlier, Murphy served in the Illinois legislature with Lincoln and he and Peters were prominent Danville lawyers. Hannegan came from Indiana, was famed as an eloquent orator and previously was a US senator and representative. Judge Davis presided and some time after the trial wrote about Hannegan in a letter to his wife, Sarah: "He was a man of high passion and carried a knife [unfortunately]... last Friday in a drunken frolic he killed his own brother-in-law at his own house.... Oh, the evils of intemperance & the horrors of an ungovernable temper."

Ninety-five witnesses were subpoenaed for the trial. After examination of the witnesses, the courtroom resounded for many hours with the ringing voices and emphatic gesticulations of the legal orators addressing the jurors. Afterward, Judge Davis instructed the jury and they retired. Shortly, the jury returned with a verdict for Fithian and awarded him $547.90 in damages. There is no indication of how the jurors arrived at the odd dollar amount for damages. Casseday paid promptly and for several years thereafter listed on his personal property tax form: "The character of Dr. Fithian, $547.90, which I bought and paid for."

With a few technological innovations, *Grubb v. John Frink & Co.* could be on the docket of any court in America today. This case involved commercial transportation, vehicle safety, medical injuries, medical care, and loss of services. On December 7, 1851, Samuel Grubb, a bridge builder by occupation, was a passenger on a stage coach trip in Illinois from Rushville to Frederickville. At four o'clock on a very dark morning the coach departed from the Rushville tavern, where the owner was the stage coach agent. Despite the darkness, the coach had no lamps. As the coach passed near a creek, it overturned and caused serious injury to Grubb. His injuries were severe enough to incapacitate him and to require recuperation under a physician's care. Grubb was confined to bed and unable to transact any business. Grubb retained Lincoln & Herndon to sue the stage coach company owners, John Frink and Martin O. Walker, for $1,000 in damages in an action of trespass on the case. Stephen T. Logan, Lincoln's former law partner, represented the stage coach company. On August 13, 1852, Lincoln wrote, signed his firm's name, and filed Grubb's declaration in this personal damage suit. In the declaration, Lincoln turned Grubb's allegations into legal language:

> said defendant...conducted themselves so carelessly, negligently and unskillfully...through the carelessness negligence, unskillfulness and default of themselves and their servants... said plaintiff...was greatly cut, bruised, and wounded...broken bones... and was very sick, weak, and distempered... for a long space of time...prevented from transacting and attending to his necessary and lawful affairs...deprived of great gains, profits and advantages...obliged to expend a large sum of money... plaintiff says he is injured and has sustained damages to the amount of one thousand dollars and therefore brings his suit.

Robert S. Blackwell, the other passenger in the coach, was deposed on February 3, 1853. Lincoln wrote parts of Blackwell's affidavit and had it sworn before Judge Samuel H. Treat. Blackwell confirmed that it was "very dark and that there were no lamps or lights of any kind about the coach." After the coach overturned, Blackwell said that Grubb "complained of great pain...seemed to be too much injured to proceed... when day light came, it was quite obvious that the over-turning of the coach might have been easily avoided if common coach lamps or lights had been with the coach; the driver complained at the time that he had been trying, but could not get the agent to furnish him with lights."

On February 7, 1853, Lincoln wrote and swore his own affidavit to take depositions from William Danner, the stage coach driver, Lewis Seligman, the tavern keeper and stage coach agent in Rushville, and Dr. Robert C. Hall, the physician who cared for Grubb. Lincoln personally redelivered the notice to take the depositions of Seligman and Hall to Lewis D. Ervin, clerk of the Schyuler County Circuit Court in Rushville. He also included a notice to take William Danner's deposition on March 15, 1853.

On February 21, 1853, Seligman and Hall were deposed in Rushville. Seligman said he kept a tavern in Rushville and was a local agent of the stage coach company. As an agent, he kept a book listing the names of passengers and the fares collected. Grubb paid fifty cents to travel the nine miles to Frederickville and Blackwell paid three dollars to go to Springfield. Seligman confirmed that the stage had four horses and left before daylight when it was very dark with passengers Grubb and Blackwell and Danner driving. Pertinent questions and answers affirmed Grubb's complaint:

> Q: Were there or were there not any lights attached to the stage that morning?
> A: There were not.
> Q: When did you next see Mr. Grubb, the plaintiff, after he left your tavern on the morning of the 7th December 1851?
> A: In about one hour he was brought back to my house apparently much injured.
> Q: How long did he remain at your house?
> A: From the 7th of December to the 27th of the same month.

Seligman said that Grubb was feeble and confined to his bed in his room. He said that Dr. Robert C. Hall attended to Grubb during his confinement. When he left the tavern on December 27, Grubb paid Seligman $33.70 for his stay.

Hall was deposed in Rushville along with Seligman on February 21, 1853. He graduated from the medical school of Maryland University in 1828 and practiced medicine for about twenty-five years in Baltimore and Rushville. As a medical expert, Hall's questions and answers specify the bodily injuries Grubb suffered:

Q: In what condition did you find the said plaintiff and what was the nature and extent of his injuries?

A: When called, I found him in bed much bruised and on examination found three of his ribs broken. He seemed to be suffering extreme pain and continued to do so for some days. It seemed as if he had been thrown onto some hard body or substance or had something heavy thrown on him.

Q: How long did you attend upon plaintiff on that occasion?

A: From the time of the accident til he left, which was about twenty days.

Q: During the time of the plaintiff's confinement how often did you visit him?

A: During the first week I visited him from two to three times a day and subsequently once a day.

Q: Was or was not the plaintiff entirely restored when he left Rushville?

A: He was not entirely recovered but such was his anxiety to get away to attend to his business that he insisted upon leaving.

Q: State your opinion as a medical man whether the plaintiff will or will not in the ordinary course of nature be restored to the same physical strength and vigor which he possessed prior to the accident for which you treated him?

A: If a young man I would say yes but considering his age I think it doubtful.

Hall concluded by stating that his bill was about $35. Grubb paid in full before he left Rushville.

William Danner was deposed for the plaintiff on March 15, 1853 in Beardstown. He was a stage coach driver for John Frink & Company from March to December 15, 1851 and was driving the day Grubb was injured. His other passenger that day was Robert S. Blackwell. Several questions and answers were particularly relevant regarding safety:

Q: Would you or not have been able to have avoided the accident had you been provided with lamps or lanterns?

A: I would have been able to have avoided the accident had I have been supplied with lamps, of that I have no doubt.

Q: Is or is it not usual and necessary for safety to have lamps or lanterns on stage coaches that do travel on night routes?

A: It is always usual and necessary to safety.

Q: Did you or not at any time call the attention of the defendants or the agent to the subject of having lamps or lanterns on your route?

A: I frequently did.

John Frink & Company failed to appear in Sangamon County Circuit Court and the court ruled for Grubb. However, the court set aside the default judgment. After that action, both parties reached an agreement and the court then dismissed the case.

On October 5, 1854, J. C. Johnson & Brother sued the Illinois Central Railroad in a *replevin* action for improper detention of a shipment of thirteen boxes, one case, and one cask of medical supplies valued at $300. A *replevin* suit is an action wherein an owner or anyone entitled to repossession of personal property may recover those goods and chattels from one who wrongfully has those goods in his possession. James B. McKinley and Lawrence Weldon represented the plaintiff company and the owners, Jonathan C. Johnson and George Johnson. McKinley and Weldon filed a declaration in DeWitt County Circuit Court complaining that the railroad "wrongfully detained the goods and chattels...and the said plaintiffs say they are injured and have sustained damages to the amount of three hundred dollars and therefore they bring their suit." Judge Davis presided in DeWitt County Circuit Court when the case was heard. Lincoln and Clifton H. Moore acted in behalf of the railroad. In response to the charges, Moore and Lincoln filed and signed pleas arguing that the railroad "did not wrongfully detain the goods of the plaintiffs, in manner and form, as in the declaration alleged...the goods mentioned in the declaration were, then and there, the property of the defendant, and not the property of the plaintiff... plaintiffs were not lawfully entitled to the procession of the goods, in the declaration mentioned." Lincoln contended that the medical supplies were the property of the railroad in their Clinton freight house until the goods were delivered, as addressed, to J. C. Johnson & Brother in Monticello, Illinois. Davis agreed and ordered that the chattels were Illinois Central Railroad property and assessed damages of $21.34 against J. C. Johnson & Brother. For his legal services in this case and a number of other suits for the Illinois Central Railroad, Lincoln billed James F. Joy, the railroad's legal counsel:

> Dear Sir: I have to day drawn on you in favor of the McLean County Bank, or rather it's cashier, for one hundred and fifty dollars. This is intended as a fee for all services done by me for the Illinois Central Railroad, since last September, within the counties of McLean and DeWitt. Within that term, and in the two counties, I have assisted for the Road, in at least fifteen cases (I believe, one or two more) and I have concluded

to bump them off at ten dollars a case. With this explanation, I shall be obliged if you will honor the draft.

When Lincoln went to Cincinnati for the Manny case, his letter had not reached Joy. He wrote again on September 19 and explained that the draft on the bank and the letter did not arrive together. Lincoln repeated his explanation of the fee and received his money shortly thereafter.

In another case, two physicians, Josiah T. Betts and Elijah S. Frazer, formed a partnership firm on October 8, 1841 "as joint dealers in the sale of drugs and medicines, each to be entitled to one half equal part of the profits...[and] each should dedicate his best efforts and his time to the business and concerns of said partnership." Both physicians agreed to contribute money or medicine to the endeavor. About eighteen months later, on Match 23, 1843, they agreed to dissolve the partnership. No resolution was reached about the dissolution of the partnership as claims and counter claims clouded the issue. Betts claimed that he "paid large sums of money for the necessary expenses of conducting the business of said firm...particularity the sum of three hundred and fifty dollars to one Thomas J. V. Owen...and the sum of three hundred dollars to one Charles Mount...while necessarily employed as agents and assistants in and about the business and concerns of said co-partnership." "From time to time [Betts] applied to [Frazer] in a friendly manner and requested him to come to a full, fair and just account with respect to said partnership...[Frazer] absolutely refused to comply with such requests" to settle the accounts.

Betts employed Charles R. Welles and Antrim Campbell to sue Frazer in Sangamon County Circuit Court in Springfield, "said court sitting in chancery." Essentially, the tribunal became a court of equity to consider the partnership rather than a court of law. Lincoln & Herndon joined with Stephen T. Logan to represent Frazer. Initially, two justices of the peace adjudicated the litigation:

John C. Sprigg and William Lavely. Moving to the higher court, this case continued for several years.

Betts charged that Frazer "hath received the sum of one thousand dollars...beyond his due proportion of the partnership profits and property...collected from debtors without accounting...never paid for use of said partnership said sum of five hundred dollars or any part thereof as aforesaid agreed to be paid by him." Continuing, Betts claimed that Frazer did not "contribute his best exertions and efforts...but on the contrary did neglect [the business]...more than three fourths of the medical and surgical business of said partnership was done by plaintiff in consequence of such negligence in ability or in attention on the part of said defendant."

In answering the bill to settle the partnership, Lincoln first agreed that Betts and Frazer did set up a partnership with each to advance $500 to begin the business, to pay half the expenses, do half the work, and receive half of the profits. "Respondent [Frazer], in good faith, intending to perform his part of said agreement, did, a short time after and out of his own funds, pay to E. B. Pense & Brothers the sum of $250 upon a bill for medicines purchased in New York, and which medicines were used by the said co-partnership in their practice." There appeared to be some confusion about the actual content of the partnership agreement. Frazer contended that the contract was never read by both parties, that the terms were not specified in conversations and that Betts may not have signed the document. Furthermore, the partnership agreement was missing. "Respondent further states that he never removed said paper from the office aforesaid; that he has never seen it elsewhere, and does not know whether it is in existence or not." Frazer denied that "Owen and Mount, or either of them, were ever employed by said co-partnership.... Owen was a relative of said complainant...both were there as students of medicine." Lincoln repudiated "all allegations in said Bill which were not herein admitted": He denied that Betts brought a large stack of medicines into the co-partnership; that Frazer did not contribute his share of the expenses; that Frazer ever refused to settle the accounts; that Betts's practice contributed highly valued "good will" to the business; and on the contrary, Frazer was injured in his professional and private reputation and suffered pecuniarily. Alleging a counter claim, Frazer charged that Betts "appropriated to himself between four and five hundred dollars beyond his just share of said co-partnership effects." Frazer did agree that he and Betts were to put additional money into the partnership to purchase drugs for resale, but Betts failed to provide his share of the funds.

With these conflicting claims by the parties involved, Lincoln arranged for the deposition of a witness to provide evidence for his client. On April 4, 1849, Norman D. Spotswood was deposed by Justice of the Peace William Lavely in Springfield. Spotswood was a former medical student in the office of Betts and Frazer. Lincoln's questions highlighted the major differences in the suit:

> Q: Did you or not read medicine in the office of Doctors Betts and Frazer while they were in partnership?
> A: I did.
> Q: Who was with you in said office at the same time?
> A: Thomas Owen, a nephew of Doctor Betts, Charles Mount and William Foster.
> Q: In what capacity were said Owen and Mount studying in said office?
> A: As students of medicine.
> Q: By whom were their studies directed? By whom were they principally instructed?
> A: They were students of both, but were mostly instructed by Doctor Frazer.
> Q: What is the custom of the county as to a physician paying, or receiving pay from students of medicine?
> A: It is the usual custom for the students or his parents to pay the physician something, and not for the physician to pay the student anything.

Q: Did you ever hear anything about Owen or Mount being employed at wages?

A: Never, never.

Q: Did you ever see anything performed by Mount or Own that would be deserving of wages?

A: I do not recollect anything that they performed except what is usual for students of medicine.

Q: Did you or not see these young men engaged about on other business in the shop except such as usual for students of medicine?

A: I did not. I frequently did the same things that they did.

Q: What is customary for students of medicine to do while they are at the office?

A: To attend to the duties of the office in preparing prescriptions, and keeping the books if requested. Preparing the prescriptions I consider to be part of their instruction.

Q: How long were you reading medicine in the office of doctors Betts and Frazer?

A: Something over a year and until the dissolution of the partnership.

Q: State whether Doctor Frazer was or was not there attending to the shop as physicians usually do waiting to attend to business?

A: So far as I have any recollection he was there as much as physicians usually are and when he went out to attend to business he usually left word where he could be found.

Q: State whether Doctor Frazer did or not take long trips to the country to see patients while he and Doctor Betts were in partnership?

A: He did. I frequently went with him myself.

Q: Which of the two did most of the country practice that required riding?

A: During the sickly months both were very busy. I cannot say which did the most.

Q: Are you now a regular graduate of medicine?
A: I am.

In his cross-examination, Welles tried to show that Spotswood was obligated to Betts. Spotswood allowed Betts and Frazer to use his physiology and pathology textbooks, valued at $40-$50, in lieu of compensation for instruction. Foster's father gave Betts a horse and Foster boarded with Betts. Welles questioned which medical students did the most work and pinpointed relevant questions:

Q: Did or not the firm keep a larger stock of medicine than physicians usually keep?
A: They kept a larger quantity that physicians usually keep in the city, but not larger than is kept by some of the country physicians.
Q: Did or did not Owen and Mount frequently prepare medicine for sale beside putting up prescriptions?
A: They prepared a few medicines sometimes. When a man came in and wanted a box of pills, they prepared them and other medicines which were used in their practice.
Q: Is it or not customary for physicians to send their prescriptions to an apothecary shop to be put up?
A: It is sometimes, when they have no shops of their own.

Lincoln concluded that Frazer realized that the partnership was a mistake after contributing large amounts of money. This case continued for several years without any resolution. When Betts died, the court dismissed the case.

Benjamin Burt charged that James F. Jennings assaulted him. He hired John H. Murphy and William D. Somers to represent him in Champaign County Circuit Court in Urbana. In Burt's declaration, Murphy and Somers detailed a colorful blow-by-blow account of the events that occurred on April 8, 1852. "Then and there with great force and violence [Jennings] seized and laid hold of the said plaintiff...with a certain pocket knife...opened in his hand did give and strike the said plaintiff with a great many stab cuts and blows on or about his neck and face near the eye and other parts of his person...plaintiff then and there did bleed and lose a great quantity of blood.... [Burt was] bruised and wounded and his eye sight [sic] much impaired and injured and [he] became and was sick, sore, lame, disabled...and so remains and continued for a long space of time from then to hither...plaintiff suffered and underwent great pain and was hindered and prevented from performing and transacting his necessary affairs...was forced and obliged to and did necessarily pay out and expend a large sum of money, to wit the sum of ten dollars...endeavoring to be cured of the cuts, stabs, bruises and wounds, sickness, severe loss of blood and injury to his eye sight [sic]." Burt charged that Jennings attacked him again that same day. "[Jennings] with force and arms made another assault on the said plaintiff, and then and there again beat, bruised, stab cut and wounded him insomuch that his life was then and there really despaired of." Burt's lawyers sued Jennings for *trespass vi et armis* and requested $1,000 in damages. Jennings retained Lincoln to defend him and Lincoln replied to the charges. Lincoln argued that Burt's lawsuit should not be allowed *actio non* because Jennings acted in self defense. "With force and arms [Burt] made an assault upon the said defendant and would then and there have beat , bruised, and ill-treated the said defendant, if he had not immediately defended himself against the plaintiff...as he lawfully might for the cause aforesaid, and in doing so did necessarily and unavoidably commit the supposed trespasses in the declaration mentioned." Murphy and Somers denied that Burt provoked the assault saying that nothing in Jenning's plea precluded Burt's action: "Defendant says *precludi non* because he says that the said defendant at the time, when he [Jennings] of his own wrong, and without cause by him [Burt] in the said plea alleged, committed the trespass in the declaration mentioned, in manner and form, as in said declaration alleged" In closing, Somers and Murphy said that the plaintiff puts himself upon the county for justice. Lincoln added a sentence on the bottom of Burt's response. "And the defendant doth the like." In a strange sense of frontier justice, the jury found for Burt and awarded him the grand sum of five cents. Perhaps, the jury believed that both men were guilty of instigating the fracas.

Between 1837 and 1861, Lincoln and his law partners handled 131 divorce cases in seventeen Illinois counties. Their female clients sued their husbands for divorce on a variety of grounds: adultery, bigamy, cruelty, desertion, drunkenness, fraud, and impotence. In eighty-two (63 percent) of Lincoln's cases, women were the plaintiff and the courts granted divorces to sixty-five (79 percent) of them. When women cited cruelty and drunkenness as the grounds for divorce, they were 100 percent successful. Women in Illinois had greater access to divorce than their counterparts in some Southern and eastern states. Divorce was a viable, legal option for women of all social classes and they experienced few legal problems obtaining a divorce. Illinois law stated very specifically that divorce did not affect the legitimacy of children and the circuit courts had the power to settle questions of alimony and child custody. Illinois granted more divorces per capita than Connecticut, Maine, Massachusetts, Missouri, or Ohio throughout the mid-nineteenth century. By 1857, Illinois led the nation in granting divorces. A review of divorce cases clearly demonstrated that Illinois women victoriously sued their husbands for divorce, obtained custody of their children, and received some level of post-nuptial support.

Two cultural factors contributed to the high rate of divorce in Illinois: social disruption associated with frontier life and an extremely mobile population. Rapid industrialization and the spread of railroads increased the mobility of Illinois inhabitants. In operational terms, three variables abetted divorces: a liberal Illinois legislature legally provided access, circuit court judges were comfortable granting divorces, and the people viewed divorce as a reasonable solution to marital difficulties.

Harriet Jackson retained Gideon Rucker along with Lincoln & Herndon and sued her husband Andrew S. Jackson for divorce in Sangamon County Circuit Court in Springfield. Judge Edward Y.

Rice presided as Harriet presented her bill for divorce, written by Rucker, and detailed several claims in her suit. She said that she was lawfully married six years ago and has "been a kind, affectionate and obedient wife to the said defendant." Within the last three years, Harriet said that Andrew "repulsed this kindness with cold, ungrateful hands disregarding the marriage vow... he utterly and entirely failed, refused and neglected to provide the necessaries of life" for her. This forced Harriet "to obtain her living [performing] base menial services." Harriet contended that Andrew married her by fraud. He misrepresented himself "as descending from a respectable family...almost of titular dignity. That he was a man of vast and accumulative wealth, all of which was untrue." Harriet stated that Andrew disregarded his sacred marriage vows and "committed adultery with a woman...being with her for five evenings and slumbering with her each night...[his adultery resulted in his having] that most loathsome and detestable disease, improper for [her] to name...detestable and loathsome to every decent respectable wedded person, male or female." Obviously, this endangered Harriet's health and reputation and "for ought she knows she has the same malady." In ending her detailed complaint, Harriet said "that the said defendant has an exceeding bad temper, treated her uncouthly and has been guilty of repeated cruelty for the past two years." Harriet prayed that Judge Rice would "decree a divorce *a vinculo matrimonii* [from the bond of marriage] and dissolve and set at naught the marriage relations subsisting between [her] and the said defendant." After several continuances, the case was stricken from the docket by the court.

In another divorce case, Lincoln & Herndon represented the husband. Acting in behalf of Sarah Kyle, Stephen T. Logan sued Joseph Kyle on the grounds of adultery in Sangamon County Circuit Court in Springfield. Judge Samuel H. Treat heard the case. Sarah charged that Joseph infected her with venereal disease. In an answer to the complaint, Lincoln wrote that Joseph provided "a state of moderate comfort" for Sarah and their daughters. About 1839, Joseph "contracted said disease in some way unknown to himself and without any illicit sexual intercourse with any one."

Pertinently, Joseph stated that Sarah had "full knowledge of all the facts in connection with his having the disease aforesaid at the time aforesaid and she continued to live and co-habit with him." Joseph denied the adultery charge while he admitted transmitting venereal disease to his wife. In his defense, Joseph "did then insist to said complainant [Sarah] that he supposed he must have caught said disease in a Springfield necessary [emergency use of an outhouse]." Joseph also denied that he committed adultery in the latter part of 1845. "He admits that about that time he did suppose himself to be again infected with the venereal disease…he doubts whether he, in fact, had said disease…he had sexual intercourse with no one except complainant [Sarah]…he had not since the June proceeding been at any place where he supposes it possible to contract venereal diseases in any indirect way…said disease, whatever it was, disappeared with little trouble and without the aid of a prescription by a physician." Although Joseph believed for a while that he contracted the disease from Sarah, he retracted his claim that she transmitted the disease to him. Pointedly, Joseph declared that he was in feeble health for many months and almost blind. He was continually at his own home or nearby in the neighborhood and "there are not, and have not been, any lewd or common women in said neighborhood, from whom he earlier contracted such a disease." In closing, Lincoln's client denied all the charges in the bill of divorce, denied Sarah's right to custody of the children and denied his wife's right to alimony. Although Lincoln didn't call any expert witnesses, contemporary venereal disease specialists agree that the disease is unlikely to be transmitted via an emergency use of an outhouse. In granting the divorce, the court awarded custody of the two minor daughters to Sarah and ordered Joseph to pay $100 in alimony.

In the almost twenty cases cited here in Lincoln's practice dealing with sex, slander and sundry suits, he tried to follow the advice of legal textbook author, Simon Greenleaf. On August 26, 1834, Greenleaf delivered a discourse at his inauguration as a professor at the Harvard University Law School and asserted: "[a lawyer] concerns himself with the beginnings of controversies, not to inflame them but to extinguish them." Applying his lawyering skills, Lincoln did exactly that when a slander charge arose during his presidency. After his house in Maryland was burned to the ground by fewer than 500 rampaging Rebels, Post-Master-General Montgomery Blair bitterly complained: "...the officers in command about Washington are poltroons [cowards]." He remarked that the Union army hugely outnumbered the Rebels and it was a disgrace that the soldiers didn't fight. General-in-Chief Henry W. Halleck sent a letter to Secretary of War Edwin M. Stanton suggesting that Lincoln dismiss Blair from the cabinet for his slander. Lincoln responded to Stanton on July 14, 1864 relative to the forwarded letter from Halleck: "I do not consider what may have been said in a moment of vexation at so severe a loss, is sufficient ground for so grave a step. Besides this, *truth* is generally the best vindication against slander." Stanton sent Halleck a copy of Lincoln's letter.

When he practiced law, Lincoln applied his own advice about truth. "In at least thirteen slander cases, Lincoln pleaded truth as a justification to the plaintiff's charges." However, this plea admitted that the defendant made the statements and required positive proof that the slanderous words were true. Obviously, there is a danger that the defendant may not be able to prove the truth and thereby augment the plaintiff's slander suit. Of his thirteen slander cases where he pleaded justification, Lincoln won three, lost eight and two cases were dismissed.

Lincoln applied reason wherever he could to resolve disputes before going into court. Often, he pointed out the technical difficulties in a case. His depositions and examination of witnesses focused upon the major points to be proven. Yet, despite all his efforts to avoid litigation when possible, Lincoln frequently appeared in court on routine matters involving small fees.

ABRAHAM AND MARY LINCOLN AND INSANITY IN THE COURTROOM

There were accepted medical and legal concepts of insanity when Abraham Lincoln practiced law in Illinois and when he was president. These principles arose in a number of Lincoln's cases dealing with alleged murderers. In *People v. Wyant,* Lincoln prosecuted a murderer when the defense plea was insanity caused by an overdose of chloroform. Referring to *People v. Sickles,* Lincoln discussed with his legal colleagues the initial use of a temporary insanity plea in a murder trial. As president, Lincoln selected an expert medical witness to determine if a convicted murderer was sane or insane. Furthermore, Lincoln and Mary Todd Lincoln were personally affected by concepts of insanity. Throughout the nineteenth century, the jurisprudence of insanity reacted and interacted with societal attitudes and behaviors.

A compilation of ideas on madness and morals in the nineteenth century included nine chapters of selections from contemporary experts that covered criminal lunatics, feminine vulnerability, heredity and character, idiocy, insanity, moral insanity, and pauper lunacy. With far ranging insight, the causes of insanity considered the effects of age, domestic troubles, education, a female's critical period, occupation, puerperal state, religion, seasons, and sex. A comprehensive book on medical jurisprudence in nineteenth-century America focused on physicians and the law covering medical testimony, malpractice, societal reactions, and the expert witness. Special attention was devoted to medically determined causes of insanity, including emotional insanity. In the 1800s, physicians equated insanity with mental illness. Legally, insane or incompetent individuals were labeled lunatics. Institutions were called lunatic asylums. Today, insanity is a legal concept; mental illness is a medical condition.

During the first half of the 1800s, attorneys and physicians seldom met professionally, except in court, to argue about testimony on matters raised in trials. Between 1867 and 1890, the medico-legal society, came into existence in five American cities: the New York Medico-Legal Society (1867); the Massachusetts Medico-Legal Society (1877); the Society of Medical Jurisprudence of New York (1884); the Rhode Island Medico-Legal Society (1885); the Chicago Medico-Legal Society (1885); and the Denver Medico-Legal Society (1890). Correlations between insanity and crime were a major discussion topic for these groups. Today, discussions of social and legal responsibilities continue with many of the same words and arguments that were used a century ago. Behavioral and attitudinal stances of the legal profession, mental health professionals, practicing physicians, the mass media, and the public endured over time.

During the nineteenth century, American physicians believed insanity resulted from two causes: the predisposing and the exciting. Predisposing causes were paramount and heredity was the most influential. Doctors thought that insanity was almost always preceded by an illness, lack of sleep, or poor nutrition. "Those weakened in body and mind became highly vulnerable to mental illness." Exciting causes included a wide variety of stressful emotional and/or physical incidents.

A preeminent American physician, Dr. Benjamin Rush believed that madness mirrored inward emotions and turned anger into illness that damaged the brain. Colorfully, Rush illustrated the observable symptoms: "A wild and ferocious countenance; enlarged and rolling eyes; constant singing; whistling and hallowing; imitations of the voices of different animals; walking with a quick step; or standing still with hands and eyes elevated towards the heavens...the madman, or maniac, is in a rage.

Theories and ideas of foreign physicians, Drs. Philippe Pinel, James Cowles Prichard, and Jean Étienne D. Esquirol, greatly

A. LINCOLN, ESQUIRE

influenced Dr. Isaac Ray in the United States. Although not legally trained, Ray's publications influenced every major development in the common law of insanity including the following: the M'Naghten rule absolving an individual if that person didn't know right from wrong; the irresistible impulse test that allowed the accused to evidence an uncontrollable urge to perform the crime; the New Hampshire doctrine that declared that an act caused by a mental illness is not a crime, a contract, or a will; and the Durham ruling dictating that the accused is not criminally resonsible if the unlawful act was the product of mental disease or mental defect. Ray created a diagnostic classification of mental illness largely derived from Esquirol. In his 1838 book on the medical jurisprudence of insanity, Ray alternated discussing the medical condition in one chapter and followed with the legal consequences in the next chapter. His topics included partial and general moral mania (disease of affect and volition), lucid intervals, simulated insanity, and the civil questions of confinement and interdiction [incompetency]. Ray defined partial moral mania: "In this form of insanity, the derangement is confined to one or a few of the affective faculties, the rest of the moral and intellectual constitution preserving its ordinary integrity." Specifically, Ray discussed the homicidal monomanic as follows: "Amid the rapid and tumultuous succession of feeling that rush into the mind, the reflective powers are paralyzed, and his movements are solely the result of a blind, automatic impulse with which the reason has as little to do, as with the movements of a newborn infant."

In a two-volume widely acclaimed 1842 medical school textbook, Dr. Robley Dunglison, dean of Philadelphia's Jefferson Medical College, discussed and defined the three commonly accepted classifications of mental alienation:

1. Mania results when the intellect is completely perverted on all subjects.
2. Monomania, or partial insanity, means that the perversion is restricted to one subject.

3. Moral insanity consists of a morbid perversion of the natural feelings, affectations, inclinations, temper, habits, moral disposition, and natural impulses without any remarkable disorder or defect of the intellect or knowing and reasoning faculties and particularly without any insane delusion or hallucination.

These medical classifications of mental alienation persisted for some time. Subsequently, the experts began to dicker about moral insanity and the necessity of organic causation for a mental illness diagnosis. Ray continued to be a leading proponent of the doctrine of moral insanity in the United States and abroad. However, during a discussion at the 1863 meeting of the Association of Medical Superintendents of American Institutions for the Insane (AMSAII) only thirteen superintendents ventured an opinion on moral insanity. Five supported the theory and eight rejected the concept. Rejections were primarily based on moralistic grounds including religious, social, and legal rationales. There was also a fear expressed that the profession's reputation would be harmed if the superintendents supported moral insanity as a defense in criminal trials. With this divided opinion among the medical mental illness experts, defense lawyers were fortunate to secure a reputable expert to testify.

Lawyers frequently bolstered their trial oratory about madness with legal, scientific, and professional references and sources such as Esquirol, Foville, Gall, Pinel, Rush, Spurzheim, a phrenology textbook, and the *American Journal of Insanity*. Occasionally, attorneys mentioned a failed attempt "by a foreign lunatic named Richard Lawrence" to kill President Andrew Jackson on January 30, 1835 and later in the late 1870s the successful assassination of President James Garfield by a mentally ill disappointed office seeker, Charles J. Guiteau. With oratorical bombast, learned counsel quoted, from memory, from Shakespeare's *King Lear* and *Richard III* to illustrate acts of madness. Medical mental illness experts contended that chronic insanity of the brain often gives no physical evidence of the disease. A monomaniac could be insane on one or two subjects and sane on all others.

Frequent spells of melancholy and depression plagued Lincoln throughout his life. A medical researcher minutely detailed Lincoln's organic and emotional neurosis. In a letter to William H. Herndon, Lincoln's last law partner, Leonard Swett, his fellow circuit-riding lawyer, asked: "What gave him [Lincoln] that peculiar melancholy?" In contrast, psychohistorian Andrew F. Rolle, professor of History, Occidental College, believed that Lincoln had no serious mental illness and was not psychotic. Nevertheless, Lincoln was surrounded by death and distress all his life: at three, his baby brother died of unknown causes; at nine, he lost his mother, Nancy Hanks; at eighteen, he lost a sister; Anne Rutledge died at age nineteen; his early relationships with women were distressing; two of his children died, Eddie at age four in 1850 and Willie at age twelve in 1862; and he suffered through the responsibility for the devastation and blood of America's Civil War. Professor Rolle surmised that Lincoln was "one on whom sorrow and care had done their worst without victory." On the plus side, Lincoln was elected five times to the Illinois legislature, once to the US Congress, was appointed a postmaster and a deputy surveyor, and established a successful law practice. Despite Lincoln's winning a number of direct elections, his defeats in running for the US Senate and for vice president overshadowed his victorious political endeavors. At one point in 1841, Lincoln wrote to Dr. Daniel F. Drake, dean of the medical department of the College of Cincinnati, and described his symptoms. Lincoln's intimate friend, Joshua F. Speed, explained the incident to Herndon in a November 30, 1866 letter:

Lincoln wrote a letter—a long one which he read to me—to Dr. Drake of Cincinnati, descriptive of his case. Its date would be in December 1840, or early in January 1841. I think that he [Lincoln] must have informed Dr. Drake of his early love for Miss [Anne] Rutledge, as there was a part of the letter which he would not read.... I remember Dr. Drake's reply, which was, that he would not undertake to prescribe for him without a personal interview.

Lincoln never followed up and no personal interview or physical examination ensued. Herndon offered a dramatically different version of this incident. In a January 1891 letter to Jessie Weik, he wrote that Lincoln had syphilis when he was a mere boy—in 1836-1837. Supposedly Lincoln had a "devilish passion" with a girl in Beardstown and caught the disease. For this reason, Herndon said that Lincoln did not let his friend Speed see the entire letter. Herndon avers that "The note to Doctor Drake in part had reference to his disease and not to the crazy spell, as Speed supposes."

After the breakup of his engagement to marry Mary Todd, Lincoln suffered a prolonged depression. In a January 20, 1841 letter to then US Congressman and law partner, John T. Stuart, Lincoln declared: "I have within the last few days been making a most discreditable exhibition of myself in the way of hypochrondrism." In later letters to his friend, Dr. Anson G. Henry, Lincoln described his ailment as "hypochondriasis-psychoneurotic-temperament-psychoneurosis." At that time hypochondriasis or psychoneurosis was classified as a disease and was later called neurasthenia.

Neurologist Dr. George M. Beard coined the term "neurasthenia" to identify a lack of nervous force, a state of nervous exhaustion afflicting the new urban "brain-workers" in America. This condition, also known as "Americanitis" or "the American disease" appeared to be unique to the US with a proclivity for women since they had "a natural tendency toward nervousness." There can be no doubt that Lincoln's collection of multiple and ambiguous symptoms paralleled this new diagnosis emerging as an epidemic in the nation. After receiving a careful reasoned explanation of his condition from Dr. Henry, Lincoln referred to his illness as a "nervous debility" and derisively as "the hypo." On January 23, 1841, Lincoln wrote to Stuart again expressing trepidation about his wretched condition:

I proceed to answer it [your letter] as well as I can, though from the deplorable state of my mind at this time, I fear I shall give you but little satisfaction.... I am now the most miserable man living. If what I feel were equally distributed to the whole human family, there would not be one cheerful face on the earth. Whether I shall ever be better, I cannot tell. I awfully forebode I shall not. To remain as I am is impossible; I must die or be better, it appears to me.... I fear I shall be unable to attend to any business here, and a change of scene might help me.

According to Herndon, Lincoln's

melancholy dripped from him as he walked and his face when in repose...was...pervaded by a look of dejection as painful as it was prominent." Herndon said that Lincoln's melancholy was "necessarily hereditary...ingrained...could not be reduced to rule or the cause arrayed...was part of his nature and could no more be shaken off than he could part with his brain.

In a November 11, 1866 letter to "Friend [Isaac N.] Arnold," Herndon made a strong assertion: "Again—did you know that Mr. Lincoln was as crazy as a loon in this city [Springfield] in 1841...that he was then deranged?" As Herndon garnered information for his book on Lincoln, informants told him that Lincoln "had bouts of mental derangement and had been suicidal on more than one occasion." Reviewing the symptoms, a contemporary medical diagnosis evolved: "Certainly, Lincoln had severe affective disorder, perhaps of the bipolar type. He would probably have received antidepressants or electroconvulsive treatments if such therapy had been available then."

After Lincoln lost the US senatorial election to Stephen A. Douglas, his lawyer friend, Henry C. Whitney, visited at his office on January 5, 1859. For many hours they sat together in gloomy companionship and Whitney found Lincoln "steeped in the bitter waters of hopeless despair."

At the trial of the conspirators in Lincoln's assassination, there was an insanity plea advanced for Lewis Thornton Powell (alias Paine or Payne), the conspirator who attacked, severely wounded, and almost killed Secretary of State William H. Seward. Dr. Charles H. Nichols, superintendent of Washington's Government Hospital for the Insane testified for the defense as an expert medical witness about Paine's insanity. However, Nichols was unable to conclude his testimony because his wife became ill and died during the June 1865 trial. Nevertheless, Paine was found sane and hanged along with George A. Atzerodt, David E. Herold, Paine, and Mrs. Mary Surratt.

In an insightful psychohistorical approach in 1877, Dr. John Frederick May diagnosed Booth as a monomaniac when he assassinated Lincoln. May surgically removed a growth from Booth's neck in April 1863 and treated him for a few weeks afterward when the adhesions broke open and left a visible ugly scar. After Booth's death, May identified his body from the mark left by his scalpel. About twenty-five years after the surgery, May wrote a learned article carefully detailing his medical rationales for Booth's insanity: heredity, physical appearance, insensitivity to heat and cold, insanity without organic disease, and self-glorification. In his conclusion, May declared that: " for the credit of our country none but *madmen* have assailed with murderous intent the Chief Magistrate of the Nation since the foundation of the Republic." Even at that late date, May was reluctant to label Booth as insane because of possible violent reactions against him in the name of patriotism. He wrote his article only five years after an obviously mentally disturbed Guiteau was hanged for assassinating President Garfield. May's article was not published until 1910, after his death. Current historical research labels Booth as a Southern patriot and not a madman.

Mary Todd Lincoln was considered unsettled, to say the least. Her troubles, real and imagined, led her into wide ranging mood swings, outbursts, possible depression and into seeking relief in the hands of mentalists and spiritualists. During one of her extended tantrums after the death of their son, Willie, Lincoln led his wife to the window of their summer quarters at the Soldiers Home, pointed to the clearly visible massive grayish-white buildings of the federal lunatic asylum and said: "Mother, do you see that large white building on the hill yonder? Try and control your grief, or it will drive you mad, and we may have to send you there." Two years before May's article diagnosed Booth as a monomaniac, insanity again intruded upon the Lincoln family. In 1875, Robert T. Lincoln consulted Leonard Swett about Mary Todd Lincoln's irrational behavior. As an example, Robert said that his mother carried $57,000 in securities in a pocket in her underclothing. Mary's lawyer cousin, John T. Stuart, Associate Supreme Court of the United States Justice David Davis and administrator of Lincoln's estate, and Swett himself all agreed that she was insane and suggested the only possible legal recourse in Illinois: a sanity trial. On May 19, 1875, a sanity trial began in Cook County Court in Chicago. Isaac N. Arnold, a friend of the former president, agreed to represent Mrs. Lincoln. Benjamin F. Ayer and Swett appeared in court for Robert. In his usual thorough style, Swett prepared for the trial by arranging for the overwhelming expert medical testimony of six physicians. All the physicians testified that Mary T. Lincoln was insane and Dr. Isham said she was *non compos mentis*.

Management personnel and employees from the Grand Pacific Hotel at Jackson Boulevard and Clark Street, where Mary stayed, testified at the trial. Additional damaging testimony came from clerks who waited on her and sales people from whom she made purchases. These witnesses used a variety of words to describe Mary's behavior: "bizarre, mentally deranged, mentally disturbed, don't think right, hard to manage, insane, suffered from nervous excitement, plain batty, manner excited, manner queer, and manner strange." Robert Lincoln testified about his mother's bizarre behavior: "She has been of unsound mind since the death of her husband, and has been irresponsible for the last ten years. I regard her as eccentric and unmanageable." When asked if he agreed with the physicians that his mother was insane, Robert replied: "My belief is the same." During the trial, Mary addressed her son gently: "Oh, Robert, to think that my son would ever have done this." Without hesitation, the jury returned a verdict of insanity and Robert was appointed conservator of her estate. On the day after the trial, Mary was taken to Bellevue Palace, an exclusive sanitarium "of the private class" in Batavia, Illinois owned by Dr. Richard J. Patterson. "More than anyone else except Robert, he [Swett] was responsible for Mrs. Lincoln's confinement." Bold black banner headlines in the May 20, 1875 edition of the Chicago *Inter-Ocean* proclaimed what happened:

CHICAGO INTER-OCEAN
MAY 20, 1875

THE WIDOW OF THE MARTYRED PRESIDENT
ADJUDGED INSANE IN THE COUNTY COURT

ONE OF THE SADDEST SPECTACLES EVER
WITNESSED IN A COURTROOM IN THIS CITY

EMINENT MEDICAL MEN PRONOUNCE HER TO BE
OF UNSOUND MIND AND INCAPABLE OF SELF-CARE

SHE WILL BE REMOVED TO-DAY TO A PRIVATE
ASYLUM AT BATAVIA, ILL.

After about four months, on September 10, 1875, Mary was allowed to leave the sanitarium to stay at the home of her sister, Elizabeth Edwards, in Springfield, Illinois. Just before she left Bellevue Palace, Robert made an entry in his disbursements ledger as his mother's conservator: "Sept. 8 Paid Dr. Andrew McFarland for professional services and expenses in going from Jacksonville, Ills. to Batavia, to visit Mrs. Lincoln.—Voucher No. 35. $100." Dr. McFarland evaluated Mrs. Lincoln's mental status. After thirteen months of being labeled a lunatic, Mary's brother-in-law, Ninian W. Edwards, petitioned for another sanity trial. On June 15, 1876, a sanity trial was held in Chicago before the same judge and took only about five minutes. Robert did not appear and offered no objection. Swett did a complete turn-around and acted as a defense counsel for Mrs. Lincoln at this second sanity trial. He appeared on behalf of Robert and said that his client would be "only too glad" to have the court decree reversed if the jury was satisfied. Dr. Patterson did not testify either. Quickly, a jury was selected with Dr. R. M. Paddock as the medical juryman. It took only a few minutes for the jury to retire and to render their verdict.

Harboring anger and resentment against Robert, Mary wrote a number of seething letters accusing her son of a "game of robbery" and of "wicked conduct." Deeply humiliated, Mary left the United States and remained abroad in Europe for four years before returning home. Eventually, she forgave Robert for the sake of her only grandchildren. After his mother's death on July 16, 1882, Robert tried to collect and burn all the bitter denunciating letters.

Some of the very same legal principles argued in Mary Todd Lincoln's sanity trial occurred in a case handled by the law firm of Lincoln & Herndon. Specifically, the trial focused upon a definition of insanity, money changing hands, and a conservator. As in Mary T. Lincoln's case, the distinction between eccentricity and insanity was blurred.

In the January 1862 term of the supreme curt of Illinois, Lincoln & Herndon participated in the long standing case of *Lilly v. Waggoner, conservator of Waggoner.* Obviously, then President Lincoln did not appear in court as William H. Herndon and Henry P. H. Bromwell represented George Waggoner, the conservator, in the appeal. In 1851, Elisha Waggoner sold eighty acres of land to Europe A. Lilly for $320. After a court ordered inquest in 1858, Elisha Waggoner was declared insane and his brother, George, appointed conservator. George sued to set aside the earlier sale of the land claiming that Elisha was insane when he sold the land. A Moultrie County Circuit Court set aside the sale and George returned the payment to Lilly with interest. Lilly appealed to the Supreme Court of Illinois and was represented by Anthony Thornton & John T. Stuart and Benjamin S. Edwards & Christopher C.

Brown. In the supreme court of Illinois, Justice Pinckney H. Walker wrote the opinion reversing the lower court judgment because the sale took place before Elisha was found to be insane. In their opinion, the supreme court of Illinois said that Elisha was insane but also experienced lucid intervals wherein the contract could have been valid. "A person may be a lunatic and yet have lucid intervals." All persons of legal age are presumed to be sane, and a deed executed several years before the maker was found to be insane, has the legal presumption of validity in its favor. Walker continued: "The law has never required the high order of reasoning powers that mark the gifted, or a large portion of the human family would be thus deprived of the legal capacity to transact their own business." While Lilly's evidence was somewhat conflicting, eight witnesses testified that Elisha Waggoner conversed rationally during business transactions. One witness was present at the time of the sale. He reported that Waggoner's wife was present, as required by statutory law, and made no objection to the sale. Nether did Samuel P. Lilly who saw his father immediately after the sale. One physician testified that based on Lilly's evidence, it is difficult to tell whether Waggoner was sane or insane. Another physician believed Waggoner to be insane, but not *non compos mentis*, and still capable of handling his business affairs. A witness testified that in 1851 Elisha was "about like the other Waggoners; was always somewhat singular from the time he first knew him." While doubt existed, George failed to establish evidence that Elisha was insane when the deed was executed in 1851. Evidence showing the insanity of a party at the time of the execution of a deed must preponderate, or the legal presumption in favor of insanity will sustain the act. Certainly, George had difficulty proving Elisha's insanity in 1851 when none of the other Waggoners, especially George, were. In the opinion on the case, supreme court of Illinois Justice Walker commented on the difficulty inherent in cases involving insanity:

It may be truly said, that there are few questions which present greater difficulties in their solution, than this of insanity. It assumes such a variety of forms, from that of the raving madman, to the monomaniac; from total dementia, to that of scarcely perceptible insanity, that it has almost been denied, that any person is perfectly sane, on every subject.

In concluding, Justice Walker said: "When all the evidence is considered, we can scarcely entertain a doubt of his sanity...there would appear to be some marks of simulated insanity...we can readily perceive a motive in the rise of this land from four to twenty dollars per acre."

In addition to the root of all evil—money—the nineteenth century legal and medical principles related to insanity appeared in the legal experiences of Leonard Swett, Wiliam H. Seward, Edwin M. Stanton, and Joseph H. Bradley, Sr. All of these lawyers interacted with Lincoln on cases involving insanity.

CHLOROFORM INDUCED INSANITY DEFENSE CONFOUNDS LAWYER LINCOLN

During an unusual 1857 trial, the defense claimed that an overdose of chloroform during an earlier surgical procedure caused the accused's insanity and absolved him of willful murder. Abraham Lincoln and Leonard Swett were the opposing lawyers.

For this murder trial, Lincoln assisted the state's attorney for the Eighth Judicial Circuit in Illinois with the prosecution. A fellow Illinois circuit-riding lawyer, Swett, was the chief defense attorney. Swett attended Waterville College (ME) for three years, served in the Mexican War, came to Bloomington (IL) in July 1848 after the war, and was an able lawyer with significant personal charm. He became a lifelong political ally of Lincoln and was one of his campaign managers during the 1860 Republican presidential nomination convention. When Lincoln became president, Swett received a consular appointment. Coincidentally, there was a strong physical resemblance between Lincoln and Swett. Both men were bony, long, and lanky with Swett having a long meditative face with a white chin beard. They had similar legal styles in the courtroom including a benign presence and a magnetic effect upon juries. After Swett's death, the *Chicago Times* published descriptive remarks by the ex-president of the Chicago Bar Association: "Tall and erect in stature, dignified and commanding in personal appearance, possessing strongly marked features, brilliant black eyes overhung by heavy, bushy brows, gifted with a powerful voice, suave manner, as an advocate Swett was one of the most persuasive who ever addressed a jury at the American bar."

To understand the medical testimony during this murder trial, the judge, lawyers, and jurors would have benefitted from learning about the historical development of medical painkillers. During surgical procedures, physicians chose from a few accepted anesthetics to ease the patient's pain. Early on physicians used nitrous oxide and in the 1850s selected either ether or chloroform.

Heated medical differences about the choice of ether or chloroform as an anesthetic appeared in professional medical journals. These articles surfaced about 1847, ten years before Lincoln prosecuted this case that included a brawl, a shooting, an amputation and a murder.

Isaac Wyant and Anson Rusk feuded belligerently for some months over a contested land boundary. After an exchange of excitable words in June 1855, several family members on both sides participated in a brutal imbroglio. Believing that Wyant threatened him with a bowie knife, Rusk shot Wyant. Wyant's left arm was badly damaged, necessitating amputation at the shoulder sixteen hours later. Attending physicians, Drs. Lemon, John Warner, and Christopher Goodbrake, administered chloroform as an anesthetic during the operation. After the amputation, Wyant was "ever after morbidly fearful that Rusk would kill him...and complained greatly about his head and exhibited many signs of being unsettled in his intellect."

Suffering continuous physical pain and emotional turmoil, Wyant stalked Rusk to the county clerk's office of DeWitt County in Clinton, Illinois, on October 12, 1855. At point blank range, in broad daylight, Wyant brutally fired four shots at Rusk, the last directly to the head, killing him. As Wyant fled the building, he was captured by the sheriff.

A grand jury indicted Wyant for murder on October 19, 1855. In preparing for an obviously sensational murder trial, Wyant's lawyers petitioned for a change of venue in the May 1856 term of the court. In granting the request, the court ordered the trial moved from Clinton in DeWitt County to Bloomington in McLean County. On September 10, 1856, Swett secured a continuance of Wyant's trial to the next court term. Without bail, Wyant remained confined in prison for about seventeen months until the trial started.

Lincoln's law associate, Ward Hill Lamon, was the state's attorney for McLean County. Their co-partnership was advertised, probably by Lamon without Lincoln's knowledge, in local newspapers such as the Iroquois Journal in Middleport, Illinois.

ABRAM LINCOLN, Springfield W. H. LAMON,
Danville
Lincoln & Lamon,
ATTORNEYS AT LAW,

Having formed a co-partnership, will practice in the Courts of the Eighth Judicial Circuit, and the Superior Court, and all business entrusted to them will be attended to with promptness and fidelity.

Office on the second floor of the "Barnum Building" over Whitcomb's Store. Denville, Nov. 10, 1852

To conduct the people's case against the murderer, Lamon secured the assistance of Lincoln, Clifton H. Moore and Harvey Hogg. To defend him, Wyant retained Leonard Swett and his partner, William Ward Orme. Newspaper accounts of the trial reveal that Lincoln handled the prosecution almost singlehandedly. Swett directed the thrust of the defense. On the afternoon of March 30, 1857, the trial began and lasted about six days. During the trial, the jury stayed at the Pike House in charge of officers. "Great interest in the progress and result of the trial was manifested by the people, and the Court House was constantly thronged."

Attracted by the spectacle of a sensational murder trial, winter dreary and work weary prairie residents converged upon the Bloomington public square. Each day, all the hitching posts were occupied and people noisily milled about on the town square. With their legal reputations well known to all, spectators jostled for seats to behold the anticipated robust fray between Lincoln and Swett.

Bloomington residents anticipated a "battle royal" between Lincoln and Swett.

Opening for the state, Lincoln presented a straightforward *prima facie* case of murder. He used a diagram of the clerk's office to show the murder site to the witnesses and the jury. All of Lincoln's six witnesses were present nearby at the time of the shooting; all heard the four shots; all saw Wyant coming or going; and Harry Kidder actually was an eyewitness to the whole affair:

> I was in the [clerk's] office when Rusk came in...first thing I saw of the difficulty was the smoke of the pistol...was in but a short time when Wyant came and opened the door and fired on Rusk...appeared about one or two o'clock.... Rusk bellowed two or three times...Rusk fell on his knees...defendant shot again.... I caught the defendant and told him he should shoot no more there...[he] shot three times...said nothing after I took hold of him...nothing passed between the defendant and Rusk before the shooting...

Three witnesses heard Wyant say that he killed Rusk. Wyant exchanged words with Constable Williams:

> Was in Taylor & Bell's store about fifty steps away...I heard the shooting and knew something was wrong and came immediately...Wyant was a few rods [about forty feet] from the court house gate when I first saw him with his pistol in his hand...He had two pistols [revolvers]; one with six loads in it and the other with two loads...I had a struggle with him to get the first pistol and he gave up the other one...I took him back to the court house...I arrested him [Wyant] and told him he had killed Rusk . He said "Well, if I have killed him, damn his soul, that is just what I came here to do...." He begged of me not to take him where he could see the dead man, for he said that his friends would shoot his poor body all to pieces.

DeWitt County Court Clerk Squire McGraw knew Rusk for a few years and noticed Wyant the day before the shooting. He saw Wyant enter the office, heard a pistol report, and a scream followed by two more shots and another scream. As Wyant came out of the clerk's office he told McGraw that "he had shot the damn rascal that had shot his arm off." McGraw had Constable Williams arrest Wyant and went to inform the coroner, Dr. Goodbrake, about the fatal shooting.

Robert Lewis was a resident of Clinton for six years. He heard the four shots and saw Wyatt after he was taken upstairs. He did not see Wyatt vomit up there. Wyatt told him that he "shot the man who murdered his arm."

Dr. Goodbrake heard the sound of four distinct shots and met McGraw outside the court house. He encountered Wyatt coming out of the court house door. "I was walking tolerably lively and [Wyatt] said something about the shooting, but I don't recollect what it was." In his testimony as the coroner, Goodbrake said:

> When I got into the office, Rusk lying on the floor with his head doubled under and his brains coming out. I examined the body and found four wounds occasioned by balls; in the head, shoulder blade, side and arm...the head wound caused the death, though the shot in the side would have terminated fatally, but not so soon...head wound ball entered above the left eye and plowed its way through the brain and lodged against the skull on the other side.... I probed the wound with a flexible Gum Catheter.

Dr. Thomas K. Edmundson first saw Rusk's body at the coroner's inquest. He agreed with Goodbrake in his description of the wounds and the cause of death. In passing, Edmundson commented that Wyatt's pistols were old fashioned with barrels that were three to four inches long.

Lincoln presented his evidence and closed for the prosecution in the evening of the first day of the trial as entered in the court record.

Presiding Judge David Davis allowed the defense to propose an insanity plea for Wyant's actions. Swett asserted: "Resting on the ground of insanity, the killing was not controverted." Innovatively, Swett stated that medical experts would testify that an overdose of chloroform resulted in damage to the brain and caused Wyant's ensuing insanity. Preparing the jury, Swett told them that evidence of commonly and professionally accepted irrational behaviors would be presented along with proof of an inherited tendency to insanity.

During the time that Lincoln practiced law, the insanity defense was well established by the 1850s. Certainly, Lincoln saw the defense used in Illinois courtrooms. Furthermore, despite heated objections, "the Supreme Court of Illinois of Lincoln's day upheld the insanity defense and met some of the same arguments that are used against it today." *People v. Wyant* was erroneously cited as the first use of medical experts in an insanity plea in the Illinois courts. Probably, the unique chloroform causing insanity rationale heightened awareness of the case. However, Dr. Edward Mead of Boston, Massachusetts reported that defense attorney Isaac N. Arnold asked him to give his opinion in a murder trial in McHenry County, Illinois in 1847 or 1848. Arnold said "it was the first that had occurred in that state of that character."

Believing that Wyant was feigning "the loss of his mentality," Lincoln strenuously objected to the defense's insanity argument. However, Judge Davis did not change his decision.

Swett augmented his insanity defense with intensive research into the medical arguments. Seeking medical expertise, Swett consulted with Dr. Luther V. Bell, Superintendent, McLean Asylum, Boston (MA). It is likely that Bell referred Swett to Dr. Isaac Ray's landmark book, *A Treatise on the Medical Jurisprudence of Insanity*, first published in 1838 and then in its third edition in 1853.

Defining mental illness, Ray declared: "Insanity is a disease, and as is the case with all other diseases, the fact of existence is never established by a single diagnostic symptom, but by the whole body of symptoms, no particular one of which is present in every case."

Scientific testimony of medical witnesses for the defense exposed Lincoln to professional concepts of insanity as caused by chloroform anesthesia. Swett displayed an extraordinary mastery of the intricacies of anesthesia, medical science, and mental disease without ever hearing the word psychiatry; the term was yet to be coined.

At the time of the trial, the insanity plea was used, but was still a novel defense. A chloroform induced insanity plea was rarer still. Supporting medical testimony for the insanity defense was said to be unique in Illinois courts.

In advocating Wyant's insanity plea Swett introduced nineteen witnesses: five relatives; five friends; six physicians; the sheriff; the county clerk; and even Swett himself. Those who were present when Wyant was shot in the arm described the raucous brawl and the mortal threats. Wyant's friends and family testified about his multiple irrational behaviors. His symptoms included: a constant fearfulness that the Rusks were going to kill him; picking his head until the scalp was bloody with festering sores; frequent and unexpected tantrums; being flighty, rambling, and unconnected; continuous talking to himself and others; and a total change in disposition. His sister surprised the jury with a grotesque fact. In an emotional outburst, Wyant demanded that his buried arm be interred from the graveyard and brought in to him. Wyant's physical complaints included: a roaring in the head; ringing in the ears; facial twitching; constipation; feverish excitement; sleeplessness; loss of appetite; and general continuous and phantom pains. Six physicians reiterated and aggrandized the medical symptoms while integrating the aberrant behaviors observed by the friends and family members.

Wyant's sister, half-brother, and an uncle told of an hereditary predisposition; two uncles were unbalanced; one went "queer in the head after not getting a girl he had sparked."

Five physicians testified about the harmful effects of too much chloroform during anesthesia. Dr. Lemon told about the amputation as well as about chloroform:

> [Wyant's] arm was fractured with wound below the elbow...arm amputated sixteen hours after the wound...Drs. Warner, Goodbrake and myself present...chloroform administered...took long time in administering it; thought it not good for anything...sent son to get bottle of ether while prisoner continued breathing the chloroform til it worked.... Books say that injury produced from chloroform causes uneasiness about the head including picking...when it [chloroform] injures the brain, it destroys the mind...there are some recorded cases of permanent insanity from the use of chloroform...insanity one of the probable effects of injury from use of it.

> [Lincoln's cross-examination of Dr. Lemon]: Did not examine bottle [of chloroform] until four or five weeks after death of Rusk...not much experience of the effects of chloroform...most of information drawn from books...inference is that anything producing insensibility affects the brain...one case of insanity mentioned in books...don't know what kind of insanity chloroform produces.

Physicians who attended Wyant's amputation and post-operative recovery visited him four or five times a day during his convalescence. Wyant's constant brooding over the loss of his left arm further unhinged his mind.

Dr. Parks recounted his experiences using a combination of ether and chloroform to make the compound less dangerous. He commented that it is probable that chloroform injures the mind. However, Parks couldn't mention a single case where a male was rendered permanently insane by the use of chloroform. In keeping with medical beliefs, Parks declared that females and nervous males are more susceptible to insanity.

Dr. Roe declared that the "tendency of chloroform is to effect the brain and nervous system...instead of deadening his [Wyant's] animal passions, it [chloroform] had the effect to revive and excite them.... I think that chloroform given in any quantities leads to insanity...picking of the head is often an accompaniment of insanity...all morbid feelings are evidences of insanity. Under Lincoln's cross-examination, Roe agreed that "It is a very difficult matter to judge insanity; the books lay down this. I know of no case of a male being made insane by chloroform, though it has occurred." He concurred that females are more susceptible, particularly during childbirth, "when there is a greater tendency to insanity."

Dr. Spencer's experience included dealing with the insane when he was in charge of the Insane Hospital in Albany (NY) for two years. He testified that "Among the symptoms of the abuse of chloroform are pain or ringing in the head, listening to fancied noises, etc. I have seen a case where this was the prominent trait of the insanity."

On seeing Wyant for the first time, Dr. Hoover "was called to him by his peculiar appearance and manner. His muscles were twitching in his face and he was picking at his head...he talked but was rambling and disconnected."

Five physicians unhesitantly agreed that Wyant was insane; of the five, two were experienced asylum superintendents. Hoover said: "I have no doubt in my mind that Wyant was insane when I saw him...satisfied from his manner that he was insane...his appearance denoted it." Agreeing, Roe declared: "I have heard the testimony in this case and from that testimony I am satisfied that Wyant was insane at the time of the commission of the offence. I think he is insane...I have no doubt of his being insane since the shooting of the arm." Spencer concurred: "From the evidence, I think Wyant was insane." Parks concluded that the "symptoms of insanity mentioned by the physicians are evidences of insanity." Dr. Andrew McFarland, superintendent for the Illinois State

Hospital for the Insane, Jacksonville, said: "There are reasonable grounds to believe from the evidence that he was insane when he killed Rusk."

During Lincoln's cross-examination of the medical experts for the defense, he questioned whether Wyant was feigning insanity. Hoover announced his position: "I don't think he was feigning insanity." McFarland's expert opinion was conclusive: "Insanity is sometimes successfully feigned, but not where there is an opportunity for experienced persons to witness the attempts at feigning. I have no fears in this case that insanity had been feigned."

McFarland was Swett's star witness. He had a medical degree from Jefferson Medical College (Philadelphia), was a former superintendent of the New Hampshire Asylum for the Insane from 1845 to 1852, Illinois state asylum superintendent since 1854, and a specialist in the study of the mind for twelve years. After all nineteen defense witnesses testified, McFarland was asked "to summarize all the points, great and small, that went to show the defendant to be insane." Speaking with self-assured authority, McFarland identified several conclusive medical rationales for Wyant's insanity: Wyant's change in character from courageous to cowardice; his wakefulness and watchfulness; the propensity of a heredity predisposition; ringing noises in the head; his picking his head constantly is of more importance than would appear to ordinary man; his vomiting after shooting Rusk evidences insanity; and his charging his sister with shooting off his arm. "I conceive it to be the natural tendency of chloroform to paralyze the brain. The secondary effect is to carry that paralyzation beyond recovery or to fatality. The first effect of it is to blunt the sensation of feeling. I consider that it effected Wyant from the amount inhaled and the length of time inhaling." McFarland told the jury that Wyant's condition used to be called a "sanguineo-nervous temperament" but physicians now ceased to talk of temperament. In addition, McFarland revealed that he had experimented with the effects of chloroform upon the mind including its use with "extremely excited maniacs."

Independent of each other, Lemon, Parks, Roe, and Spencer all expertly assented that an overdosage of chloroform injures the brain and causes insanity. A pound bottle of chloroform was used during the amputation and not touched until five weeks later. Swett was called to the witness stand, sworn, and testified that he measured the bottle and almost 2 3/8 inches of chloroform was used during Wyant's surgery. That amount certainly equals an overdosage of chloroform; equivalent to 600 to 700 drops.

Trying to depreciate the impressive accumulation of medical and lay testimony, Lincoln used folksy humor to rebut the insanity plea. In cross-examination of one defense expert physician witness, Lincoln remarked:

> You say, doctor, that this man picks his head, and by that you infer that he is insane. Now, I sometimes pick my head and those joking fellows at Springfield tell me that there may be a living, moving cause for it, and that the trouble isn't at all on the inside. It's only a case for fine-tooth combs.

Testimony of the defense's six medical experts and the concurring observations by Wyant's family and friends impressed the jury. Believing so, Lincoln rebutted with sixteen witnesses to show that Wyant had ample reasons to kill Rusk and to discredit specific defense testimony, including the concept of chloroform induced insanity.

Rusk's family members testified about Wyant's motivation to kill Rusk. They reported Wyant's frequent bluntly stated threats toward Rusk, his fights with various Rusk family members, his bullying and whipping of Rusk and others, his using a bowie knife to intimidate Rusk and his obviously seeking vengeance for his amputated arm. A witness, Mr. Nixon, said that Wyant told him he craved revenge for his injury and "it was a damn hard thing for a man to be waylaid and have his arm shot off." Two witnesses, the Court Clerk McGraw and Constable Williams, said they did not hear Wyant say anything about killing his father or anybody else's father. Robert Lewis stated that Wyant "did not look strange when we saw him upstairs after the shooting."

Pertinent and impressive testimony about Wyant's feigning insanity came from a man named Taylor, Wyant's jailor for seventeen months. Since Wyant said he was a stranger and didn't know anyone, Taylor recommended Swett as a lawyer. Taylor testified: "Swett asked Dr. Lemon in jail in the presence of Wyant if the use of chloroform would affect the brain. Dr. Lemon replied in some cases it did. Afterwards on one occasion when I took food to Wyant, he put on foolish actions. I told him he need not feign to be insane to me and afterwards he did not; he acted then as usual."

Warner, who administered the chloroform to Wyant during the amputation, testified: "I didn't think Wyant inhaled double the ordinary dose...chloroform evaporates quickly...I suppose chloroform would lose its strength during ordinary usage."

Lincoln's last rebuttal witness responded to the proposition that a chloroform overdose induced insanity. Goodbrake, then president of the Illinois State Medical Society, was present at Wyant's amputation. He said that much of the chloroform was wasted because Wyant at first refused to take it. "An ordinary dose of chloroform was given to Wyant and a bit more when he awoke during surgery." While he was awake, Wyant cried and swore and said his friends ought to have killed Rusk. Symptoms of the type mentioned were not unusual when a man lost an arm and "might be present in a sane mind as well." Goodbrake did not consider the symptoms as a sign of permanent insanity caused by chloroform. In addition, he commented: "I have examined some books on the use of chloroform...I have never found a case of permanent insanity made by chloroform." In summary, Goodbrake said that he had not seen much change in Wyant. "It impressed me that he was either a strange man or a crazy one. He was as much insane before the amputation as afterwards as it appeared to me." Lincoln's prosecution rebuttal concluded that afternoon.

On Friday, April 4, Hogg delivered a three-hour summation for the prosecution. Orme followed for the defense for almost three hours. Swett took the rest of the day starting his summation and finished on Saturday morning about noon. After lunch, Lincoln's speech began and went on until almost six o'clock.

After the summations, Judge Davis gave instructions to the jury. He relied heavily in his directions on existing legal irresistible and uncontrollable impulse precedents, the involuntary act determinations and the sound mind question. Jury members were told that if the defendant's unsoundness overwhelmed his reason, conscience and judgment, he should be found not guilty. On the other hand, if Wyant had enough mental capacity to understand the nature and consequences of his act, the right and wrong of his action, he should be found guilty. Judge Davis admonished the jury that the law presumes a man is sane and that must be rebuffed by satisfactory proof to the contrary. After immediately taking supper, the jury retired to deliberate the case.

Judge Davis's wife, Sarah, accurately forecast the next step: "A trial for murder has engaged the attention of our people for five days past.... The jury are now locked up and I fear that they will send for my better half by the middle of the night." About one o'clock on Sunday morning, the jury came back to court with the result of their deliberations:

> We the jurors duly sworn to try the cause of the People of the State of Illinois against Isaac Wyant, find on mature deliberation, that the said defendant, Isaac Wyant, is not guilty by reason of insanity. Our opinion being found principally under the fourth article of the instructions from the Court. Also the article touching evidence of medical witnesses, and we the jurors find that the aforesaid prisoner being of an unsound mind is unsafe to be at large, and therefore earnestly recommend that the Honorable Court take the necessary steps, to have him the said Isaac Wyant removed immediately to the State Lunatic Asylum at Jacksonville.

> [Court's response] It is therefore ordered by the Court that the said defendant of the above indictment be discharged and go hence without delay.

With an acquittal verdict and a recommendation for the prisoner's confinement in a lunatic asylum, Swett immediately initiated legal procedures to assure that Wyant would be sent to the Illinois State Lunatic Asylum. In response, the court convened "a jury of six good and lawful men" to hear the evidence. After hearing the evidence, the jury was satisfied that Wyant was insane and a fit person to be sent to the Illinois State Hospital for the Insane. "That his age is about thirty-five years. That his disease is not of long duration, that the disease is with him probably hereditary, that he is not subject to epilepsy, and that he is free from vermin or any infectious disease and is not a pauper." A warrant was issued for Wyatt's removal to the Illinois State Hospital for the Insane.

Sarah Davis, the judge's wife, accurately reflected the public's dubious attitude toward the verdict in a letter to her brother: "The scamp who committed the murder is in the Insane Asylum at Jacksonville, the jury having acquitted him on the plea of insanity." Like the judge's wife, Lincoln was cognizant of the skeptical attitudes of professionals and the public toward the insanity plea. Based upon his own experiences in the courtroom, Lincoln was familiar with the abilities of skillful lawyers and expert witnesses to convince a jury and to persuade the public.

A postscript to the *People v. Wyant* case came to light in a biography of Lincoln thirty-six years after the murder trial ended. Fellow Illinois attorney Joseph E. McDonald ran into Lincoln and Swett at a chance meeting in Danville, Illinois. He told them that he had defended Wyant from "every charge in the calendar of crimes…he was a weak brother and could be led into almost everything." Intrigued, Lincoln listened intently as McDonald told all about Wyant. McDonald recounted his conversation with Lincoln the next day: "He told me that he had been greatly troubled over what I related about Wyant; that his sleep had been disturbed by the fear that he had been too bitter and unrelenting in his prosecution of him." Lincoln said: "I acted on the theory that he [Wyant] was 'possuming' insanity…I fear I may have been too severe and that the poor fellow may be insane after all. If he cannot realize the wrong of his crime, then I was wrong in asking to punish him."

Holding true to his reputation, Lincoln put all his energy into the prosecution and presented the people's case with intensity and professional deftness. Lincoln drew up the indictment, made the opening and closing arguments to the jury and conducted most of the direct examination of the people's witnesses. He handled the cross-examination of the physicians who testified as to the effects of an overdose of chloroform and as to the insanity of the defendant. Considering the medical and scientific knowledge available at that time, this was a complex and perplexing assignment. Even with his extensive legal experience, Lincoln had little medical jurisprudence background. On the other hand, Swett did a much better job of medical investigation and research and emerged as a legal expert on insanity.

Lincoln recognized and emphasized the obvious legal facts. There was no doubt that Wyant murdered Rusk. However, Lincoln did not pursue the medical aspects of the chloroform induced insanity defense as relentlessly as possible. While medical literature existed to offer strong evidence of the safety of chloroform as an anesthetic, Lincoln didn't discover the material and bring it into court. Furthermore, there were other medical and asylum experts that Lincoln could have used to counter Swett's authorities on chloroform induced insanity.

Although Lincoln was "bitter and unrelenting" in the prosecution, he lost the case. His later conversation with lawyer McDonald about Wyant after the case was concluded bears evidence to his mixed emotions. Nevertheless, Abraham Lincoln applied his genius for simple, persuasive parlance, handy humor, and deft depictions in this case as he did in all others.

Immediately following this murder trial with its volume of expert medical testimony, Lincoln and Swett reversed their legal positions and met again in a medical malpractice trial. In the same McLean County Circuit Court with the same Judge David Davis presiding, Lincoln defended two accused physicians while Swett represented the injured plaintiff. Again, expert medical testimony played a major role in the arguments of both lawyers. Again, both lawyers overlooked relevant evidence. Again, Lincoln countered expert medical testimony using the folksy example of chicken bones to make his points.

LINCOLN'S CLIENT REFUSES TO PAY THE DOCTOR'S BILL FOR SERVICES

When Stuart & Lincoln dissolved their partnership, Lincoln moved directly across the street from the Hoffman's Row office to share an office with Stephen T. Logan, his new partner. Logan & Lincoln moved to the third floor of a new building. On January 4, 1844, and weekly thereafter, the *Sangamo Journal*, printed the firm's professional card on the front page:

> LOGAN & LINCOLN ATTORNEYS AND COUN-
> SELLORS AT LAW, SPRINGFIELD-OVER THE
> POST OFFICE-THIRD FLOOR.

After the Logan & Lincoln partnership ended, Lincoln & Herndon moved into the third floor office over the post office. When Lincoln went to Washington as a congressman, Herndon moved the firm to a smaller office on the third floor. Subsequently, Lincoln & Herndon moved to another location where Logan and Milton Hay also had an office on the same floor in the front of the building. A law student at Lincoln & Herndon, Gibson W. Harris, minutely described their office on the west side of the public square at 105 South Fifth Street:

> Up a flight of stairs so narrow that two people walking abreast rubbed elbows.... It was a plainly furnished back room on the second floor. The two windows looked out on a flat one-story warehouse roof, coated with tar and pebbles. On hot summer days the tar softened, and the breeze, if there

happened to be any, wafted a powerful resinous odor into the room. The office furnishings were far from elaborate. A large table in the middle of the room; two good-sized book-cases with compartments for filing and ample shelving for books—one stood on the west side between the two windows, the other midway on the south wall. The door into the office was fitted on the upper half with a window-sash divided by 8x10 glass to furnish from the office what light the entrance-hall had. A rod at the top of this carried rings attached to a curtain for closing when no interruption was desired. This curtain arrangement was seldom resorted to, but after business hours of a day full of interruptions by callers and accumulated work due an early finish, this was necessary, as all papers, briefs, etc., were prepared by pen.

As customary, Lincoln & Herndon continued to handle a large number of suits involving debts. In one such case, Lincoln's client, William H. Bissell, refused to pay Dr. Charles Ryan's $97 bill for medical services. Bissell's three nieces of his second wife, Elizabeth K. Kane, were living with him when Ryan cared for them. Witnesses for Ryan testified that Bissell's brother-in-law, William C. Kinney, his wife and their children were visiting with Bissell when Kinney's wife died. Thereafter, the children lived with Bissell and not with their father, who resided in Belleville, Illinois. When the children became ill, Bissell did not deny that he sent for the doctor to treat his nieces.

Since Ryan's claim was for less than $100, he sued Bissell in Sangamon County before Justice of the Peace William Hickman during the March 1859 term. No lawyers were involved at this stage of the suit although Bissell had a law degree. Bissell argued that the father, Kinney, was responsible for paying the bill for medical services rendered to his children. There is no explanation for the amount, but the jury found for Ryan and awarded him $13.

Obviously dissatisfied with the amount of the award, Ryan appealed to the Sangamon County Circuit Court when the fall term opened on November 16, 1859. Bissell's legal counsel consisted of

Lincoln, William H. Herndon, Milton Hay, and Stephen T. Logan. Ryan was represented by Benjamin S. Edwards, Amzi McWilliams, and John T. Stuart. Each side had one of Lincoln's former law partners, Logan for the defense and Stuart for the plaintiff. At the same time, Lincoln was busy in the US district court meeting in Springfield: On November 16, he signed a bond for costs in *Quackenbush & Co. v. Lucas*; Two days later, Lincoln warned William Dungy that the sale of certain land would leave him liable on a promissory note "and you better watch it."; in *Allen and McGrady v. Illinois River Railroad Co.*, he wrote and filed a notice of interrogatories to be asked of the defendant; on November 26, Lincoln filed a declaration and bond in *Davis & Co. V. Strosnider*. On November 3, 1859, five days before election day, Lincoln wrote to P. Quinn Harrison in Springfield urging his support for John M. Palmer for Congress. "I have reason to doubt that our friends are doing the best they can about the election. Still, you can do some more, if you will.... Pitch in and try. Palmer is good and true, and deserves the best vote we can give him. If you can make your precinct 20 votes better than it was last, we probably shall redeem the county. Try." In September 1859, Lincoln successfully defended Harrison against a murder charge and secured an acquittal. Palmer lost the election.

Before Lincoln and Bissell became close political associates, Bissell earned a medical degree from Jefferson Medical College in Philadelphia in 1834 at the age of twenty-three. He practiced medicine for three years at Painted Post in New York State before moving to Illinois. When he was elected as a Democrat to the state legislature in 1840 for one term, Bissell met Lincoln, who was also a legislator. As a politician, Bissell developed his unique charisma comprising extraordinary talent as an extemporaneous speaker, captivating powers of oratory, a charm of speech, pure elegant diction, inimitable gestures, cutting and effective satire and a sly humor. After earning a bachelor of law degree from Transylvania Law School (KY) in 1844, he was admitted to the Illinois bar that same year. Bissell practiced law in Belleville and was a district prosecutor until the outbreak of the Mexican War. During the war, he was elected colonel of the Second Regiment of Illinois Volunteers in General Zachary Taylor's army. His regiment helped turn back the Mexican Army during the two-day defensive battle of Buena Vista. Returning as a war hero, in 1848 Bissell was elected as a Democrat to the US House of Representatives for the first of his three terms. While in Congress, in 1850, Virginia Representative James A. Seddon, who became the Confederate Secretary of War, delivered a distorted version of the Buena Vista battle. Seddon contended that the Northern troops retreated under fire and only the intervention of Mississippi troops commanded by Colonel Jefferson Davis prevented a disaster. Outraged, Bissell replied with controlled anger in a masterful, hour-long speech in which he tongue-lashed Seddon and other Southerners and accused them of plotting secession. Correcting the Buena Vista allegation, Bissell retorted that Davis was a mile and a half away and that Northern and Kentucky troops turned back the Mexicans. Davis, then a US senator from Mississippi, reacted emotionally, claiming that his regiment was insulted. Intuitively, Davis challenged Bissell to a duel. Bissell accepted stipulating the use of army muskets loaded with ball and buckshot at close range. President Zachary Taylor knew both men; Bissell as a junior officer and Davis as a former son-in-law. With Taylor's intervention, Davis accepted an explanation he previously rejected and withdrew his challenge. This dueling incident made Bissell an extremely popular folk-hero in Illinois.

Incidentally, Lincoln was also involved in a duel. James Shields challenged Lincoln to a duel about September 17, 1842. It appears that Shields was grievously offended by four pseudonymous articles attacking him that were signed by Rebecca. and published in the *Sangamo Journal* between August 19 and September 8. These articles, written in a backwoods dialect, provoked Whig laughter at the expense of Democratic auditor Shields. On September 2, the newspaper published a 2,500 word essay "Letter From the Lost Townships" that poked fun at Shields and the Democrats . An amicable settlement could not be reached by Lincoln's second, Dr. Elias H. Merryman and Shields' second, General Samuel Whiteside, and a duel was proposed. Lincoln selected cavalry broadswords of the largest size as the weapons and outlined the preliminaries. On September 22, both parties proceeded to Alton and crossed the Mississippi River to the dueling grounds. Without Shields's knowledge, "his friends withdraw his first note to Lincoln, whose friends then read Lincoln's apology, and the duel is called off."

In an effort to stop the epidemic of duels, the 1848 Illinois state constitution required state officials to swear in a special inauguration oath that they had never fought or accepted a challenge to a duel or acted as a second. Legally, this requirement meant that Bissell was barred from holding office in Illinois. Bissell's serious health problems seemed to make that prohibition meaningless. By 1854, Bissell's legs were paralyzed and his crippling condition severely restricted his activities. His paraplegia was attributed to his exposure to a mysterious nervous disease while in the army. In contradiction, Bissell's ailment was described by his personal friend, Dr. Francis F. Synder, as a rheumatic or neuralgic condition and the doctor diagnosed it as caused by syphilis. "He died of the secondary effects of syphilis-he told me so himself—he contracted in Mexico."

Another national legislative event in 1854 influenced Bissell's future. Stephen A. Douglas, US senator from Illinois and chairman of the Committee on Territories, introduced the Kansas-Nebraska Act on January 4, 1854. Five months later, on May 30, 1854, the act was passed into law. That bill established a government in Nebraska and said that the territory "when admitted as a State or States…shall be received into the Union, with or without slavery, as their constitution may prescribe." Slavery was to be determined by the doctrine of "popular sovereignty." Congressman Bissell broke with his Democratic party during the debates over the extension of slavery into the new territories of Kansas and Nebraska.

Aroused and inflamed public controversy flourished over the expansion of slavery into the Kansas and Nebraska territories. On February 22, 1856, an anti-slavery conference of anti-Nebraska newspaper editors convened in Decatur to plan for the next presidential campaign. Lincoln was the only non-journalist in attendance among the thirty to forty people who attended the dinner after the meeting. This editorial gathering called for an Illinois state fusion convention at the end of May. When offered the opportunity to run for governor, Lincoln rejected the invitation on the grounds that a true Republican could not win and the candidate should be a former Democrat. A politically astute Lincoln reasoned that the anti-slavery Republican coalition would have a better chance of electing a governor if their candidate was a former Democrat. Bissell fit the bill of particulars as an anti-Nebraska Democrat, a popular folk hero regarding his duel with Davis, and a true military hero of the Mexican War.

On May 29, 1856, about 270 delegates met in Bloomington to organize the state's first Republican party. Despite Bissell's constitutional disqualification and physical handicaps, preliminary behind-the-scenes arrangements made him the unopposed candidate for governor. Bissell was willing to run for office despite his paralysis. In a letter to the editor of the *Alton Courier*, Bissell said that he could walk only with "the use of a cane and the aid of a friendly arm" but that his health and mental capacity were good. He was nominated by acclamation "with nine long, loud, and hearty cheers." Francis A. Hoffman was nominated for lieutenant governor to attract the German vote. However, Hoffman was declared ineligible because he was not a citizen for the required fourteen years. Lincoln and other Republican leaders nominated John Wood to replace Hoffman. Politically, Wood founded the town of Quincy and could take votes away from the Democrat candidate for governor, William A. Richardson, who came from Quincy. Furthermore, Wood was an abolitionist, served in the Black Hawk War, was elected mayor of Quincy several times, and even spent a year out West looking for a fortune during the California gold rush.

Nineteen days later, about June 19, the first national Republican convention was in session in Philadelphia. Lincoln did not attend the convention and Lincoln & Herndon appeared in many cases during the summer term of the Sangamon County Circuit Court. Furthermore, Lincoln was present for the entire term of the Champaign County Circuit Court in Urbana from June 17 to June 23. On June 19, John C. Frémont, known as the "Pathfinder" for his explorations of the West including the Rocky Mountains, was nominated for president. In an early June letter to Lyman Trumbull, Lincoln expressed his belief that seventy-one-year-old federal judge John McLean would be a suitable candidate for the presidency. However, there was no movement in that direction. During the selection of Frémont's running mate, Illinois delegate William B. Archer seconded Lincoln's nomination for vice-president and John M. Palmer endorsed him. In the balloting, William L. Dayton, a former US senator from New Jersey, got 253 votes to Lincoln's 110. Seeing Lincoln's support diminish, his nominators withdrew in favor of Dayton, who became Frémont's running mate. In a June 27, 1856 letter to John Van Dyke, a former New Jersey congressman, Lincoln summed up the situation: "When you meet Judge Dayton present my respects, and tell him I think him a far better man than I for the position he is in, and that I shall support both him and Colonel Frémont most cordially."

Democrats nominated James Buchanan for president and Southern rights champion, John C. Breckinridge for vice-president, while the American Party nominated ex-president Millard Fillmore for president. This American Party began in the 1840s and was usually called the Know-Nothings because of their standard reply to questions about their rituals and mysteries: "I know nothing about it." In policy, the Know-Nothings were anti-immigrant, anti-Catholic, and combated foreign influences by upholding and promoting traditional American ways. After the 1856 election, the party declined rapidly. Similarly, the Whig party disintegrated after the election. Lincoln was a Whig in the 1830s and remained so until he became a Republican in the mid-1850s. Originally, Whigs were a coalition established to contest the Democrats, especially Andrew Jackson.

Lincoln acted on his belief about the need for a former Democrat to run for Illinois governor and became a Bissell strategist during the election campaign. In the 1856 Republican presidential and gubernatorial campaigns, Lincoln made forty to fifty speeches supporting national candidates Frémont and Dayton and Illinois candidates Bissell and Wood. As a stump speaker, Lincoln did well because he had strong lungs, a hearty constitution, and a thick hide impervious to the audience's raucous sport of politician-baiting. Nearly 6,000 people attended a Frémont and Bissell meeting in Charleston on August 8, 1856. Lincoln was listened to "with marked attention and approbation." After a rally on October 18, 1856, the Republican *Belleville Advocate* commented: "The palm...belongs to Mr. Lincoln; his was the speech of the day." In sharp contrast, the Democratic newspaper, the *St. Clair Tribune* jibed Lincoln for closing his speech with the remark: "God bless the Dutch." On October 29, 1856, Lincoln followed his law partner, William H. Herndon, who made the principal speech for Frémont and Bissell. "Hon. A. Lincoln, who made a candid appeal to every opponent of the sham Democracy to cast his vote for Frémont and Dayton, Bissell and Wood, and the whole Anti-Nebraska ticket." Getting close to election day, thousands attended a Frémont and Bissell meeting in Jacksonville on November 1, 1856. "The Hon. A. Lincoln, W. H. Herndon, Swett and others addressed the crowd from different stands." At the end of an acrimonious campaign, on November 4, the Democrats won Illinois for President James Buchanan, but Bissell was elected by 4,787 votes, 46 percent of the total in the three-man field.

Toward the end of November, Lincoln was still basking in the success of the campaign that elected Bissell as he attended to his legal business. As the fall 1856 term of the Sangamon County Circuit Court opened, Lincoln & Herndon appeared in five cases on the first day of court. On the next day, ten Lincoln & Herndon cases were called, but only one was contested. On November 19, the trial of Theodore Anderson and Jane Anderson for the murder of George Anderson, uncle of Theodore and husband of Jane, began. Logan, Lincoln, and John E. Rosette defended Theodore while Stuart & Benjamin S. Edwards, Thomas Lewis, and Antrim Campbell defended Jane. Archibald McWilliams and Usher F. Linder prosecuted the case. Townspeople believed that the somewhat younger Jane tried to poison her older husband by putting strychnine in his medicine. Furthermore, they suspected that Jane participated in the lethal beating. Phebe Todd, George's sister, was a star witness for the defense. She supported Theodore's alibi and declared that on the night in question she gave her brother his medicine, not Jane. A post-mortem examination did find strychnine in the deceased's stomach. However, four physicians and others testified that death was caused by a fatal head injury during a brutal beating as George emerged from a privy in his backyard on May 15, 1856. Differing in opinion, Doctors Ryan and Bell testified that George died of strychnine poisoning. Seeking to establish a motive, the prosecution sought to prove improper relations existed between the youthful aunt Jane and her nephew Theodore. Lincoln objected and blocked that scandalous allegation. After ten days of a sensational trial, the jury retired to consider their verdict on Saturday night November 29. Jurors deliberated for several hours and returned that evening to render a not guilty verdict. Almost immediately after the close of the Anderson trial, Lincoln sat on the bench in place of Judge David Davis on December 2, 1856. Forty-five cases came before Judge Lincoln, but none were contested. He devoted his time on the bench to entering decrees and orders.

On January 12, 1857, William H. Bissell was inaugurated as the eleventh governor of Illinois. Strangely, the Democrats did not contest Bissell's election although they contended that he perjured himself by taking the anti-dueling oath. Bissell rationalized his taking the oath because the duel acceptance took place in the District of Columbia. Lincoln did not object even though the perjury took place in Illinois when the oath was administered in Springfield.

With Bissell's election, Lincoln achieved a home state power base for his future political ambitions. Lincoln savored his behind-the-scenes political power in Illinois acting as the governor's unofficial legal advisor. On January 2, 1859, Bissell sent a letter to Lincoln requesting assistance:

On getting to Springfield I shall desire to consult you as to what I should say in my message to the Legislature about Kansas.

May I ask you to write out, hastily as you please, your views on that subject, that I may make such use as I deem proper in preparing my message?

I shall be in Springfield on Monday or Tuesday next.

Since Bissell could walk only with crutches, he never entered the state Capitol during the three years of his administration. He transacted his business from a second floor room of the red brick Italianate Executive Mansion on Fifth and Jackson Streets in downtown Springfield. Illinois governors lived in the mansion beginning in 1855 and Bissell was the second governor to reside there.

On July 13, 1842, Samuel D. Marshall, a Shawneetown lawyer, hired Lincoln to defend Thomas Margrave in an appeal before the supreme court of Illinois in the case of *Grable v. Margrave*. William G. Grable was represented by James Shields and James C. Conkling. Earlier, a lower court trial in Gallatin County found Grable guilty of seducing Margrave's daughter. That jury awarded $300 to Margarve for the loss of his daughter's services. Lincoln won the appeal and the court's decision was strong and clear: "The father may not only recover the damages he has sustained by the loss of service, and the payment of necessary expenses, but the jury may award him compensation for the disgrace cast upon the family, and the loss of the society and comfort of his daughter." On the next day, July 14, Lincoln sent Marshall a letter. "Relative to the suit...I have delayed answering it til now, when I can announce the result of the case. The Judgement is affirmed. So soon as the clerk has leisure to make out a copy of the mandate of the court, I will get him to do so, and send it to you, by force of which, your clerk will issue an execution. As to the fee, if you are agreed, let it be as follows. Give me credit for two years subscription to your paper, and send me five dollars in good money or the equivalent of it in our Illinois paper." Marshall was the publisher and editor of the *Illinois Republican.*

After living at two other locations, the Lincolns moved into a house at Eighth and Jackson, a painted frame building constructed in Greek Revival style. He bought the house from Reverend Charles N. Dresser, the clergyman who married him. They signed a sales contract on January 16, 1844 for $1,200 in cash and the title to a shop where H. A. Hough did business as a cabinetmaker. Lincoln owned the grounds and building that were valued at $300. There were shade trees and wood-plank sidewalks in the residential neighborhood. About twelve years later, the Lincolns spent $1,300 as Mrs. Lincoln supervised the raising of the roof to make two full stories and added additional renovations. Lincoln frequently walked the few blocks to visit Bissell at the nearby Executive Mansion.

Isaac N. Arnold, a legal colleague, recalled the generous hospitality of the dinners and evening parties given by Mrs. Lincoln in their Springfield home. "Everything orderly and refined...a cordial and hearty Western welcome which put every guest perfectly at ease. Mrs. Lincoln's table was famed for the excellence of many rare Kentucky dishes, and in season, it was loaded with venison, wild turkeys, prairie chickens, quail, and other game, which was then abundant. Yet it was her genial manners, and ever-kind welcome, and Mr. Lincoln's wit and humor, anecdote, and unrivaled conversation, which formed the chief attraction."

On February 13, 1857, Mr. and Mrs. A. Lincoln attended a party at the Executive Mansion. "In every respect it was a delightful and magnificent entertainment, Governor and Mrs. Bissell doing the honors of host and hostess with an ease and grace which attracted and pleased all who were present.... Throughout the evening, a fine brass and string band discoursed most delicious music, and the dancers kept the cotillions filled until a late hour."

On February 17, 1857 in their office, Lincoln gave Herndon his analysis of the Democratic apportionment bill pending in the state legislature. Caught up in the rush of activities at the beginning of his term as governor, Bissell unwittingly blundered and inadvertently signed the Democratic reapportionment bill he obviously intended to veto. In effect, the reapportionment bill gerrymandered the composition of the election districts to favor the election of Democratic legislators. Reacting rapidly, Lincoln arranged a hasty conference attended by Norman B. Judd, the Republican state chairman, and Joseph Gillespie, a Whig lawyer and personal friend. Quickly, they alerted Bissell to his grave mistake. Immediately, Bissell crossed out his signature, vetoed the bill and returned it to the speaker of the Assembly. Bissell's message vetoing the apportionment bill is in Lincoln's handwriting. Democrats sought a writ of mandamus in *People ex rel. Lanphier and Walker v. Hatch* to compel Ozias M. Hatch, the secretary of state, to perform his legal responsibility to certify the reapportionment act as law.

On February 2, 1858, John A. McClernand argued the case before the supreme curt of Illinois for the Democrats. Robert Blackwell and W. C. Gundy were co-counsel. Lincoln and Jackson Grimshaw represented the Republicans. They asserted that the governor possessed the inherent power to rectify an obvious error, especially where the act had not passed from his control. A report in the *Illinois State Journal* lauded Lincoln's sagacious pleading: "The argument of Mr. Lincoln was a most able and clear exposition of the law, and in the minds of the many disinterested parties who heard it, completely removed all doubt, as to the validity of the Governor's veto."

In its February 6, 1858 decision, the Supreme Court of Illinois ruled in favor of Hatch and the Republicans. Justices noted that the governor abided by the time period specified in the state constitution for approval or veto. Continuing, the court said that while the bill is in the possession and control of the executive, it has no force of law and the governor has the right to veto the bill. Immediately after the court's verdict, Lincoln sent almost identical letters to Gillespie and Gustave P. Koerner, Bissell's former law partner, on February 7, 1858. "Let this be confidential, but [Ebenzer] Peck [court clerk] told me that in the consultation room, they unanimously declared in his presence, that even if the Gov.

had signed the Bill purposely he had a right to change his mind and strike his name off, so long as the Bill remained in his control." When president, Lincoln appointed Peck to the US Court of Claims.

Lincoln did have a personal stake in this lawsuit. He planned to run for the US Senate against Stephen A. Douglas. By law, the Illinois state legislature chose their federal senator. Obviously, a Democratic gerrymandering of the election districts created an unfair disadvantage in Lincoln's aim to be Illinois's US senator. Even the Springfield correspondent for the *St. Louis Republican,* a Democratic newspaper despite its name, reviewed the case and complimented Lincoln on his defense of Bissell: "He made one of the best arguments he ever made, and, although at the time, we differed with him in his positions, yet candor compels us to admit that he presented his case in a strong light and with much force."

One hundred thirty-four years later, on May 1, 1991, a situation similar to Governor Bissell's dilemma occurred in Los Angeles, California. Mayor Tom Bradley sued City Clerk Elias Martinez seeking to invalidate an ordinance that he signed by accident. *People ex rel. Lanphier and Walker v. Hatch* was cited as a precedent by legal counsel in this contemporary law suit. In contrast to the outcome of Lincoln's winning arguments, Judge Ronald Sohigian ruled against the mayor and the unintended law stood.

Bissell was still the Illinois governor at the time of Ryan's suit to collect his fee for medical care. Ryan's legal action originally commenced before a justice of the peace and moved through the court system. Higher court proceedings in the *Ryan v. Bissell* case occurred during the November 1859 term of the Sangamon County Circuit Court and the January 1860 term of the supreme court of Illinois.

Judge Edward Y. Rice presided in the Sangamon County Circuit Court trial. Lincoln, Herndon, and Hay continually raised objections and took exceptions to the specific rulings of the court that denied their objections. Essentially, Lincoln and his colleagues raised two technical points of law: the first on a rule of evidence regarding the determination of customary payment to physicians and the other on a violation of a statute regarding too frequent service as a juror. Ryan produced his accounts for medical attention rendered to sundry specifically named individuals. He presented evidence showing that the children lived with Bissell as part of his family ever since their mother died, that they were his nieces, that their father resided elsewhere, and that Bissell "himself and through his servants sent for the said plaintiff [Ryan] to attend on said children."

Since all the parties in the suit lived in Springfield, Dr. Meredith Helm, who practiced and lived in that city for more than twenty-five years, was called by Ryan's lawyers to testify about customary payments in similar situations. While Lincoln and Bissell's other attorneys objected to the questions put to Helm, the court overruled each objection and allowed Helm to answer questions such as the following:

> Q: When persons are living permanently in a family, and the head of the family sends for a physician, is there a custom as to who shall be charged with the bill?
> A: There is a custom amongst physicians, but [I] don't know how general it is; the custom is to charge the head of the family. In my practice I have acted on it, with some exceptions, and it has been conformed to. The exceptions, where when the person requesting the attendance directed not to charge to him but to some other person.
> Q: Is this practice universal so far as you know unless the person disclaims liability who calls for the physician?
> A: [I have] known other physicians to do it as well as myself, but do not know how universal it is.

This was the only evidence submitted regarding medical payment customs. Lincoln moved to exclude that evidence from the jury because the custom was not proven. However, the court allowed Helm's testimony to stand.

Bissell admitted that the charges were reasonable but denied any liability for payment since the children were Kinney's. Furthermore, Bissell stated that Ryan knew the children were Kinney's and that Kinney usually paid the expenses of his family while they resided with Bissell. Stridently, Bissell declared that this showed that he was "acting for Kinney in the employment of plaintiff [Ryan] to attend said children." No proof was introduced to indicate that Ryan knew that Kinney paid the bills for the children.

Ryan's attorneys submitted two instructions to the jury and the Judge so advised the jurors:

> 1. If the jury believe, from the evidence, that it was the intention of both parties that the plaintiff [Ryan] in this case should perform the services rendered to the children of his wife's deceased sister, and that the defendant [Bissell] should pay him therefor, then the defendant is liable for these charges in plaintiff's bill.
>
> 2. That in determining the intention, the jury should take into consideration the terms on which the children resided in defendant's [Bissell] family, the permanency of their abode, and the custom as proved by the witness in this cause; if they believe any such custom has been proved in this cause.

Bissell's lawyers registered an exception to the giving of the plaintiff's instructions to the jury. In contrast, Bissell's lawyers, including Lincoln, submitted four instructions for the jury:

> 1st. That notwithstanding the jury may believe, from the evidence, that the services rendered in this case to the children of Wm. C. Kinney, were rendered on the call and request of the defendant [Bissell], yet if the jury shall believe, from the evidence, that these services were rendered in the lifetime of the father of the children and that plaintiff [Ryan] knew, or had opportunity of knowing, that these

services were for the benefit of said Kinney, and that the defendant was only acting as the friend or agent for Kinney, in requesting the attendance of the plaintiff, that then the defendant would not be liable for such services.

2d. That if the jury shall believe, from the evidence, that the defendant, Bissell, in sending or calling for the plaintiff, to attend the family or children of W. C. Kinney, was acting only as the friend or agent of said Kinney, and the plaintiff from the circumstances under which the family of Kinney were residing with the defendant, knew that said Bissell was only acting for said Kinney, and as his friend and agent, in so requesting the attendance of the plaintiff, that then although the defendant may not have informed the plaintiff that he was only acting as the friend or agent of Kinney, yet he would not be liable for such services.

3d. That the jury are instructed that they must disregard any evidence of a custom amongst physicians, to charge their bills in a particular way, to or to particular persons, under any proposed state of circumstances, unless the circumstances in proof are similar to those upon which the custom is based, and unless it has been further proved that this custom is generally known.

4th. That the jury cannot take into consideration, in deciding this case, any evidence of a custom amongst physicians as to the person to whom these bills should be charged under the circumstances of this case, or under any state of supposed facts that may have been proposed to the witness by whom such custom may have been proved.

Judge Rice gave the first three defense instructions but refused to give the fourth. Lincoln and his colleagues took exception to the court's decision. On adjournment for the day, the case was submitted to the jury. Before the court adjourned and the jury retired to consider their verdict, jurors were told that they could seal the verdict and give it to the officer in charge to hold for the court the next morning. That same evening, the jury reached a verdict: "We, the jury, find for the plaintiff [Ryan]." As instructed by the court, the jury foreman sealed the verdict, handed it to the officer in charge and the jurors went home for the night. On opening the verdict the next morning, Judge Rice informed the jurors that their verdict was not in proper form and directed them to retire and reconsider. This time the jury verdict included the full amount, $97, that Ryan requested.

Upon Lincoln's advice, Bissell appealed to the supreme court of Illinois during the January 1860 term. Lincoln filed a bill of exceptions that detailed several errors in the Sangamon County Circuit Court trial. Stuart and Edwards represented Ryan. Lincoln, Herndon, and Hay continued as Bissell's lawyers and specified the technical errors in the circuit court in their appeal:

> The said Plaintiff [Bissell] now comes and says that in the Record and proceedings herein manifest error hath intervened to his prejudice as follows.
>
> 1st That the court erred in overruling the challenge for cause to the juror, Bolton, and in permitting him to be sworn upon the jury.
>
> 2d That the court erred in permitting the testimony of [Dr.] Helm in reference to a custom to go before the jury, and in not excluding the same from jury.
>
> 3d That the court erred in giving improper instructions for the Plaintiff.
>
> 4th That the court erred in refusing proper instructions for Defendant.
>
> 5th That the court erred in not discharging the jury after having separated before finding a verdict, and in permitting the jury to again retire and find a verdict.
>
> 6th That the court erred in overruling Defendant's motion for a new trial, and in rendering Judgement for Plaintiff.

Points and authorities were given for the specific errors mentioned in the bill of exceptions. In response to the defendant's bill of exceptions, Stuart and Edwards concisely answered their arguments and included the supporting legal citations:

1.There was no error in excluding the juror.

2.Substantial justice has been done by the verdict in this case; in such case the verdict will not be disturbed. *Gillett et al. vs Sweat,* 1 Gilm. 475. *Greenup vs Stoker,* 3 Gilm. 202.

The instructions given by the court when taken together, lay down the law correctly.

"All contract made in the ordinary course of business without particular stipulations express or implied are presumed to be made in reference to any existing usage relating to such practice, and it is always competent for a party to resort to such usage to ascertain and fix the terms of the contract." *Chitty on Contracts,* p. 83 in notes. 1 Smith's *Leading Cases,* 305 and seq. in notes.

It is sufficient if the custom be general and uniform and may be proved by one witness. 1 Smith's *Leading Cases,* p. 688. American notes and authorities there cited.

As to the verdict see Graham and Waterman on new trial, 1 vol. 80, 81, 85, 86. *Winslow vs Draper,* 8 Pick. 170. Horton vs Horton, 2 Cowen. 589. 3 Graham and Waterman, pp. 1403, 1404, 1406, 1407.

Regarding the juror Bolton, Lincoln, Herndon and Hay cited the April 26, 1859 Illinois state statute: "That hereafter it shall be sufficient cause of challenge to any juror called to be sworn in any cause that he has been sworn as a juror at any term of court held within a year prior to the time of such challenge."

During his *voir dire,* the preliminary examination to determine the competency of a juror, Bolton stated that he had served as a grand juror in the same court within the past twelve months. Immediately, Lincoln challenged, for cause, Bolton serving on this jury. Justice Sidney Breese delivered the opinion of the supreme court of Illinois and stated that the challenge to juror Bolton should have been allowed. He explained that the act of 1859 was designed to remedy a specific type of jury mischief:

There had grown up, in our State, a formidable corps of professional jurors; persons who, having no honest means of livelihood, or not resorting to them, if they had, were found, at every term, hanging about the court-houses, importuning the sheriffs and their deputies, and seizing every occasion, to be put upon the juries—making their living, in fact, by jury service.... This disgusting and disreputable eagerness to be upon juries, occurred at every term. The design of the act of 1859 was to put a stop to this, and plainer language could not be used to express the intention.... The act intended to break up the profession, and we will aid the law by giving it the most liberal construction to effect that end.

Lincoln, Herndon, and Hay found a citation that proclaimed that a custom cannot be established by the testimony of one witness. They argued that the testimony in reference to a custom was wholly inadmissible according to the books on evidence.

[Custom] must be known certain, uniform, reasonable and not contrary to law; that usages should be sparingly adopted by courts as rules of law, as they are often founded in mistake or in the want of enlarged and comprehensive views of the full bearing of principles. That their true office is to interpret the otherwise indeterminate intentions of parties and to ascertain the nature and extent of their contracts arising not from express stipulation, but from mere implications and presumptions and acts of a doubtful and equivocal character; and to fix and explain the meaning of words and expressions of doubtful or various senses.

To the point, Justice Breese stated that Helm's evidence of custom was not sufficient to establish the custom claimed to exist. "A usage, such as that spoken of by Dr. Helm, and he was by no means certain about it, ought to be like the practice of carrying goods for hire, which cannot be established by proof of one instance, but by an accumulation of instances. It cannot be established by evidence of opinion merely.... All the authorities concur in saying that if usage is relied upon, it must be show to be ancient, certain, uniform, reasonable, and so general as to furnish this presumption of knowledge by both parties." As far as Helm's testimony about the custom, it was very general and unsatisfactory, and fell far short of proving the custom as one known and generally acquiesced in. Helm said he did not know how general it was, even in the community in which he lived and practiced. "It will generally be desirable, when a particular usage is relied on, to establish it by the testimony of several witnesses.... All the testimony on this point should have been withdrawn from the jury."

Finally, the supreme court of Illinois did not find the recalling of the jury to put the verdict in proper form objectionable enough to warrant a reversal on that grounds alone.

Justice Breese delivered the conclusion of the supreme court of Illinois: "For the reasons given the Judgement is reversed, and the cause remanded for further proceedings, not inconsistent with this opinion."

About one month after the supreme court of Illinois trial ended, Bissell became seriously ill. During that month, in February 1860, Bissell surprisingly indicated in a private letter that he preferred Salmon P. Chase for president. He made that preference despite Lincoln's pivotal role in Bissell's becoming governor and his success acting as his lawyer. On the day before his death from pneumonia, the *Chicago Tribune* reported that Ozias M. Hatch, Illinois secretary of state, Jesse E. Dubois, state auditor, "Lincoln and Herndon have farewell interview with Governor Bissell, mortally ill and sinking rapidly." On March 22, 1860, the *Chicago Journal* described the governor's burial: "In the procession were several of the most prominent men of the State; men renowned in politics, education, military history and the law. Among them were Hon. Abraham Lincoln; his law partner, Wm. H. Herndon" and many others. Bissell was the first republican governor, the first governor to hold a college degree—actually two college degrees, the first Roman Catholic to hold the office and the first official to die in that office on March 18, 1860 at the age of forty-eight. Bissell's former law partner and German political leader, Koerner, believed that a healthy Bissell would have become president. If physically sound, Bissell's political ambitions and campaigning ability would have been a threat to Lincoln's future.

On the day after Bissell's funeral, Lincoln departed for Chicago to attend the US circuit court where the *Johnston v. Jones and Marsh* trial commenced. William S. Johnston, William Jones, and Sylvester Marsh were the principals involved in the dispute. This case dealt with the ownership of 1,200 square feet of made land, the so-called sandbar. Sand washed in by Lake Michigan accumulated along the north side of the North Pier built by the US government in 1833 along a new channel entrance for the Chicago River into the lake. Earlier in the year, on January 5, 1858, Lincoln wrote to Robert A. Kinzie, a Springfield lawyer representing a railroad having property adjoining the main land. Explaining his legal concerns, Lincoln asked Kinzie to respond to five technical questions about the location and size of the washed up land. Lincoln, John Van Arman, Samuel W. Fuller, and Van Hollis Higgins represented the defendants while Isaac N. Arnold, Isaac N. Morris, and John H. Wills appeared for the plaintiff. Judge Thomas Drummond presided at one of the trials and later evaluated Lincoln as a lawyer, "I have no hesitation is saying he was one of the ablest lawyers I have ever known." Although Lincoln stayed in Chicago at this trial until it ended on April 4, he did not spend his free time sitting in his room. He posed for sculptor Leonard W. Volk on March 29 and 30; delivered a speech at Waukegan on April 2 "at the earnest solicitation of citizens of Lake County;" and on April 3 he visited his old friend, Chicago harbormaster Julius White, in Evanston and was informally serenaded at White's house. Returning to Chicago the next day, Lincoln remained in court as the trial ended about one in the afternoon. After five hours of deliberation, the jury returned at 6:00 P.M. with a verdict for Lincoln's clients. His compensation for this case was $350 and he signed a receipt for "fee in case of *Johnston v. Jones.*"

A. LINCOLN, ESQUIRE

On April 5, Lincoln returned to Springfield and busily engaged in political activities. Lieutenant-Governor Wood succeeded Bissell to serve the remaining ten months left in his term as governor. Wood was the first bearded Illinois governor. However, Wood never even moved to Springfield, conducted his business from his hometown of Quincy, and allowed Bissell's widow to continue living in the executive mansion. Interestingly, at the end of February 1860, Judge Davis wrote to Springfield lawyer Henry E. Drummer about the Republican nomination for president. "Of course, I shd like it, if Lincoln could be nominated, but I am afraid that is a foregone conclusion. It seems to me from this standpoint now, as if it would either be Mr. Bates or Gov. Seward." Despite his feelings, Davis strenuously worked to secure the nomination for Lincoln. After Lincoln's nomination for president at the Republican convention in Chicago on May 18, Wood made a generous offer to Lincoln on May 22, 1860: "As I do not expect to occupy the Executive Office in the State House at present, I invite you to take and use the same at your pleasure, until it may be wanted for executive purposes."

Wood allowed nominee and later president-elect Lincoln to take over the governor's one-room office in the statehouse to conduct his political and pre-inauguration activities. An announcement in the *Illinois State Journal* alerted the public: "Today, and til further notice, Mr. Lincoln will see visitors at the Executive Chamber in the State House from 10 to 12 A.M. and from 3 1/2 to 5 1/2 P.M. each day." In residence at the state house, Lincoln received a steady stream of a combination of well-wishers and favor seekers. After his term expired on January 14, 1861, Wood never ran for state office again. During the Civil War, Wood served as state quartermaster general for two years. In 1863, at age sixty-four, Wood became a colonel of the 137th Illinois Regiment doing picket duty in Memphis.

LINCOLN POLITICALLY SELECTS THE MEDICAL EXPERT ON INSANITY

Two years into the presidency of Abraham Lincoln, Washington, DC exhibited drastic changes in living conditions, apparently not for the betterment of its residents. Toward the end of February 1863, the *New York Times* commented on the social condition of the district. This editorial remarked that the capitol's population jumped from 40,000 to 100,000 causing a shortage of housing and hotels. "The condition of our National Capitol is a public disgrace. If its overcrowding and filthiness are continued, it will be in danger of a scourge by pestilence." New York City newspaper editor Horace Greeley agreed: "Washington is not a nice place to live in. The rents are high, the food is bad, the dust is disgusting, the mud is deep, and the morals are deplorable." Rooms in Washington cost $3-$10 per week and full room and board ranged from $5-$25 per week. Food prices were rising rapidly: a loaf of bread, 10 cents; milk, 16 cents a quart; sugar, 35 cents per pound; meat, 25-30 cents per pound; two dozen eggs, 30 cents; coffee, 70 cents per pound; and twelve ears of green corn, 25 cents. Horse drawn cabs cost $12^{1/2}$ cents per mile and a minstrel show charged 35 to 50 cents for a reserved seat. New York's Albany Argus published its Washington correspondent's degrading observations:

> Washington is becoming unhealthy. No wonder. The agglemeeration [sic] of antagonistic humanity there; the heterogeneous mass of respectable crime and criminal respecta-bility; the all-pervading army; the poisonous water and the deadlier liquor; the seething heat and the blinding dust, all combine to

make Washington an epitome and model of all that is disagreeable.

In the summer of 1863, a confederate civilian physician shot and killed a white Union officer who was training colored troops in Norfolk, Virginia. A military commission conducted a trial and the murderer was convicted. With no question as to guilt, President Lincoln responded to a rash of emotional clemency appeals. He chose a medical expert to conduct a professional examination to determine whether or not the murderer was sane or insane. His own legal experiences in cases such as *People v. Wyant* and *Fleming v. Rogers and Crothers* involved selecting expert medical witnesses to testify on behalf of his clients.

However, in this case, both legal and political factors conceivably influenced Lincoln's decision. Lincoln considered law and politics interrelated, mutually dependent, and wholly inclusive. During his law practice, Lincoln was a prosecutor in a case where the insanity plea was used as a defense. Two influential cabinet members, Secretary of State William H. Seward and Secretary of War Edwin M. Stanton, also had legal experience involving the insanity plea in murder trials. Being an experienced and competent trial lawyer, Lincoln was cognizant of the legal precedents and of the public's skeptical attitudes toward the insanity plea. He was familiar with the abilities of skillful lawyers such as Seward, Stanton, and Leonard Swett, his adversary in the *People v. Wyant* and *Fleming v. Rogers and Crothers*, to use expert witnesses to convince a jury and to persuade the public. In addition to the legal aspects, Lincoln faced serious politicallysensitive issues such as the deadly draft riots, the military necessity to recruit emancipated slaves into the Union army, the impact of Union Negro soldiers upon the troops from the border states, the morale and discipline of the army, and the upcoming uncertain 1864 presidential election.

Compounding the legal and political difficulties, President Lincoln suffered unremitting odious attacks on his character from the North, the South, and from England. Two London newspapers were brutal in their attacks. In the *Herald*: "Mr. Lincoln is a vulgar, brutal boor, wholly ignorant of political science, of military affairs, of everything else which a statesman should know." It was not better in the *Standard*: "Never were issues so momentous placed in so feeble a hand; never was so great a place in history filled by a figure so mean." Epithets in the newspapers explicitly reflected the contemporary public's passionate emotions that held Lincoln in low esteem: aimless punster, ape, baboon, bigot, blackguard, charlatan, degenerate, despot, eunuch, gorilla, lunatic, mole-eyed monster, moral dwarf, obscene clown, political coward, racist, simple Susan, slang-wanging stump speaker, smutty joker, traitor, tyrant, unmentionably diseased, and woodenhead. After Lincoln delivered his short but memorable address at the dedication of a cemetery in Gettysburg in November 1863, an indignant *Chicago Times* reporter added to the invective: "The cheek of every American must tingle with shame as he reads the silly, flat, dishwatery utterances of the man who has to be pointed out to intelligent foreigners as the President of the United States."

These epithets and diatribes highlight the obvious distinction between Lincoln's analogous ambivalent reputation and his subsequent complete adulation. A sociological analysis compared Lincoln's ambiguous reputation before and during the Civil War with his image after his assassination. Researchers concluded that the impassioned national mourning transformed the martyred president into a sanctified icon. In contrast to being a "sanctified icon" during his own lifetime, Lincoln was a model local politician and a faithful practitioner of patronage while in the White House. "He was a total political operator—a party hack. But so what?…the wiles and commitments of the party activist and regular are, therefore, not easily denigrated." On Lincoln's death, Representative J. M. Ashley of Ohio spoke for a number of legislators: "The decease of Mr. Lincoln is a great national bereavement, but I am not sure it is so much of a national loss."

To comprehend Lincoln's decision-making process, the facts about the lieutenant's murder must be considered along with the legal and political issues. These stressful events began shortly after the Union victory as the bloody, momentous Battle of Gettysburg in Pennsylvania ended during early July 1863. Reactions to the lieutenant's murder came from both sides. Union adherents denounced the murder as an "undefended assassination." Confederates condemned the military commission's death verdict as the consequences of "abolition malice." However, the murder, the trial, and the outcome took place and were rooted in happenings that took place in Norfolk, Virginia about fourteen months earlier.

With a white handkerchief tied to a pole, the citizen representatives from Norfolk waited in two carriages just beyond a little bridge across Princess Anne Avenue, a short distance beyond Chapel Street. As the Union troops clad in dark blue uniforms approached, Mayor William W. Lamb, George W. Camp, Captain James Cornick, Charles H. Rowland, and J. B. Whitehead met Major-General John E. Wool and negotiated the city's surrender. Norfolk was occupied by Union forces on May 10, 1862. In the afternoon of the next day, Lincoln and Secretary of War Stanton sailed up the James River to briefly look at the city. After the Emancipation Proclamation on January 1, 1863, about 500 Norfolk Negroes staged a parade on Main Street. There were people-filled horse drawn carriages and an old butcher wagon in which Negro women trampled and tore the Confederate flag. After burning an effigy of Confederate President Jefferson Davis and burying it in the cemetery, the celebration ended with a march to the house of the military governor, Major-General Egbert L. Viele. Federal marshals mounted on horses decorated with red, white and blue sashes directed all the activities. Natives of Norfolk reported: "No person of any respectability holds any intercourse whatever with the Yankees. Our contempt for them cuts." Norfolk remained in Union hands until the end of the Civil War.

On Saturday, July 11, 1863, Dr. David Minton Wright celebrated two milestones; his wife's birthday and their thirtieth wedding anniversary. About 4:00 P.M., a white officer, Second Lieutenant Alanson L. Sanborn, Company B, 1st Regiment, US Colored Volunteers, marched at the head of his company as they drilled on the sidewalks of Main Street in Norfolk. Although the lieutenant was sometimes called Anson, the official Army Register lists him as Alanson. Before joining the Army in May 1863, Sanborn was a schoolteacher from Whitford Centre, Vermont. He actively recruited blacks into the Union army during the prior two months as the regiment was organized in Washington, DC. Wright, a tall erect man with long gray hair, a full beard and a moustache, stood on the street watching the lieutenant drill the colored troops. He was emotionally overwrought by the spectacle of former slaves jostling Southern men, women, and children off the sidewalk into the gutter. A vigorous secessionist, Wright owned six slaves; three females aged sixty, forty, and sixteen; two males aged sixty and one male aged forty-six. He was incensed at seeing the former slaves, now soldiers, clad in blue uniforms and armed with muskets and bayonets. Wright backed into a store doorway to avoid the marching troops.

Although witnesses differ on the exact scenario, heated and/or insulting words and gestures were exchanged between Wright and the lieutenant. In one version, Wright clenched his fists and exclaimed: "Oh, you dastardly coward!" or called Sanborn "a son of a bitch." Approaching Wright, some said threateningly with sword raised as if to strike, Sanborn bellowed: "You are under arrest." Wright warned Sanborn to "stand off" but Sanborn continued advancing toward Wright. With emotions boiling over on all sides, a general mêlée ensued. Knowing that Wright was always unarmed, a friend in the crowd passed a gun to him to defend himself. As Sanborn approached him, Wright produced a five-chamber Colt revolver from behind his back and fired two shots, fatally wounding Sanborn. Staggering forward pursuing Wright, Sanborn stumbled into Foster and Moore's dry goods store and fell to the floor. As Sanborn lay on the floor, Wright struggled with the soldiers who captured him and yelled: "Let me go; let me do something to help this man." Sanborn died several minutes later. Immediately, Provost-Marshall Alexander E. Bovay sent a telegram to Major-General John A. Dix: "Lieutenant Sanborn, of the colored regiment, was shot at the head of his company on Main Street this p.m. by Doctor Wright and died immediately. Doctor

Wright is in jail heavily ironed." A series of bold declaratory headlines in the *Brooklyn Daily Eagle* dramatically presented the events:

BROOKLYN DAILY EAGLE
Two Cents Tuesday,   July 14, 1863

FROM FORTRESS MONROE
A US Officer Shot at Norfolk, Va.
HE IS KILLED WHILE DRILLING A NEGRO
MILITARY COMPANY IN MAIN STREET
ARREST OF THE ALLEGED MURDERER

During his trial, Wright revealed the intensity of his feelings toward the colored troops: "Is it to be supposed that a citizen of Norfolk, himself an owner of slaves, not knowing but what even one of my slaves was in that company, would submit to be arrested by Negroes and marched off to the guardhouse? No sir, I could not submit to that!"

Immediately after the shooting, Wright was jailed in the customs house, not too far from his own home. As Wright was questioned, his eldest daughter, Miss Pence (Penelope) stood by him for about one hour without any of the Union guards gallantly offering her a seat.

Although a civil government existed and was able to try Wright, a special military commission was established for the trial. Lucius H. Chandler and Lemuel Bowden served as attorneys for Wright. Chandler was the US attorney for the Eastern District of Virginia. Bowden was a US senator representing Virginia. A bit later, Joseph Eggleston Segar joined the defense representing Wright. Segar was in the US House of Representatives in the 37th Congress in 1862-1863. At the time, eastern Virginia was included in the Union and West Virginia became a state on June 20, 1863.

Two days after the shooting, on July 13, 1863, the Portsmouth (VA) City Council passed a resolution denouncing "the brutal murder of a Union officer by a rabid Secessionist." Military authorities were urged "to bring to speedy and condign punishment the author of this foul crime and treasonable act to his country and his God." Furthermore the council sought "to remove from our midst the foul-mouthed traitors who infest the street corners and market-places of our city, plotting treason and even contemplating such deeds of bloodshed as we are now called to reflect on."

While in prison awaiting trial, Wright wrote to his wife: "I am to be tried by a military commission to-day or to-morrow. I suppose the verdict will be the same as that of the provost marshal, made before he had examined the first witness." Although the name of the court was different, the rules and regulations of a military court martial applied in a trial by a military commission. This trial distinction is consequential. Compared to civil courts, military commissions were often biased. Worse yet, military commissions could send the accused to the gallows while a conviction by a civilian jury generally resulted in imprisonment.

On July 20, 1863, the trial began in the customs house. Wright's lawyers emphatically argued that Norfolk was under civil government and the military had no jurisdiction to try him. His lawyers protested that Wright was a noncombatant civilian and a March 3, 1863 act of Congress prohibited a military trial. All the defense arguments failed to convince the military commission and the prosecution prepared to present their witnesses.

Personally, Lincoln felt that civil courts were powerless to deal with individual insurrectionary activity and trial by military commission was constitutional. That opinion was reinforced by Lincoln's experiences with the courts in Washington, DC shortly after he assumed the presidency. Secretary of the Navy, Gideon Welles, pinpointed the problem in his diary: "Unfortunately the hearts and sympathies of the present judges are with the Rebels." Massachusetts Senator Henry Wilson said that the chief judge's "heart is sweltering with treason." On May 23, 1862, the Congress introduced a bill to reorganize the district's courts. About 3000 and almost all the lawyers in Washington, forty-nine, opposed the measure stating: "They believe that this measure is not called for by any public necessity, and that it would not be acceptable to the great mass of the people in the District." On February 20, 1863, Kentucky Senator Garrett Davis placed the opposition memorial before the Senate and the House. Lincoln supported the reorganization and the bill was passed on March 5, 1863 with nineteen Republican senators in favor and sixteen opposed and in the House by 86 to 59. Promptly, Lincoln signed the bill and on March 23, 1863 appointed four-new judges loyal to the Union cause: David Kellogg Cartter from Ohio became chief justice. Cartter was a campaign manager when Lincoln gained the presidential nomination in Chicago; associate justices named were Abram B. Olin of New York; George P. Fisher of Delaware; and Andrew Wylie of Washington, DC. Wylie was the only avowed Republican in Alexandria, Virginia, to vote for Lincoln in 1860 despite threats of violence if he did so. After Lincoln's election, Wylie was sitting on his porch relaxing in a rocking chair. A shot was fired that shattered the glass he was holding in his hand. Immediately thereafter, he moved to the district. Ohio Congressman Albert G. Riddle delivered a descriptive epilogue: "The Supreme Court of the District of Columbia was a court of our creation and for which we cleared the ground by sweeping the alleged disloyal Circuit Court from the boards." Lincoln had only one justification for his policy; necessity justified the exercise of arbitrary power by the president. While he was no dictator, Lincoln certainly did exercise the powers of the president boldly. However, Lincoln's friend David Davis, then an associate justice of the Supreme Court of the United States, apprized him during the war that military trials in areas where the federal courts were functioning freely were "unconstitutional and wrong." Furthermore, Davis told Lincoln that the Supreme Court of the United States should not uphold such trials. Davis firmly believed that military commissions had no jurisdiction over civilians.

In a later disagreement, the 1866 Supreme Court of the United States decision in the *Ex Parte Milligan* case affirmed the illegality of military commissions to determine the guilt of civilians. In keeping with his own judicial opinion, Davis wrote the decision for the court. Paradoxically, Lincoln appointed his Illinois colleague, Judge David Davis, to the Supreme Court of the United States on October 21, 1862 to commendation from the *Daily National Intelligencer*: "Our worthy President has made a wise selection in the appointment...Davis is a fine lawyer as well as an honorable, able, warm-hearted man who has no selfish motives." In a letter to Swett, Davis said "I feel great trepidation in going on the Supreme Bench. I cannot throw it off." When Lincoln was looking to appoint a chief justice in 1864, the *New York Times* erroneously declared that "Justice Davis...will all but certainly be Chief Justice." Davis knew that he was not in the running and former Secretary of the Treasury Salmon P. Chase was appointed.

When the military commission prosecution rested, defense lawyer Bowden began by cross-examining Provost Marshall Bovay. On the evening of the shooting, Bovay admitted that he interviewed Wright. Pointedly, Bowden asked Bovay to describe Wright's conduct and appearance during the conversation that evening. After a prosecution objection, the court ruled that no further evidence would be admitted as to Wright's conduct or appearance after his arrest. With court back in session, Wright's lawyers requested a half-hour for consultation. After the time expired, Bowden and Chandler, much to the surprise of everyone present, announced their withdrawal from the case and left the courtroom. With this tactic, the lawyers hoped to postpone the trial to gain time to plan to save Wright from the inevitable gallows.

Immediately, the court asked Wright if he wished to obtain other counsel or if he prefer that his trial proceed. He responded by asking for a day to consider. After agreeing, the court adjourned. Next day, Wright presented a written statement declaring that he could not and did not wish to obtain further counsel, nor did he wish to introduce any new evidence on his own behalf. Court adjourned to allow Wright to prepare a concluding statement. On the last day of the trial, Wednesday, July 29, 1863, Wright addressed the court. Standing awkwardly before the five member military commission, Wright denied their jurisdiction, denounced the testimony of witnesses as erroneous, and stated that his actions were based upon self-defense. He questioned the "logic" of having colored troops in Norfolk, suggesting that the soldiers were there to provoke and harass white citizens. Furthermore, Wright questioned Sanborn's motives and commented that Sanborn directed offensive remarks to him. Finally, Wright reminded the court that he immediately offered medical care to Sanborn after he was wounded.

In his closing, Judge Advocate John A. Bolles mentioned Wright's possible insanity. If that were so, he insisted that Wright should be confined in an asylum until cured. However, Bolles declared that the shooting of Sanborn was deliberate and unprovoked. Succinctly, Bolles advised the court that they were soldiers and knew what "the good of the service demanded."

Upon reaching a verdict, the court unanimously condemned Wright to be "hung by the neck until he be dead." Place and time of execution to be selected by the Fortress Monroe commander, Major-General John G. Foster, or by the president of the United States.

Hurriedly, defense lawyer Chandler met with Lincoln at the White House and appealed to him to suspend "a speedy enforcement of the judgement of the Military Commission" until he could "give the case a full examination." On August 3, 1863, Lincoln telegraphed Foster: "If Dr. Wright, on trial at Norfolk, has been, or shall be convicted, send me a transcript of his trial and conviction, and do not let execution be done upon him, until my further order." Foster replied: "Your orders will be strictly obeyed. The trial is concluded. General [Henry M.] Naglee informs me that the proceedings, findings & sentence have been forwarded to you for your revision and approval." Reacting to the court's verdict, President Lincoln was beleaguered by "petitioners surpassing in number those of any other pardon appeal during the war for the privilege of a fair and impartial trial" for Wright. John S. Millson and ninety-four other citizens from Norfolk sent a telegram to "His Excellency ABRAHAM LINCOLN" on July 28, 1863: "The undersigned respectfully request that Dr. D. M. WRIGHT, of this city, charged with the murder of Lieutenant Sanborn, be restored to his home and family or be delivered over to civil authorities or some other tribunal where he can have the privilege of a fair and impartial trial, which right belongs to every human being." More than 340 Norfolk citizens, including nine ministers, eleven physicians, five lawyers and consular representatives from Portugal and Austria, signed a petition to pardon or commute the death sentence. N. B. Webster, a New Hampshire native and then a Norfolk educator, delivered a clemency plea that stressed Wright's medical services to the community. Defense lawyers, Bowden, Chandler, and Segar telegraphed Lincoln on August 7 from Norfolk:

> I most respectfully request that so soon as the record in the case of Dr. D. M. Wright, charged with the murder of Lieutenant Sanborn, shall be laid before you, you will telegraph the Hon. L. H. Chandler and myself, fixing some day when we may appear before you and present the mass of testimony which has been taken to prove the insanity of Doctor Wright, and also to present such statements in regard to the manner of conducting his trial, and to the facilities afforded him for making anything like a fair defense, as the facts of the case will justify.

On August 7, 1863, Mrs. Stark A. W. Preighton of Edenton, North Carolina, Wright's niece, wrote to the Confederate States of America President Jefferson Davis asking "if anything can be done by our Government for Doctor Wright." Her letter was endorsed by CSA Secretary of War J. A. Seddon who was doubtful the CSA could help and might "probably prejudice it [Wright's cause] with our brutal foes." President Davis responded to a similar letter from the former CSA Attorney General Thomas Bragg on September 1, 1863 stating: "I have been unable to devise any method which seemed likely to render him [Wright] effective service."

On August 15, 1863, "a committee of five gentlemen chosen by the Union League, Washington Council No. 4, had a very pleasant and impartial interview with his Excellency" concerning Sanborn. A document was read to the president to argue for justice for the

Sanborn shooting and for a warning to others. This document noted that the president had the sealed verdict to review and that Dr. Wright's friends were petitioning for a pardon. Committee members were instructed to "beseech you, for the sake of justice and humanity, and as a suitable warning to all future offenders against the majesty of the law." After listening to the sometimes bombastic phrases read by the draft club representatives, Lincoln commented: "An example would prove a great benefit to the cause."

Legislation passed on July 17, 1862 created the office of judge advocate general to provide supervision of proceedings of courts-martial and military commissions. Shortly after the legislation, Lincoln appointed Joseph Holt to the position. Judge Advocate General Holt sent Lincoln his review of the evidence in Wright's case on August 19, 1863. Holt asserted that the military commission followed proper legal procedure and conducted a fair trial. Testimony on Wright's conduct and appearance was disallowed because an insanity defense was never seriously proposed. After citing case references, Holt declared: "It will be seen, therefore, by this examination of his [Wright's] address that the accused himself not only disclaims the idea of insanity as an answer to his crime, but actually sets up another, that of self-defense." Holt concluded: "The crime then stands in the record as a homicide committed without just cause or provocation, an undefended assassination, and therefore fully meriting the sentence imposed by the court."

On August 28, 1863, Lincoln telegraphed General Foster: "Please notify, if you can, Senator Bowden, Mr. Segar, and Mr. Chandler, all, or any of them, that I now have the record in Dr. Wright's case, and am ready to hear them. When you shall have got the notice to them, please let me know." Foster replied the same day: "I have notified Mr. Chandler of your wishes & he will start for Washington this evening. I have also sent notice to Senator Bowden. Mr. Segar is not here but is understood to be in Washington." Lincoln gave a full hearing to Wright's lawyers, examined the trial transcript and considered Judge Advocate General Holt's report. His remarks illustrate his thought processes: "…being satisfied that no proper question remained open except as to the insanity of the accused, I caused a full examination to be made on that question…by an expert of high reputation in that professional department."

Letters in the Lincoln's presidential papers raise intriguing legal and political means and ends questions regarding how Lincoln caused a full insanity examination. On September 2, 1863, Secretary of State Seward wrote to Lincoln: "Dr. Nicholl's surroundings are so disloyal as to shake public confidence in himself. Dr. Gray of Utica occurs to me as a very proper person." A logical inference is that Lincoln was choosing between two physicians recommended by Seward, a Dr. Gray and a Dr. Nicholl. It is also reasonable to deduce that Lincoln had information about both doctors, that he and Seward discussed the matter and that Seward investigated and made a choice. However, it is not exactly clear what Seward meant when he wrote that Dr. Gray was "a very proper person." Were Dr. Nichols' "surroundings so disloyal" as to interfere with his professional judgment?

In certainty, Seward's note must unquestionably refer to Dr. Charles H. Nichols, superintendent of the Government Hospital for the Insane in Washington, DC. Dr. John P. Gray was superintendent of the Utica (NY) Lunatic Asylum. Both, Gray and Nichols were specialists in the study of the mind and colleagues in the Association of Medical Superintendents of American Institutions for the Insane (AMSAII), the precursor to the American Psychiatric Association. Despite being colleagues, these two "experts of high reputation" could not have been more different in their professional and philosophical approach to the question of sanity or insanity.

Pertinent to the choice of a medical expert, there were subsequent theoretical and courtroom confrontations between Gray and Nichols relating to sanity/insanity determinations. Confrontations occurred when Mary Harris killed Adoniram J. Burroughs in 1865 and in the 1882 trial of President James Garfield's assassin, Charles J. Guiteau. On both of these occasions, Gray discounted insanity pleas while Nichols supported the defense arguments. Nichols prevailed as Harris was acquitted while Gray convinced jurors and Guiteau was hanged.

At the recommendation of Dorothea Lynde Dix, President Millard Fillmore appointed Nichols the first superintendent of the Government Hospital for the Insane in 1852. His wife, Ellen, was a daughter of Washington's former mayor, John W. Maury, allegedly a secessionist. A number of her relatives chose to serve in the Confederate forces. Dabney H. Maury and Matthew F. Maury were prominent in doing so. Perhaps, these were the "disloyal surroundings" Seward referred to in his note to Lincoln. Active in political and social circles in the Capitol, Nichols served on the board of school commissioners, the Levy court, the Metropolitan Police Board, the American Colonization Society, and the Columbian University Board. During the Civil War, he administered a hospital for wounded Union soldiers on the grounds of the insane asylum.

On March 3, 1863, Nichols and his friend, Dr. Pliney Earle, attended a levée at the White House and called on "Abraham and Mary Anne." When the AMSAII met in Washington in 1864, Nichols arranged an appointment for members with the president that resulted in "considerable conversation." There is no question that Lincoln personally knew Nichols and was aware of the asylum. From a window of the Lincolns' summer residence at the Soldiers' Home, the President could easily see the massive whitish, gray sandstone buildings of the Government Hospital for the Insane.

At the seventeenth annual meeting of the AMSAII on May 19, 1863 at the Metropolitan Hotel in New York City the attending superintendents extensively discussed forms of insanity. Nichols confessed his surprise that one-half of the association members declined to express any views on moral insanity, a type of insanity that could occur without detectable organic brain damage. Of those who did vote, five supported and eight rejected the concept of moral insanity. At one point in the debate, Nichols announced: "I have no hesitation in acknowledging my belief in moral insanity as one of two distinct forms of mental derangement...[moral insanity occurred when individuals had] an irrepressible disposition to do morally wrong acts…there have been attempts to palliate crime by calling it moral insanity, I grant." Dr. Isaac Ray, superintendent, Butler Hospital for the Insane, Providence, Rhode Island, clarified the point: "Although there may be no intellectual aberration or impairment visible, yet it does exist; it is there, though we do not see it."

In attendance at the AMSAII meeting, Gray diametrically opposed Nichols' position. By 1863, Gray had already served as the editor of the *American Journal of Insanity* for nine years. Gray defined insanity as: "A physical disease of the brain with mental phenomena as symptoms…The exciting causes of insanity…are physical; that is, no moral or intellectual operations of the mind induce insanity apart from physical lesion…. Moral insanity has not a single symptom to distinguish it from moral depravity." With these views, Gray earned a reputation as a staunch upholder of traditional morality, social order, and religion. To meet their own specific legal needs, jurists sought Gray's testimony to exploit his avowed conservative opinions on moral insanity.

Significantly, Lincoln's choice of a medical expert on insanity was likely influenced by his own prior legal experiences as well as those of Seward and Stanton. Importantly, Stanton's personal interactions with medicine and the medical profession were relevant. He was severely asthmatic and was treated by doctors since childhood. His father, brother and brother-in-law were physicians.

During 1846, Seward volunteered to defend two murderers who were prisoners in the Auburn (NY) penitentiary. Henry G. Wyatt murdered another prisoner. William Freeman murdered John G. Van Nest, his wife, their two-year-old son, his mother-in-law, and badly wounded the hired man. Both, Wyatt, and Freeman were Negroes and Seward's defense for both was insanity caused by brutal beatings. "His conduct is unexplainable on any principle of sanity…. Freeman is a demented idiot made so by blows [in prison] which extinguished everything in his breast but a blind passion of revenge." During the three months that he devoted to these cases, Seward greatly enhanced his proficiency on the subject of insanity and medical expertise. Particularly, Seward benefitted from working with Dr. Amariah Brigham, medical superintendent of the Utica Lunatic Asylum and editor of the *American Journal of Insanity*. Brigham was Seward's prime witness, the only real medical expert on insanity at the trial, and his personal consultant on insanity.

Following an initial hung jury, Wyatt was executed after a second trial. Six medical authorities found Freeman sane while seven expert witnesses declared him insane. Freeman was found guilty and died in jail after a new trial was ordered by the supreme court of New York. A post-mortem examination confirmed that "Freeman had disease of the brain, and was deranged in mind...until the time of his death." Seward's *Argument in Defense of William Freeman* was published from his notes and went through four printings.

On March 30, 1857, Lincoln aided the prosecution in a murder trial where the defense was insanity due to an overdose of chloroform during surgery. Isaac Wyant brutally killed Anson Rusk in broad daylight in front of numerous witnesses. Leonard Swett, the defense lawyer, proposed the insanity plea supported by expert medical testimony. Rendering an acquittal, the jury recommended commitment to the asylum. During the trial, Lincoln thought that Wyant was "possuming" insanity.

In April 1859, Stanton played a pivotal role on a legal defense team in a scandalous murder trial in Washington, DC. Seward and Lincoln were exposed to a new theory of moral mania: "For the first time in American jurisprudence, the defense set up the plea of a brain-storm or temporary aberration of mind." A cuckolded Daniel E. Sickles cold-heartedly shot and killed his wife's lover, Philip Barton Key, in Lafayette Park across from the White House. Key, forty-two, was the US attorney for the District of Columbia, one of the eleven children of Francis Scott Key, the author of "The Star-Spangled Banner" and himself a three time US attorney for the District of Columbia. Sickles, thirty-seven, was a US congressman from New York City's Third District and a former first secretary of the American Legation in London.

Seward knew Sickles and the murder occurred in full view in front of his house. With the sensational murder case receiving coverage on the front pages of virtually every major newspaper in the nation, Lincoln read about it and discussed it with other lawyers. Fellow circuit lawyer Henry C. Whitney was with Lincoln while the 1859 murder trial was going on in Washington. Lincoln reacted to the published testimony from defense witness John B. Haskin that he and his wife called on Mrs. Sickles when her husband was absent: "I found Mrs. Sickles and Mr. Key seated at a round table with a large bowl of salad on it; she was mixing it; there was a bottle of champagne and glasses on the table [laughter]...Mrs. Sickles got up, blushed, and invited us to take a glass of wine with her...on entering the carriage, my wife said that Mrs. Sickles was a bad woman. Whitney said : "That expression [Mrs. Sickles was a bad woman] tickled Lincoln's fancy. I have heard him tell it over and over again."

Sickles's defense included the "unwritten law" allowing a husband to avenge the despoiling of his marriage bed, lay people testifying as to his state of frenzy, and testimony about his resultant temporary insanity. Jurors took seventy minutes to find Sickles not guilty. George Templeton Strong's diary summed up the public's opinion: "Were he not an unmitigated blackguard and profligate, one could pardon any act of violence on such provocation. But Sickles is not the man to take the law into his own hands and constitute himself the avenger of sin.... One might as well try to spoil a rotten egg as damage Dan's character."

On the day after Seward wrote to Lincoln recommending Gray as the medical expert, on September 3, 1863, Francis H. Pierpont, Union governor of Eastern Virginia, wrote to Lincoln. He urged support for Wright's death sentence and claimed that his execution would aid in the recruitment of black soldiers for the Union army. Besieged on all sides, Lincoln added a note to Seward's September 2, 1863 letter and sent it back to him to take action: "Please telegraph Dr. Gray asking him whether he could come and serve the government one month more or less, & how soon."

After learning of Gray's willingness to serve, Lincoln had a lengthy interview with Gray at the White House. When they met the contrast between the two was striking. Gray was broad shoul-dered, short and stout, weighing more than 300 pounds. He was convivial, genial, kind, and enjoyed criminal trials. Lincoln towered over Gray and looked like a sorrowful scarecrow as they sat and talked. After the meeting, Lincoln appointed Gray a special com-missioner and gave him a letter of instruction dated September 10, 1863:

> ...The record is before me; and a question is made as to the sanity of the accused...take in writing all evidence which may be offered on behalf of Dr. Wright, and against him.... All said evidence to be directed to the question of Dr. Wright's sanity or insanity, and not to any other questions...you will report... your own conclusions as to Dr. Wright's sanity both at the time of the homicide and the time of your examination.... If you deem it proper, you will examine Dr. Wright personally...

A few days later, on September 13, 1863, Lincoln telegraphed Gray who was already in Norfolk: "The names of those whose affidavits are left with me on the question of Dr. Wright's sanity are as follow: Mrs. Jane C. Bolsom, Mrs. M. E. Smiley, Moses Hudgin, J. D. Ghislin, Jr., Felix Logue, Robert B. Turnstall, M.D., Mrs. Elizabeth Rooks, Dr. E. D. Granier, Thomas K. Murray, William J. Holmes, Miss Margaret E. Wigeon, Mrs. Emily S. Frost." While Lincoln listed twelve names, Gray reported on testimony from thirteen witnesses for each side. Eventually, Gray dismissed the testimony for the accused because those witnesses were outside of Wright's social sphere and the statements were "too few, too disconnected, and too insignificant, to afford reasonable found-ation upon which to establish the fact of insanity." Prosecution testimony found more favor with Gray: "On the contrary, those of the witnesses who knew him [Wright] intimately, and met him in the familiar intercourse of social life, testify to his sanity."

During his examination, Gray conducted two personal interviews with Wright. Each interview lasted about two hours and Gray recounted Wright's comments about his history and his attitudes:

> Was born April 21, 1809 in Nansemond County, Virginia to David and Mary [Armistead] Wright...attended Captain Patrick's military school in Middletown, Connecticut...was there imbued more or less with Northern ideas in regard to slavery...read medicine with Dr. William Warren in Edenton, North Carolina...graduated from University of Philadelphia Medical School in 1833...practiced in Edenton for 18 years...married Penelope Creecy of Edentown, [NC] in 1833...moved to Norfolk about 1854...rendered heroic service during the Yellow Fever epidemic of 1855...he changed his opinion on the subject of slavery and conscientiously believed it to be in accordance with the scriptures, and the true welfare of the negro, and that he looked upon the attempted destruction as a wrong to both races...though at times he was depressed, he could not say the depression was frequent or great...at the commencement [of the rebellion] he was a Union man, but gradually went into the current Southern feeling...he voted for secession...he thought the arming of slaves a great wrong...he saw those colored troops, and this officer at their head, coming towards him, in an instant he felt the most unconquerable and desperate impulse to shoot him, and got a pistol...immediately afterwards, he felt the most awful agony of mind...In giving this account, he at times wept, and was greatly overcome by his emotions.

Gray found Wright to be "perfectly coherent, and presented no indications of aberration of mind in conversation, manner, or appearance." Furthermore, Gray carefully considered Wright's statement that he committed the murder under "a most unconquerable and desperate impulse." He decided: "It has been impossible for me to arrive at the conclusion that this impulse was an insane one, and uncontrollable in the sense in which an insane man's impulses are beyond his control." Earlier court decisions allowed for the "irresistible impulse" defense in a murder trail. In an 1844 Massachusetts trial, *Commonwealth v. Rogers,* Judge Lemuel Shaw ruled that: "One is not responsible for an act done under an uncontrollable impulse which is the result of mental disease." In contrast, Gray was dogmatic in his disbelief of the irresistible or uncontrollable impulse.

Based on all the testimony, his own interviews and his observations, Gray reported to Lincoln: "I am of the opinion that Doctor David M. Wright was not insane prior to the 11th day of July, 1863, the date of the homicide of Lieutenant Sanborn; that he has not been insane since, and is not insane now."

Gray concluded his examination on September 26, 1863 and General Foster notified Lincoln the next day. Foster gratuitously took the opportunity to state his own military biases:

> I deem it a proper opportunity for me to forward to you my convictions in the case and my most respectful sug-gestions...the homicide was a deliberate and cold-blooded murder...looking to the nature and character of the troops of which Lieutenant Sanborn was an officer, I deem it essential to discipline and proper feelings of pride and self-respect among the officers of colored troops that Doctor Wright should pay the penalty to which he was sentenced by court-martial.

Foster's remarks reiterated the prosecution's closing com-ments. Judge Advocate Bolles admonished the military court members to do what "the good of the service demanded." Without the death sentence for Wright, white officers might decline to command colored troops. Former slaves and free men might be reluctant to volunteer to serve in the Union army. All told, the Union might flounder in its efforts to defeat the rebels.

On October 7, 1863 Lincoln approved Dr. Wright's sentence. Lincoln noted that an "expert of high reputation in that professional department" reported to him that Wright was not insane prior to or on the day of the homicide and has not been insane since and is not insane now. He concluded: "I therefore approve the finding and sentence of the military commission, and direct that the major-general in command of the department including the place of the trial, and wherein the convict is now in custody, appoint time and place and carry said sentence into execution." Taking action, Foster ordered that Wright be hanged on Friday, October 16, 1863 at 10:00 A.M. Learning of his fate, Wright designed his own coffin. Shaped like an immense wedge, there was a raised area near the head where Wright placed daguerreotypes of his whole family. Inspecting the coffin and expressing his satisfaction, Wright "wrote his name on the lid with a lead pencil in a good, bold hand."

Defense lawyer Bowden telegraphed the president on October 15: "Hon. L. H. Chandler has this moment informed me that Doctor Wright is ordered for execution in the morning, and that it is very desirable he should be granted a respite of one week in order to the arrangement of his private affairs and the making of provision for his afflicted family." Wright had a wife and eight children ranging in age from seven to twenty-three. Lincoln immediately telegraphed General Foster: "Postpone the execution of Dr. Wright to Friday the 23rd Inst. [October]. This is intended for his preparation and is final."

As part of his preparations, Wright asked to witness the long planned marriage of his daughter, Elizabeth, who was engaged to William H. Talbott. Accordingly, on Saturday evening, October 17, 1863, the ceremony took place in the prison with Rev. Mark L. Cheevers, the Methodist chaplain from Fortress Monroe officiating. About thirty invited guests attended. "The sad circumstances...drew tears from the eyes of even the Federal attendants."

On the same day as the wedding Foster telegraphed Lincoln: "The Hon. Mr. Chandler has made application for Mr. William Talbot and Mrs. Dr. Wright to proceed to Washington for the purpose of having an interview with you in behalf of her husband who is sentenced to be executed. My rules are not to allow any one to leave the Department who are not willing to take the oath of allegiance, but as you have postponed the execution one week I feel it my duty to forward the application to you for your decision." Wright's wife, accompanied by her new son- in-law, attempted to gain a personal audience with Lincoln to plead for her husband's life. Lincoln's reply was curt: "It would be useless for Mrs. Dr. Wright to come here. The subject is a very painful one, but the case is settled."

Wright's defenders argued that Lincoln's decision was prompted by his real concern that he might lose the upcoming presidential election. Reflecting upon the 1864 election, Lincoln said: "I should not have been elected" if the Democrats waged a different campaign. It was possible for General George McCellan to be elected with a swing of only 31,500 votes in eight states. Lincoln's reelection jitters combined with his zealous nationalistic aim to preserve the Union at all costs.

Defense lawyers Bowden and Chandler remained steadfast up to the end. Bowden claimed a possible bias on the part of a member of the military commission. He had an October 22, 1863 dispatch from the attorney general of Virginia which stated: "I have the signed certificate of a commissioned officer, US Army, declaring that a member of the military commission which tried Doctor Wright expressed himself unfavorable to that individual before the prisoner was arraigned or he had heard any of the testimony. Answer immediately." In a letter to the president dated October 22, 1863, Chandler enclosed a copy of the dispatch to Bowden with a urgent plea of his own: "To proceed with the execution when such doubt as to the fairness and impartiality of his trial... would destroy the proceeding...I received...information... which precluded the chances of an impartial trial, but was restrained by a pledge of secrecy and confidence from making any use of the information communicated to me...I entertain the belief that proof can be exhibited...the trial was not before such a tribunal as could be safely trusted with the liberties and lives of the people." It was reiterated that Wright was "of unsound mind" and urged that he be confined for life. They suggested that Wright be exchanged for a Northern physician, Dr. William P. Rucker, who was a Confederate prisoner in Richmond.

Penelope, Wright's eldest daughter, devised an audacious plan for her father's escape. On the evening of October 21, in the semidarkness of the cell and directly under the watchful eye of the guard, she used a master key to open his manacles. Penelope deftly draped some of her garments, including a face veil, over her father to transform him into a woman. She slipped on his boots and lay on the cot under the blanket with only her booted feet showing. In his disguise, Wright left with his other visitors and headed toward a waiting carriage. He managed to get about fifty feet away before a sentry became suspicious of the "tall woman" and "her gait." Lieutenant Cook, the officer of the guard, hurried after the "woman," lifted her veil and declared: "That's played out; I know you Dr. Wright." Without embarrassment, Wright replied: "Desperate means are pardonable under desperate circumstances." Numerous fires were reported in Norfolk that night. Possibly, the blazes were meant as a distraction for the escape.

Surreptitious efforts to free Wright continued. A Union war department telegrapher, Richard O'Brien, was supposedly offered a bribe to send a bogus telegram of reprieve to Fortress Monroe. He was offered $20,000 in gold and a free passage to England on a blockade runner. O'Brien refused the bribe.

During the morning of October 23, 1863, "soulless blacks, and senseless, vulgar whites, thronged Church Street as the cortege passed to the Federal gibbet" at the Fair Grounds at 18th Street. Norfolk newspapers described the thousands of spectators as "mostly Federals, white riff-raff and Negroes." Dressed in a dark coat, pants, buff vest and white necktie, Wright presented a dignified and self-processed appearance before the assembled clamorous crowd. Responding to rumored threats of a Confederate rescue attempt, a hollow square of massed Union troops surrounded the gallows in the center of the race track. Wright's final words consisted of a single sentence: "The deed I committed was done without malice." At 11:30 A.M., General-in-Chief Henry W. Halleck received a telegram from General Foster: "Dr. Wright was executed this morning at Norfolk according to orders. Everything passed off very orderly."

During his period of about four months pondering the death sentence for Wright, Lincoln frequently signed orders commuting death sentences for desertion, disobeying orders, mutiny, shootings, spying, stealing, and assorted high crimes. When Lincoln reviewed the military courts-martial during the Civil War, he would usually give the man a second chance. On Saturday, July 18, 1863, Lincoln and Holt spent six hours going over courts martial verdicts. Lincoln's assistant secretary John Hay observed that the president "caught any fact" to justify saving a life. In addressing a meeting of the Union Veterans Club in Chicago, Lincoln's close friend and fellow lawyer, Leonard Swett recalled that he said that an approval of the death penalty tore his heart most. Lincoln told Swett that he went through the submitted papers to see "if I can't find something by which I can let them off." That sentiment is echoed in Samuel K. Jackson's 1893 letter to the *Landmark,* a Norfolk journal. Jackson was an intimate friend of Wright's until he moved in 1857. After correcting two minor errors in a prior article, Jackson recalled that "it was said at the time that Pres. Lincoln wanted an excuse to pardon him [Wright]." Lincoln's compassionate attitude is illustrated in his reply to a man who was weeping because his son's execution was merely suspended rather than receiving a pardon : "My dear man, if your son lives until I order him shot, he will live longer than ever Methuselah did."

There was a funeral service for Wright on October 24, 1863 at Christ Church, Freemason and Cumberland. His coffin was profusely decorated with white flowers and evergreens and the lid was open as hundreds viewed his face. The Reverends E. M. Rodman, Parkman and M .A. Okeson performed the Episcopal solemnities. Wright was interred at Elmwood Cemetery with this inscription on his tombstone:

DR. DAVID MINTON WRIGHT
Born April 21st 1809
Died October 23rd 1863

Not for the dead in Christ we weep,
Their sorrows now are o'er,
The sea is calm, the tempest past
On that eternal shore.
Their peace is sealed, their best is sure
Within that better home,
A while we weep and linger here
Then follow to the tomb.

Ironically, on the same day as Wright's funeral a Major Crosby received a letter from Assistant-Adjunct General George H. Johnson, by command of Union General James Barnes. That letter ordered Wright's release upon his giving a bond of $1,000.00 to guarantee his appearance before Federal authorities as required. It is supposed that Wright was to be released to await a second trial. General Barnes allowed Wright's family to leave Norfolk and they arrived within Confederate lines at Petersburg, Virginia.

Mrs. Wright died on May 13, 1889 and was buried beside her husband in Norfolk. Wright's children remained in the South. Penelope [Pencie] married Alexander Watson Weddell of Petersburg. He was a captain in the Confederate army, a lawyer, a journalist, and finally the rector of historic St. John's Church in Richmond. Their son, Alexander Wilburne Weddell was the US ambassador to Argentina and the president of the Virginia Historical Society. At twenty-one, Minton Augustus Wright died in the Battle of Gettysburg but Wright's family decided not to tell him the sad news while he was in jail. Mary married Frederick A. Fetter. John [Joshua] C. Armistead was a midshipman on the *CSS Patrick Henry* in 1863 and in 1892 he was unmarried. Sallie [Sarah] married Thomas Warren. William married Sarah Coke.

Thirty-eight years after Wright's death, on May 8, 1901, the city council of Portsmouth expunged from the records the earlier denunciations. "Aspersions by an official body of sycophants and scalawags on a heroic and spotless gentleman are forever blotted out." Nevertheless, a Southern historian categorized Dr. Wright's execution as the "most agonizing tragedy of the occupation, the one that shocked Norfolk more than any other single incident, the one that has lived vividly in the memory of many Virginians."

A distinguished Norfolk physician, Dr. L. B. Anderson, reviewed Wright's case in 1892 and concluded he was unblemished: "Rest, our most worthy compatriot and professional brother, though abolition malice has striven to fix a stigma upon thy name and a blot upon thy character; it has only enshrined thy virtues more securely in the hearts of thy countrymen and engraved thy name more deeply upon their memories forever."

In retrospect, Lincoln plausibly considered a web of related circumstances and disparate factors beyond the "undefended assassination" and the sanity or insanity of Wright. A number of political interrelated events occurred before, during and after Wright's "undefended assassination" trial, guilty verdict, death sentence, sanity determination, and public hanging.

On July 22, 1862, Lincoln told his cabinet that emancipation was "a military necessity absolutely essential to the preservation of the Union." On January 1, 1863, the Emancipation Proclamation announced that freed slaves and "…such persons of suitable condition, will be received into the armed services of the United States to garrison and defend forts, positions, stations, and other places, and to man vessels of all sorts in said service." A lengthy, mainly favorable, *New York Times* editorial eight days later debated the pros and cons of the Union's recruiting black soldiers.

After emancipation, intensive efforts sought to enlist emancipated slaves and free blacks into the Union army as volunteers. At the same time, Lincoln was deeply concerned about keeping the border states of Kentucky, Maryland, and Missouri loyal to the Union. He said: "There are fifty thousand bayonets in the Union armies from Border Slave States. Will they go over to the rebels if slaves become soldiers?"

In May 1863, the congress of the Confederate States of America passed a joint resolution on retaliation ordering that white commissioned officers commanding or training negroes will be "deemed as inciting service insurrection, and shall, if captured, be put to death…" Would that edict unnerve Union officers?

Lincoln regularly read the Washington, DC *Daily National Intelligencer* and absorbed a heavy dose of articles about the need for more troops, the enrolling of black troops, the continuous difficulties recruiting and/or drafting Union troops, and the growing conscription chaos including the spectacularly bloody carnage in the mid-July 1863 draft riots in New York City.

Abolitionist Frederick Douglass had urged the use of black soldiers since the war's beginning. Douglass met with Lincoln in August 1863, before Lincoln selected a medical expert to determine Wright's sanity. They discussed issues regarding Negro troops: equal pay and equal promotion; prisoner-of-war status for captured troops; and retaliation if colored troops were murdered. Lincoln reassured Douglass about each item.

On September 7, 1863, Major-General Henry M. Naglee reported that Confederate guerrillas in Virginia blew up bridges and fired on Union soldiers. He ordered the most prominent, influential, restless secessionists to repair the bridges and also forced them to be the advance guides for the Union troops. How would the decision on Dr. Wright affect that insurgency?

These interrelated events reflected the sensitive political climate at this point in the Civil War. Amid the turmoil, Lincoln remained tenaciously determined to preserve the Union and the nation. Lincoln's dilemma in the Wright case was deftly described by a *New York Times* book reviewer: "Nothing poses the question of justifiable ends and means in politics more poignantly than the problems Lincoln faced in suppressing a proslavery Southern rebellion by mobilizing a Northern constituency hostile to both slavery and black people." Lincoln himself added a caveat to explain his legal and political means and ends actions: "A measure made expedient by a war is no precedent for times of peace."

Lincoln agreed with Seward's recommendation of Gray as the "very proper person" over Nichols whose "surroundings are so disloyal." In so doing, Lincoln's political choice bolstered military discipline and morale, calmed Frederick Douglass, stimulated enlistments and allowed the Union to eventually recruit 179,985 colored troops.

Sanborn's public assassination severely damaged Union troop recruiting efforts in eastern Virginia for months. Between March and the end of August, 1863, comments to and from Lincoln proclaimed the concrete value of Negro troops to the Union cause and set a precedent for hanging verdicts. These communications took place before Lincoln made his decision about Wright's execution on October 7, 1863.

Learning that Tennessee Governor Andrew Johnson was thinking of raising a Negro military force, Lincoln encouraged him to do so in a private letter on March 26, 1863: "The colored population is the great available, yet unavailed of, force, for restoring the Union. The bare sight of fifty thousand armed, and drilled black soldiers on the banks of the Mississippi, would end the rebellion at once. And who doubts that we can present that sight, if we but take hold in earnest?" On May 22, 1863, Union army General Order No. 143 established the Bureau for Colored Troops at 531 17th Street in Washington. Major Charles W. Foster was appointed Bureau Chief. Lincoln wrote to the Secretary of War Stanton on July 21, 1863: "I desire that a renewed and vigorous effort be made to raise colored forces along the shores of the Mississippi."

Commanding General U. S. Grant, praised the soldierly ability of Negroes, writing to Lincoln on August 23, 1863: "By arming the negro we have added a powerful ally. They will make good soldiers, and taking them from the enemy weakens him in the same proportion they strengthen us."

On August 27, 1863, Lincoln allowed Major-General George G. Meade to determine the "…punishment as being indispensable to the service." Meade decided on "a prompt execution." Five men, paid draft substitutes, took the money, deserted, became "bounty jumpers" and were shot as an example to others. In the March 3, 1863 act establishing the draft, seven types of exemptions were listed. Section 13 allowed every drafted person "to purchase his own exemption" and to furnish an acceptable substitute for about

$300 to $500. An editorial in the *New York Times* applauded the "humanity in the law" allowing individuals to buy a substitute. Although not eligible for the draft, even Lincoln paid for a "representative recruit" to represent him in the war. John Summerfield Staples bore the president's musket in the Civil War.

On August 31, 1863, Lincoln wrote to state legislator James C. Conkling in Springfield, Illinois: "...some of the commanders of our armies in the field, who have given us our most important successes, believe the emancipation policy, and the use of colored troops, constitute the heaviest blow yet dealt to the rebellion; and that, at least one of those important successes, could not have been achieved...but for the aid of black soldiers." Lincoln's December 8, 1863 annual message to the 38th Congress reviewed the year and declared: "Of those who were slaves at the beginning of the rebellion, full one hundred thousand are now in the United States military services, about one-half of which number actually bear arms in the ranks;...So far as tested, it is difficult to say they are not as good soldiers as any."

At one point, colored troops constituted 10 percent of the Union army and fought in 449 engagements, including 39 major battles. During the war, 37,300 black soldiers died. In addition, the Congressional Medal of Honor was awarded to twenty-one blacks serving the Union: seventeen soldiers and four sailors.

Two days before Wright was to be hanged, another "undefended assassination" occurred. On October 21, 1863, secessionist John H. Sothoron and his son shot and killed Second Lieutenant Eben White, 7th US Colored Troops, at Benedict, Maryland. White and his colored troops were enrolling blacks who were working on Sothoron's plantation into the army. After the shooting, the Sothorons fled to Richmond for sanctuary and were never prosecuted. A delegation from Maryland's southern St. Mary's County visited Lincoln to give him the "facts." They stated that colored troops "by their presence, with arms in their hands, are frightening quiet people, and producing great confusion." From Baltimore, Major-General Robert C. Schenck informed Lincoln that the delegation grossly misrepresented matters and added: "I beg that the President will not intervene and thus embolden them." Lincoln telegraphed a reply to Schenck: "The fact of one of our officers being killed on the Patuxent, is a specimen of what I would avoid. It seems to me we could send white men to recruit better than to send negroes, and thus inaugurate homicides on punctilio [a fine point of etiquette]."

About one week after Wright was hanged, Lincoln choose Gray as a medical expert again. On October 31, 1863, Union army Private Lorenzo C. Stewart was in jail for desertion. That evening he put morphia in the guards' whiskey to induce sleep so he could escape. However, two guards died and others became sick. Stewart was tried and sentenced to death for desertion and for the murders. After clemency appeals from the citizens of Elmira, New York, President Lincoln again appointed Gray to examine Stewart as to his sanity. Characteristically, Gray concluded: "He has a certain moral infirmity, not amounting to insanity; he is an eccentric, peculiar, and in some respects, a weak man, but, in no proper sense of the word, an insane man." Despite Gray's conclusion, Lincoln commuted Stewart's sentence to imprisonment in the penitentiary at hard labor for ten years.

Shortly after receiving Gray's opinion about Lorenzo, Lincoln attended Ford's Theatre. On November 9, 1863, Lincoln sat in the President's box and "applauded the actor rapturously." His secretary, John Hay, noted the event in his diary: "Spent the evening at the theatre with President, Mrs. Lincoln, Mrs. Hunter, Cameron and Nicolay. J. Wilkes Booth was doing the Marble Heart. Rather tame than otherwise." An article in the *Washington Chronicle* reported that Booth, a "popular young tragedian... appears to have taken the citizens by storm...The performance of these characters by Mr. Booth has won the highest encomiums from the press and the public wherever he has appeared."

EPILOGUE

After four years, the bloody and devastating American Civil War was winding down as the new year began in 1865. Americans reacted individually and publicly to a variety of happenings affecting them and the nation. Adhering to his lifelong habit, President Abraham Lincoln carefully read the newspapers and noticed the meaningful as well as the insignificant events.

At the end of 1864, Walter Whitman was a federal government clerk in the Bureau of Indian Affairs. Secretary of the Interior James Harlan discovered a copy of Whitman's book of poetry, *Leaves of Grass*, on his desk. Harlan found Whitman's poetry offensive and fired him. Strong and emotional public support for Whitman from friends and admirers coalesced and they fought for another position for him. William Douglas O'Conner wrote a stirring pamphlet in Whitman's defense entitled *The Good Gray Poet*. On the first day of the new year, Whitman, "the good gray poet," began work as a clerk in the office of the Attorney General at a salary of $1,200 per year.

From a clerk's office at the Supreme Court of the United States at three in the afternoon, Lincoln's friend and fellow lawyer, Orville H. Browning, watched a terrible tragedy as a raging fire destroyed the Smithsonian Institution in late January 1865.

On the first day of February, Lincoln was aware of a monumental event taking place at the Supreme Court of the United States. Recently appointed Chief Justice Salmon P. Chase presided as U.S. Senator Charles Sumner of Massachusetts moved for the admission of John S. Rock, "a colored lawyer of Massachusetts" to practice before the Supreme Court of the United States bar. Chase approved and Rock became the first Negro admitted to that prestigious position.

On February 22, 1865, Washington newspapers published a contentious long open letter addressing both the U.S. Senate and the U.S. House of Representatives. Acting on behalf of federal government clerks, William D. O'Conner requested a temporary increase in their salaries. He pointed out that current salaries ranged from $1,200 to $2,000 per year. Of the 1,500 clerks in the Treasury Department, 900 [60%] received $1,200 per year. While complaining about inflation, O'Conner said that the dollar was worth only fifty cents.

An article in the *Daily National Intelligencer* reported that "we have examined samples" of safety matches. "Ingenious and valuable invention, ignited by rubbing on the outside of the box, considered perfectly safe." They "predicted large sales for this useful item."

In Congress, the legislators discussed the coinage of new three cent pieces. These coins would be a little larger than the five cent piece, of silver color, and with the Goddess of Liberty on the face surrounded by the words, "United States of America." On the back of the coin, the letter "three in Roman letters" was enclosed in an olive branch. "In God We Trust" was added by the Congressional Act on March 3, 1865.

Early in the year, on February 3, 1865, Lincoln and Secretary of State William H. Seward prepared to meet with confederate peace ambassadors on the President's steamer, *River Queen*, in Hampton Roads [VA]. Confederate Vice President Alexander H. Stephens headed the Southern delegation accompanied by John A. Campbell, Assistant Secretary of War and Robert M.T. Hunter, a prominent Virginia Senator. These peace ambassadors talked earnestly for four hours but their mission was fruitless. On February 7, 1865, Seward reported that "the conference came to an end by mutual acquiescence, without producing an agreement."

Even as the combatants sought to negotiate the end of the war, this peace initiative shared space on the front page of the local Washington newspapers with stories about a shocking murder in the U.S. Treasury Building. As the southern delegates returned home, the tragedy in the U.S. Treasury continued to receive intense press coverage. As a lawyer, Lincoln realized the possible impact of the murder case upon legal precedents. Personally knowing the lawyers involved, Lincoln anticipated the insanity plea defense and this was confirmed in newspaper reports. However, this murder case marked the first time in the U.S. that expert medical testimony supported a temporary insanity plea. Lincoln's own legal experience touched on the insanity plea, the selection of the expert medical witness, and on convincing jurors to arrive at the correct verdict. Significantly, the murder took place in a federal building, a federal clerk was murdered, federal employees were witnesses to the murder, and a federally employed physician, Dr. Charles H. Nichols, was the only expert medical witness supporting the insanity defense. As the chief federal executive and as a lawyer, it is most likely that Lincoln followed the legal aspects of the trial

When the facts of the murder appeared in the newspapers, it is conceivable that Lincoln was reminded of his own legal experiences in the *People v Wyant* and in the military commission trial of Dr. David M. Wright. Another reminder about legal experiences took the bodily form of General Daniel E. Sickles. He was warmly welcomed by the Lincolns into their social circle and frequently hobbled about the White House on his crutches. Sickles' lower leg was blown off during the battle of Gettysburg in July 1863. Since Sickles was acquitted of murdering Philip Barton Key in 1859 on the grounds of temporary insanity caused by severe emotional distress, he personally understood the evolving tragedy. It is conceivable that Sickles encouraged Mrs. Mary Todd Lincoln to be sympathetic toward the imprisoned murderess.

In a note in the trial transcript, the court reporter stated that Mrs. Abraham Lincoln sent flowers to Harris; a beautiful bouquet whose centre flower signified, in botanical language, *Trust in me.* While not mentioning her name, a defense lawyer alluded to the flowers sent to Harris' cell while she was in jail.

Her prison abode has been brightened by the presence of the noblest and purest of her own sex, and delicate flowers from the loftiest station in the world have mingled their odors with the breath of her captivity.

Coincidentally, this murder trial involved people Lincoln met during prior legal encounters: Dr. Charles H. Nichols and Dr. John

P. Gray from the trial of Dr. David M. Wright; Justice Andrew Wylie whom Lincoln appointed to the supreme court of the District of Columbia; Joseph H. Bradley, Sr. from the trial of Sickles and as a prominent Washington lawyer opposed Lincoln's reorganization of the District court; Edward C. Carrington, a Virginian whom Lincoln appointed U.S. Attorney for the District of Columbia; James Hughes whom Lincoln appointed as an Associate Justice to the U.S. Court of Claims; Charles Mason, a former Commissioner of the U.S. Patent Office; Daniel W. Voorhees, a legal colleague Lincoln encountered in the county circuit courts of Illinois; and even Dr. John Frederick May, who appealed to Lincoln for leniency for an imprisoned relative.

During the afternoon of April 14, 1865, President Lincoln had a long chat with his old friend Richard J. Oglesby, the governor of Illinois. As President and Mrs. Lincoln were getting ready to leave, another old friend from Illinois, U.S. Congressman Isaac N. Arnold, walked up to them. Lincoln excused himself and told Arnold to come see him tomorrow morning. Exiting the White House, the Lincolns traveled to Ford's Theatre on Tenth Street to see the comedy farce, *Our American Cousin*, starring Laura Keene. After a number of rejections, the Lincolns arranged to be accompanied by Clara Harris, the daughter of U.S. Senator Ira Harris of New York, and her fiancee, Major Henry R. Rathbone. Arriving about 8:30 PM, after the play had already started, the Presidential party proceeded to their private box. As Lincoln appeared at the balcony railing holding his silk top hat in his hand, the band stopped to play *Hail to the Chief*. Henry C. Ford, brother of the theatre owner, thoughtfully furnished a rocking chair for Lincoln as well as a couch and comfortable chairs for the others. Laughter could be heard coming from the Presidential box as the play continued. Being a well-known actor to the employees at Ford's, John Wilkes Booth easily and stealthily gained access to the Presidential box. He propped up the door to block the entrance. At about 10:15 P.M., Booth pointed his single-shot .44 caliber derringer at the left side of the back of Lincoln's head. From about two feet away, Booth fired one lead ball into Lincoln's head as he sat in his rocking chair enjoying the play. That single mortal lead ball traveled through Lincoln's brain and lodged behind his right eye. Immediately, Lincoln lapsed into unconsciousness. He was attended by a number of physicians as he precariously hung on to life for more than nine hours. After being moved to a nearby house, Lincoln died at 7:22 early the next morning. Newspapers published the sorrowful details in heavily black-bordered columns on the front pages. A state of official and private mourning prevailed in the nation.

When Abraham Lincoln died, Secretary of War Edwin M. Stanton solemnly declared that "Now, he belongs to the ages." Now, thousands of previously unknown documents have been discovered by *The Lincoln Legal Papers* project. That new evidence comprehensively delineates Lincoln's career as a practicing attorney for almost twenty-five years. That wealth of information can assist in enlightening the ages of Lincoln's pre-presidential work life as a lawyer.

REFERENCES AND NOTES

CHAPTER 1
REVERENCE FOR THE LAW: A POLITICAL RELIGION

For Lincoln they were complimentary: C. Davis, 1994c, 72; Tyson, 12.

Mr. Lincoln was: Hertz, 1938, 425.

He took up the law: G. W. Harris, November 1903.

Forty lawyers held office: C. Davis, 1994c, 65.

the craftiest and most dishonest: Donald, 1956.

A huckster in politics: Donald, 1956.

Mr. Chairman, this movement: Lincoln speech, January 11, 1837; Basler, 1:27.

Lincoln a party man: Historian David H. Donald made this point in a radio
conversation, *Think Tank Transcripts*, 7

He was an upwardly: Parshall, 71.

the slow, cautious: Historian David H. Donald in a radio conversation, *Think
Tank Transcripts*, 8.

I claim not to: Current, 299; Williams, Pederson, and Marsala, illuminate the
multiple dimensions of Lincoln's leadership including his "classical
prudence," his cerebral pragmatism, his building upon Democratic
principles and his "active-flexible" style.

a mere politician: Kazin.

Lincoln opposed compromise: Historian Eric Foner in a radio conversation,
Think Tank Transcripts, 5.

likely to vote for politician they know: Wald, 1.

First political announcement; lost the election: Abraham Lincoln's First, March
9, 1832, website; Basler 1953, 1:5–9.

miles of canals: Growth of Nation, 42, website.

railroad growth; *Tom Thumb*; train routes: Growth of Nation, 42, website.

telegraph; printing press; cotton gin; reaper; labor organizations: An Outline of
History, website.

Prohibition will work: Honest Abe, website.

temperance; women's rights; Seneca Falls; only 100 signed: Growth of Nation,
50, website.

one flourishing town after another: An Outline of American History, Sectional
Conflict, website; de Tocqueville, introduction.

Kingdom of God: An Outline of History, Role of Philosophy & Literature, 1,
website.

golden age of literature: An Outline of History, website.

read several chapters: Burlingame, Ettinger, 293.

panic of 1837; land sales; bank notes: Growth of Nation, 33, website.

alleged frauds; monopoly; ruinous expansion: Growth of Nation, 33, website.

US population: An Outline of History, Culture & Industry, website.

immigration by decade: NPG, website.

the most influential and potent: G.W. Harris, November 1903.

Lincoln and I: Hertz, 1938, 96.

newspaper subscription: Herndon, Weik, 1893, 2:32; Basler, 3:385.

mobs; hanging; burning; murder: Lincoln, The Perpetuation, January 27, 1838, website; Basler, 1:108–15.

We had a society: Lincoln, The Perpetuation, website; Basler, 1:108–15.

Law is a form: Aristotle, Book 7, Chapter 4, Section 5.

civil and religious; rule of law; I hope I am over wary: Lincoln, The Perpetuation, 2, website; Basler, 1:108–15.

Whatever, then, their cause: Lincoln, The Perpetuation, 2, website; Basler, 1:108–15.

What has this; it has much; burn churches: Lincoln, The Perpetuation, 4 website; Basler, 1:108–15.

attachment of the people: Lincoln, The Perpetuation, website ; Basler, 1:108–15; Burt and Strozier, 1990, and M. L. Wilson review interpretations of the Lyceum address; Cuomo & Holzer; expound on Lincoln on Democracy to illustrate his principles.

Let every American: Lincoln, The Perpetuation, 4, website ; Basler, 1:108–15.

There is no grievance: Lincoln, The Perpetuation, 5, website.

Reason, cold, calculating: Lincoln, The Perpetuation, website ; Basler, 1:108–15.

Legislation and adjudication: Nicolay, Hay, 1894, 3: 239.

A house divided; alike lawful: Lincoln, House Divided speech June 16, 1858, website; Basler, 2:461–69.

No law is stronger: Tracy, 120–21.

I have never: Lincoln, Independence Hall speech, February 22, 1861, website; Basler, 4:440–46.

I am exceedingly anxious: Lincoln, New Jersey Senate speech, February 21, 1861, website; Basler, 4:235–36.

Laws of the United States: Lincoln , Proclamation Calling Militia, April 15, 1861, website.

swore in his presidential: Kleinfield, 1997.

I have no purpose: Lincoln, First Inaugural address, March 4, 1861, website; Basler, 4:249–79.

suspended *habeas corpus*: Basler, 5:436

Are all the laws: Lincoln, Special Message to Congress, July 4, 1861; Rehnquist; Basler, 4:421–41.

In this case: Mitgang, February 13, 1994, 40.

four articles of impeachment: Seligman, 355.

President did not have power, arrest unconstitutional: Seligman, 359.

I think history will: Seligman, 371.

cross-examination of Foner: Seligman, 377.

They want to tear: Seligman, 384.

It is obvious: Seligman, 387.

If there is any thing: Kleinfield.

Is it doubted: Lincoln, Annual Message to Congress, December 1, 1862, website; Basler, 5:518–37.

peace has been preserved: Lincoln, Thanksgiving Proclamation, October 3, 1863, website; Basler, 6:496–97.

there may be some irregularities: Lincoln, speech to 164th Ohio Regiment, August 18, 1864, website; Basler, 7:504–505.

a body of gentlemen: Leitch.

honorary LL.D. degrees: Basler, 3: 50; *New York Times*, June 27, 1861; *New York Tribune*, June 27, 1861.

Both parties deprecated war: Lincoln, Second Inaugural, March 4, 1865, website; Basler, 8:332–33.

re-inauguration of the national authority: Lincoln, Last Public Address, April 11, 1865, website; Basler, 8:399–405.

I have, for a quarter of a century: Rankin, 306–307.

The true spirit of the law: Legal History, website.

Wherever law ends: Locke, 1690, Sec. 202; also attributed to Pitt, *Case of Wilkes*: Speech, January 9, 1770.

The law embodies: Holmes, *The Common Law*, lecture 1, 1881; Holmes ordering Lincoln: Burlingame, Ettinger, 357.

Law is the crystallization: Stevenson, 1080.

Codex Hammurabi minutiae: Spiegel, Springer, 1997.

dynamic and symbiotic relationship: C. Davis, 1989, 2.

CHAPTER 2

A. LINCOLN, ESQUIRE: THE EVOLUTION OF A LAWYER

He was not a folksy: Key.

the rise of a truly: C. Davis, 1994e, 8. Marshall, Chief Justice, Supreme Court of the United States; Kent, Chief Justice, Supreme Court of New York; Shaw, Chief Justice, Supreme Court of Massachusetts; Webster, noted lawyer, statesman and orator.

Lincoln seldom disappointed: E. Johnson, March 11, 1996.

The courtrooms: Arnold, 1885, 56; Moores, 488.

juggled law and politics: C. Davis, 1994a, 26.

When he rose to speak: Herndon to T. H. Bartlett July 19, 1887 in Hertz, 1938, 191–92; Shestack, March 21, 1992.

Lincoln was, upon the whole: Arnold, 1885, 84.

Simplicity and economy: C. Davis, 1994c, 72.

legal system reflected life: K. L. Hall, 1989, vii.

There is no mystery: Hertz, 1938, 428.

Case of the $3 hog: *Byrne v. Stout*, 15 Ill 180: Evans, 14.

impeachment of Justice Browne: H. E. Pratt, 1939e; Duff, 87–89; L. Rogers, 1997; McDermott. Neely, 1982b, reported on Lincoln as a major Whig leader in Illinois who rallied members to support issues.

$5 for legal services: *Hemdon v. Smith*, Lincoln Legal Papers case file.

Commencement of Lincoln's: Stuart & Lincoln Fee Book, Lincoln Legal Papers; Donald, 1995, 74.

the matter you speak: Basler, 1:229–30.

volume of bankruptcy cases: H. E. Pratt, 1943a; Bresnan tells how "the long nine" legislators arranged to move to Springfield; Beringer presents a pioneer portrait of Lincoln in Vandalia.

one of the ablest: Herndon, Weik, 1893, 1:250; Arnold, 1885, 66.

Logan not loveable: Donald, 1948, 18.

a little shriveled-up: Hertz, 1938, 430.

Logan's influence on Lincoln: Herndon, Weik, 1893, 1:250; Masters, 1931, 83.

He would get a case: Lincoln-Herndon Law Office, website.

Lincoln a case lawyer: Herndon, Weik, 1893, 2:6.

We are not: Basler, 1:325; Globe Tavern: Angle, 1935, 87.

Lincoln's only house: Donald, 1995, 95–96.

recovery of a legal fee: *United States v. Farnsworth et al.*; *Logan & Lincoln v. Atchison*, Lincoln Legal Papers case file.

Lincoln encouraged Herndon: Donald, 1948, 17–18.

a lawyer's lawyer; *He was regularly*: Stage, 212; Mitgang, February 13, 1993, A12:1.

In his examination: *Danville Illinois Citizen*, May 29, 1850 in D. Davis MSS, Chicago Historical Society; cited by Donald, 1995, 150.

Mr. Lincoln usually called: Reported by Charles S. Zane, a law student at Lincoln & Herndon, in Newton, 252.

Not even judge Davis: Thomas, 1954, 57.

Herndon charged Lincoln for books: Donald, 1948, 22.

The furniture, somewhat dilapidated: G. W. Harris, December 1903; Weik, 1922, 106–107; Newton 42; Abraham Lincoln's Law Office, website

in my old; *When you can't*: misplaced documents: Herndon, Weik, 1893, 1:315; 318.

rarely consulted others: Lamon, 313–14; Kyle, 61.

Lincoln worked long hours: Burlingame, 321.

Lincoln did his reading: Bledsoe; Donald, 1948, 38.

Herndon had thriving practice: W. D. Beard, 1999.

more time on law than politics: Herndon, Weik, 1893, 1:247–48.

Yet, Mr. Lincoln: Hertz, 1938, 426.

emphasized the necessary: W. D. Beard, 1992b, 219.

success due to slow thinking: Herndon, Weik, 1893, 2:6; Whitney, 235–36

thought slowly and acted slowly: Herndon, Weik, 1893, 2:6; Hertz, 1938, 427.

But it was: Hertz, 1938, 427; Herndon, Weik, 1893, 2:7.

statute of limitations not expired: *Thomas Lewis, administrator of Moses*
    Broadwell v. William Lewis for the use of Nicholas Longworth, Lincoln Legal
    Papers case file, 48 US (7 Howard) 776 (1849); *American Bar Association*
    Journal; Krock.

focused on presidency: Lupton, 1999.

Lincoln filed documents for other lawyers: *Shepherd v. Walker, 1858,* Lincoln
    Legal Papers case file; Basler, 2: 431.

Lincoln refused job: J. W. Starr, 126–31.

sand bar case: *Johnston v. Jones & Marsh,* 1860, Lincoln Legal Papers case file;
    Duff, 241–42; Basler, 2:430; Arnold, 1881, 149.

Manny cases: *McCormick v. Talcott et al.,* Lincoln Legal Papers case file; Duff,
    324. Manny died and Talcott, a partner in the firm, was sued.

Lincoln's income: Arnold, 1885, 83.

Lincoln & Herndon caseload: Donald, 1948, 44.

earnings per week in given term: Donald, 1995, 106.

description of court house: Tarbell, 1900 Part 1, 245.

He occupied very much: Fox, 1927.

Lincoln wrote the bill: Basler, 11: 7.

Lincoln's days on the road: J. H. Baker, 1987, 108.

Horrible travel conditions: Arnold, 1885, 56, 59.

Lincoln enjoyed circuit life: W. L. King, 71; Arnold, 1885, 56, 59

orgmathorial court: Whitney, 67.

Lincoln's fees too small: J. H. Cooper, February 23, 1987; W. L. King, 89.

set up law offices: Donald, 1948, 45.

circuit-riding image: Strozier, 1982, 143.

Lincoln's technicality: *People v. Bantzhouse,* 1858, Lincoln Legal Papers case file;
    Tyson.

Yes, I have bought: M. Freedman, February 19, 1996; *People v. Harrison,* 1860,
    Lincoln Legal Papers case file; Hertz, 1938, 107; Mitgang, February 20, 1989

A list of partnerships cites more than seventy different lawyers practicing with
    Lincoln in twelve counties: Hertz, 1930, 17–18; *Hoped to secure:* Herndon,
    Weik, 1893, 1:390.

Decreed divorces, awarded settlements: Martha Benner quoted in Mitgang, July 4,
    1993, Section l, 14:4.

If, after all: Basler, 4:35; *People v. Musick et al.,* Lincoln Legal Papers case file; Miers, 2:176.

Lincoln bought railroad stock: J. W. Starr, 84–85.

miss a fee: Basler, 2:202.

Lincoln sued for his fee: *Lincoln v. Illinois Central RR,* Lincoln Legal Papers case file; Duff, 225.

Lincoln's railroad defenses: *Illinois Central RR v. Allen; Allen v. Illinois Central RR,* four cases, 1855, 1859, 1859, 1862, Lincoln Legal Papers case files.

knotty land cases: Stevens, 42.

honest answer and low fee: Chrisman, 15–16.

almanac discredited witness: *People v. Armstrong,* 1858, Lincoln Legal Papers case file; Duff, 350–59.

Murder trial: *People v. Goings,* 1859, Lincoln Legal Papers case file; East, 1953; Duff, 347–50.

Oh no, Bob: Duff, 349; East, 1953; *He told one:* Burlingame, Ettinger, 64, 306.

bastardy case: *People ex rel. Neighbor v. Hall; Neighbor v. Hall,* 1859, Lincoln Legal Papers case file.

hated long trials, favored settlements: Lamon 313–14; Whitney, 173.

I have heard him: Herndon, Weik, 1:315–19.

dismissed cases: Steiner, 1995, 1.

Lincoln unwilling to violate law: Weik, 1922, 198.

Matson slave case: *In re Bryant et al., 1847,* Lincoln Legal Papers case file; Duff, 130–32; Weik 1897; McIntyre; Chroust.

Peoria bridge obstruction: *Columbus Insurance Co. v. Peoria Bridge Co.,* 1853, Lincoln Legal Papers case file; *Illinois State Register* December 20, 1851; Duff, 235–36. Earlier in this case, the insurance company sued Curtenius et al.

Lincoln for the railroad: *Hurd v. Rock Island Bridge Co.,* 1857, Lincoln Legal Papers case file; Duff, 332–44.

Lincoln appears for both sides: *Hall v. Perkins* 5 Ill. 549 (1843); *Perkins v. Hall,* Lincoln Legal Papers case file.

seen and heard: A. B. Clough Papers, Chicago Historical Society, Illinois.

did not prepare; a lawyer who: Masters, 1931, 119, 121.

Was as hard to beat: Woldman, 1936, 231.

In all the elements: Hertz, 1938, 425; Lamon 313–14; Kyle, 6.

It is good policy: Basler, 1:453.

As *a lawyer:* Browne, 145.

He was not: Whitney, 87–88.

As *he entered the trial:* Herndon, Weik, 1893, 2:3; Basler, 2:281.

Lincoln's advice to would-be lawyers: Basler, 2:327, 535; 3: 344; 4:121.

had a large practice; If not: W. Gilbert to Lincoln, October 17, 1860, Robert T. Lincoln Collection, Library of Congress.

unfailing vein of humor: Lamon, 313–14.

Its gone to h--l: J. D. Wickizer to Herndon November 25, 1866 in Hertz, 1938, 320; Wilson, Davis, 1998, 424.

never failed to produce: Burlingame, 1994, 11.

unusual sense of humor: K. Burns.

Gentlemen of the jury: Herndon, 288; Lincoln's Own Yarns and Stories, website.

That reminds me: F. T. Hill, 218.

It looks very much: Frank, 182; *Johnston v. Jones & Marsh*, 1860, Lincoln Legal Papers case file; Duff 241–42.

Lincoln disrupted court with comments: *Farni v. Tesson*, 1859, Lincoln Legal Papers case file; Chase, 65.

Lincoln acting: Bergen, 392.

Lincoln was an outstanding: Frank, 172; Shestack, 1992a, 12

Five qualities: Frank, 97–98.

CHAPTER 3

LINCOLN'S CLIENT ASSAULTED: HE QUESTIONED HIS PHYSICIAN'S MEDICAL SCHOOL GRADUATION

plaintiff's affidavit filed: Tazewell County Circuit Court, July 24, 1851

appearance bond: Tazewell County Circuit Court, July 24, 1851.

infamously false; without any; made an assault; used by none other; such an instrument; by profession: Plaintiff's affidavit, Tazewell County Circuit Court, July 24, 1851.

Edward Jones, Plaintiff: Plaintiff's declaration, Tazewell County Circuit Court, September 1, 1851.

conform to the writ: Miers, 2:59.

I want you to open: F. T. Hill, 186.

at said time; large cane; did necessarily and unavoidably; prayed for judgment: Defendant's plea, Tazewell County Circuit Court, September 23, 1851.

did have sexual intercourse: Thompson v. Henline, McLean County Circuit Court, defendant's plea, October 3, 1851; Steiner, 1995; Miers, 2:60.

Judge Logan and myself: Basler, 1:270.

Stuart & Lincoln bank account: Basler, 1:267.

Of this we have expended: Basler, 1:285.

Lincoln's separate bills: Basler, 2:69.

Herndon's fondness for drink: Rankin, 265.

was an excellent: Newton, 18.

Hated Herndon; *Pointedly drew her voluminous:* Tilton, 210; Randall, 1954, 50.

This is in return: Randall, 1955, 12; In his lecture Herndon [1945, 39] stated that Abraham Lincoln loved Ann Rutledge.

Herndon Springfield Mayor: *Illinois State Journal*, March 9, 17 and April 5, 1854; Donald, 1948, 168–73; Miers, 2:118.

I also heard them: Charles S. Zane in material prepared for Newton, 251.

Lincoln as a lawyer: Frank, 168–73.

Mr. Lincoln was the plainest man: Shestack, March 21, 1994.

most reticent & mostly: Randall, 1954, 50.

Lincoln's business card: American Memory, Printed Ephemera Collection, website.

only three states required more than a diploma: Burrow, 10.

collapse of license laws; *no legal restrictions*: Warner, 237; Abram, 17.

Discourage litigation: Lincoln 1850; Basler, 2:81.

I never want the reputation: Tilton, 181.

the respectable attorney: New York Legal Observer, 395.

attire and physical habits: J. H. Cooper, February 23, 1987.

David Davis biography: *Bibliographic Record*, 9.

Jacobus v. Kitchell et ux.: Tazewell County Circuit Court, declaration, September term 1851.

census data on Maus: Bloomington-Normal Genealogical Society, 180, 184.

Maus not listed as a graduate of Jefferson: Gayley, 49.

CHAPTER 4
FIRED FOR INCOMPETENCY: ASYLUM'S MEDICAL
    SUPERINTENDENT SUES

trustees appeal lower court decision: Bannister, 1992, 172.

Lincoln consulted on the case: Miers, 2:101.

Lincoln's letter in reply: Basler, 2:197–98.

Quo Warranto explained: California Attorney General's Office

evil-minded and other complaints: Ranney, 249.

protest gained little for AMSAII : Pitts, 58.

AMSAII reluctant to protest; no risk with Nichols: Pitts, 58.

Nichols called a *rank abolitionist*: Schultze letter, March 12, 1858.

Nichols labeled a *secessionist*: J. M. W. letter to Lincoln, April 12, 1861

Nichols called a *copperhead*: Machett letter, April 19, 1861.

Nichols declared *incompetent*: N. S. Davis letter, November 1869.

On motion of A. Lincoln: Barnhart, 1954.

slander case of *Martin v. Underwood*: Vermilion County Circuit Court, *trespass on the case/slander*, April 1858 term.

used, uttered, spoke and published: Vermilion County Circuit Court, plaintiff's declaration, October 1857 term.

the said plaintiff: Vermilion County Circuit Court, defendant's plea, October 1857 term.

A. LINCOLN, ESQUIRE

asking for a continuance: Miers, 2:204.

We the jury find: Vermilion County Circuit Court, verdict, April 1858 term.

good, true, honest, just: Vermilion County Circuit Court, plaintiff's declaration, October 1857 term.

because they were political: American Journal of Insanity, 29:247.

asylum expenditures: Rammelkamp, 65.

irregular meetings; unlawful: Dexter, Craven.

Shall have charge of: Peck, 129; Watters, 14.

On the twelfth August: Illinois State Hospital, 1st report, 48.

after many contentious: Illinois State Hospital, Special Report, 9.

with a salary of: Illinois State Hospital, 1st report, 71–72.

The successful candidate: Illinois State Hospital, Special Report, 9.

long before the building: Rammelkamp, 65.

took strong grounds: Rammelkamp, 65–66.

Higgins biography: W. B. Atkinson, 56.

Higgins listed in legislature; Lincoln & Herndon notice: *Sangamo Journal*, August 27, 1846, 2.

AMSAII visitations in Boston; Higgins's paper *called up*: American Journal of Insanity, 7:77.

content of Higgins's paper: *American Journal of Insanity*, 7:64.

intrigue of fraud: Illinois State Hospital Record, March 1, 1851.

AMSAII visitations in Philadelphia: *American Journal of Insanity*, 8:82–88.

appeared and took his seat; AMSAII visitations in New York City: *American Journal of Insanity*, 9:67.

Did the authors: Illinois State Hospital, 3d Report, 103.

six specific criticisms: Holmes, Morton, et al, Protest, 1852, 3; *Morganville Journal*.

gratifying results presented: Illinois State Hospital, 3d Report, 98.

The superintendent has been: Illinois State Hospital, 3d Report, 106.

patient's death and asylum fire: Illinois State Hospital, 3d Report, 117; Watters, 10.

no one ought to expect: Illinois State Hospital, 3d Report, 105–107.

request for names of patients: Journal of the Senate, 1853, 9. Letter, Higgins to R. E. Goodell, January 20, 1853.

report to Senate; *apparent inequality*: 1853, 1–3.

appointment of new trustees: *Illinois State Journal*, February 14, 1853, 2.

Whereas ,this institution: Supreme Court of Illinois, Abstract filed by Stuart & Edwards for the Plaintiffs in Error, 1853.

Four resolutions of the trustees: Supreme Court of Illinois Abstract, 1853.

That Thomas Delny: Tazewell County Circuit Court, May 1853 term, Indictment; Luthin, 1960, 169–70; Miers, 2: 98, identifies the rapist as Watlen.

A mob came near, awful crime: Daily Register [Springfield], May 14, 1853, 3; *Will your Excellency, Please let this man*; Lincoln Legal Papers case file.
amount of indebtedness: Illinois Journal, June 8, 1853, 2.
Dr. Higgins asked: Illinois Journal, June 8, 1853, 2.
That the President: Illinois Journal, June 8, 1853, 2.
That Dr. James M. Higgins: Illinois Journal, June 8, 1853, 2.
corrections in the resolutions; *and whereas, while the said*: Supreme Court of Illinois Abstract, 1853.
Higgins not qualified: Supreme Court of Illinois, Information filed by Cyrus Eppler, October 26, 1853.
contrary to; State's attorney prayeth: Supreme Court of Illinois, Information filed by Cyrus Eppler, October 26, 1853.
equally potent before: Richards, February 11, 1909.
could split hairs: Bruce, 14; Mitgang, 1997; W. D. Beard, 1993. ii.
the governor, the judges: Peck, 129.
the substance is the same: Peck, 136.
We have no doubt: Peck, 130.
I do not believe: Peck, 131.
In cases of this sort: Peck, 133.
Such a proceeding: Peck, 133.
removal only for infidelity; does not possess; Unless the board: Peck, 136.
The duties of that office: Peck, 136.
If it is substantially: Peck, 136–37.
trustees' minority report; *immediate attention; precipitate, unlawful; alarming...incorporation of evils; its rue weal*: Craven, Dexter, February 13, 1854.
Dr. Andrew McFarland: Illinois State Hospital, 4th Report, 152; *American Journal of Insanity*, 12: 367–70.
letter to Yates: Angle, 1930, 131.
Hon. Richard Yates: Angle, 1930, 131; Basler, 2:226.
in the Autumn: Basler, 4:67.
incredible quantity of hard liquor: Duff, 378, note 7.
Yates is beaten; insane asylum: Basler, 2:286.
in the event: R. P. Howard, 124.
stirring speech: R. P. Howard, 124.
Trumbull biography: Trumbull website.
I am trying: Basler, 4:40.
Yates drunk: R. P. Howard, 124.
sending 197,360 men: R. P. Howard, 125.
Old Abe was too slow: R. P. Howard, 127.

CHAPTER 5
LINCOLN SECURES A CHARTER FOR A
   HOMEOPATHIC MEDICAL SCHOOL

Resolved. That any such unnatural: American Medical Association, 1958, 146.
We never fought: Kaufman, 1971, 158.
expulsion of AMA members: Coulter, 3:206–209.
Seward's physician a homeopath: P. Starr, 1982, 98.
named as trustees: Laws of 1855, 531.
members of the medical school Board: W. H. King, 2:348.
first female medical college: W. H. King, 2:159.
respected American advocates of homeopathy: W. H. King, 2:14
Dr. Rush endorses bloodletting: Coulter, 3:39.
800,000 leeches imported: Coulter, 3:70.
law of simila; like cures its like: Hahnemann, 1810; Hahnemann, 1828.
domestic homeopathy kit, $5: Numbers, 46.
Scammon and Hoyne lay homeopaths: Andreas, 469.
Hoyne's wife daughter of a homeopath: Andreas, 468.
Chicago educated the most homeopaths: W. H. King, 1:345 and 3:213.
first national medical society: Coulter, 3:124.
AMA first organized: N. S. Davis, 1855; Fishbein, 1947, 3.
bitter feud between allopaths and homeopaths: Coulter.
exchange of letters: Andreas, 469.
Your Committee thinks: W. H. King, 2:341.
variety of alternative healers: Gevitz; Burrow, 3.
to rush into practice: Jacobi, 368.
Fifty thousand dollars: Laws of 1855, 532.
charter for a private corporation: Blake, 359.
Hoyne took the Doctor: Andreas, 471.
Mr Hoyne, the district attorney: Miers, 2:103; *Register* July 6, 1853.
federal practice of Lincoln & Herndon: Duff, chapter 13, 221–42; Thomas,
   1935a.
Thomas Hoyne biography: T. Hoyne, 1877; T. Hoyne, 1884; T. Hoyne, 1878;
   Higginson, 1883.
active and efficient: In Memoriam, 1883, 88.
constant fidelity to one: In Memoriam, 1883, 88.
Temple S. Hoyne biography: Pamphlets-Homeopathic, 1850–1893; T. S. Hoyne,
   1868; T. S. Hoyne, 1873; T. S. Hoyne, 1878; T. S. Hoyne, 1883.
Thomas Hoyne elected Chicago Mayor: *Chicago City Manual,* 1911, 46; *Chicago
   City Manual,* 1916, 202; *In Memoriam,* 1883; Chicago Historical Society,
   1884.
he was more indebted: Nicolay papers, interview, February 20, 1875.
Judd complained to Lincoln: Nicolay, Hay, 1894, 5:290.

There is not one: Edwards, 8.

If it shall not incommode: Basler, 4:187.

Judd biography: Edwards, 19.

One year after date: D. L. Wilson, 1948, 50.

The court is of the opinion: D. L. Wilson, 1948, 51.

Scammon v. Cline: 3 Ill 456; Bannister, 1994, 153–54; Duff, 248–49.

prejudiced jury favored Cline: Luthin, 1960, 65–66.

Robert T. Lincoln's apprenticeship and Scammon: Palmer, 1:74.

conducted with great ability; out but a few moments: Alton Telegraph December 14, 1844.

Chapman perjury case: *Alton Telegraph*, December 14, 1844; Palmer, 1:168; Memorials...Logan, 30; Duff. 233.

Lincoln's role in the passage of railroad legislation: J. W. Starr, 25, 112.

Father of the Illinois Central: Brown, 124–25, 149.

Bissell and Brayman first attorneys: Brown, 127.

Lincoln & Herndon represented railroads: Lueckenhoff, 393; In 1905, the Illinois Central Railroad published 200 copies of a thirteen-page booklet commemorating Lincoln as their attorney.

Lincoln lobbied legislators: Brown, 130.

Lincoln's first railroad case: Basler, 2:194, 202, 205.

ICRR tax in charter: Brown, 130.

As this will be: Tracy, 47; Basler, 2:202; Luthin, 1960, 158.

He was an absolute: Key, 83 quoting Cullom Davis

I am now free: Fehrenbacher, 1989, 299; Basler, 2:205.

within the constitutional power: Illinois Central Railroad v. County of McLean, 17 Ill 290; J. W. Starr, 62.

the decision was worth: 17 Ill 291; Basler, 3:331.

trouble collecting fee: Townsend, 1924, 86.

increase fee and sue: Donald, 1948, 284; Duff, 315.

new bill and endorsements: Nicolay, Hay, 1894, 1:219. Some sources list six lawyers and others eight.

had to threaten seizure: Townsend, 1924, 86.

Joy's legal fee: Angle, 1947, 179.

comparative earnings: Brown, 134; Thomas, 1952, 92.

lawyers for Hurd: Duff, 336.

$500,000 for the lawsuit: *Chicago Daily Press*, September 26, 1857; Page, 5.

McClellan and Illinois Central Railroad tax case: Brown, 146, 149, 150–53.

Effie Afton case: Duff 338. Judd's letter was destroyed in a fire.

What mood was the steamboatmen: Page, 6.

Every bushel of wheat: Page, 6.

people along the river: Saltonstall, 64.

united in saying; Lincoln chipped a piece of wood: *Cincinnati Enquirer,* September 17, 1857; Saltonstall, 64.

Gentlemen, I have not: Luthin, 1960, 165–66.

Mr. A. Lincoln: Chicago Daily Press, September 25, 1857; Basler, 2:415–22.

first stenographer: F. T. Hill, 260.

bridge litigation ended: Page, 10; Basler, 2:422; Luthin, 1960, 163–65.

Judd's land as payment: Duff, 345.

bribed to run into bridge: F. T. Hill, 260.

Dr. Davis S. Smith biography: Holloway, 420.

first homeopathic pharmacy: Zeuch, 242.

Dr. Smith's offices in Association: *Journal of the American Institute of Homeopathy,* 2:189.

body politic; to give instruction: Laws of 1855, 530–31.

make, create and endow; No person shall be appointed: Laws of 1855, 531–32.

prescribe and regulate: Laws of 1855, 532.

all rights, privileges and powers: *Laws of 1855,* 532–33; W. H. King, 2:341.

CHAPTER 6
VICTORIAN PHYSICIANS, IMPROPERLY HEALED FRACTURES AND AMERICA'S FIRST MEDICAL MALPRACTICE CRISIS, 1835–1865

Much of the hostility: Ficarra, 21.

malpractice virtually unknown: Mohr, 255.

contagion of law suits: Mohr, 112.

A respected Buffalo surgeon: DeVille, 44.

nine of ten physicians suffered malpractice suit: Mohr, 117.

occur almost every month: Western Journal of Medical Sciences, 309.

There can hardly: Elwell, 83.

Elwell bio: Shastid, 94.

legal study of state supreme court cases: C. R. Burns, 41.

states used English common law: H. W. Smith, 116:2149.

Blackstone's *Commentaries:* Blackstone, 1803, 122–23.

Injuries affecting a man's: H .W. Smith, 116:2490.

Cross v. Guthrie: Root, 2:90–92; American Decisions, 1:61.

his costs and expenses; contrary to all: Gordon, 73.

case law decision rationales: C. R. Burns, 50–51. All the quotes within the five rationales are from this source.

no texts dealt with malpractice: Frey, 56; *Lincoln Legal Briefs, 1989,* 1.

reference texts: Farr; Beck; Coley; Chitty; A. S. Taylor, 1848; Ray; Dean; Wharton, Stillé.

to furnish the medical man: Elwell, i.

law and medicine; None of the previous: New York Medical Press, 141.

for the cause: Foster, 119.

healers and fractures: Hippocrates; Desault; Eliason, 65; Mulvania, Johanson, 853; De Moulin, 54.

Better suffer a little: Eliason, 65.

It was generally believed: De Moulin, 54.

A man must be: Kirkland, 2.

Compound fractures of the limbs: Rutkow, 321.

principal medical reference: A. P. Cooper, 1832.

Text: S. D. Gross, 1830.

The title was unfortunate: S. D. Gross, 1887; Norman, 66.

Formerly, and with: A. P. Cooper, 1835, 616.

nine-tenths of all: Elwell, 55.

antisepsis introduced: Lister, 1:1867 and 2:1867.

An amputation that would: Elwell, 54.

tolerably well-versed: cited in Frey, 56; Griggs, 178.

low quality of medical education: Spiegel, 1993, 293.

Indian doctors, urine doctors: Wood, 395.

Text: Ordonaux, 1869.

the quack, the pill-vender: Ordonaux, 1860, 400.

that the chances are altogether: Western Medical and Surgical Journal, 346.

lax state license laws: DeVille, 225.

Ignorant and impudent pretenders: Wood, 395.

four reasons why better physicians were sued more often: Mohr, 114.

the avarice of those: Wood, 395.

that many men abandoned: F. H. Hamilton, 1886, 98.

mutually incompatible professions: New York Medical Press, 141.

CHAPTER 7
DEFENSE LAWYER, A. LINCOLN, USES CHICKEN BONES IN A
   MALPRACTICE CASE

The dressing of both limbs: McLean County Circuit Court, Deposition of Freese, August 24, 1857.

Fleming's sister nursed him: Illinois Historical Library, Springfield, David Davis papers, BV-6.

was getting along first-rate: McLean County Circuit Court, Deposition of Freese, August 24, 1857.

they were crooked as: McLean County Circuit Court, Deposition of Freese, August 24, 1857.

For God's sake: McLean County Circuit Court, Deposition of Freese, August 24, 1857.

he would not: Illinois Historical Library, Springfield, David Davis papers, BV-6.

swore that he would: McLean County Circuit Court, Deposition of Freese, August 24, 1857.

he would rather: McLean County Circuit Court, Deposition of Freese, August 24, 1857.

I then understood: McLean County Circuit Court, Deposition of Freese, August 24, 1857.

A layer of muslin: Illinois Historical Library, Springfield, David Davis papers, BV-6.

the interests and prejudices: Wood, 395.

juries have seemed: Boston Medical & Surgical Journal, 1852, 264.

A jury of laboring men: Scalpel, 311.

And the said defendants: McLean County Circuit Court, defendants plea, April 7, 1857.

Lincoln requests a continuance: McLean County Circuit Court, defendants plea, April 9, 1857; Miers, 2:166, 178.

this cause stand: McLean County Circuit Court, defendants plea, April 10, 1857.

numerous medical malpractice phrases in complaint: McLean County Circuit Court, declaration filed March 28, 1856, amended August 27, 1856.

commanded to summon; personally to appear: McLean County Circuit Court, September 8, 1856.

Lincoln requests another continuance: McLean County Circuit Court, defendants affidavit, September 10, 1856.

granted *at the costs*: McLean County Circuit Court, September 10, 1856.

Hamilton's *fracture tables* and publications; expert witness: F. H. Hamilton, 1849; F. H. Hamilton and Boardman, 1853; F. H. Hamilton, 1854; F. H. Hamilton, 1855a,b; F. H. Hamilton, 1860.

erect something like: American Journal of Medical Sciences, 39, 422.

fracture of the thigh bone; Neither in Great Britain: F. H. Hamilton, 1855a, 8–10.

They may hesitate: F. H. Hamilton, 1855a, 9.

Surgeons themselves believed: New Hampshire Journal of Medicine, 20.

On the circuit: J. L. King, 166:186.

It is true that: C. Davis, 1989, 6:1.

toted books and hunted: Donald, 1948, 22, 38.

Lincoln's advice to aspiring lawyers: Basler, 3:344 and 4:121.

legal text: Blackstone, 1803. There was an 1841 edition published by W. E. Dean in New York.

legal texts: Chitty, 1842; Greenleaf, 1842; Story, 1836; Story, 1838; Chitty, 1834; A. S. Taylor, 1836; Wharton, Stillé, 1855.

legal text in Lincoln's office: Dean, 1850; *Lincoln Legal Briefs*, 1:1. This book is now the property of the US National Park Service, Lincoln Home, Springfield, Illinois.

It abundantly proves: J. W. Hamilton, 11:53.

medical malpractice not in texts: *Lincoln Legal Briefs*, 1:2–3.

to acquaint physicians: Elwell, 1860, i; Elwell biography, Shastid, 4:94.

summons for plaintiff's witnesses: McLean County Circuit Court, February 20, 1857; March 6, 1857; March 18 1857.

Swett's insanity defense: Ray, 1838.

insane, not guilty: Spiegel, Kavaler, 1997b,145.

possuming insanity; have been too: Woldman, 52.

Lincoln and the insanity plea: Spiegel, 1994, 60.

summons for defendant's witnesses: McLean County Circuit Court, April 7, 1857; April 9, 1857.

types of physicians advertising: *Weekly Pantagraph*; Bloomington City Directory, 1855–1856; Prince, Burnham, *History of McLean County*, 1908; *Biographical record of McLean County*, 1899.

Hubbard and Hamilton: *Bibliographic Record*, 809–11.

This bone has; Can you walk?: Wakefield, 1936, 54–56; letter from daughter Lulu Crothers to Wakefield, *New York Times*, July 12, 1958.

the slight defect: DeVille, 101.

medical malpractice crisis: Spiegel, Kavaler, 1997a, 283.

logical analysis and rhetorical flourishes: *Lincoln Legal Briefs*. 1:1.

the skill, ingenuity: Boston Medical and Surgical Journal, 1854, 73.

After all one can do: Pray, 289.

compound dislocations of the: Pray, 51:189.

to set the leg: McCandless v. McWha, 22 Penn. 261, 1853, 263.

doctor wins malpractice case: *Buffalo Medical Journal and Medical Reports*, 135.

Hamilton testifies, doctor wins: *Ohio Medical & Surgical Journal*, 13.

After a few questions: Scalpel, 311.

jury *being unable to agree*: McLean County Circuit Court, proceedings, April 7, 1857. While the docket is dated April 7, the trial ended April 10.

newspaper report on trial: Bloomington *Daily Pantagraph*, April 14, 1857, 3.

Lincoln requests another continuance: McLean County Circuit Court, continuance granted, June 15, 1857.

at present engaged: McLean County Circuit Court, deposition of Freese, August 24, 1857.

Lincoln's seven deposition questions for Freese: McLean County Circuit Court, defendant's interrogatories, August 1, 1857.

to be holden; summons for plaintiff's witnesses: McLean County Circuit Court, August 8, 1857.

Lincoln's five deposition questions for Small: McLean County Circuit Court, defendant's interrogatories, August 21, 1857.

Swett's thirteen sensational interrogatories for Freese: McLean County Circuit Court, plaintiff's interrogatories, August 24, 1857.

fully advised on the premises: McLean County Circuit Court, continuance granted, September 8, 1857.

Small's five questions and responses: McLean County Circuit Court, deposition of Small, November 10, 1857.

fee for Small's deposition: McLean County Circuit Court, November 10, 1857.

summons for plaintiff's witnesses: McLean County Circuit Court, November 16, 1857.

change of venue requested: McLean County Circuit Court, plaintiff's affidavit, December 20, 1857.

the venue of this case: McLean County Circuit Court, change of venue granted, December 21, 1857.

court papers sent to Logan County Circuit Court: McLean County Circuit Court, clerk's entry, December 26, 1857.

fees charged by the court: Logan County Circuit Court, March term, 1858.

as per agreement on file: Logan County Circuit Court, dismissal of case, March 15, 1858.

court papers destroyed in fire: H. E. Pratt, 1936, 45.

he was not more; Lincoln was great: Angle, 1929, 40.

Lincoln's biggest legal fee: Bloomington *Weekly Pantagraph*, July 1, 1857; H. E. Pratt, 1936, 51.

Eli and Marie Crothers biography: *Biographical Record*, 471.

my old personal friend: Basler, 5:358, 451 and 6:294.

I personally wish: Basler, 7:11.

I will be personally: Basler, 7:203.

Dr. J. R. Freese, now editor: Basler, 8:12.

Please let the appointment: Basler, 8:25–26.

CHAPTER 8
BROKEN WRIST WITHOUT DUE CARE: LINCOLN DEFENDS THE PHYSICIAN

Watson was a good legal fixer: Luthin, 1960, 160.

Lincoln hired and given retainer: Hinchcliff, 361; Emerson, 361; Parkinson; Duff, 323.

During my stay in Chicago: Tracy, 58–59; Basler, 2:315.

Lincoln writes to Manny & Co.: Tracy, 61.

A long, lank creature: Luthin, 1960, 162; Herndon, Weik, 1893, 2:24.

Why did you bring: Herndon-Weik collection, Herndon to Weik, January 6, 1887; Donald, 1995, 186.

Lincoln remained in Cincinnati: Dickson.

roughly handled by that: Herndon, Weik, 1893, 2:356.

Lincoln appointed the best man: Beveridge Papers, Dowse to Beveridge, October 10, 1925. William H. Dowse was an associate in Harding's law firm from 1878 to 1890; Duff, 325.

medical malpractice suit initiated: Bannister, 1992, 220; Morse, 7; Sandor, 1951, 705; DeVille, 49, 184.

on motion and by agreement: Continuance granted, Hancock County Circuit Court, October 8, 1855.

Now comes the defendant: Affidavit for security, Hancock County Circuit Court, March 4, 1856.

Now comes the defendant: defendant's pleas and plaintiff's security filed, Hancock County Circuit Court, March 6, 1856.

Now comes the plaintiff: Demurrer filed, Hancock County Circuit Court, March 7, 1856.

Now come to be heard: Demurrer sustained, Hancock County Circuit Court, March 11, 1856.

a three day trial: Court docket for June 10–12, 1856, Hancock County Circuit Court.

cases in Springfield, Summer 1856: Miers, 2:171.

request for change of venue: Motion granted, Hancock County Circuit Court, October 8, 1857.

Continuance granted: Adams County Circuit Court, October 20, 1857.

fee book: Hancock County Circuit Court, October term, 1856.

Lincoln campaigning for candidates: Miers, 2:181.

jury named: Adams County Circuit Court, March 23, 1858.

verdict; request for a new trial: Adams County Circuit Court, March 25, 1858.

Goings bondsman: East 1953; Miers, 2:213, 231.

hearing for a new trial; granting appeal to Supreme Court of Illinois: Adams County Circuit Court, April 10, 1858.

We the jury; appeal; *an official security bond:* Adams County Circuit Court, April 16, 1858.

Professional card column: *Daily Illinois State Journal,* January 13, 1857, 1:1.

Ritchey v. West: Peck, 329.

Biography of Elliott Herndon: Palmer, 1:84–85; *History of Sangamon County,* 106–107; Donald, 1948, 136–37, 158.

fracture tables: F. H. Hamilton, Boardman, 1853.

handwritten bill of exceptions: Long, 1993, 55.

No question can arise: Peck, 329.

a want of reasonable care: Peck, 329.

must be held to employ: Peck, 329.

medical evidence resplinting: F. H. Hamilton, Boardman, 1853.

would have tended: Peck, 329.

the wrist received no injury: Peck, 329.

a new trial will not: Peck, 329.

Upon the whole: Peck, 329.

judgment form: supreme court of Illinois, January term, 1860.

fee book: supreme court of Illinois, January term, 1860.

dismantled his shifty; But being thoroughly: D. L. Wilson, 1994.

Peachy Quinn Harrison case: Mitgang, February 10, 1989, B7:3; Duff, 363–64; Hertz, 1938, 107–108; Basler, 3: 492–93.

Dred Scott decision: *Illinois State Register*, March 12, 1857; Duff, 346; Donald, 1948, 100.

respect and obey, but erroneous: Duff, 747.

with a certain piece; with a certain hard substance: Mason County Circuit Court, indictment, October term, 1857; Townsend, 1925. At times, articles erroneously label the weapon a slingshot. Lincoln gave prosecutor J. Henry Shaw the slungshot as a remembrance, Hertz, 1938, 306.

he fears that: severance and change of venue, Mason County Circuit Court, October term, 1857.

Lincoln's letter to Hannah: Tracy, 1917, 79. Luthin, 1960, 165, contends that this letter is spurious and was actually written after Lincoln's death. In her statement to Herndon, Hannah said that she wrote to Lincoln first, Hertz, 1938, 369.

Lincoln played and rocked Duff Armstrong: Duff, 111.

how Lincoln chose jurors: Weaver, 1926, 1; Oates, 1977, 100–101

sat with his head: Bergen, 390; Counsel Quest.

Lincoln's cross-examination of Allen: Counsel Quest; T. J. Fleming, 1985, 20.

Lincoln, with his usual care: Bergen, 393.

almanac and witness: Counsel Quest

the almanac floored: Shaw to Herndon, August 22, 1866, Herndon-Weik Collection; While the astronomical facts remain constant, several different almanacs have been cited including Ayer's, Goudy's, and Jayne's, Hertz, 1938, 340.

additional evidence: Woldman in Angle, 1947, 175–79; Bergen, 394.

most persuasive testimony: Harriot statement, undated, Herndon-Weik Collection.

Dr. Stephenson founded GAR: Heiple, website.

he began to talk: Bergen, 390.

whole testimony and picked it: Woldman in Angle, 1947, 177.

I have never seen: Walker to Herndon, June 3, August 27, and September 17, 1866, Herndon-Weik Collection; Duff, 357.

Lincoln's instructions to the jury: Cass County Circuit Court, May 1857; Duff, 357.

Aunt Hannah: T. J. Fleming, 1985, 20.

Duff Armstrong murder trial: Tarbell, August 1896, 277; Counsel Quest; Duff, 350–59; Gridley.

jurors say 1857 almanac used: Duff, 358.

was 2 days: F. T. Hill, 234.

questions about the almanac: Olson, Doescher, 1990.

Yours of the 14th of July: Fehrenbacher, 1989, 485.

Lincoln's letter to Hannah Armstrong: Basler, 6:462.

Come see Stephen: Treasure Chest: The Fifth Artifact, website.

in broiling summer heat: Holzer, 1996, 61; Neely, 1982, 4, 117, 123, 167, 228, 249.

Douglas's *withering sarcasm*: Holzer, 1996, 61.

onlookers set off cannons: Holzer, 1996, 62.

The fire flew some: Holzer, 1996, 62.

made by boiling the shadow: Parshall, 74.

gave great satisfaction; *Lincoln's Heart Fails*: Mitgang, October 8, 1992, 26.

campaign expenditures, popular vote and legislative vote: Mitgang, October 8, 1992, 26.

Lincoln-Douglas debates: Nicolay, Hay, 1894, 276–96; Mitgang, October 8, 1992, 26; Holzer, 1996, 61; Reilly examined the role of press coverage at the debates; Holzer, 1994, edited the first complete unexpurgated text of the debates.

The mode is very simple: Basler, 4:121.

so awful ugly: K. Burns, 5.

shingle and professional card: Donald, 1948, 157; Woldman, 109.

Your of January 30th: Basler, 5:118.

Herndon sent fees to Lincoln: Herndon and Weik, 1889, 2:266; Miers, 3:313; H. E. Pratt, 1943b, 134–35.

Upon the election: *Everybody's Advertiser*, Springfield, September 1, 1861.

Let it hang there: Herndon and Weik, *1889*, 3:482; Weik, 1922, 298; Woldman, 271.

CHAPTER 9

LINCOLN'S CASES OF SEX, SLANDER, AND SUNDRY SUITS

Lincoln handled sixty-eight slander suits: Steiner, 1995, 2.

definition of slander: Bannister, 1994, 117.

Dr. Lehman's letter: *Lehman v. Schroeder* case file, Lincoln Legal Papers.

Mark me down: Basler, 2:444.

Schroeder biography: *Biographical Record McLean County*, 596–99; *History of McLean County*, 819.

And now this day: McLean County Circuit Court, judgment and execution docket, January 8, 1859; Basler, 2:444; Miers, 2:216.

False, scandalous, malicious: plaintiff's declaration, Christian County Circuit Court, November term, 1847.

He caught my old sow: Christian County Circuit Court, November term, 1847.

False, scandalous, malicious: plaintiff's declaration, Christian County Circuit Court, November term, 1847.

Lincoln and Herndon received $25: Lincoln Legal Papers, case file.

Commit the infamous: McLean County Circuit Court, defendant's plea, October 3, 1851.

Two trials, hung jury, case dismissed: McLean County Circuit Court, docket entry, April 21, 1851.

Good name, fame: Woodford County Circuit Court, plaintiff's declaration, February 7, 1852.

Good and worthy; falsely and maliciously: Woodford County Circuit Court, plaintiff's declaration, February 7, 1852.

Wickedly and maliciously: Woodford County Circuit Court, plaintiff's declaration, February 7, 1852.

False, slanderous, malicious: Woodford County Circuit Court, plaintiff's declaration, February 7, 1852.

Good, true, honest: Woodford County Circuit Court, plaintiff's declaration, February 7, 1852.

$2,000 award: Woodford County Circuit Court, declaration and praecipe , judgment, April 15, 1852.

Graphically, falsely and maliciously: Tazewell County Circuit Court, plaintiff's affidavit, August 6, 1851.

On October 1, 1850: Tazewell County Circuit Court, plaintiff's declaration, September 1, 1851.

Elizabeth is not guilty: Tazewell County Circuit Court, defendant's plea and demurrer, September 1, 1851.

will either leave; be compelled: Tazewell County Circuit Court, affidavit, August 6, 1851.

Twelve witnesses: Lincoln Legal Papers, case file.

They or either: Steiner, 1995.

For a considerable: Tazewell County Circuit Court, defendant's affidavit, September 1, 1851.

rogued; after skin: Menard County Circuit Court, defendant's declaration, May 25, 1843.

and his denunciation: letter from Parks to Herndon, March 25, 1866, Herndon-Weik Collection.

We the jurors: Menard County Circuit Court, *Cabot v. Regnier* verdict, November 7, 1843.

he did not believe: Menard County Circuit Court, affidavit, November 17, 1843.

new trial and change of venue: motion, Menard County Circuit Court, November 8, 1843.

Lincoln filed demurrer March 14, 1844: Miers, 1:224.

Do you not think: Morgan County Circuit Court, Bennett deposition, March 12, 1844; Duff, 91.

jury awarded $1,600 on March 15, 1844: Miers, 1:224.

went out to find: Morgan County Circuit Court, Bowen affidavit, March 16, 1844.

at a late hour: Duff, 91.

Justice Purple wrote the opinion: Gilman, 2:34–43.

By the weight: Gilman, 2:40.

In my judgment: Gilman, 2:41.

Upon the whole: Gilman, 2:42.

struck by the shockingly: Duff, 92–93.

labor, care, diligence: Menard County Circuit Court, Reginer's declaration, April 18, 1855.

We of the jury: Menard County Circuit Court, verdict, May 29, 1855.

It appeared there was due: DeWitt County Circuit Court, justice of the peace transcript, July 3, 1841.

court costs: DeWitt County Circuit Court, fee book, October term, 1841.

court costs: DeWitt County Circuit Court, fee book, May term, 1842.

physician's fees for services: Menard County Circuit Court, account, January 11, 1845.

delivering lady…sewing and dressing: Menard County Circuit Court, account, 1846.

We the jury: Menard County Circuit Court, justice of the peace transcript, December 16, 1845.

court costs reimbursed: Menard County Circuit Court, justice of the peace transcript, December 16, 1845.

court costs: Menard County Circuit Court, fee book, June 7, 1846.

said justice to certify: Woodford County, petition for writ, justice of the peace court, July 11, 1843.

the Hon Samuel H. Treat: Woodford County Circuit Court, petition for *certiorari,* September 15, 1843.

said judgment is unjust: Woodford County Circuit Court, petition, September 15, 1843.

statement of libel; *whereas the said:* Barnhart, 5.

And now, fellow citizens: Barnhart, 6.

He was a man: Davis to his wife, May 11, 1852, David Davis collection.

The character of Dr. Fithian: Barnhart, 7.

Lincoln filed Grubb's declaration: Miers, 2:80.

said defendant: plaintiff's declaration, *Grubb v. John Frink & Co.*, Sangamon County Circuit Court, August 13, 1852.

Lincoln wrote parts of Blackwell's affidavit, February 3, 1853: Miers, 2:92.

very dark and: Sangamon County Circuit Court, Blackwell's deposition, February 3, 1853.

complained of great pain: Sangamon County Circuit Court, Blackwell's deposition, February 3, 1853.

Lincoln wrote and swore; affidavit: Sangamon County Circuit Court, February 7, 1853; Miers, 2:93.

Lincoln delivered notices: Miers, 2:92.

depositions taken: Sangamon County Circuit Court, February 21, 1853.

Were there or were there not: Sangamon County Circuit Court, Seligman's deposition, February 21, 1853.

In what condition: Sangamon County Circuit Court, Hall's deposition, February 21, 1853.

fee for taking deposition: Sangamon County Circuit Court, clerk's bill, February 21, 1853.

Would you or not: Sangamon County Circuit Court, Danner's deposition, March 15, 1843.

Wrongfully detained the goods: DeWitt County Circuit Court, plaintiff's declaration, October 5, 1854.

did not wrongfully detain: DeWitt County Circuit Court, defendant's plea, May 18, 1855.

I have to day drawn: Basler, 2:325.

Lincoln sent another letter: Basler, 2:326.

as joint dealers: Sangamon County Circuit Court, bill to settle partnership, December term, 1850.

paid large sums of money: Sangamon County Circuit Court, bill to settle partnership, December term, 1850.

From time to time: Sangamon County Circuit Court, Bill to settle partnership, December term, 1850.

hath received the sum: Sangamon County Circuit Court, bill to settle partnership, December term, 1850.

contribute his best exertions: Sangamon County Circuit Court, bill to settle partnership, December term, 1850.

Respondent in good faith: Sangamon County Circuit Court, defendant's answer, December term, 1850.

Respondent further states: Sangamon County Circuit Court, defendant's answer, December term, 1850.

Owen and Mount: Sangamon County Circuit Court, defendant's answer, December term, 1850.

appropriated to himself: Sangamon County Circuit Court, defendant's answer, December term, 1850.

Deposition questions and answers: Sangamon County Circuit Court, Spotswood's deposition, December term, 1850.

Relevant questions: Sangamon County Circuit Court, Spotswood's deposition, December term, 1850.

was by me duly sworn: Sangamon County Circuit Court, Spotswood's deposition, December term, 1850.

Then and there: Champaign County Circuit Court, plaintiff's declaration, May term, 1852.

With force of arms: Champaign County Circuit Court, defendant's plea, May term, 1852.

With force of arms: Champaign County Circuit Court, defendant's plea, May term, 1852.

Committed the trespass: Champaign County Circuit Court, plaintiff's amended declaration, May term, 1852.

And the defendant: Champaign County Circuit Court, defendant's replication, May term, 1852.

women victoriously sued: *Lincoln Legal Briefs*, 45[2]:2, 1998.

cultural factors in divorce: *Lincoln Legal Briefs*, 45[2]:2, 1998.

divorce suit initiated: Sangamon County Circuit Court, bill of divorce, August term, 1858.

been a kind, affectionate: Sangamon County Circuit Court, bill of divorce, August term, 1858.

repulsed this kindness: Sangamon County Circuit Court, bill of divorce, August term, 1858.

to obtain her; living: Sangamon County Circuit Court, bill of divorce, August term, 1858.

as descending from: Sangamon County Circuit Court, bill of divorce, August term, 1858.

committed adultery: Sangamon County Circuit Court, bill of divorce, August term, 1858.

for ought she knows: Sangamon County Circuit Court, bill of divorce, August term, 1858.

That the said defendant: Sangamon County Circuit Court, bill of divorce, August term, 1858.

decree a divorce: Sangamon County Circuit Court, bill of divorce, August term, 1858.

A state of moderate: Sangamon County Circuit Court, defendant's answer, March term, 1846.

In some way unknown: Sangamon County Circuit Court, defendant's answer, March term, 1846.

Full knowledge of all: Sangamon County Circuit Court, defendant's answer, March term, 1846.

Did then insist: Sangamon County Circuit Court, defendant's answer, March term, 1846.

He admits that about: Sangamon County Circuit Court, defendant's answer, March term, 1846.

that there are not: Sangamon County Circuit Court, defendant's answer, March term, 1846.

concerns himself with the beginnings: Greenleaf, August 26, 1837 discourse.

the officers in command: Basler, 7:439–40.

I do not consider: Basler, 7:440.

In at least thirteen: Steiner, 1995, 10.

Lincoln's wins and losses: Steiner 1995, 12.

CHAPTER 10
ABRAHAM AND MARY LINCOLN AND INSANITY IN THE COURTROOM

madness and morals in the 1800s: Skultans.

medical jurisprudence and insanity: Mohr.

medico-legal societies: Tighe, 231.

Those weakened in body: Dwyer, 61.

A wild and ferocious: Rush, 1812, 27; Quen, 1983, 527.

In this form of; Amid the rapid: Ray, 1838, 186, 261; Hughes.

three classifications of mental alienation: Dunglison, 351.

vote on moral insanity: *American Journal of Insanity*, 20:63, 98.

insanity texts: Esquirol, 1838; Foville, 1844; Gall, 1835; Pinel, 1809; Rush, 1835; Spurzheim, 1836.

phrenology text: Gall, 1804.

foreign lunatic: Growth of Nation, website

spells of melancholy; Curfman, 2; In a medical journal, Kempf concluded that Lincoln "was never free for a day from the tendency to melancholy."

What gave him: Letter from Swett to Herndon, February 14, 1866; D. L. Wilson, 49.

surrounded by death and distress: Nevins, Stone, 1962.

one on whom sorrow: G. Abrams, 1.

Lincoln's failures and successes: Morel, website.

Lincoln wrote; to prescribe without: Joshua Speed interview with Herndon in 1866. Herndon, Weik, 1893, 114. No copy of this letter to Dr. Drake has been found.

devilish passion: Hertz, 1938, 259.

The note to Dr. Drake: Hertz, 1938, 259.

I have within the last: Shutes, 26.

hypochondriasis-psychoneurotic-temperament: Curfman, 2.
Dr. Beard coined word neurasthenia: G. M. Beard, 1869, 217.
Americanitis; American disease: Haller, 1971, 473.
a natural tendency: Gosling.
symptoms of neurasthenia: Haller, 1970, 2489.
nervous debility; the hypo: Shutes, 28.
I proceed to answer your letter: Shutes, 29.
Melancholy dripped from him: Beveridge quoting Herndon, 523–24.
necessarily hereditary: Herndon, Weik, 1893, 190.
Again did you know: Hertz, 1938, 37.
had bouts of mental derangement: D. L. Wilson, 1997, 39.
Certainly, Lincoln had severe: Hudgens, 110.
steeped in the bitter waters: Whitney, 153.
Booth's insanity, *for the credit of our country:* May, 51; Brooks, 1997, 3.
Mother, do you see: Keckley, 104.
Mrs. Lincoln *non compos mentis:* New York Times, May 20, 1875.
Payments to consultant physicians: Croy, 141.
testimony, *bizarre, mentally deranged:* Croy, 74.
She has been of unsound: Mearns, 1948, 71.
My belief is the same: Croy, 93.
Oh Robert, to think: New York Times, May 20, 1875; R. P. Randall, 1995, 98.
More than anyone: Neely, McMurty, 142.
newspaper headlines: R. A. Ross, 313.
Dr. McFarland's consultation: Croy, 133, 142.
another sanity trial for Mrs. Lincoln: Croy, 129.
only too glad: New York Times, June 16, 1876.
We, the undersigned: Croy, 129, 131; R. P. Randall, 1955, 10.
Lilly v. Waggoner: Bannister, 238; 27 Ill Reports, 395.
It may be truly said: 27 Ill Reports, 395.

CHAPTER 11
CHLOROFORM INDUCED INSANITY
    DEFENSE CONFOUNDS LAWYER LINCOLN
Lincoln and Swett similarities: Hendrick, 110–11.
medical textbooks existed: Rutkow, 1988, 22–26; medical texts: Sargent, 1848;
    Flagg, 1851; *produces the desired effect:* J. D. Gross, 391. *employed*
    chloroform: Atlee, 389; *Beyond comparison, the best:* R. L. Howard, 324;
    uniform success with: Eve, 324; *chloroform in all important:* Twitchell, 324.
to none has it: J. P. Gray, 5:73; Ray also used Etherization: Ray, 11:164; used for
    puerperal insanity: Waters, 13:341; *feigned insanity is detected:* Bucknill,
    13:354; case of pretended insanity: Bucknill, 12:301; Dr. Snow administered

to 450 patients: R. S. Atkinson, 197;Snow administered to Queen Victoria: Lee, R. S. Atkinson, 4; 15 drops for the Queen: Richardson, 239; *chloroform à la reine*: Lee, 4; Snow used chloroform 2,000 times: Snow, 1858; *dire; unfortunate*: Warren, 1849.

description of Swett: *Chicago Times*, June 9, 1889.

change of venue requested: DeWitt County Circuit Court, May 1856 term.

change granted, moved to Bloomington, continuance: DeWitt County Circuit Court, September 10, 1856.

Lincoln & Lamon advertisement: *Iroquois Journal*, July 6, 1853.

jurors selected; *Great interest*: *Weekly Pantagraph*, April 8, 1857, 1.

crowded courtroom; *battle royal*: *Weekly Pantagraph*, April 8, 1857, 1; H. E. Pratt, 1944a, described Lincoln's defense in his first murder trial in 1838 where the defendant was acquitted; McMurtry reported that in 1839, Lincoln defended a murderer who was hanged for his crime.

I was in the office: *Weekly Pantagraph*, April 15, 1857, 1.

Was in Taylor & Bell's: *Weekly Pantagraph*, April 15, 1857, 1.

he had shot; shot the man: *Weekly Pantagraph*, April 15, 1857, 1.

I was walking tolerably: *Weekly Pantagraph*, April 15, 1857, 1.

When I got into: *Weekly Pantagraph*, April 15, 1857, 1.

Lincoln presented evidence and closed: McLean County Circuit Court, indictment, April 2, 1857.

Resting on the ground: *Weekly Pantagraph*, April 15, 1857, 1.

the Supreme Court of Illinois: *Lincoln Lore*, 2.

it was the first; earlier insanity plea: *American Journal of Insanity*, 33:254.

the loss of his mentality: Woldman, 151.

consulted Dr. Bell: Neely, McMurty, 10.

Insanity is a disease: Ray, 1838, 50.

queer in the head: Duff, 304.

arm was fractured: *Weekly Pantagraph*, April 15, 1857, 1.

Dr. Parks's testimony: *Weekly Pantagraph*, April 15, 1857, 1.

tendency of chloroform; It is very difficult; when there is: *Weekly Pantagraph*, April 15, 1857, 1.

Among the symptoms: *Weekly Pantagraph*, April 15, 1857, 1.

was called to him: *Weekly Pantagraph*, April 15, 1857, 1.

I have no doubt: *Weekly Pantagraph*, April 15, 1857, 1.

I have heard: *Weekly Pantagraph*, April 15, 1857, 1.

From the evidence; symptoms of insanity: *Weekly Pantagraph*, April 15, 1857, 1.

There are reasonable grounds: *Weekly Pantagraph*, April 15, 1857, 1.

I don't think: *Weekly Pantagraph*, April 15, 1857, 1.

insanity is sometimes: *Weekly Pantagraph*, April 15, 1857, 1.

to summarize all the points: McFarland, 7.

I conceive it; extremely excited maniacs: *Weekly Pantagraph*, April 15, 1857, 1.

You say, doctor: McFarland, 7.

It was a damn hard: Weekly Pantagraph, April 15, 1857, 1.

did not look strange: Weekly Pantagraph, April 15, 1857, 1.

Swett asked Dr. Lemon: Weekly Pantagraph, April 15, 1857, 1.

I didn't think: Weekly Pantagraph, April 15, 1857, 1.

Dr. Goodbrake biography: W. B. Atkinson, 340.

An ordinary dose; might be present; I have examined; It impressed me: Weekly Pantagraph, April 15, 1857, 1.

A trial for murder: W. L. King, 93.

We the jurors: McLean County Circuit Court, jury verdict, April 11, 1857.

recommended an asylum: F. T. Hill, 236.

Swett moves for confinement: McLean County Circuit Court, warrant issued, April 11, 1857.

court costs: McLean County Circuit Court, clerk's file, March 1857.

The scamp who: W. L. King, 93.

every charge in; He told me; I acted on: Herndon, Weik, 1893, 2:13.

Lincoln was a practicing lawyer for about twenty-four years, tried at least 5,000 cases, and more than 400 of those before the supreme court of Illinois: McWhirter, D1.

CHAPTER 12
LINCOLN'S CLIENT REFUSES TO PAY THE
DOCTOR'S BILL FOR SERVICES

Up a flight of stairs: G. W. Harris, December 1903; Former Lincoln & Herdon law student John H. Littlefield gave a similar description of the office in the *Brooklyn Eagle*, October 16, 1887.

US district court cases: Miers, 2:265–66,

I have reason to doubt: Basler, 3:492; Miers, 2:265.

Bissell's characteristics: *Portrait & Biography*, 150–52; R. P. Howard, 110.

his friends withdraw: Miers, 2:190–92; *Sangamo Journal.* October 14, 1842; Basler, 1:291–97, 299–302; Nicolay, Hay, 1894, 1:68–71.

Bissell's mysterious disease: *Portrait & Biography*, 150–52.

He died of: Walton 1962; R. P. Howard, 111.

when admitted as: Potter, Fehrenbacher, 1976, chapter 7 gives a detailed account of the Kansas-Nebraska arguments.

the use of a cane: R. P. Howard, 112.

with nine long, loud: McLean County Historical Society, 155.

John Wood nominated: Selby, 1912; R. P. Howard, 112.

Wood biography: R. P. Howard, 119.

Lincoln leaned toward Mclean for president: Basler, 2:342.

Lincoln for vice-president: Weik, 1908; C. W. Johnson, 1893, 63–64; Gienapp; Wentzell

When you meet Dayton: Miers, 2: 172; Basler, 2:289, 346; Nicolay, Hay, 1894, 1:219.

I know nothing: American Memory: website; C. G. Hamilton explains the connection between Lincoln and the Know Nothing movement.

Stump speaker necessities: Maple, 19.

with marked attention: Miers, 2:175; *Illinois State Journal,* August 18, 1856.

The palm…belongs: Miers, 2:181; *Belleville Advocate,* October 22, 1856; Basler 2:379–80.

God bless the Dutch: Miers, 2:181; *St. Clair Tribune,* October 25, 1856.

Hon. A. Lincoln: Miers, 2:182; *Illinois State Journal,* October 30, 1856.

The Hon. A. Lincoln: Miers, 2:183; *Illinois State Journal,* November 3, 1856.

election results: R. P. Howard, 112, *Portrait and Biographical Album,* 150–52.

Anderson murder trial: *Illinois State Register,* November 24 and 25, 1856; Miers, 2:183–85; Duff, 330–31; Jane raised $300 for her lawyers and they in turn each contributed $25 to pay Lincoln $75 to participate in the defense: Pratt, 1943b, 39.

Judge Lincoln: Miers, 2:185.

dueling oath perjury: R. P. Howard, 112.

On getting to Springfield: Mearns, 1:223.

Grable v. Margrave 4 Ill 372; *The father may:* Luthin, 1960, 68.

Relative to the suit; five dollars plus newspaper: Basler, 1:290; Miers, 1:176, 187.

Lincoln's Springfield home: Buehrer, 34–40; Ward, 68–78; W. T. Anderson, 26–32; 9.

sales contract in Basler, 1:331.

shade trees and wood planks: Executive Mansion Where Abraham Lincoln Visited: website.

renovations to home: Kunhardt, 70.

Everything orderly and refined: Arnold, 1881, 137–38.

In every respect: Miers, 2:189; *Illinois State Journal,* February 16, 1857.

Lincoln analyzes the apportionment bill: Miers, 2:190.

reapportionment favored Democrats: Mearns, 1948, 224.

in Lincoln's handwriting: Miers, 2:244; R. P. Howard, 113; Basler, 1:225, 3:364–65.

writ of mandamus: People ex rel. Lanphier and Walker v. Hatch, Secretary of State, 19 Ill 283; Duff, 262–63; Woldman, 158.

right to rectify error: Luthin, 1960, 150.

The argument of Mr. Lincoln: Reapportionment Hearings, *Illinois State Journal,* February 3, 1858, 1.

supreme court of Illinois decision: 19 Ill 283.

Let this be confidential: Basler, 2:432–33. Peck appointment: Pratt, 1944b, 112.

Lincoln's personal stake in reapportionment: Luthin, 1960, 150.

He made one of the best: Illinois State Journal, February 18, 1858, 1.

Mayor Bradley suit in Los Angeles: Perez-Pena, 43.

himself and through his: supreme court of Illinois, Abstract, January 20, 1860.

Helm biography: Holloway, 208; Sangamon County Genealogical Society, 188.

Helm allowed to answer questions; *When persons:* supreme court of Illinois, Abstract and Brief in Error, January 20, 1860.

acting for Kinney: supreme court of Illinois, Abstract and Brief in Error, January 20, 1860.

If the jury believe: supreme court of Illinois, Abstract and Brief in Error, January 20, 1860.

Lincoln's instructions to jury: supreme court of Illinois, Abstract and Brief in Error, January 20, 1860.

seal the verdict; *We the jury:* supreme court of Illinois, Abstract and Brief in Error, January 20, 1860.

Lincoln specifies six technical errors: supreme court of Illinois, Abstract and Brief in Error, January 20, 1860.

responses to the errors: supreme court of Illinois, Abstract and Defendants Brief in Error, January 20, 1860.

custom proved by one witness: J. W. Smith, 688.

That hereafter it shall be: Laws of State of Illinois, 1859, 154.

juror challenged; *There has grown up:* Peck, 23 Ill 520.

legal cites for custom needing more than one witness: *Halmerson v. Cole; 1 Speers 321; 1 Rep. Con. Ct. 309; Wood v. Hicock; 2 Wend. 501.*

custom *must be known:* Greenleaf, 1853, 2 sec. 251.

a usage; such as: Peck, 23 Ill 521.

It will generally be: Peck, 23 Ill 522.

For the reasons given: Peck, 23 Ill 523.

court costs: supreme court of Illinois, fee book, January 1860.

Bissell favored Chase: R. P. Howard, 115. Davis's choices: Pratt, 1944b, 23.

Lincoln and Herndon: Chicago Tribune, March 17, 1860; Miers, 2:276.

In the procession: Chicago Journal, March 22, 1860; Miers, 2:276.

Bissell first: R. P. Howard, 108–15.

Kinzie letter: Basler, 2:430–31. In 1837, Kinzie complained to Lincoln that he never received $80 owed to him, Nicolay, Hay, 1894, 1:37, 41.

I have no hesitation: Browne, 143. Judge Drummond and all the counsel dined at the home of I. N. Arnold: Barnard & Miller, 4.

at the earnest: Miers, 2:277.

fee in case of: Miers, 2:278; *Chicago Tribune,* April 5, 1860.

offer to use Executive Office: Mearns, 1:248.

Today and til: Illinois State Journal, November 14, 1860, 1.

Wood first with beard: R. P. Howard, 117–19.

A. LINCOLN, ESQUIRE

Lincoln's patronage, Dayton appointment: Hertz, 1931, 2:810; The Political Graveyard, website.

Frémont liberation order and biography: Basler, 4:406, 517; Carte de Visite, website.

CHAPTER 13
LINCOLN POLITICALLY SELECTS
THE MEDICAL EXPERT ON INSANITY

The condition of our: New York Times, February 28, 1863, 4; Forman, Lowry reproduce an 1865 map of Washington, DC, showing streets, points of interest, buildings, and Booth's escape route.

Washington is not a nice place: Federal Writers Project, 16; Lowry, 1994 and 1997, even reproduces a map of the locations of the bawdy houses in Washington, DC.

Prices for food and leisure: McMaster, 555.

Washington is becoming unhealthy: Albany Argus, July 12, 1865, 2.

law and politics interrelated: C. Davis, 1994a, 72,

uncertain presidential elections: Waugh.

Mr. Lincoln is a vulgar, Never were issues: Kazin.

epithets used for Lincoln: Keiser; Donald 1956; Kazin; *Think Tank Transcripts;* B. Schwartz, 1994, found Lincoln to be simultaneously "interrogated & commemorated, condemned & canonized and profaned & sanctified."

The cheek of every: K. Burns.

martyred president into sanctified icon: B. Schwartz, 1991, 1998; Holzer, Boritt, Neely, 1984, explore Lincoln's image in the popular print.

He was a total: Silbey; Safire, 1986; Carman, Luthin focus upon Lincoln and the patronage.

The decease of Mr. Lincoln: Donald, 1956.

Lincoln looks at Norfolk: L. B. Anderson; Chambers, 132.

Emancipation Proclamation celebration: Dabney, 330; Wertenbacker, 220.

No person of any: Jordan, vii–viii; Wertenbacker, 220.

Birthday and anniversary celebrated: Squires.

Biography, Lt. Sanborn: Jordan, 8; Official Army Register, 169.

Biography, Dr. Wright: Blanton, 311; Jordan, 6–8; Graber, 249–56. Dr. Wright's mother was Mary Armistead.

differing murder scenarios: *Lynchburg Daily Virginian,* July 23, 1863, 2; Jordan, 66–68; Chambers, 131; Sandburg, 3:487; Dabney, 330–31; Blanton, 310–11.

Let me go: Squires.

Lt. Sanborn of the colored regiment: War of the Rebellion, 2, 6:106.

Is it supposed: Jordan, 30; Records of Judge Advocate.

Wright jailed: *War of the Rebellion,* 2, 6:106; L. B. Anderson, 331.

no seat for Pencie: Jordan, 12.

Biography, Chandler: Jordan, 14; Wertenbacker, 239; US Congress, 288.
Biography, Bowden: *National Cyclopediia*, 4:377; Sifakis, 64; Jordan, 14; US Congress, 288, 72.
Biography, Segar: Jordan, 38; US Congress, 279, 288, 1793.
West Virginia becomes state: Basler, 6:181.
brutal murder; bring to speedy; to remove: Squires.
I am to be tried: George, 199; L. B. Anderson, 331; Squires.
Lincoln believed civil courts powerless: Gambone, 246; Frank, 149.
Unfortunately the hearts: Secretary of the Navy Gideon Welles in Beale, Brownsword; cited in Bullard.
Heart is sweltering: Senator Henry Wilson quoted in Bullard.
They believe that: bill introduced on May 23, 1862 in Bullard.
opposition noted in Congress: *Congressional Globe*, 37th Congress, 3d Session, Part 2, February 20, 1863, 1185.
Wylie shot at; broke glass: Bryan, 2:4.
The Supreme Court of the District: Bullard, 117–20.
Lincoln's justification: Silver, 119.
unconstitutional and wrong: Herndon, Weik, 1893, 3:556.
no jurisdiction: Silver, 228.
Davis wrote *Ex Parte Milligan*: Frank, 148–49.
Our worthy President: *Daily National Intelligencer*, November 10, 1862, 3.
Justice Davis will: *New York Times*, November 28, 1864, 4.
I feel great: Pratt, 1944b, 99; Davis not in running: Silver, 189; Carman, Luthin, 181.
Good of the service: Jordan, 30–31.
A speedy enforcement: Presidential Papers Microfilm, #25256, August 1, 1863.
If Dr. Wright: Basler, 6:362; *War of the Rebellion*, 2, 6:170; Nicolay, Hay, 1894, 9:53.
Your orders will be: Basler, 6:362.
petitioners surpassing in number: Sanburg, 3:487
the undersigned respectfully: *War of the Rebellion*, 2, 6:157.
more than 340 sign a petition : *Lynchburg Daily Virginian*, September 8, 1863; Jordan, 29, 46, 69; Presidential Papers #s 27295, 27297, 27303 [October 17, 1863], # 27368 [October 21, 1863]; Millson telegram, *War of the Rebellion*, 2, 6:157.
Plea for clemency: Squires.
I most respectfully: *War of the Rebellion*, 2, 6:187.
If anything can be: *War of the Rebellion*, 2, 6:188.
I have been unable: *War of the Rebellion*, 2, 6:245.
Committee meets with president: *Philadelphia Inquirer*, August 18,1863, 1.
Holt named judge-advocate: Silver, 133.
It will be seen; the crime then stands: *War of the Rebellion*, 2, 6:216.

Please notify; I have notified: War of the Rebellion, 2, 6:233; Basler, 6:419.
being satisfied that: War of the Rebellion, 2, 6:36.
Dr. *Nicholl's surroundings:* Presidential Papers #25985 [September 2, 1863], 26202 [September 9, 1863]; Basler, 6:249. Furthermore, the citation indicated that "Dr. Nicholl has not been identified."
Biographical information about Dr. Nichols: W. B. Atkinson, 693; *American. Journal of Insanity*, 46:416–22; Johnson, Malone, 489; Spiegel, M. S. Spiegel, 1991; *New York Herald*, December 18, 1889, 1; *New York Times*, December 18, 1899, 3.63
Biographical information about Dr. Gray: Hutchings, 1944a, 34–36 ; Kaufman, Galishoff, Savitt, 303; Kelly, Burrage, 488; Tucker, 540–44; Waldinger, 163–79; Walsh, 1:234, 4:20; *New York Herald*, November 30, 1886, 19; *New York Daily Tribune*, November 30,1886, 5; *New York Times*, November 30, 1886, 1.
Harris/Burroughs case: Spiegel, M. S. Spiegel, 1991.
Guiteau trial: Rosenberg, 1968.
Dix recommended Dr. Nichols: Synder, 137.
Dr. Nichols attends White House party: Sanborn, 248.
considerable conversation: Bond, 1947, 111.
saw asylum from windows: J. H. Baker, 212.
vote on moral insanity: Dain, Carlson, 795–801.
I have no hesitation: American Journal of Insanity, 20:63, 67.
Although there may be: American Journal of Insanity, 20:79. Dr. Ray's book was extensively cited as the basis for the principle of "knowing right from wrong" when insanity was alleged. See Isaac Ray, 1838.
Dr. Gray opposed Dr. Nichols: American Psychiatric Assn., 205–11, 342–49, 366, 651–54; *American Journal of Insanity*, 22:333–69 [No author but most likely written by Dr. J. P. Gray]; Rosenberg, 190; Jordan, 39; Spiegel, M. S. Spiegel, 1991, 55; Waldinger, 178.
A physical disease: J. P. Gray, 29: 275; American Psychiatric Assn., 205–11; J.P. Gray, 1865, 333–69.
Gray's reputation: Waldinger, 163–79.
Lincoln's prior legal experience: A local newspaper, the *Weekly Pantagraph*, reported comprehensively on the Wyant/Rusk trial on April 15, 1857, 1; Woldman, 151; Neely, McMurtry, 10; McFarland, *Chicago Tribune*, June 20, 1889, 7; Duff, 304–307.
Stanton's medical history: Thomas, Hyman, 1962.
Seward's prior legal experiences: Books by Conrad and B. F. Hall detail the Wyatt/Freeman trials. Seward was Lincoln's most influential cabinet member: Bancroft, 357.
His conduct is unexplainable: F. W. Seward, 809–810; Bancroft, 175.
Brigham biography: Hutchings 1944b; Carlson, 831 and 911.

Freeman had disease: B. F. Hall, 499.

four printings of *Argument*: Blatchford, 1846; J. M. Taylor, 59, 74; Lothrop, 43; Van Deusen, 94.

Stanton's prior legal experience: Court reporter Fontaine reported on Stanton's role in the Sickles/Key murder trial. T. J. Fleming, 1967, recounted the husband's revenge. and Brandt, 1991, discussed the Congressman who got away with murder. Balderston, Kelly, R. B. Morris, and Pinchon also reported on the trial.

For the first time: Knappman, 127–32; Nevins, 2:438.

were together when: Whitney, 823.

I found Mrs. Sickles: Fontaine, 70.

that expression tickled: Whitney, 182–83.

unwritten law, defiler: Swanberg, 64.

Were he not: Nevins, 2:438; Nevins, 4:422; T. J. Fleming, 1967, 67, 75.

Sickles reconciled with Teresa: *New York Times*, July 7, 1859, 4.

Governor Pierpont urged death sentence: Jordan, 38; Presidential Papers, #26018 [September 3, 1863]; Roy, 46–49, discusses Lincoln's political and military motivations in recruiting more than 178,000 blacks into the Union army.

Please telegraph Dr. Gray: Basler, 6:429.

Gray's lengthy interview: Sandburg, 3:488.

Gray described: Hutchings, 1944a.

The record is before me: Nicolay, Hay, 1894, 9:114; Presidential Papers, #26178 [September 10, 1863]; *War of the Rebellion*, 2, 6:447.

The names of those: Nicolay, Hay, 1894, 9:119; Basler, 6:443; *War of the Rebellion*, 2, 6:443.

Too few; On the contrary: Both quotes are from J. P. Gray, 1864, 284–300.

Was born April 21, 1809: J. P. Gray, 1864, 293, 294, 299; Williman gave an account of the 1855 Yellow Fever epidemic in Norfolk in 1856. Selden and a committee of physicians did likewise in 1857. Both references are cited by Numbers, Savitt, 235, 244.

perfectly coherent; It has been impossible: J. P. Gray, 1864, 284.

One is not responsible: *Commonwealth v. Rogers*, 1844

I am of the opinion: J. P. Gray, 1864, 300.

I deem it proper: *War of the Rebellion*, 2, 6:323.

expert of high; I therefore approve: Dr. Wright's defenders argued that Lincoln's decision was prompted by his concern that he might lose the 1864 presidential election combined with his zealous nationalistic aim to preserve the Union at all costs.

Foster ordered hanging: *War of the Rebellion*, 1:29, Part 2:322.

wrote his name: *Philadelphia Inquirer*, October 21, 1863, 2.

Hon. L. Chandler: *War of the Rebellion*, 2, 6:380.

Wright's family members: US Department of the Interior, Eighth Census of the US, 1860 Census Population Schedules, Virginia, City of Norfolk, Free Inhabitants, Microfilm Roll 298, 67.

Postpone the execution: War of the Rebellion, 2, 6:390; Basler, 6:514

The sad circumstances: Lynchburg Daily Virginian, October 24, 1863, 2.; Jordan, 46; L. B. Anderson, 331.

The Hon. Mr. Chandler; It would be useless: War of the Rebellion, 2, 6:426; Presidential Papers, #27291 [October 17, 1863]; Basler, 6:522.

I should not: W. C. Harris; Rawley; Hertz, 1931, 2:912; Basler, 6:505; *War of the Rebellion,* 2, 6:361; Roy, 46.

I have the signed; to proceed with; exchange for Rucker: War of the Rebellion, 2, 6:409; *Daily Examiner* [Richmond VA], September 26, 1863, 1; *Philadelphia Inquirer,* October 28, 1863, 1; Presidential Papers, #27368-9 [October 21, 1863].

escape plan a failure: *Lynchburg Daily Virginian,* November 4, 1863, 2.

bribe offered to telegrapher: Sandburg, 3:489.

The deed I committed: Daily Examiner [Richmond VA], October 27, 1863, 1; *Lynchburg Daily Virginian,* October 29, 1863, 2; *New York Herald,* October 25, 1863, 1; L. B. Anderson, 334.

Dr. Wright was executed: War of the Rebellion, 1, 29, 2:370.

Lincoln's commutations: *caught any fact:* Burlingame, Ettinger, 64; Scarborough, *Chicago Tribune,* February 12, 1992, 17; Basler, 5:475, 476, 6:335–40, 347, 364, 529; Alotta, 1989, 21; Lowry, 1998 and 1999, discusses the courts-martial of fifty officers and Lincoln's balance of sternness and compassion in dispensing military justice.

If I can't find: Journal of Civil War Medicine, 22; *New York Times,* May 1, 1880, 3.

It was said: Jackson, February 17, 1893.

My dear man: Rice, 1895, 434.

Wright's funeral: *Lynchburg Daily Virginian,* November 10, 1863, 2.

Wright's tombstone inscription: Jordan, 70.

Wright's supposed release: US War Dept, Records of the Adjutant General's Office, Compiled Military Service Records, Colored Troops Division, Letters Received, S22[Ct], Record Group 94, National Archives Microfilm. Johnston to Crosby [October 24, 1863].

Wright's family after his death: L. B.Anderson, 337.

Aspersions by an: Richmond News, May 10, 1901, 5.

most agonizing tragedy: Chambers, 142

Rest, our most worthy: L. B. Anderson, 337.

a military necessity: Freedman, 85.

such persons of suitable: Basler, 6:23.

favorable newspaper comment on Negroes as soldiers: *New York Times* [editorial], January 9, 1863, 4.

There are fifty thousand: Basler, 5:356; Carle, 80.

deemed as inciting: US House of Representatives. Report on the Treatment of Prisoners of War by the Rebel Authorities During the War of the Rebellion. Washington, DC: Govt. Printing Office, 1869. [40th Congress, 2nd Session, Report No. 45], 461.

Lincoln read newspapers: Safire, 1987a, 15.

Lincoln and Douglass meet: *New York Daily Tribune*, July 5, 1885, 3.

confederate guerrillas: US War Records Office, *War of the Rebellion*, Series 1, 27:845.

Nothing poses the question: Mayer, February 12, 1989, 24.

A measure made expedient: Safire, 1987b, 28–29.

number of colored troops: McPherson, 237.

recruiting damaged: Glatthaar, 69.

The colored population: Graf, Haskins, 6:194; Basler, 6:149.

Bureau for Colored Troops: Cornish, 138.

I desire that: Basler, 6:342.

By arming the Negro: R. R. Wilson, 170.

the punishment; prompt execution: Basler, 6:23.

to purchase; humanity of the law: New York Times, March 3, 1863, 3.

Lincoln's representative recruit: Spiegel, 1991a.

Some of the commanders: Basler, 6:423; Carle, 1992.

Of those who were: Basler, 7:49.

Congressional Medals of Honor: McPhearson, 237.

another undefended assassination: Daily Examiner [Richmond VA], October 28, 1863, 1; Basler, 7:28.

By their presence: Basler, 6:530.

I beg that: Basler, 6:530.

The fact of one: Basler, 6:532.

He has a certain: J. P. Gray, 1865, 380–90.

Applauded the actor: New York World, April 19, 1865; *Spent the evening*; Burlingame, Ettinger, 110; Dennett, 118; George, 1957.

A popular young tragedian: Washington Chronicle, April 29, 1863; Berkelman; Grover, a theater owner, discusses Lincoln's interest in the theater.

EPILOGUE

Whitman gets clerical job: Kaplan, 298.

Smithsonian up in flames: *New York Times*, January 24, 1865, 1.

first Negro lawyer admitted to practice before the Supreme Court of the United States: Silver, 209.

Salaries of clerks: *Daily National Intelligencer*, February 22, 1865, 2.

We have examined samples: Daily National Intelligencer, February 22, 1865, 3.

New three cent coin: *Evening Star*, April 21, 1865, 1.

tragedy in the Treasury: *Daily National Intelligencer*, January 31, 1865, 1.

the conference came to an end: Nicolay, Hay, 1894, 2:650; Basler, 8:254-255; Carr; Riddle, 1895, 327; Hubbard, 1998, elaborates on Confederate diplomacy before and during the conflict.

Sickles case: Fontaine, 1859. This is the court reporter's official transcript; Kelly, 73.

come see me tomorrow morning: Arnold, 1885, 431.

A. LINCOLN, ESQUIRE

BIBLIOGRAPHY

UNPUBLISHED SOURCES

Barnhart, J. H. "Fithian v. Cassedy Trial." Unpublished manuscript, Danville IL, 1954. In author's possession.

Allen B. Clough Papers. Chicago Historical Society, Illinois.

Challiss, W. L. Collection of Lecture Admission Cards and Related Material from Jefferson Medical School, 1847-1848. College of Physicians of Philadelphia.

Craven, W. L. and D. Dexter. Special Report of the Minority of the Board of Trustees of the Illinois State Hospital for the Insane to the General Assembly of the State of Illinois, Jacksonville, Illinois, February 13, 1854. Springfield, Illinois, Illinois State Archives, RS 600.1.

Davis, C. Abraham Lincoln, Esq.: The Symbiosis of Law and Politics Abraham Lincoln and the Political Process. Papers, Seventh Annual Lincoln Colloquium, 1994a: 25-33.

Davis, N. S. to Hon. J.D. Cox, Secretary of the Interior, November 1869, Record Group 48, Box 125, National Archives, Washington, DC.

Dowse, W. H. to A. J. Beveridge, October 10, 1925, Beveridge Papers, Library of Congress, Washington, DC.

Herndon-Weik Lincoln Collection, Library of Congress, Manuscript Division.

James Herriott statement, undated, Herndon-Weik Collection, Library of Congress.

Hertz, E. Abraham Lincoln. The Legal Phase of the First American. Radio address, WRNY, February 12, 1927.

J. M. W. to Abraham Lincoln, April 12, 1861, Record Group 48, Box 137, National Archives, Washington, DC.

Jordan, E. L. "A Painful Case: The Wright-Sanborn Incident in Norfolk Virginia, July-October 1863." M.A. Thesis, Old Dominion University, 1979.

Lebenshon, Z. M. Personal correspondence based upon Dr. Lebensohn's research notes on Mary Harris, June 2, 1980.

Abraham Lincoln Papers, microfilm, Presidential Papers, Washington, DC: Library of Congress, 1959.

Robert T. Lincoln Collection, Library of Congress, Washington, D.C.

Matchett, W. B. to Hon. Caleb R. Smith, Secretary of the Interior, April 19, 1861, Record Group 48, Box 137, National Archives, Washington, DC.

Municipal Reference Collection, Chicago. Compilation of material on Thomas Hoyne including inaugural address, May 18, 1876.

Nicolay, John G. Papers, Library of Congress, Manuscript Division.

Official Army Register: Volunteer Force of the US Army 1861-1865, Part 8, July 16, 1867 Washington, DC: Government Printing Office.

Pamphlets: Homeopathic, 1850-1893. Bradford Collection, University of Michigan.

Pitts, J. A. "The Association of Medical Superintendents of American Institutions for the Insane." Ph.D. dissertation, University of Pennsylvania, 1979.

Price, J. Notes on the Lectures of Thomas D. Mutter taken at Jefferson Medical School, 1848-1849. Collection at the College of Physicians of Philadelphia.

Records of the Investigation by the Board of Visitors: Certain Charges Preferred Against the Superintendent, Dr. C. H. Nichols Washington, DC. 1869. Government Hospital for the Insane Archives.

Remey, C. M. Life and Letters of Charles Mason, Chief Justice of Iowa 1804-1882. Typescript. Washington, DC: Library of Congress, 1939.

Schultze, F. S. to James Buchanan, March 12, 1858 Record Group 48, Box 125, National Archives, Washington, DC.

J. Henry Shaw to William H. Herndon, August 22, 1866, Herndon-Weik Collection, Library of Congress.

Sims, J. M. to Hon. J.D. Cox, Secretary of the Interior, November 1869, Record Group 48, Box 125, National Archives, Washington, DC.

Steiner, M. E. "Abraham Lincoln and the Antebellum Legal Profession." Ph.D. Thesis, University of Houston, Texas, 1993.

Toner, J. to Hon. J. D. Cox, Secretary of the Interior, November 1869, Record Group 48, Box 125, National Archives, Washington, DC.

Turner, T. R. "Public Opinion, the Assassination of Abraham Lincoln, the Trial of the Conspirators and the Trial of John Surratt." Ph.D. dissertation, Boston University, 1971.

US Department of the Interior. Eighth Census of the US, 1860 Census Population Schedules, Virginia, City of Norfolk, Free Inhabitants, Microfilm Roll 298.

US War Department. Records of the Adjutant General's Office, Compiled Military Service Records, Colored Troops Division, Letters Received, S22[Ct], Record Group 94, National Archives Microfilm. Johnston to Crosby [October 24, 1863].

US War Department. Records of the Office of the Judge Advocate General. [Army] Court Martial Case Files 1863-1865 [MM-631, Record Group 30, Dr. David M. Wright], National Archives Microfilm, Washington, DC.

Vasnicka, R. National Archives and Records Administration, Economic and Natural Resources Branch, Washington, DC, Personal Communication, July 16, 1987.

Walker, William to William H. Herndon, Letters, June 3, August 27, and September 17, 1866, Herndon-Weik Collection, Library of Congress.

Watters, M. The Beginnings of Mental Health Service in Illinois, Unpublished paper from the notes of Dr. Watters. Manuscript. 1995. Springfield, Illinois, Illinois Department of Human Services.

Wiley, J. Notebooks on Medical Education, Jefferson Medical School, 1835-1837, Collection at College of Physicians of Philadelphia.

Legal Records

Adams County Circuit Court [Quincy, Illinois]. *West v. Ritchey*, Jury named, March 23, 1858; Jury allowed to separate, March 24, 1858; Verdict of $700 for the plaintiff, March 25, 1858; Overruled new trial; appeal to Illinois Supreme Court granted with posting of bond, April 10, 1858; Final Order and Bond, [Verdict of Jury, Appeal Petition, and Security Bond of $1, 500] filed April 16, 1858; Appeal not filed in time, January 7, 1859.

Champaign County Circuit Court [Urbana, Illinois]: *Burt v. Jennings* Defendant's plea and replication, October term, 1852; Amended declaration, October term, 1852.

Christian County Circuit Court [Taylorville, Illinois]: *Torrance v. Galloway*, Declaration of plaintiff, November term, 1847; Court docket, dismissal, November term, 1847.

Commonwealth v. Mosler, 4 Pa. 264 1846.

Commonwealth v. Rogers, 7 Met. 500 MA 1844.

Congressional Globe. 37th Congress, 3d Session, 1862-63, Part 2, February 20, 1863, 1185.

DeWitt County Circuit Court [Clinton, Illinois]: *Winn v. Stipp*, Transcript of the Justice of the Peace, July 3, 1841; Fee book, October term 1841; *J. C. Johnson & Bro. v. Illinois Central Railroad*, Plaintiff's declaration, October 5, 1854; Plea of defendant, May 18, 1855; Justice's Court, Warrant for Isaac Wyant, October 13, 1855; *People v. Isaac Wyant*, Indictment for Murder, October 18, 1855; Change of Venue, May Term, 1856.

Halmerson v. Cole, 1 Speers 321. Rep. Con. Ct. 309.

Hancock County Circuit Court [Carthage, Illinois]: *West v. Ritchey*, Continuance granted, October 8, 1855; Request for plaintiff security, March 4, 1856; Defendant's pleas files; Plaintiff files security, March 6, 1856; Plaintiff's demurrer to defendant's pleas sustained, March 11, 1856; Continuance granted, June 9, 1856; Jury named and issue joined, June 10, 1856; Trial concluded, jury retired, instructed to seal the verdict, June 11, 1856; Jury cannot agree, June 12, 1856; Defendant's change of venue granted to Adams County, October 2, 1856; Continuance granted, October 20, 1857; Fee bill, October term, 1856.

Illinois Supreme Court [Springfield, Illinois]: *Stevenson v. Higgins*, Information [Declaration] filed by Cyrus Eppler, state's attorney, October 26, 1853;

Abstract filed by Stuart & Edwards for the Plaintiffs in Error in 1853; *Bissell v. Ryan*, Abstract and Brief of Plaintiff in Error, January 20, 1860; Defendant's brief, January 20, 1860; Fee book, January 1860; Execution, January term, 1860; *Ritchey v. West*, Execution, January term, 1860; Plaintiff's costs, January term, 1860.

Laws of State of Illinois Passed by the 19st General Assembly Convened January 1, 1855. Springfield: Lanphier & Walker, 1855; Passed by the 21st General Assembly Convened January 3, 1859. Springfield: Bailhache & Baker, 1859.

Lilly v. Waggoner, 27 Ill Reports, 1863, 395.

Logan County Circuit Court [Lincoln, Illinois]: *Fleming v. Rogers & Crothers*, Case dismissed, March 15, 1858.

McLean County Circuit Court [Bloomington, Illnois]: *Thompson v. Henline*, Court docket entry, case dismissed, April 21, 1851; Defendant's plea, replication, October 3, 1851; *People v. Wyant*, Subponea for witnesses for the People, October 6, 1855; Subponea for witnesses for the People, October 16, 1855; Receipt for Isaac Wyant, October 26, 1855; Subponea for witnesses for the People, April 28, 1856; Indictment for murder, March 31, 1857; Docket of judgments & executions, March 1857; Indictment for murder, April 2, 1857; Indictment for murder, April 4, 1857; In the Matter of Isaac Wyant Alleged to be Insane, April 6, 1857; *Fleming v. Rogers & Crothers* Declaration filed, March 28, 1856. Amended and filed August 27, 185; Ruling on request for continuance, April 10, 1856; Subponea for witnesses for the plaintiff, September 8, 1856; Ruling on request for continuance, September 10, 1856; Subponea for witnesses for the plaintiff, February 20, 1857; Subponea for witnesses for the plaintiff, March 6, 1857; Subponea for witnesses for the plaintiff, March 18, 1857; Subponea for witnesses for the defendant, April 7, 1857; Subponea for witnesses for the defendant, April 9, 1857; Continuance granted June 15, 1857; Subponea for witnesses for the plaintiff, August 8, 1857; Interrogatories of Isaac M. Small, August 21, 1857; Deposition of Jacob R. Freese, August 24, 1857; Continuance granted, September 8, 1857; Deposition of Isaac M. Small, November 10, 1857; Subponea for witnesses for the plaintiff, November 16, 1857; Copy of records sent to Logan County Circuit Court. December 26, 1857; Fee bill certified by court clerk, December 26, 1857.

Menard County Circuit Court [Petersburg, Illinois]: *Cabot v. Regnier*, Defendant's declaration, May 25, 1843; Affidavit of Bennett Abell for the plaintiff, November 7, 1843; Jury verdict, November 7, 1843; Plaintiff's motion for new trial, November 8, 1843; *Powell v. Worth*, Iven Worth's account, January 11, 1845; Iven Worth's account, November 29, 1845; Justice of the Peace transcript, December 16, 1845; Justice of the Peace transcript, December 29, 1845; Iven Worth's account, March 7, 1846; Fee book, June 1846; *Regnier v. Druet*, Plaintiff's declaration, April 18, 1855; Jury verdict and cause continued, May 29, 1855.

Morgan County Circuit Court [Jacksonville, Illinois]: *Cabot v. Regnier*, Deposition of Maria Bennett for defendant, March 12, 1844; Affidavit of John D. Bowen for plaintiff, March 17, 1844.

Sangamon County Circuit Court [Springfield, Illinois]: *Kyle v. Kyle* Defendant's answer, March term, 1846; *Betts v. Frazer* Defendants answer, December term, 1850; Deposition, December term, 1850; Bill to settle partnership, December term, 1850; *Grubb v. John Frink & Co.*, Plaintiff's declaration, August 13, 1852; Deposition of Robert S. Blackwell, February 3, 1853; Affadavit for depositions, February 7, 1853; Deposition of Lewis and Dr. Hall, February 21, 1853; Deposition of William March 15, 1853; *Jackson v. Jackson* Bill for divorce, August term, 1858.

State v. Thompson: 90 Ohio 622 1834.

Tazewell County Circuit Court [Pekin, Illinois]: *Jones v. Maus*, Plaintiff's affidavit [declaration], July 24, 1851; Complaint, September 1, 1851; *Jacobus v. Kitchell et ux.* Plea, demurrer, September term, 1851; Plaintiff's affidavit, September term, 1851; Declaration, September term, 1851; Defendant's affidavit, September term, 1851; *People v. Delny*, Indictment, May term, 1853.

Vermilion County Circuit Court [Danville, Illinois]: *Martin v. Underwood*, Declaration of plaintiff, October term, 1857; Defendant's response to declaration, October term, 1857; Jury verdict, April term, 1858.

Woodford County Circuit Court [Metamora, Illinois]: *Davidson v. McGhilton*, Plaintiff's declaration, praecipe, February 7, 1852; Court docket entry, default judgment, April 15, 1852; *Cassell for use of Crocker v. Robinson* Petition for certiorari, September 15, 1843.

Woodford County Justice of the Peace Court: *Cassell for use of Crocker v. Robinson* Petition for certiorari, July 11, 1843.

PUBLISHED SOURCES

Books

Alotta, R. I. *Civil War Justice. Union Army Executions Under Lincoln.* Shippensburg PA: White Mane Pub. Co, 1989.

American Medical Association. *History of Medical Schools, 20th Edition.* Chicago: American Medical Association, 1958.

———. *Digest of Official Actions, 1846-1958.* Chicago: American Medical Association, 1959.

American Psychiatric Association. *One Hundred Years of American Psychiatry.* New York: Columbia University Press, 1944.

Andreas, A. T. *History of Chicago* Chicago: privately published, 1884.

Angle, P. M. "When Lincoln Practiced Law" in *Lincoln Centennial Association Papers.* Springfield IL: Lincoln Centennial Association, 1928a.

———. *One Hundred Years of Law. An Account of the Law Office Which John T. Stuart Founded in Springfield, Illinois a Century Ago.* Springfield: Brown, Hay and Stephens, 1928b.

———. "Abraham Lincoln: Circuit Lawyer," Springfield IL: Lincoln Centennial Association Papers, 1929.

———. *New Letters and Papers of Lincoln.* Boston: Houghton, Mifflin Co., 1930.

———. *Lincoln 1854-1861: Being the Day-by-Day Activities of Abraham Lincoln from January 1, 1854 to March 4, 1861.* Springfield IL: Abraham Lincoln Association, 1933.

———. *Here I Have Lived: A History of Lincoln's Springfield 1821-1865.* New Brunswick NJ: Rutgers University Press, 1935.

———. *The Lincoln Reader.* New Brunswick: Rutgers University Press, 1947.

Apple, R. D. *Women, Health and Medicine in America.* New York: Garland Pub. Co., 1990.

Aristotle. *Politics.* Cambridge: Harvard University Press, 1972.

Arnold, I. N. "Reminiscences of the Illinois Bar Forty Years Ago: Lincoln and Douglas as Orators and Lawyers," in *Early Illinois.* Fergus Historical Series. Chicago: Fergus Printing Co., 1881. Pages 132-54.

———. *The Life of Abraham Lincoln.* Chicago: Jansen, McClurg & Co., 1885.

Atkinson, W. B. *The Physicians and Surgeons of the U.S.* Philadelphia: Charles Robson, 1878.

Baker, J. H. *Mary Todd Lincoln, A Biography.* New York: W. W. Norton & Co., 1987.

Bancroft, F. *The Life of William H. Seward.* New York: Harper & Brothers Publishers, 1900.

Bannister, D. W. *Lincoln and the Common Law A Collection of Lincoln's Supreme Court Cases From 1838-1861 and Their Influence On the Evolution of Illinois Common Law.* Springfield IL: Human Services Press, 1992.

———. *Lincoln and the Supreme Court.* Springfield IL: privately published, 1994.

Baringer, W. E. *Lincoln's Vandalia: A Pioneer Portrait.* New Brunswick NJ: Rutgers University Press, 1949.

Basler, R. P. *The Collected Works of Abraham Lincoln.* 11 volumes. New Brunswick NJ: Rutgers University Press, 1953.

Beale, H. K. and A. W. Brownsword. *Diary of Gideon Welles, Secretary of the Navy Under Lincoln and Johnson.* New York: W. W. Norton & Co., 1960.

Beard, W. D. Foreword in J. Long, *The Law of Illinois. Lincoln's Cases Before the Illinois Supreme Court.* Shiloh: The Illinois Co., 1993.

Beck, T. R. *Elements of Medical Jurisprudence.* Albany NY: Webster & Skinner, 1823.

Beecher, H. F. and M. D. Altschule. *Medicine at Harvard. The First Three Hundred Years.* Hanover: University Press of New England, 1977.

Beverdige, A. J. *Abraham Lincoln 1809-1858.* 2 volumes. Boston: Houghton Mifflin Co., 1928.

Biographical Record of McLean County, Illinois. Chicago: S. J. Clarke Pub. Co., 1899.

Bittinger, B. F. *Historic Sketch of the Monument to Dr. Samuel Hahnemann.* New York: Knickerbocker Press, 1900.

Blackstone, W. "Of Wrongs and Their Remedies, Respecting the Rights of Persons, in Private Wrongs," in *Commentaries on the Laws of England.* Philadelphia: William Birch Young and Abraham, 1803.

Blanton, W. B. *Medicine in Virginia in the Nineteenth Century.* Richmond: Garrett & Massie, Inc., 1933.

Blatchford, S. *Argument of William H. Seward in Defence of William Freeman on His Trial for Murder at Auburn, July 21st and 22nd, 1846.* Auburn: J. C. Derby & Co., 1846.

Bordley, J. and H. A. McGehee. *Two Centuries of American Medicine 1776-1976.* Philadelphia: W. B. Saunders Co., 1976.

Boulton, T. B., R. Bryce-Smith, M. K. Sykes, and G. B. Gillett. *Proceedings of Fourth World Congress of Anesthesiology.* Amsterdam: Excerpta Medica Foundation, 1970.

Bousfield, R. M. and R. Merrett. *Report of the Trial of Daniel M'Naughton at the Central Criminal Court, Old Bailey (On Friday, the 3rd, and Saturday, the 4th of March 1843) for the Wilful Murder of Edward Drummond, Esq.* London: H. Renshaw, 1843.

Bouvier, J. *A Law Dictionary Adapted to the Constitution and Laws of the United States of America.* Philadelphia: Childs & Peterson, 1856.

Brandt, N. *The Congressman Who Got Away With Murder.* Syracuse: Syracuse University Press, 1991.

Briefs. Abraham Lincoln's Last Case in Chicago. Chicago: Barnard and Miller, 1933.

Browne, F. F. *The Every-Day Life of Abraham Lincoln.* Chicago: Browne & Howell Co., 1913.

Bruce, R. V. *Lincoln and the Riddle of Death.* Fort Wayne IN: Louis A. Warren Lincoln Library and Museum, 1981.

Bryan, W. B. *A History of the National Capitol, 1815-1878.* New York: The Macmillian Co., 1916.

Burgess, L. *A Day With Mr. Lincoln.* Redondo Beach CA: Rank and File Pub., 1994.

Burlingame, M. *The Inner World of Abraham Lincoln.* Urbana: University of Illinois Press, 1994.

———— and J. R. T. Ettinger. *Inside Lincoln's White House. The Complete Civil War Diary of John Hay.* Carbondale: Southern Illinois University Press, 1997.

Burnham, J. H. *History of Bloomington and Normal in McLean County, Illinois.* Bloomington: privately published, 1879.

Burrow, J. G. *American Medical Association. Voice of American Medicine.* Baltimore: Johns Hopkins University Press, 1963.

Busey, S. C. *Personal Reminiscences and Recollections of Forty-six Years' Membership in the Medical Society of the District of Columbia.* Washington, DC: The Medical Society of the District of Columbia, 1895.

Camac, C. N. B. "William Thomas Green Morton, 1819-1868," in *Classics of Medicine and Surgery.* New York: Dover Pub., 1936.

Carman, H. J. and R. H. Luthin. *Lincoln and the Patronage.* New York: Columbia University Press, 1943.

Carr, J. S. *The Hampton Roads Conference.* Durham NC: self published, 1917.

Chicago City Manual. Chicago IL, 1911 and 1916.

Chicago Historical Society. *Memorial Addresses Commemorative of the Lives and Characters of Hon. Isaac N. Arnold...and Hon. Thomas Hoyne Delivered October 21, 1884.* Chicago: Fergus Printing Co., 1884.

Chitty, J. *A Practical Treatise on Medical Jurisprudence.* London: Butterworth, 1834.

————. *A Treatise on the Parties to Actions, and on Pleading.* 2 volumes. Springfield MA: G. & C. Merriam, 1842.

Chrisman, C. *Memoirs of Lincoln.* Mapleton IA: Mapleton Press, 1927.

Clendening, L. *Anesthesia, Source Book of Medical History.* New York: Dover Publications, 1942.

Clephane, J. O. *Official Report to the Trial of Mary Harris Indicted for the Murder of Adoniram J. Burroughs.* Washington, DC: W. H. and O. H. Morrison, 1865.

Coffin, A. I. *A Botanic Guide to Health and the Natural Pathology of Disease.* Manchester: Wm. Irwin, 1846.

Coley, H. *A Treatise on Medical Jurisprudence Comprising the Consideration of Poisons and Asphyxia.* New York: William Stodart, 1832.

Conrad, E. *Mr. Seward for the Defense.* New York: Rinehart & Co., 1956.

Cooke, N. F. *Valedictory Address to the Graduating Class of Hahnemann Medical College and Hospital, Delivered February 15, 1865.* Chicago: Beach & Barnard, 1865.

Cooper, A. P. *A Treatise on Dislocations and On Fractures of the Joints.* London: Longman, 1822.

————. *The Lectures of Sir Astley.* Philadelphia: E. L. Carey & A. Hart, 1835.

Cornish, D. T. *The Sable Arm. Negro Troops in the Union Army 1861-1865.* New York: W. W. Norton, 1966.

Coulter, H. L. *Divided Legacy: The Conflict Between Homeopathy and the American Medical Association.* Berkeley: North Atlantic Books, Homeopathic Educational Services, 1982.

Courville, C. B. *Untoward Effects of Nitrous Oxide Anesthesia.* Mountain View CA: Pacific Press Publication Association, 1939.

Cross v. Gutherie in A. C. Freeman, *American Decisions.* (San Francisco: Bancroft and Co., 1882) 1:61-62.

Croy, H. *The Trial of Mrs. Abraham Lincoln.* New York: Duell, Sloan and Pearce, 1962.

Cuomo, M. M. and H. Holzer. *Lincoln On Democracy.* New York: HarperCollins, 1990.

Current, R. N. *The Political Thought of Abraham Lincoln.* Indianapolis: Bobbs-Merrill Co., 1967.

Dabney, V. *Virginia the New Dominion.* Garden City NY: Doubleday & Co., 1927.

Dain, N. *Concepts of Insanity in the U.S. 1789-1865.* New Brunswick NJ: Rutgers University Press, 1964.

Davis, C. *The Public and Private Lincoln: Contemporary Perspectives.* Carbondale: Southern Illinois University 1979.

————. "The Little Engine That Knew No Rest: Lincoln's Career in Law," in L. Burgress *My Day With Mr. Lincoln.* Redondo Beach CA: Rank and File Publishing, 1994b.

————. *Abraham Lincoln and the Golden Age of American Law.* Historical Bulletin No. 48, Racine: Lincoln Fellowship of Wisconsin, 1994e.

————. "The Law Practice of Lincoln," in *The Universal Lincoln.* Edited by Y. D. Lew. Taipei, Taiwan:Chinese Cultural University Press, 1995.

Davis, N. S. *History of the American Medical Association From Its Organization Up to January 1850.* Philadelphia: Lippincott & Grambo, 1855.

Davidson, M. H. Armstrong: *The Evolution of Anaesthesia.* Baltimore, Williams & Wilkins, 1965.

Davy, H. *Researches Chemical and Philosophical, Chiefly Concerning Nitrous Oxide, or Dephlogisticated Nitrous Air, ...and Its Respiration.* London: J. Johnson, 1800.

Dean, A. *Principles of Medical Jurisprudence. Designed for Professions of Law & Medicine.* New York: Gould, Banks and Gould, 1859.

Dennett, T. *Lincoln and the Civil War in the Diaries and Letters of John Hay.* New York: Dodd, Mead & Co., 1939.

Desault, P. J. *A Treatise on Fractures, Luxations and Other Affections of the Bones.* Philadelphia: Lea & Blanchard, 1805.

DeVille, K. A. *Medical Malpractice in Nineteenth-Century America. Origins and Legacy.* New York: New York University Press, 1990.

Donald, D. H. *Lincoln's Herndon.* New York: Alfred A. Knopf, 1948.

———. *Lincoln.* New York: Simon & Schuster, 1995.

Donnelly, M. C. *The American Victorian Woman: The Myth and the Reality.* New York: Greenwood Press, 1986.

Donovan, J. W. *Modern Jury Trials and Advocates: Containing Condensed Cases with Sketches and Speeches of American Advocates; The Art of Winning Cases and Manner of Counsel Described, with Notes and Rules of Practice.* New York: Banks & Brothers, Law Publishers, 1882.

Dripps, R. D., J. E. Eckenhoff, and L. D. Vandam. *Introduction to Anesthesia. The Principles of Safe Practice.* Philadelphia: W. B. Saunders, 1988.

Duff, J. J. *A. Lincoln, Prairie Lawyer.* New York: Rinehart & Co., 1960.

Duis, E. *The Good Old Times in McLean County, Illinois containing 261 Sketches of Old Settlers.* Bloomington IL: Leader Pub. & Printing House, 1874.

Dunglison, R. *The Practice of Medicine; or A Treatise on Special Pathology and Therapeutics.* Philadelphia: Lea & Blanchard, 1842.

Edwards, E. *Sketch of the Life of Norman B. Judd.* Chicago: Norton & Leonard, 1891.

Eliot, C. W. *Harvard Memories.* Cambridge: Harvard University Press, 1923.

Elwell, J. J. *A Medico-Legal Treatise on Malpractice, Medical Evidence, and Insanity, Comprising the Elements of Medical Jurisprudence.* New York: John S. Voorhis, 1860.

Emerson, R. W. *Representative Men.* Boston: Phillips, Samson & Co., 1849.

Esquirol, J. E. D. *Des Maladies Mentales Considerèes Son Les Rapports Mèdicale: Hygiènique et Mèdico-Legal.* Paris: J. B. Ballière, 1838.

Evans, F. T. and J. C. Gray. *General Anaesthesia, Second Edition.* Volume 1. London: Butterworths, 1965.

Evans, H. O. *Abraham Lincoln As a Lawyer.* Pittsburgh: Smith Bros, 1928.

Evans, W. A. *Mrs. Abraham Lincoln. A Study of Her Personality and Her Influence on Lincoln.* New York: Alfred A. Knopf, 1932.

Farr, S. *Elements of Medical Jurisprudence.* London: T. Becket, 1788.

Federal Writers Project [WPA]. *Washington City and Capitol.* Washington, DC: Govt. Printing Office, 1937.

Fehrenbacher, D. E. *Abraham Lincoln. Speeches and Writings, 1832-1858 & 1859-1865.* New York: Library of America, 1989.

Fehrenbacher, D. E. and V. Fehrenbacher. *Recollected Words of Abraham Lincoln.* Stanford: Stanford University Press, 1996.

Ficarra, B. J. "A History of Legal Medicine," in *Legal Medicine Annual.* Edited by C. Wecht, New York: Appleton-Century Crofts, 1976.

Fiedler, G. *The Illinois Law Courts in Three Centuries, 1673-1973.* Berwyn IL: Physicians' Record Co., 1973.

Fish, D. *Lincoln Biography: A List of Books and Pamphlets Relating to Abraham Lincoln*. New York: F. D. Tandy Co., 1905.

Fishbein, M. *A History of the American Medical Association 1847-1947*. Philadelphia: W. B. Saunders Co., 1947.

Flagg, J. F. *Ether and Chloroform; Their Employment in Surgery, Dentistry, Midwifery, Therapeutics, etc.* Philadelphia: Lindsay & Blakiston, 1851.

Flexner, A. *Medical Education in the U.S. and Canada. A Report to the Carnegie Foundation for the Advancement of Teaching*. New York: Carnegie Foundation, 1910.

Fontaine, F. *Trial of Hon. Daniel E. Sickles for Shooting Philip Barton Key, Esq.* New York: R. M. Dewitt Pub., 1859.

Forman, S. M. and T. P. Lowry. *Abraham Lincoln's Washington DC Civil War Map*. Bethesda MD: Paradocs Pub., 1997.

Foville, A. L. *Traite Complet de L'anatomie, de la Physilogie et de la Pathologie du Systeme neveux Cebro-Spinal*. Paris: Fortin & Masson, 1844.

Frank, J. P. *Lincoln As a Lawyer*. Urbana: University of Illinois Press, 1961.

Freedman, R. *Lincoln, A Photobiography*. New York: Ticknor & Fields, 1987.

Freeman, N. L. and W. L. Gross. *Report of the Cases Determined in the Supreme Court of the State of Illinois Nov. 1859-Apr. 1859-Jan. 1860*. Chicago: Callaghan and Co., 1876, 23 Ill. 517.

Gall, F. J. *Manual of Phrenology; Being an Analytical Summary of the System of Dr. Gall on the Faculties of Man and the Functions of the Brain*. Philadelphia: Carey, Lea & Blanchard, 1835.

Garrison, F. H. *An Introduction to the History of Medicine, Fourth Edition*. Philadelphia, W. B. Saunders Co., 1929.

Gayley, J. F. *A History of the Jefferson Medical School of Philadelphia with Biographical Sketches of the Early Professors*. Philadelphia: Joseph H. Wilson, 1858.

Gevitz, N. *Other Healers. Unorthodox Medicine in America*. Baltimore MD: Johns Hopkins University Press, 1988.

Gienapp, W. E. *The Origin of the Republican Party, 1852-1856*. New York: Oxford University Press, 1987

Gilman, C. *Reports of Cases Argued and Determined in the Supreme Court of the State of Illinois*. Volume 2. Chicago: Callaghan & Co., 1888.

Glatthaar, J. T. *Forged in Battle. The Civil War Alliance of Black Soldiers and White Officers*. New York: Free Press, 1990.

Goodhart, A. L. "Lincoln and the Law," in A. L. Goodhart, *Lincoln and the Gettysburg Address: Commemorative Papers* Urbana: University of Illinois Press, 1964.

Graber, V. A. *The Armistead Family 1635-1910*. Richmond VA: self published, 1910

Graf, L. P. and R. W. *The Papers of Andrew Johnson*. Volume 6. Knoxville: University of Tennessee Press, 1983.

Gray, J. C. *General Anaesthesia, Second Edition*, Volume 1. London, Butterworths, 1965.

Greenleaf, S. *A Discourse Pronounced at the Inauguration of the Author as Royall Professor of Law in Harvard University, August 26, 1834*. Cambridge: James Munroe & Co., 1837.

————. *A Treatise on the Law of Evidence, 2 Vols*. Boston: C. Little & James Brown, 1842.

Greenstone, J. D. *The Lincoln Persuasion: Remaking American Liberalism*. Princeton: Princeton University Press, 1993.

Griggs, S. C. *History of Medical Education and Institutions in the United States*. Chicago: privately published, 1851.

Gross, S. D. *The Anatomy, Physiology and Diseases of the Bones and Joints*. Philadelphia: J. Grigg, 1830.

Haehl, R. *Samuel Hahnemann: Sein Leben und Schaffen*. Leipzig: Dr. Willmar Schwabe, 1922.

Hahnemann, S. *Organon der Rationellen Heilkunde*. Dresden: Arnold, 1810.

Hahnemann, S. *Die Chronischen Krankheiten, Ihre Eigenhumliche Naturund Homoopathische Heilung*. Dresden, Leipzig: Arnold, 1828.

Hahnemann Medical College. *First Annual Announcement*. Chicago: Hyatt Brothers, 1860.

Hall, B. F. *The Trial of William Freeman For the Murder of John G. Van Nest*. Auburn NY: Derby, Miller & Co., 1848.

Hall, K. L. *The Magic Mirror: Law in American History*. New York: Oxford University Press, 1989.

Hamilton, C. G. *Lincoln and the Know Nothing Movement*. Washington: Public Affairs Press 1954.

Hamilton, F. H. *Fracture Tables Compiled from Dr. Hamilton's Notes with a Supplement by Dr. Boardman Comprising in All An Analysis of 461 Cases of Fractures*. Buffalo: Jewett, Thomas & Co., 1853.

————. *Deformities After Fractures*. Philadelphia: T. K. & P. G. Collins, 1855a.

Harris, G. W. *Pennsylvania State Reports*, 22:261-74. Philadelphia: Kay, 1855.

Hendrick, B. J. *Lincoln's War Cabinet*. Gloucester MA: Peter Smith, 1965.

Herndon, W. H. and J. W. Weik. *Abraham Lincoln, The True Story of a Great Life*. New York: D. Appleton & Co., 1893.

————. *Herndon's Lincoln. The True Story of a Great Life*. 3 volumes. Chicago: Belford, Clarke & Co., 1889.

Herndon, W. H. *Lincoln and Ann Rutledge and the Pioneers of New Salem. A Lecture by William H. Herndon*. Herrin IL: Trovillion Private Press, 1945.

Hertz, E. *Abraham Lincoln, A New Portrait* New York: Horace Liveright, Inc., 1931.

————. *The Hidden Lincoln from the Letters and Papers of William H. Herndon.* New York: Viking Press, 1938.

Higgison, G. M. *Papers of Thomas Hoyne 1817-1883.* Chicago: Chicago Historical Society, 1883.

Hill, F. T. *Lincoln the Lawyer.* New York: The Century Co., 1906.

History of Sangamon County. Chicago: Interstate Pub. Co., 1881.

Holloway, L. M. *Medical Obituaries: American Physicians' Biographical Notices in Selected Medical Journals Before 1907.* New York: Garland Pub., 1981.

Holmes, J. T., J. Morton, A. Becraft, and J. B. Turner. *Protest In Behalf Of Illinois Hospital for the Insane by Members of the Board.* Jacksonville: Morgan Journal & Book Office, 1852.

Holmes, O. W. "The Young Practitioner," in W. H. Davenport, *The Good Physician.* New York: MacMillian, 1962.

Holzer, H., G. S. Boritt, and M. E. Neely. *The Lincoln Image: Abraham Lincoln and the Popular Print.* New York: Scribner Press 1984.

Holzer, H. *The Lincoln-Douglas Debates.* New York: Harper Perennial 1994.

————. *Lincoln As I Knew Him: Gossip, Tributes and Revelations From His Friends and Worst Enemies.* Chapel Hill NC: Algonquin Books, 1999.

Hooker, W. "Report of the AMA Committee on Medical Education," in *Transactions of the AMA, Volume 2.* Philadelphia: T. K. & P. G. Collins, 1849.

Horowitz, M. *The Transformation of American Law, 1780-1860.* Cambridge, MA: Harvard University Press, 1977.

Houston, R. M. *Charge of the Graduates of Jefferson Medical School of Philadelphia, March 28, 1849.* Philadelphia: Merrihew & Thompson, 1849.

Howard, R. P. *Mostly Good and Competent Men. Illinois Governors, 1818-1988.* Springfield: Illinois State Historical Society, 1988.

Hoyne, T. *Historical Sketch of the Origin and Foundation of the Chicago Public Library.* Chicago: Beach, Barnard & Co., 1877.

————. *Bibliographical; Memoir of the Hon. George Manierre.* Chicago: Chicago Historical Society, April 16, 1878.

————. *The Early History of Illinois.* Chicago: E. B. Myers & Co., 1884.

Hoyne, T. S. *Classification of a Few of the "New Remedies" According to the Parts of the Body Acted Upon: After the Plan of Bonninghausen.* St. Louis: H. C. G. Luyties, 1868.

————. *Hoyne's Annual Directory of Homeopathic Physicians in the State of Illinois for the Year 1873.* Chicago: Sinclair & Blair, 1873.

————. *Clinical Therapeutics.* Chicago: Duncan Brothers, 1878-1880.

————. *Venereal and Urinary Diseases.* Chicago: Halsey Brothers, 1883.

Hubbard, C. *The Burden of Confederate Diplomacy.* Knoxville: University of Tennessee Press, 1998.

————. *Lincoln and His Contemporaries.* Macon GA: Mercer University Press, 1999.

Hughes, J. S. *In the Law's Darkness: Isaac Ray and the Medical Jurisprudence of Insanity in Nineteenth Century America.* Dobbs Ferry NY: Oceana Pub., 1986.

Illinois Central Railroad Company. *Abraham Lincoln As Attorney for the ICRR.* Chicago: Ginthrop Warren Printing Co., 1905.

Illinois State Hospital for the Insane [Jacksonville]: *First Biennial Report of the Trustees and Treasurer, 1847-'48.* Chicago: F. Fulton & Co., 1863.

————. *Third Biennial Report of the Trustees, Superintendent, and Treasurer, 1851-'52.* Chicago: F. Fulton & Co., 1863.

————. *Fourth Biennial Report of the Trustees, Superintendent, and Treasurer, 1854.* Chicago: F. Fulton & Co., 1863.

In Memoriam. Sketch of the Life and Character of Thomas Hoyne, LLD, With the Proceedings of Public Bodies on the Occasion of His Death, and Memorial Addresses. Chicago: Barnard & Gunthorp, 1883.

Jefferson, T. *The Writings of Thomas Jefferson.* Washington, DC: Thomas Jefferson Memorial Association, 1907.

Johnson, A. and D. Malone. *Dictionary of American Biography.* New York: Charles Scribner's Sons, 1931.

Johnson, C. W. *Proceedings of the First Three Republican National Conventions of 1856, 1860 and 1864.* Minneapolis: C. W. Johnson, 1893.

Kaplan, J. *Walt Whitman, A Life.* New York: Simon & Schuster, 1980.

Kaufman, M. *Homeopathy in America. The Rise and Fall of a Medical Heresy.* Baltimore: Johns Hopkins Press, 1971.

————. *American Medical Education. The Formative Years 1765-1910.* Westport CT: Greenwood Press, 1976.

Kaufman, M., S. Galishoff, and T. I. Savitt. *Dictionary of American Medical Biography.* Westport CT: Greenwood Press, 1984.

Keckley, E. *Behind the Scenes, or, Thirty Years a Slave, and Four Years in the White House.* New York: G. W. Carleton & Co., 1868.

Kelly, H. A. and W. I. Burrage. *Dictionary of American Medical Biography.* New York: D. Appleton & Co., 1928.

Kelly, T. *Murders. Washington's Most Famous Murder Stories.* Washington, DC: Washingtonian Books, 1976.

King, W. H. *History of Homeopathy and Its Institutions in America.* New York: Lewis Pub. Co., 1905.

King, W. L. *Lincoln's Manager, David Davis.* Cambridge, Harvard University Press, 1960.

Kirkland, T. *Thoughts on Amputation, being a supplement to the letters on compound fractures and a comment on Dr. Johann Ulrich Bilguer's book on this operation.* London, 1780.

Knapp, G. E. *Lincoln the Lawyer*. Springfield IL: Illinois State Historical Society, 1929.

Knappman, E. W. *Great American Trials*. Detroit: Visible Ink Press, 1994.

Kunhardt, P. B., P. B. Kunhardt III, and P. W. Kunhardt. *Lincoln. An Illustrated Biography*. New York: Library of America, 1989.

Kyle, O. R. *Abraham Lincoln in Decatur*. New York: Vantage Press, 1957.

Lamon, W. H. *Life of Abraham Lincoln: From His Birth to His inauguration as President*. Boston: James R. Osgood & Co., 1872.

Lawson, J. D. *American State Trials*. Volume 12. St. Louis: F. H. Thomas Law Book Co., 1919.

Lee, J. A. and R. S. Atkinson. *A Synopsis of Anaesthesia*. Baltimore: Williams & Wilkins Co., 1964.

Leech, M. *Revillie in Washington, 1860-1865*. New York: Harper & Bros., 1941.

Leitch, A. *A Princeton Companion*. Princeton: Princeton University Press, 1978.

Linder, U. F. *Reminiscences of the Early Bench and Bar of Illinois*. Chicago: Chicago Legal News Co., 1879.

Locke, J. *Second Treatise of Government*. Indianapolis: Hackett Pub. Co., 1980.

Long, J. *The Law of Illinois. Lincoln's Cases Before the Illinois Supreme Court, Volume 1*. Shiloh: The Illinois Co., 1993.

———. *The Law of Illinois. Lincoln's Cases Before the Illinois Supreme Court, From His Return to the Practice of Law Until His Return to Politics Volume 2*. Shiloh: The Illinois Co., 1996.

Lowry, T. P. *The Story the Soldiers Wouldn't Tell: Sex in the Civil War*. Mechanicsburg PA: Stackpole Books, 1994.

———. *The Civil War Bawdy Houses of Washington, DC*. Fredericksburg VA: Sergeant Kirkland's, 1997.

———. *Tarnished Eagles: The Courts-Martial of Fifty Union Colonels and Lieutenant Colonels*. Mechanicsburg PA: Stackpole Books, 1998.

———. *Don't Shoot That Boy! Abraham Lincoln and Military Justice*. Mason City IA: Savas Pub., 1999.

Ludlam, R. *Valedictory Address to the Graduating Class of Hahnemann Medical College and Hospital, Delivered March 19, 1874*. Chicago: Sinclair & Blair, 1874.

Luthin, R. H. *The Real Abraham Lincoln*. Englewood Cliffs NJ: Prentice-Hall, 1960.

Mansfield, E. D. *Memoirs of the Life and Services of Daniel Drake, MD*. Cincinnati: Applegate and Co., 1855.

———. *Lincoln the Man*. New York: Dodd, Mead & Co., 1931.

Matthews, E. W. *Lincoln As a Lawyer: An Annotated Bibliography*. Carbondale: Southern Illinois University Press, 1991.

McCool, C. M. *Dr. Mary Walker: The Little Lady in Pants*. New York: Vantage Press, 1962.

McGrew, R. E. *Encyclopedia of Medical History*. New York: McGraw-Hill Book Co., 1985.

McLean County Historical Society. Volume 3 of *Transactions of the McLean County Historical Society*. Bloomington IL: Pantagraph Printing Co., 1858.

McMaster, J. B. *A History of the People of the United States During Lincoln's Administration*. New York: D. Appleton & Co., 1927.

McPherson, J. M. *The Negro's Civil War*. Urbana: University of Illinois Press, 1982.

Mearns, D. C. *The Lincoln Papers*. Garden City NY: Doubleday & Co., 1948.

Memorials of the Life and Character of Stephen T. Logan. Springfield: H. W. Rokker, 1882.

Miers, E. S., W. E. Barringer, and C. P. Powell. *Lincoln Day by Day. A Chronology 1809-1865*. Washington, DC: Lincoln Sesquicentennial Commission, 1960.

Mohr, J. C. *Doctors & The Law: Medical Jurisprudence in Nineteenth Century America*. New York: Oxford University Press, 1993.

Morris, R. B. *Fair Trial. Fourteen Who Stood Accused*. New York: Alfred A. Knopf, 1953.

Morse, H. N. *Lawyer Lincoln—Accounts of Six Cases in Which Abraham Lincoln Participated as Counsel*. Atlanta: Peachtree Pub., 1900.

Morton, W. T. G. *On the Psychological Effects of Sulfuric Ether, and its Superiority to Chloroform*. Boston: David Clapp, 1850.

Nadelson, C. C. Foreword in *The American Victorian Women: The Myth and the Reality* New York: Greenwood Press, 1986.

National Cyclopedia of American Biography. New York: James T. White & Co., 1897.

Neal, T. *Lawyer On the Circuit*. Los Angeles: Dawson's Book Shop, 1945.

Neely, M. E. *The Abraham Lincoln Encyclopedia*. New York: McGraw-Hill Book Co., 1982a.

————. *The Extra Journal: Rallying the Whigs in Illinois*. Fort Wayne IN: Louis A. Warren Library and Museum, 1982b.

————. *Lincoln and the Constitution*. Madison: Lincoln Fellowship of Wisconsin, 1983.

————. *The Last Best Hope on Earth: Abraham Lincoln and the Promise of America*. Cambridge: Harvard University Press, 1993.

Neely, M. E., and R. G. McMurty. *The Insanity File. The Case of Mary Todd Lincoln*. Carbondale: Southern Illinois University Press, 1986.

Nevins, A. and M. H. Thomas. *The Diary of George Templeton Strong. Volume 2, The Turbulent Fifties 1850-1859*. New York: Macmillan Co., 1952.

Nevins, A. and I. Stone. *Lincoln: A Contemporary Portrait*. Garden City NY: Doubleday, 1962.

Newton, J. F. *Lincoln and Herndon*. Cedar Rapids IA: Torch Press, 1910.

Nicolay, J. G. and J. Hay. *Abraham Lincoln, A History.* New York: The Century Co., 1890.

———. *Complete Works of Abraham Lincoln.* 2 volumes. New York: The Century Co., 1894.

Norman, J. *Morton's Medical Biography.* Brookfield VT: Gower Pub. Co., 1991.

Norwood, W. F. *Medical Education in the United States Before the Civil War.* Philadelphia: University of Pennsylvania Press, 1944.

Numbers, R. L. "Do-It-Yourself the Sectarian Way," in *Send Me a Lady Doctor.* Edited by R Abram. New York: W. W. Norton & Co., 1985. Pages 43-54.

Numbers, R. L., and T. L. Savitt. *Science and Medicine in the Old South.* Baton Rouge: Louisiana State University Press, 1989.

Oakleaf, J. B. *Abraham Lincoln As a Criminal Lawyer.* Rock Island IL: Augustana Books, 1923.

Oates, S. B. *With Malice Toward None.* New York: Harper & Row, 1977.

———. *A Woman of Valor. Clara Barton and the Civil War.* New York: Free Press, 1994.

Ordronaux, J. *The Jurisprudence of Medicine in its Relation to the Law of Contracts, Torts and Evidence* Philadelphia: T. & J. W. Johnson, 1869.

Ownsbey, B. J. *Alias Paine, Lewis Thornton Powell, The Mystery Man of the Lincoln Conspiracy.* Jefferson NC: McFarland & Co. 1993.

Packard, R. D. *A. Lincoln, Successful Lawyer.* Cleveland OH: Carpenter Printing Co., 1948.

Palmer, J. M. *The Bench and Bar of Illinois: Historical and Reminiscent.* Chicago: Lewis Pub. Co., 1899.

Peck, E. *Report of the Cases Determined in the Supreme Court of the State of Illinois November 1855-June 1856, 1861 and 1862.* Chicago: Callaghan and Co., 1886.

Phillips, W. *Speeches, Lectures and Letters.* Second series. Boston: Lee & Shephard, 1894.

Pinchon, E. *Dan Sickles, Hero of Gettysburg and Yankee King of Spain.* Garden City: Doubleday Doran & Co., 1945.

Pinel, P. *Traite Mèdico-Philosophique Sur L'Alienation Mentale.* Second edition. Paris: J. A. Brosson, 1809.

Pollak, K., and E. A. Underwood. *The Healers. The Doctor, Then and Now.* London: Thomas Nelson and Sons, Ltd., 1968.

Portrait and Biographical Album of McLean County, Illinois. Chicago: Chapman Brothers, 1887.

Potter, D. M., and D. E. Fehrenbacher. *The Impending Crisis, 1848-1860.* New York: Harper & Roe, 1976.

Power, J. C. *History of Early Settlers, Sangamon County, Illinois.* Springfield IL: Phillips Bros. Press, 1970.

Pratt, F. *Stanton, Lincoln's Secretary of War.* Westport CT: Greenwood Press, 1970.

———. *Lincoln 1840-1846: Being the Day-to-Day Activities of Abraham Lincoln.* Springfield: Abraham Lincoln Association, 1939b.

———. *The Personal Finances of Abraham Lincoln.* Springfield: Abraham Lincoln Association, 1943b.

———. *Concerning Mr. Lincoln in Which Abraham Lincoln is Pictured as He Appeared to Letter Writers of His Time.* Springfield: Abraham Lincoln Association, 1944b.

Prichard, J. C. *A Treatise On Insanity.* London, Marchant, 1833.

Prince, E. M. and J. H. Burnham. "History of McLean County," in *Historical Encyclopedia of Illinois.* Volume 2. Edited by N. Bateman and P. Selby. Chicago: Munsell Pub. Co., 1908.

Rankin, H. B. *Intimate Character Sketches of Abraham Lincoln.* Philadelphia: J. B. Lippincott, 1924.

Ray, I. *A Treatise On the Medical Jurisprudence of Insanity.* Boston: Charles C. Little & James Brown, 1838.

Reese, D. M. *Humbugs of New York: Being a Remonstrance Against Popular Delusion; Whether in Science, Philosophy, or Religion.* New York: J. S. Taylor, 1893.

Rehnquist, W. H. *All the Laws But One: Civil Liberties in Wartime.* New York: Alfred A. Knopf, 1998.

Rhodes, J. A. *Jauchius: The Trial of Mary Todd Lincoln.* Indianapolis: Bobbs-Merrill, 1959.

Rice, A. T. *Reminiscences of Abraham Lincoln By Distinguished Men of His Time.* New York: North American Publishing, 1880.

Richards, J. T. *Abraham Lincoln, the Lawyer-Statesman.* New York: Houghton-Mifflin Co., 1916.

Richardson, B. W. *Disciples of Aesculapius.* New York: E. P. Dutton & Co., 1901.

Riddle, A. G. *Recollections of War Times.* New York: G. P. Putnam's Sons, 1895.

Rolle, A. F. *Lincoln As Man and Myth.* Redlands CA: Lincoln Memorial Shrine, 1985.

Root, J. *Reports of Cases Adjudged in the Superior Court and in the Supreme Court of Errors in the State of Connecticut, 1793 to 1798.* Volume 2. n.p., 1802.

Rosenberg, C. E. *The Trial of the Assassin Guiteau. Psychiatry and Law in the Gilded Age.* Chicago: University of Chicago Press, 1968.

Rothstein, W. G. *American Physicians in the Nineteenth Century. From Sects to Science.* Baltimore: Johns Hopkins University Press, 1972.

———. *American Medical Schools and the Practice of Medicine.* New York: Oxford University Press, 1987.

Rush, B. *Medical Inquiries and Observations Upon the Diseases of the Mind.* Fifth edition. Phila: Grigg & Elliot, 1835.

Rutkow, I. M. *The History of Surgery in the U.S. 1775-1900*. San Francisco: Norman Publishing Co., 1988.

―――. *Surgery. An Illustrated History*. St. Louis: Mosby, 1993.

Safire, W. *Freedom. A Novel of Abraham Lincoln and the Civil War*. Garden City NY: Doubleday & Co., 1987a.

Sandburg, C. *Abraham Lincoln, The War Years*. Volume 3. New York: Harcourt, Brace & Co., 1939.

Sargent, F. *On Bandaging and Other Operations of Minor Surgery*. Philadelphia, Lea & Blanchard, 1848.

Scammon, J. Y. *Report of the Cases Determined in the Supreme Court of the State of Illinois December 1839-December 1840*. Chicago: Callaghan and Co., 1886.

Schuckers, J. W. *The Life and Public Services of Salmon Portland Chase*. New York: D. Appleton & Co., 1874.

Seward, F. W. *Autobiography of William H. Seward*. New York: D. Appleton & Co., 1877.

Sharp, H. S. *Footnotes to American History. A Bibliographic Source Book*. Metuchen NJ: Scarecrow Press, 1977.

Shaw, A. A. *The Lincoln Encyclopedia*. New York: Macmillan Co., 1950.

Shestack, J. J. *Abe Lincoln As a Circuit Lawyer*. Philadelphia: Wolf, Block, Shorr & Solis-Cohen, 1992.

Shutes, M. H. *Lincoln and the Doctors*. New York: Pioneer Press, 1933.

Sifakis, S. *Who Was Who in the Civil War*. New York: Facts On File Pub., 1988.

Silver, D. M. *Lincoln's Supreme Court*. Urbana: University of Illinois Press, 1956.

Simon, J. Y., H. Holzer, and W. D. Pederson. *The Lincoln Forum: Lincoln, Gettysburg and the Civil War*. Mason City IA: Savas Pub., 1999.

Simpson, J. Y. *Account of a New Anaesthetic Agent, As a Substitute for Sulfuric Ether in Surgery and Midwifery*. New York: Rushton, Clarke & Co., 1848.

Skultans, V. *Madness and Morals: Ideas on Insanity in the Nineteenth Century*. London, Routledge & Kegan Paul, 1975.

Smith, B., and C. Webb. *Lawyer Lincoln. A Comedy in One Act*. Evanston IL: Row, Peterson and Company, 1954.

Smith, J. W. *A Selection of Leading Cases, On Various Branches of the Law: with Notes*. Fourth American edition. Philadelphia: T. & J. W. Johnson, 1852.

Snow, J. *On Chloroform and Other Anesthetics: Their Action and Administration*. Edited with a Memoir of the Author by Benjamin W. Richardson. London, John Churchill, 1858.

Spurzheim, J. C. *Observations on the Deranged Manifestations of the Mind, of Insanity, with addition by Dr. Amariah Brigham*. Third edition. Boston: Marsh, Capen & Lyon, 1836.

Starr, J. W. *Lincoln and the Railroads: A Biographical Study*. New York: Dodd, Mead & Co., 1927.

Starr, P. *The Social Transfoirmation of American Medicine*. New York: Basic Books, 1982.

Stevens, W. B. *A Reporter's Lincoln*. St. Louis: Missouri Historical Society, 1916.

Story, J. *Commentaries on Equity Jurisprudence, 2 Vols*. Boston: Hilliard Gray & Co., 1836.

———. *Commentaries on Equity Pleadings*. Boston: C. C. Little & J. Brown, 1838.

Strozier, C. B. *Lincoln's Quest for Union*. New York: Basic Books, 1982.

Styple, W. *The Little Bugler: The True Story of a Twelve Year Old Boy in the Civil War*. Kearny NJ: Belle Grove Pub. Co., 1998.

Sutton, R. *The Trial of John H. Surratt for Crimes and Misdemeanors On An Indictment for Murder of President Lincoln*. Washington, DC: Govt. Printing Office, 1867.

Swanberg, W. A. *Sickles the Incredible*. New York: Charles Scribner's Sons, 1956.

Swett, L. H. *A Memorial of Leonard Swett: A Lawyer and Advocate of Illinois*. Aurora IL: Phillips Press, 1895.

———. *The Life of Abraham Lincoln*. New York: Lincoln Memorial Association, 1900.

Taylor, A. S. *Elements of Medical Jurisprudence*. London: Deacon, 1836.

———. *On Poisons, in Relation to Medical Jurisprudence and Medicine*. Edited with notes and additions by R. E. Griffith. Philadelphia: Lea and Blanchard, 1848.

Taylor, J. M. *William Henry Seward. Lincoln's Right Hand*. New York: Harper Collins, Pub., 1991.

Thomas, B. P. *Lincoln and the Courts, 1854-1861*. Springfield: Abraham Lincoln Association Papers, 1933.

———. *Lincoln's New Salem*. Springfield: Abraham Lincoln Association, 1934.

———. *Abraham Lincoln*. New York: Alfred A. Knopf, 1952.

——— and H. M. Hyman. *Edwin M. Stanton. The Life and Times of Lincoln's Secretary of War*. New York: Alfred A. Knopf, 1962.

Thomson, S. *New Guide to Health: or, Botanic Family Physician, containing a Complete System of Practice*. Second edition. Boston: self published, 1825.

de Tocqueville, A. *Democracy in America*. New York: New American Library, 1956.

Tracy, G. A. *Uncollected Letters of Abraham Lincoln*. Boston: Houghton Mifflin Co., 1917.

Trall, R. T. *The Hygienic System*. Battle Creek MI: The Office of the Health Reformer, 1872.

American Medical Association. Volume 2 of *Transactions of the American Medical Association*. Philadelphia: TK & PG Collins, 1849.

Tree, L. *Side-Lights On Lincoln*. Santa Barbara: University of California, 1911.

Tucker, W. G. "Memoir of John Purdue Gray, M.D., LL.D.," in *Transactions of the Medical Society of the State of New York.* Syracuse: Syracuse Journal Co., 1888.

Turner, J. G. and L. L. Turner. *Mary Todd Lincoln Her Life and Letters.* New York: Alfred A. Knopf, 1972.

Turner, T. R. *Beware the People Weeping: Public Opinion and the Assassination of Abraham Lincoln.* Baton Rouge: Louisiana State University Press, 1982.

———. *The Assassination of Abraham Lincoln.* Malabar FL: Kreiger Pub., 1999.

Underwood, E. A. *The Healers. The Doctor, Then and Now.* London: Thomas Nelson and Sons, Ltd., 1968.

US Congress. *Biographical Dictionary of the American Congress.* Washington, DC. Government Printing Office, 1950.

US House of Representatives. *Report on the Treatment of Prisoners of War By the Rebel Authorities During the War of the Rebellion.* Washington, DC: Govt. Printing Office, 1869.

U.S. Official Register. Washington, DC: Govt. Printing Office, 1870.

US War Records Office. *War of the Rebellion.* Washington, DC: Govt. Printing Office, 1884-1889.

Vandam, L. D. *Introduction to Anesthesia. The Principles of Safe Practice.* Seventh Edition. Philadelphia: W. B. Sanders Co., 1988.

Van Deusen, G. G. *William Henry Seward.* New York: Oxford University Press, 1967.

Voohees, D. W. *Argument Before the Committee on Expenditures in the Interior Department, in Defence of Dr. C. H. Nichols. Superintendent, Government Hospital for the Insane, July 15, 1876.* Washington, DC: Joseph L. Pearson, 1876.

Wakefield, S. D. *How Lincoln Became President.* New York: Wilson-Erikson Inc., 1936.

Walsh, J. J. *History of Medicine in New York.* New York: National Americana Society, 1919.

Walton, C. C. *John Francis Synder: Selected Writings.* Springfield: Illinois State Historical Society, 1962.

Warner, J. A. "Medical Sectarianism, Therapeutic Conflict and the Shaping of Orthodox Professional Identity in Antebellum American Medicine," in *Medical Fringe and Medical Orthodoxy 1750- 1850.* Edited by W. F. Bynum and R. Porter. London: Croom Helm, 1987.

Warren, J. C. *Effects of Chloroform and of Strong Chloric Ether, as Narcotic Agents.* Boston: William D. Ticknor, 1849.

Watson, J. *A Lecture on Practical Education in Medicine and On the Courses of Instruction at the New York Hospital.* New York: J & H. G. Langley, 1846.

Waugh, John C. *Reelecting Lincoln. The Battle for the 1864 Presidency.* New York: Crown Publishing, 1998.

Weik, J. W. *The Real Lincoln. A Portrait.* Boston: Houghton Mifflin Co., 1922.

Weiss, H. B. and H. R. Kemble. *The Great American Water-Cure Craze: A History of Hydropathy in the United States.* Trenton: Past Times Press, 1967.

Wershub, L. P. *One Hundred Years of Medical Progress.* Springfield IL: Charles C. Thomas, 1967.

Wertenbacker, T. J. *Norfolk, Historic Southern Port.* Durham NC: Duke University Press, 1931.

Wharton, F. and M. Stillè. *A Treatise on Medical Jurisprudence.* Philadelphia: Kay, 1855.

Whitney, H. C. *Life On the Circuit With Lincoln.* Boston: Estes and Lauriat, 1892.

Wilder, A. *History of Medicine. A Brief Outline of Medical History and Sects of Physicians, from the Earliest Historic Period: With an Extended Account of the New Schools of the Healing Art in the Nineteenth Century, and Especially a History of the American Eclectic Practice of Medicine, Never Before Published.* New Sharon ME: New England Eclectic Publishing Co., 1901.

Williams, F. J., W. D. Pederson, and V. J. Marsala. *Abraham Lincoln: Sources of Style and Leadership.* Westport CT: Greenwood Pub., 1994.

Wills, G. *Lincoln Before Washington. New Perspectives on the Illinois Years.* Urbana: University of Illinois Press, 1997.

Wilson, D. L. and R. O. Davis. *Herndon's Informants: Letters, Interviews, and Statements About Abraham Lincoln.* Urbana: University of Illinois Press, 1998.

Wilson, R. R. *Uncollected Works of Abraham Lincoln.* Elmira NY: Primavera Press, 1948.

———. *Lincoln in Caricature.* New York: Horizon Press, 1953.

Woldman, A. A. *Lawyer Lincoln.* Boston: Houghton Mifflin Co., 1936.

Zane, J. M. *Lincoln the Constitutional Lawyer.* Chicago: Printed for the Caxton Club, 1932.

Zeuch, L. H. *History of Medical Practice in Illinois.* Chicago: Book Press, Inc., 1927.

Periodicals

Abraham Lincoln Quarterly. Donald, D. H. "Billy, You're Too Rampant," 3:375-407, 1945; Parkinson, R. H. "The Patent Case that Lifted Lincoln Into a Presidential Candidate," 4:105-22, 1946.

Albany Argus. "Local Affairs," July 8, 1865; "Condition of the Capitol," July 12, 1865.

Alton Telegraph. "Chapman Convicted," December 14, 1844.

American Bar Association Journal. "Lincoln's Oral Argument: Text of Notes for His Only Supreme Court Case," 34:791-94, 1948; Townsend, W. H.

"Lincoln the Litigant," 86:83-88, 1924; "Lincoln's Defense of Duff Armstrong," 11:81-84, 1925; "Lincoln's Law Books," 15:125-26, 1929; Bullard, F. L. "Lincoln and the Courts of the District of Columbia," 63:117-20, 1938; Key, J. A. "Lincoln As a Lawyer," 80:82-84, 1994.

American Heritage. Carle, G. L. "The First Kansas Colored," 43:78-91, 1992; Dunn, J. T. "Crazy Bill Had a Down Look," 6:60-65, 1955; Fleming, T. J. "A Husband's Revenge. Verdicts of History," 18:65-75, 1967; Holzer, H. "A Legacy of Excellence: the Lincoln-Douglas Debates," 47[6]:61-63, 1996; Randall, R. P. "When Mary Lincoln Was Adjudged Insane," 6:10-11, 96-99, 1955; Ward, G. C. "The House At Eighth and Jackson," 40:68-78, 1989; Wills, G. "A Most Abandoned Hypocrite" 45:36-46, 1994.

American History. Hubbard, C. M. "Lincoln and the Chicken Bone Case," 32:30-34, 69, 1997.

American History Illustrated. Anderson, W. T. "Mr. Lincoln's Springfield," 24:26-32, 1989; Balderston, T. "The Sad Shattered Life of Teresa Sickles," 17:41-45, 1982; Cooney, C. F. "The General's Badge of Honor," 20:16-17, 1985.

American Journal of Forensic Psychiatry. Spiegel, A. D. and M. S. Spiegel. "J. Wilkes Booth As a Patient, As a Corpse To Be Identified and Diagnosed As a Monomaniac," 20:53-86, 1999.

American Journal of Insanity. "Proceedings of Annual Meeting," 7:64-69, 77-82, 1850; "Proceedings of Annual Meeting," 8:82-88, 1851; "Proceedings of Annual Meeting," 9:67, 1852; "Reports of State Asylums," 12:367-70, 1856; "Proceedings of Annual Meeting," 20:63, 67, 98, 1863-1864; "Proceedings of the 21st Annual Meeting, Association of Medical Superintendents of American Institutions for the Insane, Philadelphia PA, May 25, 1867," Harrisburg: Theo. F. Scheffer Printer and Bookseller, 21-22:124-27, 1867-1868; "Proceedings Annual Meeting," 33:160-323, 1876; "The Guiteau Trial," 38:416, 1881-1882; "Assault on Dr. Gray," 38:466, 1881-1882; "Obituary. Charles H. Nichols, M.D., LL.D." 46:416-22, 1890; Brigham, A. "Moral Treatment," 4:1-15, 1847; Bucknill, J. C. "Extraordinary Case of Pretended Insanity," 12:301, 1855; "Feigned Insanity," 13:354-367, 1856-1857; Gray, J. P. "Inhalation of the Vapor of Sulfuric Ether in Cases of Insanity," 5:73-74, 1847; "The Case of Dr. David M. Wright, for the Murder of Lieutenant Sanborn—Plea, Insanity," 20:284-300, 1864; "Homicide: Plea Insanity, Case of Lorenzo C. Stewart," 21:380-90, 1865a; "The Trial of Mary Harris," 22:333-69, 1865b-1866; "Thoughts on the Causation of Insanity," 29:275, 1872; Ranney, M. "Proceedings of the 26th Annual Meeting," 29:249-57, 1872; Ray, I. "Etherization in the Treatment of Insanity," 11:164-69, 1854; "The Insanity of Women Produced by Desertion or Seduction," 23:263-74, 1866-1867; Waters, A. T. H. "On The Use of Chloroform in the Treatment of Puerperal Insanity," 13:341-53,

1857; Nichols, C. H. Proceedings of the 26th Annual Meeting. Comments of Dr. Nichols. 29:247-48, 1872.

American Journal of Legal History: Ireland, R. M. "Insanity and the Unwritten Law," 32:157-72, 1988.

American Journal of Legal Medicine: Chroust, A. H. "Abraham Lincoln Argues a Pro-Slavery Case," 5:299-308, 1961.

American Journal of Medicine Sciences: Medical School Advertisement 18:575, 1849; "Review of Frank Hamilton's Works," 39:422, 1860; Wood, W. W. "Thoughts on Suits for Malpractice, Suggested by Judicial Proceedings in Erie County, Pennsylvania." 18:395-400, 1849.

American Journal of Psychiatry: Carlson, E. T. "Amariah Brigham: Life and Works" [Part 1], 112:831-36, 1956; "Psychiatric Thought and Practice" [Part 2], 113:911-16, 1957; Dain, N. and Carlson, E. T. "Moral Insanity in the U.S.," 118:795-801, 1962; Hudgens, R. W. "Mental Health of Political Candidates: Notes on Abraham Lincoln," 130:110, 1973; Hutchings, R. H. "John P. Gray," 100:34-36, 1944a; "Amariah Brigham," 100:29-33, 1944b.

American Literature: Basler, R. P. "Abraham Lincoln's Rhetoric," 11:167-82, 1939.

American Medicine: Shastid, T. H. "A Short Biography of Dr. John J. Elwell," 4:94-96, 1909.

America's Civil War: Spiegel, A. D. "John Sumerfield Staples Bore the President's Musket in the Civil War," 4:16-17, 1991a.

Annals of Medical History: Jacobi, A. "The New York Medical College," 1:368-73, 1917.

Archives of Neurology & Psychiatry: Kempf, E. J. "Abraham Lincoln's Organic and Emotional Neurosis," 67:419-33, 1952.

Arena Magazine: Weik, J. W. "Lincoln and the Matson Negroes," 752-58, April 1897.

Arizona Law Review: Seligman, J. "The Impeachment Trial of President Abraham Lincoln," 40:351-87, 1998.

Atlantic Monthly: Donald, D. H. "Getting Right With Lincoln," 1956; Thomas, B. P. "Abe Lincoln, Country Lawyer," 193:57-61, 1954; Villard, H. "Recollections of Lincoln," 93:165-74, 1904.

Boston Medical and Surgical Journal: "Prosecuting Surgeons," 46:264-65, 1852; Beard, G. M. "Neurasthenia, or Nervous Exhaustion," 3:217, 1869.

Boy's Life: Fleming, T. J. "Lincoln's Favorite Case: Abraham Lincoln Defends Duff Armstrong," 75:20, 1985.

Brooklyn Daily Eagle: "A U.S. Officer Shot At Norfolk, Va.," July 14, 1863.

Buffalo Medical Journal Medical Reports: Hamilton, F. H. "Prosecution for Alleged Mal-Practice," 4:275, 1848-1849.

Bulletin of the Abraham Lincoln Association: Pratt, H. E. "The Genesis of Lincoln the Lawyer," 57:3-10, 1939a; "In Defense of Mr. Justice Browne," 56:3-8,

1939c; Thomas, B. P. "Lincoln's Earlier Practice in the Federal Courts, 1839-1854," 39:3-9, 1935a; "The Eighth Judicial Circuit," 40:3-10, 1935b.

Bulletin of the History of Medicine: Burns, C. R. "Malpractice Suits in American Medicine Before the Civil War," 43:41-56, 1969.; Carlson, E. T. "Dain N: The Meaning of Moral Insanity," 36:130-40, 1962; Jarcho, S. "Edwin Stanton and American Medicine," 45:153-58, 1971; Legan, M. S. "Hydropathy in America: A Nineteenth Century Panacea," 45:267-80, 1971; Quen, J. M. "An Historical View of the M'Naghten Trial," 42:43-49, 1968; Waite, F. C. "American Sectarian Medical Colleges Before the Civil War," 19:148-66, 1946.

Bulletin of the Los Angles County Medical Association: Sandor, A. A. "Abraham Lincoln and Malpractice," 81:705, 1951.

Caduceus: Karst, F. "Homeopathy in Illinois," 4:1-33, 1988; Spiegel, A. D. and F. Kavaler. "Abraham Lincoln, Medical Jurisprudence, and Chloroform Induced Insanity in an 1857 Murder Trial," 10:145-60, 1994.

Case & Comment: Fox, E. J. "The Influence of the Law in the Life of Abraham Lincoln," 33:3-6, 1927.

Century Magazine: Grover, L. "Lincoln's Interest in the Theater," 943-53, April 1909; Saltonstall, F. G. "A Recollection of Lincoln in Court," 636-37, February 1897; Weik, J. W. "Lincoln As a Lawyer With An Account of His First Case," 68:279-89, 1904; "Lincoln's Vote for Vice-President in the Philadelphia Convention of 1856," 76:186-89, 1908.

Charleston Medical Journal and Review: Williman, A. B. "An Account of the Yellow Fever Epidemic in Norfolk During the Summer of 1855" 11:1856.

Chicago Daily Press: "Lincoln's Defense of Bridge," September 25, 1857.

Chicago Daily Tribune: "Trial of Mrs. Abraham Lincoln for Insanity," May 20, 1875; "The Case of Mrs. Lincoln," May 21, 1875.

Chicago Times: "Leonard Swett Dead," June 9, 1889.

Chicago Tribune: "Married: A. Judson Burroughs to Amelia L. Boggs," September 16, 1863; "Married: Mary G. Harris to Charles H. Devlin," November 12, 1863; "The Burroughs-Harris Tragedy," February 2, 1865; "The Washington Tragedy, The Prisoner's Statement of Her Relations With the Diseased—Representations of Friends of the Diseased," February 4, 1865; "A Homicidal Heroine Wedded to Her Aged Legal Advisor," November 3, 1883; Kirby, J. A. "New Light on Honest—But Cagey—Abe," July 21, 1994; McFarland, A. "Insanity As a Defense. The Late Leonard Swett One of Its Most Successful Advocates," June 20, 1889; Parsons, C. "The Lincoln Log: After Years of Study, Historians Are Ready to State Their Case on Lincoln's Legal Career," Sec. 10, 16., February 8, 1998; Scarborough, I. E. "Lincoln and the Power of Principle," February 12, 1992; Swett, L. "Abraham Lincoln, The Story of His Life," February 21, 1876.

Christianity Today: Kazin, A. "The Gorilla," 29:17-18, 1985.

Christian Science Monitor: Tyson, J. L. "Lincoln's Legal Papers Are a Case in Shrewdness," March 22, 1994.

Cincinnati Enquirer: "The Effie Afton Case," September 17, 1857.

Civil War History: Gambone, J. G. "*Ex Parte Milligan*. The Restoration of Judicial Prestige?," 16:246-59, 1970; George, J., Jr. "The North Affair: A Lincoln Administration Military Trial," 33:199-218, 1987; Harris, W. C. "Conservative Unionists and the Presidential Election of 1864," 38:298-318, 1992; Rawley, J. "The Nationalism of Abraham Lincoln," 9:283-98, 1963; Strozier, C. "On the Verge of Greatness: Psychological Reflections On Lincoln At the Lyceum," 36:137-48, 1990; Wilson, D. L. "Abraham Lincoln and That Fatal First of January," 38:101-30, 1992; Wilson, M. L. "Lincoln and Van Buren in the Steps of the Fathers: Another Look At the Lyceum Address," 29:197-211, 1983.

Civil War Times Illustrated: Roy, C. A. "Was Lincoln the Great Emancipator?," 3:46-49, 1994.

Clinton Transcript: Swett, L. "Letter from Leonard Swett, Esq.," May 6, 1857.

Connecticut Law Tribune: Freedman, M. "Lincoln: Model for the 21st Century?," February 19, 1996, 21; Shestack, J. J. "Resolve to be Honest At All Events," March 21, 1994.

Connecticut Medicine: Gordon, V. M. "The Origin, Basis and Nature of Medical Malpractice Liability," 35:73-77, 1970.

Daily Examiner [Richmond VA]: "Dr. Rucker," September 26, 1863; "The Execution of Dr. Wright," October 27, 1863; "Safe In Dixie," October 28, 1863;

Daily Illinois State Journal [Springfield]: Advertisement for Lincoln & Herndon, January 13, 1857.

Daily National Intelligencer [Washington, DC]: "An Interesting Report," September 26, 1862; "Judge David Davis" [Editorial], November 10, 1862; "Execution of Dr. Wright," October 26, 1863; "Another Terrible Tragedy—A Deliberate Murder of a Treasury Clerk—A Woman the Assassin," January 31, 1865; "A Recent Scene in the Supreme Court," February 10, 1865; "Safety Matches," February 22, 1865; "Salaries of Clerks," February 22, 1865, 2:3; "The Conspiracy Trial of the Accused," June 7, 1865; "Mrs. D. E. Sickles Dies," February 12, 1867.

Daily National Intelligencer and Express [Washington, DC]: "Personal," December 24, 1869.

Daily Pantagraph [Bloomington IL]: "Circuit Court," April 14, 1857.

Daily Register [Springfield]: "An Awful Crime and Speedy Punishment," May 14, 1853.

Documentary Editing: Beard, W. D. "American Justinian or Prairie Pettifogger? Lincoln's Legal Legacy: Documenting the Law Practice of Abraham

Lincoln," 14:61-64, 1992; Davis, C. and W. D. Beard. "Brief of Argument in *Abraham Lincoln vs. Illinois Central Railroad*," 11:27, 1989.

Early American Life: Buehrer, B. B. "Lincoln's Springfield Homes," 20:34-40, 1989.

The Economist: "Abraham Lincoln: Dreaded Abe Wins Case," June 8, 1991, 31.

Evening Star [Washington, DC]: "The Tragedy in the Treasury Building—Clerk Shot Dead by a Female—Her Statement As To the Incentive for the Terrible Deed," January 31, 1865; "The Murder of Mr. A. J. Burroughs," February 1, 1865; "The Treasury Building Tragedy—Statement of the Prisoner," February 1, 1865; "Testimony of Dr. C. H. Nichols for the Accused," June 2, 1865; "Testimony of Dr. Jas. O. Hall for the Accused," June 13, 1865; "Bradley-Harris Wedding: The Tragedy and Trial of Which the Marriage is a Sequel," November 3, 1883; "Joseph H. Bradley Dead," April 4, 1887.

Everybody's Advertiser: "Announcement of Herndon & Zane," September 1, 1861.

Forum: Shaw, T. "Lincoln As a Lawyer," 77:220-29, 1927.

Frank Leslie's Illustrated Newspaper: Sketch of Lincoln in the Governor's room in the Illinois State House, SpringField, November 24, 1860; Abraham Lincoln's First Law Office and Present Law Office and Sketchs of both, December 22, 1860; Sketch of Mary Harris shooting Burroughs, February 18, 1865; "Can Women Commit Murder?," August 12, 1865.

Green Bag: Chittenden, L. E. "Legal Reminiscences. Lincoln As a Lawyer," 266-68, 1894; Wright, A. H. "A New Light On Lincoln As an Advocate," 78-80, February 1908.

Harper's New Monthly Magazine: "The Washington Tragedy," March 19, 1859; "The Sickles Story" [editorial],"Explanation by Daniel E. Sickles," July 30, 1859; Dickson, W. M. "Abraham Lincoln At Cincinnati," 69:62-66, 1884; Flint, A. "Medical and Sanitary Progress," 53:71, 1876.

Historic Traveler: Holzer, H. "The Land of Lincoln," April 1998.

History Today: Kleinfeld, J. "The Union Lincoln Made; Political and Legal Aspects of Suspension of Writ of Habeus Corpus by President Lincoln During Civil War," 47[11]:24-30, 1997.

Illinois Appellate Law Review: Davis, C. "A. Lincoln On Appeal," 6:44-49, 1994d.

Illinois Bar Journal: Pratt, H. E. "Lincoln and the Bankruptcy Law," 31:201-206, 1943a; "Lincoln's Supreme Court Cases," 32:25-35, 1943c; Sprecher, R. A. "Lincoln As a Bar Examiner," 918-22, 1954.

Illinois Central Magazine: Drennan, J. G. and A. Lincoln. "Once Illinois Central Attorney," 10:7-8, 1922.

Illinois Historical Journal: Bridges, R. D. "Three Letters from a Lincoln Law Student," 66:79-87, 1973.

Illinois History Journal: Beard, W. D. "Lincoln As a Railroad Lawyer," 85: 209-10, 1992; "'I Have Labored Hard To Find the Law': Abraham Lincoln for the Alton and Sangamon Railroad," 85:209-20, 1992.

Illinois Journal: "Illinois State Hospital for the Insane," 2:1, June 8, 1853.

Illinois Law Review: McIntyre, D. T. "Lincoln and the Matson Slave Case," 1:386-91, 1906.

Illinois Medical Journal: Pearson, E. F. "Abraham Lincoln—Health, Habits and Doctors," 147:143-47, 174, 1975.

Illinois State Historical Society Journal: Brown, C. L. "Abraham Lincoln and the Illinois Central Railroad, 1857-1860," 36:121-63, 1943; Carpenter, R. V. "Lincoln's First Supreme Court Case," 4:317-23, 1911; East, E. E. "Lincoln and the Peoria French Claims," 42:40-56, 1949; Masters, E. L. "Days in the Lincoln Country," 18:779-92, 1926.

Illinois State Journal: "Illinois Legislature," February 14, 1853; "Illinois State Hospital for the Insane," June 8, 1853; "Reapportionment Hearing," February 3, 1858; "Reapportionment in the Court," February 18, 1858; "Mr. Lincoln at State House," November 14, 1860; "Seventh Annual Report, 1863-4 Springfield, Illinois; " Weaver, W. H. "Lincoln Favored Fat Men But Disliked Blond Jurors, Aged, Speaker Tells Club," February 16, 1926.

Illinois State Register: "Dred Scott's Case," March 12, 1857.

Independent: Rice, A. T. "Incidents of President Lincoln's Sympathy," 47:434, 1895; Weldon, L. "Reminiscences of Lincoln As a Lawyer," 47:450-52, 1895.

Indiana Historical Society Publications: Moores, C. W. "Abraham Lincoln, Lawyer," 7:483-535, 1922.

Indiana Lawyer: Maple, S. M. "Lincoln Biography Portrays President Superbly," March 20, 1996, 19.

International Journal of Law and Psychiatry: Tighe, J. A. "The New York Medico-Legal Society: Legitimating Union of Law and Psychiatry. 1867-1918," 9:231-43, 1986.

Iroquois Journal [Middleport IL]: Professional Advertisement, July 6, 1853.

Journalism Quarterly: Reilly, T. "Lincoln-Douglas Debates of 1858 Forced New Role on the Press," 55: 734-43, 752, 1979.

Journal of the Abraham Lincoln Association: Beard, W. D. "Dalby Revisited: A New Look at Lincoln's Most Far-Reaching Case in the Illinois Supreme Court," 20:1-16, 1999; Steiner, M. E. "The Lawyer as Peacemaker: Law and Community in Abraham Lincoln's Slander Cases," 16:1-22, 1995.

Journal of the American Institute of Homeopathy: "Proceedings," 2:179-80, 189, 1910; "General News—Illinois," 17:652, 1924.

Journal of the American Medical Association: "Statistics of Medical Colleges in the U.S. and Canada, 1921-1922," 79:651, 1922 and 1922-1923, 81:563, 1923; Gage, E. C. "Women Kept Out of Salt Lake Medical Society," 270:2770,

1993; Sandor, A. A. "The History of Professional Liability Suits in the United States," 163:459-66, 1957; Smith, H. W. "Malpractice: Something of the Anatomy of the Law," 116:2149-59, 1941a; "Legal Responsibility for Medical Malpractice. Forgotten Ancestors of the American Law of Medical Malpractice," 116:2490-94, 1941b.

Journal of Alternative and Complimentary Medicine: Burns, J. L. and S. B. Burns. "Photoessay. Homeopathic Physician, 1855," 1:321-22, 1995.

Journal of Civil War Medicine: "Historians Find Trove of Signatures by Lincoln," 2:22, 1998; Curfman, D. R. "The Medical History of Abraham Lincoln," 2:2-4, 1998.

Journal of Community Health: Spiegel, A. D. "New York Medical College. An Early Center of Excellence in American Medical Education," 18:293-315, 1993; "Abraham Lincoln and the Insanity Plea," 19:201-20, 1994; Spiegel, A. D. and F. Kavaler. "America's First Medical Malpractice Crisis, 1835-1865," 22:283-308, 1997a; Spiegel, A. D. and C. R. Springer. "Babylonian Medicine, Managed Care and Codex Hammarubi, Circa 1700 BC," 22:69-79, 1997; Spiegel, A. D. and P. B. Suskind. "Mary Edwards Walker, M.D. A Feminist Physician A Century Ahead of Her Time," 21:211-35, 1996.

Journal of History of Medical Allied Science: "A Comprehensive Discussion of Gray's Views," 163, 1979.

Journal of the History of Medicine: Waldinger, R. S. "Sleep of Reason: John P. Gray and the Challenge of Moral Insanity," 34:163-79, 1979.

Journal of the Illinois State Historical Society: Chase, C. M. "Lincoln Tries a Suit Well," 47:63-66, 1954; East, E. E. "The Melissa Goings Murder Case," 46:79-87, 1953; Gridley, J. N. "Lincoln's Defense of Duff Armstrong," 3:24-44, 1910; Gilbert, B. "Attorney for William Baker Gilbert," 46:290-93, 1953; Hinchcliff, E. "Lincoln and the Reaper Case," 33:361-68, 1940; Pratt, H. E. "The Repudiation of Lincoln's War Policy in 1862—Stuart-Swett Congressional Campaign," 24:3-14, 1931; "Abraham Lincoln in Bloomington, Illinois," 29:42-69, 1936; "Abraham Lincoln's First Murder Trial," 37:242-49, 1944a; "The Famous 'Chicken Bone' Case," 45:164-67, 1952; "Judge Abraham Lincoln," 48:28-30, 1955; Ross, R. A. "Mary Todd Lincoln, Patient at Bellevue Place, Batavia," 63:5-34, 1970; Selby, P. "The Editorial Convention of 1856," 5:343-49, 1912.

Journal of Medical Education: Norwood, W. F. "American Medical Education from the Revolutionary War to the Civil War," 32:433-47, 1957.

Journal of the State Historical Society: Rammelkamp, C. H. "The Memoirs of John Henry, a Pioneer of Morgan County," 18:39-76, 1925.

Lancet: Lister, J. "On a New Method of Treating Compound Fracture, Abscess, etc. with Observations on the Conditions of Suppuration," 1:326-29, 357-59, 387-89, 507-509; 2:95-95, 1867; Simpson, J. Y. "On a New Anesthetic

Agent More Efficient Than Sulfuric Ether," 2:549-50, 1847; Stanley, F. "Poisoning by the Inhalation of Impure Nitrous Oxide Gas," 1, 1842.

The Landmark: Jackson, S. K. "Letter to the Editor," February 2, 1893.

Law, Medicine and Health Care: Frey, E. F. "Medicolegal History: A Review of Significant Publications and Educational Developments," 10:56-60, 1982.

Ledger Dispatch [Norfolk, VA]: Squires, W. H. T. "Norfolk in By-Gone Days. Our Confederate Martyr," April 13, 1939.

Legal Intelligencer: Shestack, J. J. "Abe Lincoln: Circuit Lawyer," February 11, 1994, 3.

Legal Times: Johnson, E. "Abraham Lincoln Didn't Fish for Clients," March 11, 1996, 28.

Lincoln Herald: Bray, R. "The P. Quinn Harrison Murder Trial," 99:59-79, 1997; George, J., Jr. "The Night John Wilkes Booth Played Before Abraham Lincoln," 59:11-15, 1957; Lufkin, R. F. "Mr. Lincoln's Light From Under a Bushel—1850," 52:2-29, 1950; Lupton, J. A. "Basement Barrister: Abraham Lincoln's Practice Before the United States Supreme Court," 101:47-58, 1999; Page, E. L. "The Effie Afton Case," 58:3-10, 1956; Spiegel, A. D. and F. Kavaler. "Chicken Bones, Defense Lawyer A. Lincoln and a Malpractice Case," 99:156-70, 1997b; Suppinger, J. E. "The Intimate Lincoln. Lawyer and Politician, Part 8," 84:222-36, 1982.

Lincoln Legal Briefs: "Recent Discovery re Peachy Quinn Harrison," 8:1, 1988; "Postscript, *People v. Harrison,* 9:1, 1989; "Lincoln in the Federal Courts," 9:2, 1989; "Lincoln's $5, 000 Fee," 9:3, 1989; "Lincoln, Medical Law, and Chicken Bones," 12:2-3, 1989; "Judge Lincoln," 24:3, 1992; "'Too Deep for Me, '" 33:1, 1995; "Murder and Capital Punishment," 34:2-4, 1996; "Bibliography," 43:1-4, 1997; "A. Lincoln, Divorce Lawyer," 45[2]:2-3, 1998; "Perjury"; "Top Ten Cases," 45[3]:2-4, 1998; "Preview," 46[1]: 2, 1999.

Lincoln Legal Papers: S. Wise to W.H. Bissell, February 11, 1859; W. H. Bissell to O.M. Hatch, February 12, 1859.

Lincoln Lore: "The Insanity Defense in Lincoln's Illinois," 1727:1-4, 1982; McMurtry, R. G. "The Only Murderer Defended By Lincoln Who Was Hanged For His Crime," No. 1459:1-3, 1959.

Los Angeles Times: Abrams, G. "New Historic Insights Into Lincoln, A Man of Tragedy," February 2, 1986.

Lynchburg Daily Virginian: "Brutal Murder of a U.S. Officer by a Secesh Citizen," July 23, 1863; "From Norfolk" [Petitions to Lincoln], September 8, 1863; "Latest from Norfolk," October 24, 1863; "The Execution of Dr. Wright of Norfolk," October 29, 1863; "Northern Account of the Execution of Dr. Wright," November 4, 1863; "Funeral of Dr. Wright at Norfolk," November 10, 1863.

Magazine of History with Notes and Queries: "Lincoln and Dr, Crothers," 173:28-29, 1861; Hertz, E. "Abraham Lincoln: His Law Partners, Clerks and Office Boys," 44:11-26, 1930.

Maryland State Medical Journal: Rappeport, P. J. "The Insanity Plea: Getting Away With Murder," 32:263-74, 1983.

McClure's Magazine: Tarbell, I. M. "Lincoln As a Lawyer," 171-81, July 1896; "Lincoln's Important Law Cases," 272-81, August 1896.

Medical & Legal Journal: Andoh, B. "The M'Naghten Rules—The Story So Far," 61:93-102, 1993.

Minnesota Medicine: Mulvania, R. L. and J. E. Johanson. "History of the Treatment of Compound Fractures," 54:853-60, 1971.

Mississippi Valley History Review: Shryock, R. H. "Sylvester Graham and the Popular Health Movement," 18:172-83, 1931.

Missouri Law Review: Lueckenhoff, S. K. A. "Lincoln, A Corporate Attorney and the Illinois Central Railroad," 61:393-428, 1996.

National Electric Light Association Bulletin: Fowle, F. F. "A Famous Interference Case: Lincoln and the Bridge," 14:612-22, 1927.

National Intelligencer and Express [Washington, DC]: "Personal," December 24, 1869.

National Law Journal: "A Lawyer's Lawyer" [editorial], 9[26]:A22, 1997; Cooper, J. H. "Abraham Lincoln Wasn't A Yuppie," February 23, 1987, 13; Perez-Pena, R. "What Would Honest Abe Have Done?," May 13, 1991, 43; Weidlich, T. "Lincoln As a Lawyer: A Portrait," A15, October 9, 1995.

National Magazine: Horner, W. N. "Abraham Lincoln's Law Cases," 52ns:551-55, 1924.

National Republican [Washington, DC]: "Escape of Mary Harris from the Insane Asylum," July 9, 1873; "Mary Harris Caught: She is Arrested in Philadelphia and Brought Back," July 26, 1873; Ford, W. D. "'Abe' Lincoln the Lawyer," February 13-15, 1938.

Netherlands Journal of Surgery: DeMoulin, D. "The Treatment of Compound Fractures in the Eighteenth Century," 37:54-59, 1985.

New York Daily Herald: "Letter to the Editor," April 15, 1859.

New York Daily Tribune: "Mr. Graham's Opening" [editorial], April 11, 1859; "Defense Tactics," April 16, 1859; "Sickles Acquitted," April 27, 1859; "Comments on Trial," April 28, 1859; "Southern Medical Students Seceding From the University," December 21, 1859; "News of the Day," September 5, 1862; "Abraham Lincoln. Frederick Douglass's Reminiscences." July 5, 1885; "Obituary, Dr. John Purdue Gray," November 30, 1886.

New Yorker: Mitgang, H. "The Hairsplitter," February 17, 1997.

New York Evening Post: "The Sickles Tragedy," March 8, 1859.

New York Herald: "The Sickles Trial" [editorial], April 4, 1859; "Interesting from Fortress Monroe," July 25, 1863; "Execution of Dr. Wright," October 25, 1863; "Military Courts Versus Civil Courts As Illustrated At Washington" [editorial], July 22, 1865; "Obituary" [Dr. Gray], November 30, 1886; "Joseph H. Bradley Dead," April 4, 1887; "Death Notice. Dr. Nicholas," December 18, 1889.

New York Journal of Medicine: Ordronaux, J. "Review of Elwell's Text," 8:400, 1860.

New York Legal Observer: "Examination of Students," 3:395-96, 1845.

New York Medical Journal: Davis, N. S. "On Medical Education," 5:415-18, 1845.

New York Medical Press: "Notice of Elwell's Malpractice," 3:141-42, 1860.

New York State Journal of Medicine: Haller, J. S. "Neurasthenia. Medical Profession and Urban Blahs,". 70:2489-97, 1970; "Neurasthenia. The Medical Profession and the New Woman of Late Nineteenth Century," 71:473-82, 1971; Spiegel, A. D. "Mary Edwards Walker, MD: The Only Woman Ever Awarded the Congressional Medal of Honor," 91:297-304, 1991b.

New York Times: "Sickles Indicted for Murder," March 18, 1859; "News of the Washington Bar," March 24, 1859; "Sickles Trial Opens," April 4, 1859; "Sickles Trial," April 13, 1859; "Personal," July 7, 1859; "Letter to the Editor," July 21, 1859; "The Sickles Story" [editorial], July 21, 1859; "The Medical Stampede in Philadelphia," December 22, 1859; "Medical Education in New York" [editorial], October 18, 1860; "The Employment of Refranchised Negroes as Soldiers" [editorial], January 9, 1863; "Social Condition of Washington," February 28, 1863; "The Execution of Dr. Wright," October 25, 1863; "Justice Davis for Chief," November 11, 1864; "Smithsonian Destroyed by Fire," January 24, 1865; "The Verdict in the Mary Harris Case," July 20, 1865; "Escape From a Lunatic Asylum," July 9, 1873, 1:1; "Mrs. Abraham Lincoln," May 20, 1875; "Mrs. Abraham Lincoln," May 22, 1875; "Mr. Lincoln's Widow," May 24, 1875; "Recovery of Mrs. Lincoln," August 22, 1875; "Mrs. Lincoln Full Recovery Denied," August 26, 1875; "Mrs. Abraham Lincoln," August 30, 1875; "Mrs. Abraham Lincoln's Health," June 16, 1876; "Reminiscences of Lincoln," May 1, 1880; "Joseph H. Bradley Marries Mary Harris: He's 81 and She's 39," November 4, 1883; "Death of Dr. John P. Gray," November 30, 1886; "Joseph H. Bradley Dead," April 4, 1887; "Obituary, Dr. Charles Henry Nicholas," December 18, 1889; "Miss Lulu M. Crothers," December 24, 1940; "Rachel Crothers Dramatist Dead," July 6, 1958; Lehmann, M. G. "The Cases that Lawyer Lincoln Took," March 5, 1992; Hertz, E. "When Lincoln the Lawyer Rode the Circuit," February 7, 1937; Krock, A. "Lincoln's Clear Legal Mind Shown By Rare Text of His Notes in Suit," 1, February 12, 1948; Mitgang, H. "Lincoln as Lawyer: Transcript Tells

Murder Story," February 10, 1989; "Under the Dust, A New Luster for A. Lincoln, Esq.," February 9, 1992; "1858 Debates: No Makeup, No Moderator," October 8, 1992; "Document Search Shows Lincoln the Railsplitter was Polished Lawyer," February 15, 1993; "Newly Found Lincoln Files Show Wide Range of Early Legal Work," July 4, 1993; "Document Reveals Lincoln's Deft Legal Mind," February 13, 1994; "Heritage of Lincoln the Lawyer," February 11, 1998; "Adding a New Word to Lincoln's Eloquence: Internet," February 12, 1998; Patton, P. "Lincoln Fueled the Railroad Era's Engine," February 24, 1992; Wakefield, S. D. "Lincoln-Crothers Incident," July 12, 1958.

New York Times Book Review: Mayer, H. "Abe, Honestly and Otherwise," February 12, 1989.

New York Times Magazine: Safire, W. "Lincoln Meets the Press," August 23, 1987b.

New York Tribune: "Mrs. Abraham Lincoln," September 3, 1875; "Mrs. Lincoln Restored to Reason," June 16, 1876.

New York World: "Trouble in Norfolk," July 15, 1863; "Epidemic of Crime," July 11, 1865; "Mrs. Lincoln," May 21, 1875; "Mrs. Lincoln," May 22, 1875.

North American Review: Bergen, A. "Abraham Lincoln As a Lawyer," 166:186-95, 1898; King, J. L. "Lincoln's Skill As a Lawyer," 166:186-95, 1898.

Ohio Bar Association Report: Hill, W. J. "Lincoln the Lawyer," 6:241-46, 1933.

The Outlook: Weik, J. W. "A Law Student's Recollection of Abraham Lincoln," 97:311-14, 1911.

Pantagraph [Bloomington]: White, R. "Psychiatrist Reconstructs Lincoln Era Court Drama," February 12, 1966.

Papers of the Abraham Lincoln Association: Silbey, J. "Always a Whig in Politics," 8:21-42, 1986.

Petrus: Galtrius: Guidi, G. "Vidus and E. Chirugia. Graeco in Lantinum Conversa," 1544.

Philadelphia Inquirer: "The Murder of Lt. Sanborn—Interview With the President," August 18, 1863; "Our Norfolk Letter," October 21, 1863; "Escape of Surgeon Rucker," October 28, 1863; "Medical Parade Disrupted," October 29, 1893.

Philadelphia Magazine of History and Biography: Rogers, N. "The Proper Place of Homeopathy: Hahnemann Medical College and Hospital in an Age of Scientific Medicine," 4:179-201, 1984.

Political Science Quarterly: Luthin, R. H. "Abraham Lincoln Becomes a Republican," 59:420-38, 1944.

Press Tribune [Chicago]: Hahnmann Medical College, October 15, 1860.

Prologue: Burton, S. J. "Lincoln At the Bar. New Documentation of Abraham Lincoln's Law Career," 22:198-203, 1990.

Psychiatric Clinics of North America: Quen, J. M. "Isaac Ray and the Development of American Psychiatry and the Law," 6:527-37, 1983.

Psychiatric Quarterly: Spiegel, A. D. and M. S. Spiegel. "Not Guilty of Murder By Reason of Paroxysmal Insanity: The "Mad" Doctor vs 'Common-Sense' Doctors in an 1865 Trial," 62:51-66, 1991.

Quarterly Journal of Ideology: Davis, C. "Law and Politics: The Two Careers of Abraham Lincoln," 17:61-75, 1994c.

Records, Columbia Historical Society: May, J. F. "The Mark of the Scalpel," 13: 51-68, 1910.

Resident & Staff Physician. Ladenheim, J. "The Chicken Bone Case," 32:105, 1986.

Richmond News: "Expunged Record of an Old Tragedy," May 10, 1901.

San Francisco Chronicle: "Honest Abe Lincoln for the Defense," February 19, 1989.

Sangamo Journal: "Rail Road Meeting," January 5, 1832; "Illinois Legislature," August 27, 1846.

Saturday Review: Randall, R. P. "With Malice Toward None...[Except Lincoln's Wife]," 37:11-12, 50-51, 1954.

Scalpel: "The Greenpoint Malpractice Case," 8:311-15, 1856.

Science. Chapman, C. B. "Doctors and Their Autonomy: Past Events and Future Prospects," volume 200 [4344]:851-56, 1978.

Shakespeare Quarterly: Berkelman, R. "Lincoln's Interest in Shakespeare," 2: 303-12, 1951

Sky & Telescope: Olson, D.W. and R. Doescher. "Astronomical Computing: Lincoln and the Almanac Trial," 80:184-88, 1990.

Social Forces: Schwartz, B. "Mourning and the Making of a Sacred Symbol: Durkheim and the Lincoln Assassination," 70:343-64, 1991; "Postmodernity and Historical Reputation: Abraham Lincoln in Late Twentieth-Century American Memory," 77:63-103, 1998.

Sociological Abstracts: Schwartz, B. "Remembering the Emancipator: Ritual and Symbol in the Black Community of Memory," 42:480, 1994.

Southern Historical Society Papers: Anderson, L. B. "The Execution of Dr. David M. Wright By the Federal Authorities at Norfolk, Virginia," 21:326-37, October 23, 1863.

Southern Review: Bledsoe, A. T. "Book Review of Lamon's Lincoln," 13:328-68, 1873.

Springfield Clinic Medical Bulletin: Davis, C. "Abraham Lincoln and the Medical Profession," 18:17-20, 1991.

Springfield Sun: "Researcher Finds Lincoln Perturbed Over Prosecuting Mentally Ill Man," April 7, 1966.

Star-Ledger [Newark, NJ]: Kilian, M. "On the Trail of Lincoln's Assassin," April 5, 1998; Wald, D. "Poll: Voters Mistrust Pols, But Prefer Devils They Know," October 19, 1998.

St. Louis Post-Dispatch: McDermott, K. "Lincoln Defended Judge in 1843 Case That Parallels 1997," May 4, 1997, 7; McWhirter, C. "Lincoln the Lawyer," November 30, 1993; Rogers, L. "Earlier Justice Hired Lincoln for Defense," 2, April 30, 1997.

Surratt Courier: Brooks, R. "Insane? Or Ill?," 22:3-9, 1997.

Tamkang Journal of American Studies: Davis, C. "Crucible of Statesmanship. The Law Practice of Abraham Lincoln," 6:1-19, 1989.

Time Magazine: Wills, G. "Dishonest Abe," 40:41-42, 1992.

Transactions of the American Medical Association: Atlee, W. L. "On Anesthetic Agents," 3:389-90, 1850; Eve, J. A. "Chloroform Use," 3:323-26, 1850; Gross, J. D. "On the Use of Chloroform," 3:391-93, 1850; Gross, S. D. "Report of the Committee on Medical Education," 18:363-68, 1867; Hamilton, F. H. "Report on Deformities After Fractures," 8:347-93, 1855b; 9:69-233, 1856; 10:239-453, 1857; Hooker, W. "Report of the AMA Committee on Medical Education," 4:409-41, 1851; Twitchell, A. "On Anesthesia," 3:323-26, 1850; Howard, R. L. "Anesthesia," 3:323-26, 1850.

Transactions of the Illinois Historical Society: Tilton, C. C. "Lincoln and Lamon: Partners and Friends," 38:175-228, 1931.

Transactions of the Illinois Medical Society: "Christopher Goodbrake," 20-21, 1891.

Transactions of the Ohio State Medical Society: Hamilton, J. W. "Report on Difficulties Growing Out of Alleged Malpractice in the Treatment of Fractures," 11:53-64, 1856.

Transactions and Studies of the College of Physicians of Philadelphia: Blake J. B. "Homeopathy in American History: A Commentary," 3:83-92, 1981; Eliason, E. L. "A Saga of Fracture Therapy," 11:65-76, 1943.

Tyler's Quarterly Magazine: Ashe, S. A. "Lincoln the Lawyer," July 1934, 15-20.

Virginia Magazine of History & Biography: Chambers, L. "Notes on Life in Occupied Norfolk, 1862-1865," 73:131-44, 1965.

Wall Street Journal: Keiser, T. "The Illinois Beast: One of Our Greatest Presidents," February 11, 1988.

Washington Chronicle: "The Washington Tragedy," February 1, 1865.

Washington Post: "A Romance of the Court: Marriage of an Aged Attorney to His Fair Client," November 3, 1883; "Death of Mr. Bradley," April 4, 1887.

Weekly Pantagraph [Bloomington IL]: "Local Matters. The Trial of Wyant," April 8, 1857; "Trial of Isaac Wyant," April 15, 1857; "Railroad Law Suit Settled," July 1, 1857.

Western Humanities Review: Burt, J. "Lincoln's Address to the Young Men's Lyceum: A Speculative Essay," 51:304-20, 1997.

Western Journal of Medical and Physical Sciences: Reviews 28:309, 1853.

Wisconsin Magazine of History: Gunderson, R. G. "'Stoutly Argufy': Lincoln's Legal Speaking," 46:109-17, 1963.

Woman's Home Companion: Harris, G. W. "My Recollections of Abraham Lincoln, Four Part Article," pages 9-11, November 1903, pages 14-15, December 1903, pages 13-15, January 1904, pages 10-11, 24, February 1904.

University of Detroit Mercy Law Review: Steiner, M. E. "Lawyers and Legal Change in Antebellum America: Learning from Lincoln," 74:427-64, 1997.

USA Weekend: Burns, K. "Too Human to Be Heroes?," July 31-August 2, 1998, 4-7.

U.S. News & World Report: Parshall, G. "Who Was Lincoln?," 113:70-77, 1992.

Virginia Medical Journal: Selden, W., et al. "Report on the Origin of the Yellow Fever Epidemic in Norfolk During the Summer of 1855," 9:91, 1857.

Websites

American Memory: Examiner's Questions for Admission to American Party. http://lcweb2.loc.gov/cgi-bin/query/r?ammem/mcc:@field (DOCID+@lit(mcc/062)).html.

Barnes, D. Dairy and Notes, Law Student at the University of North Carolina, 1840. http://www.unc.edu/lib/mssinv/rxhibits/legal/barnes.html.

Bresnan, A. L. *The Long Nine*. http://www.frontiernet/~brez13/original.html.

California Attorney General's Office: *Quo Warranto Applications*. http://caaq.state.ca.us.opinions/quo.html.

California Attorney General's Office: *Nature of the Remedy*. http//caaq.state.ca.us.opinions/nature.html.

Counsel Quest: Abraham Lincoln's Infamous Cross-Examination As Defense Counsel On a Murder Case. http://www.counselquest.com/Lincoln.html.

Douglas, S. A. Biography. http://encarta.msn.com/index/concise/OvolOF/01c36000.asp

Executive Mansion Where Abraham Lincoln Visited:. http://www.netins.net/showcase/creative/lincoln/sites/mansion/html.

John C. Frémont, Carte De Visite:. http://www.npg.si.edu/exh/brady/gallery/88gal.html.

Growth of the Nation: History. http://www.libarts.sfasu.edu/history/133_Unit3.html.

Heiple, R. Brief History of the Early GAR. http://pages.prodigy.com/CGBD86A/pg8hist.html.

Hippocrates. *On Fractures* [Francis Adams, Translator], 400 B.C. http://classics.mit.edu/Hippocrates/fractur.mb.txt.html.

History Place: Abraham Lincoln Timeline. http://www.historyplace.com/lincoln/index.html.

Thomas Jefferson University: A Brief History.
http://jeffline.tju.edu/SMI/archives/history/index.html.
Thomas Jefferson University: History and Development.
http://jeffline.tju.edu/tjuweb/tju/hist.html.
Jefferson Medical College: Famous Faculty.
http://jeffline.tju.edu/SMI/archives/history/faculty.html.
Jefferson Medical College: Ten Notable Alumni and Past Faculty.
http://jeffline.tju.edu/SMI/archives/history/notables.html.
Lincoln A. First Political Announcement, New Salem, Illinois, March 9, 1832.
http://www.netins.net/showcase/creative/lincoln/speeches/1832.html.
———. The Perpetuation of Our Political Institutions Springfield, IL: Address
to the Young Men's Lyceum, January 27, 1838.
http://www.netins.net/showcase/creative/lincoln/speeches/lyceum.html.
———. Prohibition, Speech, Illinois General Assembly, December 18, 1840.
http://www.deoxy.org/prohib1.html.
———. Notes on the Practice of Law, July 1, 1850.
http://www.patente.com/ethics.html.
———. Short Autobiography, 1859.
http://www.historyplace.com/lincoln/autobi-1.html.
———. Speech to the State Republican Convention, June 16, 1858.
http://scom.tamu.edu/pres/speeches/abehouse.html.
———. Address to the New Jersey Senate, February 21, 1861.
http://www.netins.net/showcase/creative/lincoln/speeches/trenton1.html.
———. Address in Independence Hall, February 22, 1861.
http://www.netins.net/showcase/creative/lincoln/speeches/philad el.html.
———. First Inaugural Address, March 4, 1861.
http://libertyonline.hypermail.com/Lincoln/lincoln-1.html.
——— Proclamation Calling Militia and Convening Congress, April 15, 1861.
http://www.historyplace.com/lincoln/proc-1.html.
———. Annual Message to Congress—Concluding Remarks, Dec. 1, 1862.
http://www.netins.net/showcase/creative/lincoln/speeches/congress.html.
———. Order of Retaliation, July 30, 1863.
http://www.historyplace.com/lincoln/retal.html.
———. Proclamation of Thanksgiving, October 3, 1863.
http://www.netins.net/showcase/creative/lincoln/speeches/thanks.html.
———. Speech to 164th Ohio Regiment, August 18, 1864.
http://www.netins.net/showcase/creative/lincoln/speeches/ohio.html.
———. Second Inaugural Address, March 4, 1865.
http://www.netins.net/showcase/creative/lincoln/speeches/inaug2.html.
———. Last Public Address, April 11, 1865.
http://www.netins.net/showcase/creative/lincoln/speeches/last.html.

Lincoln Legal Papers: An Emerging Reappraisal of Lawyer Lincoln.
    http://www.fgi.net/lincolnlegalpapers/emerging.html.
Lincoln Legal Papers: Lincoln's Legal Career.
    http://www.fgi.net/LincolnLegalPapers/carrer.html.
Lincoln Sites: Lincoln-Herndon Law Offices.
    http://www.state.il.us/HPA/LINCHERN.html.
Morel, L. Abraham Lincoln's Failures and Successes.
    http://www.netins.net/showcase/creative/lincoln/speeches/failures.html.
NPG: US Immigration Levels by Decade.
    http://www.npg.org/facts/us_imm_decade.html.
Oglesby, Richard J. Biography.
    http://cyberschool.4jlane.edu/people/fa..s/O/RichardJOglesby/RichardJOgl
    esby.html.
An Outline of American History wysiwyg://40/http://odur.let.rug.nl/-
    usa/H/1990/
The Political Graveyard. http://www.potifos.com/tpg/bio/daya-debo.html.
Stroup, G. Where Did Homeopathy Come From?.
    http://www.dfnet.com/glenda/where.html.
Think Tank Transcripts: Who Was Abraham Lincoln? February 16, 1996.
    http://www.pbs.org/thinktank/archive/transcripts/transcript247.html.
Three Centuries of Broadsides and Other Printed Ephemera.
    http://memory.loc.gov/cgi-bin/a..uffrg, horyd, wtc&linkText=0.html
Treasure Chest: The Fifth Artifact:.
    http://vangogh.bergen.org/~abrwon/treasure/artifact05/html.
Lyman Trumbull: Biography.
    http://encarta.msn.com/index/concise/Ovol11/01147000.asp.
Norton, R. V. S. John Surratt.
    http://members.aol.com/RVSNorton/Lincoln37.html.
———. Judge Abraham Lincoln.
    http://members.aol.com/RVSNorton/Lincoln53.html.
Ullman, D. A Condensed History of Homeopathy.
    http://www.homeopathic.com/intro/his.html.
Wentzel, J. A. The History of the Republican Party.
    http://www.geocities.com/CapitolHill/7552/Republican_Party_History.html.

Record of the Illegal Board and Protest Against It. Jacksonville, March 1, 1851.

*Special Report of the Trustees in a Review of a Report of a Legislative Committee
    Appointed by the Twenty-Fifth General Assembly.* Springfield, Illinois, 1868.

INDEX

Beckwith, Corydon
asks Lincoln to rescue relative 104; lawyer 97
Bell, Luther V.
asylum superintendent 211; consulted with Swett 126, 211
Bennett, Maria 170
Bergen, Abram
Lincoln acting in court 48; Lincoln and eye witness 156
bestiality
Davidson v. McGhilton 168; *Thompson v. Henline* 54, 167; *Torrence v. Galloway* 167
Betts, Josiah T. 183
Betts v. Frazer
court costs 185; deposition 185; testimony 183, 185
Bigelow, Henry J.
experience with fractures 130
Bissell, William H.
apportionment bill 233; candidate for Illinois governor 145, 227; career 224; died from syphilis 226; died in office 241; elected governor 229; favored Chase for president 241; health problems 226; Illinois Central Railroad 94, 98; inauguration 226, 230; law degree 224; Lt. Gov. ineligible 83; Lincoln wrote veto message 233; Lincoln is advisor 228, 230; medical debt 223; medical degree 224; Mexican War 224; mortally ill 241; nominated by acclamation 227; oath re dueling 226, 230; paraplegia of legs 226; pardoned rapist 75; potential presidential candidate 242; unopposed for governor 227; used executive mansion 231
Blackstone, William
Commentaries 107, 124, 163; Of Wrongs 125; *mala praxis* defined 107
Blackwell, Robert 233
Blackwell, Robert S. testimony of 96, 178
Bledsoe, Albert T.
Herndon read for Lincoln 31; Herndon was man Friday 31
Bolles, John A.
decision for good of service 253, 263; shooting deliberate 253; Wright's insanity 253

Booth, John Wilkes
assassination of Lincoln Elog; Lincoln sees him perform 273; highest encomiums 273; insanity of 200
Bovay, Alexander 248
Bowden, Lemuel 249; Lincoln hears him 254; Lincoln told of Wright's insanity 254; military commission bias 265; requests respite for Wright 264
Bradley, Sr., Joseph H. insanity experience 205; opposed DC court reorganization Elog
Bradley, Tom 234
Bradley v. Martinez cited *People v. Hatch* 234; court ruled law stood 234; Mayor signed Bill 234
Bragg, Thomas 254
Brayman, Mason 94, 95
Brayton, Benjamin 98
breach of contract 144
Breckinridge, John C. presidential candidate 147, 163; vice presidential candidate 228
bridge obstruction
Columbus Insurance Co. v. Peoria Bridge Co. 43; *Hurd v. Rock Island Bridge Co.* 43, 97
Brigham, Amariah editor, *American Journal of Insanity* 259; insanity expert 252, 259
Breese, Sidney customary medical payment 240; father of Illinois Central Railroad 94; Lincoln as a lawyer 15-16; professional jurors 240; railroad bias 98
Brockman, John M. 163
Bromwell, Henry P. H. 203
Brown, Christopher C. 203
Brown, William 77
Browne, Thomas C.
debt 58; impeached 21
Browning. Orville Hickman 82, 96, Elog
Bryant, William Cullen
favored homeopathy 85; newspaper editor 85
Byrne v. Stout xii, 21
Buchanan, James 228-229
Bunn v. Bays 144
Bunn, John
few slavery cases for Lincoln 42
Burns, Ken
Lincoln not electable today 163
Burt, Benjamin 187

commutations 267, 273; and
Confederate peace ambassadors Elog;
criminal law 40; cross-exam expertise
128, 157-158, 216; debt collection 22;
Declaration of Independence 9-10;
diatribes against 246; District of
Columbia court reorganization 250;
dishonest 1; duel 225-226; eminent
lawyer 49, 233, 234; epithets for 246;
explains self-defense 47; expedience in
war 270; fees 39, 96, 38, 142, 155, 231;
federal law 9, 33; General Assembly
service 151, 153; Gettysburg Address
criticized 246; *habeas corpus* 11; honest
politicians 2; honorary degrees 3, 15;
house divided speech 10; house
ownership 27, 231; humor 46, 47, 48,
57, 216; hypochondriac 198, 199;
impeachment of 12; inaugural 11, 15;
income 34; and jury 57, 156, 160, 238;
largest fee of $5,000 39, 96, 138; law
firms 54; law and politics 1, 19, 245; law
and society 8, 17, 21; and law students 1,
7, 30, 41, 56, 161, 163-164, 222, Elog; as
lawyer 10, 18-20, 26, 29, 32, 44, 46, 48,
53, 56, 59, 138, 216, 234, 242; a lawyer's
lawyer 28, 95; legal associates 54, 208;
leadership style 2, 124, 126; malice
toward no one speech 15; married 24,
27; melancholy 197; Mexican War 58;
mob law 8-9; newspapers 270;
nicknames 246; notes for law case 10,
59; number of cases 22; New Salem
speech, 1832 3; a party hack 246;
peacemaking 59; and physicians 59, 61;
picking a jury 156; pleading 45; political
religion 9, 39; political strategist 90, 145,
228, 230, 245, 269; posed for sculptor
242; and possuming insanity 126, 219,
259; prohibition 4; as prosecutor vi, 74,
259; and railroads 22, 39. 95, 96, 98,
182; as rainmaker 56; resembled Swett
206; re-election 265; and representative
recruit in war 272; Republican Party
organization 154; reputation 240, 245,
246; settling cases 41; shrewd,
sophisticated 18; slavery 11, 42, 154,
269, 272; split hairs 77; and EM Stanton
142-143; State Bank speech 2; stump
speaker 229; success rate 49; Supreme

court 27, 32; treason 11, 250; truth in
slander cases 192; types of cases viii,
165; U.S. Representative 152; U.S.
Senate race 154, 161, 234; Vice-
Presidential nominee 154, 229; Young
Men's Lyceum speech 1838 8
Lincoln, Mary Todd
    Bellevue Place sanitarium 202-203; at
    Bissell's party 232; bizarre behavior 201;
    engagement broken 24, 198; and M
    Harris Elog; hated Herndon 55 -56; WH
    Herndon a drudge, an inebriate 56;
    hospitality 232; and insanity 201-203;
    lunatic asylum 201; married 27; new
    insanity trial 203; reaction to RT
    Lincoln's testimony 202; renovated
    house for $1,300 232; saw J W Booth in
    play 273; and DE Sickles Elog;
    spiritualists 201; and J T Stuart 22;
    unsettled 201
Lincoln, Robert T.
    born in Globe Tavern 27; consulted
    Swett re mother's insanity 201; firm
    hires Scammon's son 93; hired law firm
    re mother's insanity 201; internship
    with Scammon 93; testified against
    mother 202
Lincoln-Douglas debates
    descriptions 162; expenses 163; style 162
Lincoln & Herndon
    cases 31, 32, 52, 70, 84, 94, 144, 167,
    168, 203, 229; continuing practice 164;
    debt collection 31, 33; fees 55, 167;
    finding documents 31; formed 28;
    Herndon's duties 56; in Illinois
    Supreme Court 32; jurisprudence text in
    office 125; large practice 35; law
    students 1, 7, 30, 41, 46, 56, 161, 163-
    164, 222, Elog; number of cases 31;
    office 29-30, 147, 222; office
    management 30; professional card 164;
    sign 163-164
Lincoln & Lamon 208
Lincoln, Timothy D. 97, 100
Linder, Usher F.
    cases 41, 176, 229; Lincoln's advice on
    pleadings 45
Lister, Joseph 112
litigious society 21
Littlefield, John 30, 41